TARGETED:

BEIRUT

TARGETED: BEIRUT

THE 1983 MARINE BARRACKS BOMBING AND THE UNTOLD ORIGIN STORY OF THE WAR ON TERROR

JACK CARR

AND JAMES M. SCOTT

**SIMON &
SCHUSTER**

London · New York · Sydney · Toronto · New Delhi

First published in the United States by Emily Bestler Books,
an imprint of Simon & Schuster, LLC, 2024

First published in Great Britain by Simon & Schuster UK Ltd, 2024

1 3 5 7 9 10 8 6 4 2

Simon & Schuster UK Ltd
1st Floor
222 Gray's Inn Road
London WC1X 8HB

Simon & Schuster: Celebrating 100 Years of Publishing in 2024

www.simonandschuster.co.uk
www.simonandschuster.com.au
www.simonandschuster.co.in

Simon & Schuster Australia, Sydney
Simon & Schuster India, New Delhi

A CIP catalogue record for this book
is available from the British Library

Hardback ISBN: 978-1-3985-4082-8
eBook ISBN: 978-1-3985-4084-2

Interior design by Silverglass

Printed and Bound in the UK using 100% Renewable
Electricity at CPI Group (UK) Ltd

MIX
Paper | Supporting
responsible forestry
FSC
www.fsc.org   FSC® C171272

For them all

*"Blessed are the peacemakers, for they shall
be called the children of God."*

—MATTHEW 5:9, KING JAMES VERSION

"Beirut is not hell, but you can see it from here."

—DESCRIPTION COMMON AMONG U.S.
SERVICE MEMBERS IN LEBANON

"Lebanon is a harsh teacher."

—WILLIAM B. QUANDT, MIDDLE EAST EXPERT

Contents

Preface

Welcome to Beirut 1983.

A place of turmoil. A place of death.

By the mid-seventies, the "Paris of the Middle East" had become a battle-ground, with Maronite Christians, Druze Muslims, Shiite Muslims, Sunni Muslims, militias, and terrorist groups all vying for a piece of the rubble. Tensions had already hit their boiling point, but there was more destruction to come.

Bombings, assassinations, and kidnappings were the order of the day on terrain where the CIA, not far removed from the reorganization following the Church Committee and Pike Committee Hearings, would ply their trade in this emerging battleground of the Cold War. But war in Lebanon was anything but cold.

In 1982, the United States Marines entered the arena. They were called "Peacekeepers." Having spent time on the ground in Afghanistan and Iraq, and now having had the honor of speaking to the Marines who deployed to Lebanon, I can say with utmost certainty that they were most certainly in combat, regardless of the labels placed upon them by the administration.

As a lifelong student of war, for me the 1983 Marine headquarters and barracks bombing has long loomed large in my consciousness. I remember watching news of the event on television with my parents and remember the *Time* and *Newsweek* magazine covers on our kitchen table. They used the same powerful photograph of Marines carrying a wounded comrade, devastation evident in the background. The *Time* magazine cover read "Carnage in Beirut." *Newsweek* led with "The Marine Massacre." I remember our daily newspaper bringing the latest information each morning as my dad had his coffee and read the pages, setting them aside for me when he was finished. What had happened? Why had it happened? Who was responsible? Why were we in Lebanon? What were we going to do about it? Would we hit back? If we did, would we be going to war?

Targeted: Beirut allowed me to answer those questions.

The attack of October 23, 1983, would also cast a shadow over United States foreign policy writ large, one that still influences our initiatives and decisions on the international stage more than forty years later.

As my understanding of world events matured through academic study and the practical application of martial policy, I found myself wondering what our enemies had learned from our misadventure in Lebanon. Did they learn that terrorism works?

The goal of my new Targeted series is to explore history's most devastating terrorist attacks and examine their enduring global impacts. When I started the process, I wrote down every terrorist attack of the past fifty years and spread them out on a table. I kept coming back to Beirut 1983 as the place to begin. It was clear to me that to understand the "why" behind the intent of many international terrorist attacks today, we need to study the Beirut of yesterday. Beirut 1983 would set the tone for all that was to follow.

I planned to study the attack from the tactical, operational, and strategic perspectives to both humanize the experience of those who served there— who dug their buddies out of the rubble, worked to save lives and identify bodies—and to understand its broader context. It was also extremely important to me to honor and respect the families who lost loved ones in what would prove to be the seminal attack of the era.

To do this story justice, I wanted to partner with an established military historian, and there was one person I wanted to work with: author, military historian, and Pulitzer Prize finalist James Scott. James is the critically acclaimed author of *Black Snow: Curtis LeMay, the Firebombing of Tokyo, and the Road to the Atomic Bomb, Rampage: MacArthur, Yamashita, and the Battle of Manila, Target Tokyo: Jimmy Doolittle and the Raid That Avenged Pearl Harbor, The War Below: The Story of Three Submarines That Battled Japan,* and *The Attack on the Liberty: The Untold Story of Israel's Deadly 1967 Assault on a U.S. Spy Ship.* As an admirer of his work, I set up a call and was delighted to discover that not only was James a brilliant historian, but he was also a genuinely kind and thoughtful man as well. What started as a professional partnership quickly turned into a genuine friendship. Without James Scott this book would not be in your hands today. It was a true honor to work with him on this project.

The 1983 Marine barracks bombing would prove to be the largest single day loss of life for the United States Marine Corps since Iwo Jima in World War II. How do we ensure that those who fought and died in Beirut will not have died in vain? We learn. That is how we honor their memory. We remember them and their stories so that their experience in Lebanon will not fade from public conscious. *Targeted: Beirut* is for all of us; it is as much for citizens as it is for military flag officers and intelligence officials who advise elected representatives and lawmakers whose duty it is to effectively direct and control our military.

There are lessons and warnings in the pages that follow. It is up to us to heed them and evolve them going forward into wisdom so that those who step up to serve our country in uniform or in our intelligence services will not have to relearn those lessons in blood.

I remain hopeful that the story in these pages will not be forgotten, that the legacy and heroism of those who fought and died in Lebanon will add to our foundational knowledge of warfare.

We can honor the sacrifice of those who died, and of those whose lives were irrevocably altered, by remembering, by learning, and by applying the lessons of the past to problem sets of the present and future.

We owe our fallen, their families, and service members of the future nothing less.

Semper Fi.

Jack Carr

Rescuers probe the wreckage of the destroyed Battalion Landing Team
headquarters on October 24, 1983. Visible in the background is the
control tower of Beirut International Airport.
AP Photo

PART I

April 1983–September 1983

You are about to embark on a mission of great importance
to our nation and the free world.

—PRESIDENT RONALD REAGAN

August 25, 1982

Captain Richard Zilmer leads his troops ashore from the landing
ship Saginaw at the port of Beirut on September 29, 1982.
Marine Corps

CHAPTER 1

Beirut has become synonymous with death and destruction.
—*PITTSBURGH POST-GAZETTE* EDITORIAL
April 20, 1983

The black GMC pickup truck idled alongside the curb of Beirut's seashore drive at 12:43 p.m. on April 18, 1983. Secured in the truck bed and hidden under a canvas tarp sat enough pentaerythritol tetranitrate—a high-powered explosive favored by militaries, quarry blasters, and, of course, terrorists—to rival two thousand pounds of TNT. The hefty payload, as one witness would later tell investigators, forced the rear of the late-model pickup to sag.

The driver scanned the midday traffic that crawled through the Lebanese capital, spotting a dated green Mercedes in the oncoming lane. The German car's headlights flashed three times, signaling the truck driver to shift into gear and ease back into traffic.

The mission was a go.

A mile away, towering over the corniche with a view of the Mediterranean's cool blue waters, loomed the American Embassy, a rose-colored monolith that had dominated the Beirut skyline since it originally opened its doors as a hotel three decades earlier. The crescent-shaped embassy that fronted the palm-lined Avenue de Paris employed 341 people who helped overseas Americans, processed visas, and advanced diplomatic relations.

It had been a quiet Monday in Beirut, a welcome reprieve in a city battered by eight years of civil war, foreign invaders, and sectarian violence that had torched businesses, leveled apartment blocks, and claimed the lives of 100,000 men, women, and children. The arrival of American Marines six months earlier—based at the airport as part of a multinational peacekeeping force—had helped restore a semblance of calm that reminded war-weary residents of the halcyon days when the city was known as the Paris of the Middle East. Shoppers browsed stores along Hamra Street—dubbed the Fifth Avenue of Lebanon—that once again offered everything from designer jeans and caviar to the latest electronic games. Others queued up outside cinemas where Bill Murray's comedy *Stripes* had proven a popular hit. "People," as *New York Times* reporter Thomas Friedman observed, "were just starting to relax in Beirut, daring to believe that the presence of American troops meant the war was finally over."

But America's flatlining efforts to pressure Israeli and Syrian forces to withdraw from Lebanon had sparked an uptick in violence, one that reminded residents of the potential savagery that lurked beneath the veneer of peace. In the previous month, gunmen had attacked patrols of the Italian, French, and American peacekeepers, wounding fourteen, including five Marines. Only four days earlier on April 14, an assailant fired a rocket-propelled grenade at the American Embassy, which hit an empty office. The time for peace was running out.

A dusting of snow still capped Mount Lebanon, climbing nearly two miles above the capital, even as the last of the season's cool weather threatened to give way to the oppressive heat of summer. The morning drizzle had subsided, replaced by the midday sun, which burned off the haze. Locals in search of visas lined up outside the first-floor consular offices, which assisted an average of 150 people per day. Others strolled down the scenic seaside promenade. Up on the embassy's sixth floor, workers rolled out and installed new carpets.

The day before, many of the embassy staff had participated in the Beirut marathon, including general services officer Robert Essington, who had charged across the finish line in four hours and two minutes. The race coupled with the after-party had exhausted many, prompting Ambassador Robert Dillon to offer participants a day off to recover.

But few took him up on the deal.

Lance Corporal Robert "Bobby" McMaugh wished he could have stayed in bed rather than man Guard Post One at the embassy's main entrance. The twenty-one-year-old Marine, who nursed a hangover, had been a star running back and kicker at Osbourn High School in Manassas, Virginia. Off the field, he proved equally as popular, a humble and warm personality who had insisted on taking his younger sister to her first high school dance because no one else was good enough. That same kindness motivated Bobby on the mornings he stood guard to present female employees with a flower. Much to his father's frustration, Bobby had postponed college to enlist in the Marines, where he volunteered for duty in Beirut, hoping that a posting to one of the world's hot spots might catapult his career. During his recent downtime, however, he had survived a car bombing on the streets of the capital, which, he later confided in a call to his mother, marked the first time in his life he had ever been scared.

Bobby had pushed those fears out of his mind the night before when he and a few fellow Marines feasted on spaghetti and champagne at the home of Letitia "Tish" Butler, a staffer with the U.S. Agency of International Development. He had returned to the embassy at 1 a.m. for a final beer before collapsing atop his bunk fully clothed. "I'll give you three hundred Lebanese lira," he pleaded with one fellow Marine, "if you stand my duty today."

But no one would accept his offer.

Despite his hangover, Bobby stood armed with a rose when embassy secretary Dorothy Pech appeared in front of his bulletproof-glass booth Monday morning.

"How are you doing, Bob?" she asked.

"I don't feel too good," he confessed.

"You guys are going out too much," she chided him.

The young Marine would have no doubt agreed.

"Well," Pech added, "maybe today will be a short day."

The pickup truck closed the distance.

Elsewhere in the embassy, Robert Ames of the Central Intelligence Agency huddled on the fifth floor with the embassy's spooks. The bespectacled father of six served as the clandestine agency's top Middle East expert, often tasked to personally brief President Ronald Reagan. At first glance, Ames appeared an unlikely intelligence officer. The forty-nine-year-old Philadelphian, who stood six feet three inches tall, had grown up the son of a Pennsylvania steelworker. A basketball scholarship had earned him an education at La Salle University, while a stint in the Army had introduced him to the world of signals intelligence. Over the years, as he pinballed between Yemen and Iran, Kuwait and Lebanon, he not only mastered Arabic but developed an unrivaled insight into the volatile region. Ames accomplished this while balancing time with his family in the Washington suburb of Reston, Virginia. He imitated Donald Duck's voice for his children, coached youth basketball, and liked to relax in his favorite rocking chair to the tunes of the Beach Boys. "He was," as his wife Yvonne later said, "the cornerstone of the family."

Frustration in Washington over the president's apparent stillborn peace initiative for the region had landed Ames back in Beirut, where he had touched down the day before. The veteran operative had attended a dinner that night with his colleagues where the intractable reality cast a shadow over the evening. Those tensions had turned contentious Monday morning as Ames met with the agency's entire team. Station Chief Ken Haas, whose wife, Alison, brought him lunch most days, emerged from the session upset. He phoned her to pop by early, where the couple ate a sandwich. She started to peel an apple, but her husband was too distressed to eat more.

"I've got one more cable to write," he said. "I don't know how I'm going to do it; you go ahead and go home and take a nap and I'll be home when I finish."

Alison Haas rose and approached her husband, who grabbed her face with both of his hands and delivered a dramatic kiss, one she would re-member for decades.

"See you later," she said.

Up on the eighth floor, Ambassador Dillon seized on the break in the rain to swap his business suit for workout clothes. One of his bodyguards waited for him to change while others prepared his convoy for the trip over to the American University of Beirut. His security detail would then close the field, allowing him to jog three miles around the track. The United States took the ambassador's safety seriously—and with good reason. During the Lebanese Civil War in 1976, assailants kidnapped and shot then ambassador Francis Meloy. Four years later, gunmen in a speeding Mercedes ambushed Ambassador John Dean, though an armored limou-sine saved his life. But protecting the ambassador was far easier than secur-ing the embassy, which operated out of a leased location with no setbacks in the heart of the congested capital. America had begun construction in 1973 of a more secure compound, but Lebanon's civil war had put that project on hold. In the meantime, the United States had invested $1.5 million to improve security, but only so much could be done to retrofit a decades-old hotel. In addition, much of the focus was on preventing a potential mob at-tack, similar to the 1979 seizure of the American Embassy in Iran. Workers had added tear gas ports in the walls of the lobby, installed fortified doors, and covered windows with protective Mylar to prevent shattering.

The fifty-four-year-old Dillon, who boasted a head full of silver hair, was mindful of the dangers. He had started his career in the CIA before migrating over to the foreign service. In his nearly three-decades-long career Dillon had served around the world, including posts in Venezuela, Turkey, and Egypt. That afternoon the ambassador had brushed off a call with a German banker. Dillon felt guilty as he slipped out of his clothes. His run could wait. He picked up the phone to call him back at the same time as he struggled to pull on a Marine T-shirt, which he had been given in his role as the honorary manager of the leathernecks' softball team.

Down in the first-floor cafeteria, Anne Dammarell ate a chef's salad in the back at a table with her colleague Bob Pearson. The forty-five-year-old Dammarell, who worked with the U.S. Agency for International Development, had served for the past two and a half years in war-torn Beirut. The experience had proven tiresome, prompting her to request a new post. She was scheduled to leave the following Monday for an assignment in Sri Lanka. Dammarell had spent that morning at her apartment meeting with two contractors to obtain quotes to ship her belongings by sea and air. An unfinished report lured her back to the embassy around noon, where she bumped into Pearson, who was planning her farewell party.

"Let's go down to the cafeteria and get something to eat," he suggested.

Over lunch the conversation drifted, as so many did, to the stalled efforts to secure peace. "This is either the end of the world," Pearson said, "or the Second Coming."

At 1:04 p.m., the driver of the GMC slowed to a crawl as he approached the intersection in front of the embassy, waiting for a lull in the oncoming traffic to cross.

Horns blared.

A brief break in the midday gridlock offered a window. The driver, who witnesses later reported wore a black leather jacket, punched the accelerator and shot across the busy avenue. He did not bother to brake, but wheeled right, pulling into the east exit of the horseshoe-shaped drive. The ambassador's limousine was parked in front of the embassy's main entrance, wedged between two security vans, where guards patiently waited for Dillon to finish his call with the banker. Just inside the building, Bobby McMaugh nursed his hangover, Anne Dammarell picked at her salad, and Ken Haas typed his cable, his last assignment for the day before he could head home and into the arms of his wife.

The truck blew past the Lebanese security checkpoint. Only ten yards stood between the GMC and the embassy's front portico, a distance it covered in less than two seconds.

There was no time to raise a rifle, pick up a phone, or even run.

The vehicle rammed the embassy in front of the lead security van at 1:05 p.m. and detonated its explosive payload, sending a bright orange fireball hundreds of feet into the heavens. The explosion blew out windows as far as a mile away. American sailors aboard the amphibious assault ship *Guadalcanal* five miles offshore felt the shudder. The blast scorched visa applicants in the consular office, flipped cars upside down and set them ablaze, and shattered the Mylar-covered windows throughout the eight-story building. The front of the embassy's center wing collapsed like a house of cards, burying the lobby under an avalanche of broken concrete, rebar, and splintered desks and file cabinets. The attack would prove to be not only the bloodiest assault on an American Embassy but the opening salvo in the nation's four-decade war on terrorism. "Everything," as one survivor recalled, "went black."

CHAPTER 2

I don't know how the hell I survived.
—JOHN REID, PUBLIC AFFAIRS OFFICER
April 23, 1983

Sirens wailed.

Black smoke curled skyward, blocking the midday sun and hiding the gouged front of the American Embassy. In an instant, the cascade of concrete had buried the lobby, including Guard Post One, where Bobby McMaugh enjoyed passing out roses.

Gone, too, was the embassy's cafeteria, Information Service Library, personnel and consular sections, as well as all the individual offices stacked above them.

The explosion had knocked out power and severed phone lines. Water gushed from broken pipes. Pulverized concrete dust clouded the air, choking the survivors who crawled out from under toppled desks, bookshelves, and file cabinets. Into the noxious mix wafted tear gas from ruptured canisters in the armory. "I thought what might kill me," recalled consular officer Dundas McCullough, "aside from the explosion, was suffocation."

Many never heard the blast but felt only the sudden and violent shake of the building, reminiscent of an earthquake, followed by a rush of searing heat that hurled them to the floor, through walls, or in the case of Chief Warrant Officer Rayford Byers, out of a fifth-floor window. Byers miraculously survived the fall, though he lost his left eye, broke both collarbones and arms, and suffered fourteen broken ribs and a crushed skull.

Others remembered what sounded like a clap of thunder, as walls, floors, and ceilings suddenly split apart. The explosion blew doors off hinges, tossed air conditioners across offices, and wrenched open safe doors, spewing classified documents into the air. Vaporized windows sliced up survivors and riddled them with shards of glass, including Robert Essington, who would later count more than five hundred pieces embedded in his body.

But that was only one of his problems.

"Mr. Essington, Mr. Essington," he heard his secretary holler at him in the immediate aftermath of the bomb. "Here's your ear!"

Survivors struggled to orient themselves in the dark and rubble-strewn landscape, one now filled with dangerous pitfalls, as communications officer Faith Lee discovered up on the sixth floor. "When I came out of the office, there was nothing there. You could see the sea," she recalled. "It had just been all blown away. I mean it was just nothing."

My god," she thought. "*How are we going to get out of here?*"

Lee wasn't the only one.

Corporal Ronnie Tumolo had just sat down to enjoy a lunch of rice with chili in the Marine mess hall when the terrorist's bomb exploded, showering him with glass. Seconds later Tumolo's radio crackled with the voice of fellow Marine security guard Charles Pearson. "Holy shit, we've been hit big-time," Pearson exclaimed. "React! React!"

That was the code word for the Marines to grab their rifles and form up. Tumolo raced up the stairs to retrieve his gear from his room. When he arrived, he tried the door, only to find it wouldn't budge, no doubt a result of the blast. Tumolo took a few steps back and charged, ramming his shoulder into it, but again the door held. In a final effort, he kicked the handle. "My bedroom door flung open," Tumolo said. "All I could see was the Mediterranean." The Marine stood in awe. "Everything," he recalled, "from my room down was gone."

Down on the first floor, Staff Sergeant Charles Light woke up after being thrown through a wall only to discover that the blast had robbed him of his boots. His solid oak desk, which had taken seven men to install, was little more than splinters. The embassy's commissary and armory had erupted in flames. Rounds cooked off from the heat while smoke and tear gas permeated the air. "Even though I'd been in that building for nine months, I didn't know where I was," Light recalled. "I couldn't orientate myself." The explosion had toppled walls and reduced the concrete support piers to rebar skeletons. The Marine stumbled through the rubble. "My hearing came back," he said. "I started hearing screams and moans and pleas for help."

Light encountered a woman stumbling down the stairs from the second floor. The blast had left her face barely attached to her skull. Light comforted her amid the smoke and confusion, promising he could get her out of the embassy, even though he had no idea how.

Through the smoke, the sergeant spotted an opening amid the debris. He crawled through, pulling her out behind him. In the crescent-shaped driveway, Light spotted a severed leg from the ambassador's driver, Cesar Bathiard, who roasted just steps away inside one of the burning security vans. Bathiard's friend and fellow guard, Mohammed, used a rebar rod that resembled a crook to try to yank him from the vehicle, but he succeeded only in stripping away Bathiard's flesh. "Just as I looked at him," the sergeant recalled, "his eyes popped out of his head."

The guard's efforts were hopeless. "Mohammed took out his pistol and shot Cesar between the eyes and killed him," Light testified. "Put him out of his misery."

Light grabbed the wounded woman and pulled her toward the corniche, a once-peaceful coastal promenade. Bodies smoldered on the ground around them while others floated in the sea. The sergeant waved down a cab, whose driver sized up the battered duo and tried to escape, no doubt wanting to avoid a bloody mess. Light flashed his handgun. The Marine helped the woman into the back seat and fished a wad of Lebanese cash from his pocket, which he tossed inside.

"*Mostashfa*," he demanded. "Hospital."

Up on the eighth floor, Ambassador Dillon's T-shirt, which he pulled over his head the moment the bomb detonated, saved his face when the window imploded in front of him. "Everything," Dillon said, "seemed to happen in slow motion." The wall behind his desk collapsed, burying his legs beneath a masonry slab that measured five feet long by two wide. Smoke, dust, and tear gas filled his office, convincing him initially that another rocket-propelled grenade had hit the embassy. Deputy Chief of Mission Bob Pugh, secretary Dorothy Pascoe, and administrative counselor Thomas Barron charged in covered with dust. Unable to lift the slab, the trio used a flag staff to pry up the wall, allowing the ambassador to wriggle free. "We all started to cough and retch from the tear gas," Dillon said. "Someone vomited."

The explosion had destroyed the embassy's central staircase, forcing them to climb down an alternative stairwell crowded with debris. On the descent, the group picked up other bloodied survivors. This was far worse, the ambassador realized, than a rocket-propelled grenade attack. "We were astounded to see the damage below us," Dillon recalled. "With each second, the magnitude of the explosion became clear."

In the back of the cafeteria, Anne Dammarell felt heat like an oven the second the bomb exploded. She opened her eyes moments later to see blue sky. The ground-floor cantina had absorbed some of the worst of the terrorist's blast. Dammarell and her lunch partner Bob Pearson were the only two to survive. The blast had left Dammarell with nineteen broken bones, including one foot, both arms, multiple ribs, and her pelvis and scapula.

"Relax," she told herself, "just remain calm."

Her wait was fortunately short. Within minutes, several rescuers found her, removing the debris that pinned her legs before lifting her up. Ambassador Dillon watched as the men carried her out to an ambulance. "She looked," he recalled, "like a piece of hamburger."

"*She's not going to make it,*" he thought.

Students from the neighboring American University of Beirut were some of the first to arrive along with several taxi drivers along the corniche, who offered to transport wounded to the hospital. French peacekeepers pulled up within minutes, cordoning off the area. The senior officer asked who was in charge. A staffer directed him to Bob Pugh, who had just escaped along with the ambassador. The officer saluted the deputy chief of mission.

"May we enter your embassy?" he asked.

Pugh welcomed them.

Red Cross and Lebanese civil defense volunteers followed. Medical teams rushed inside to help free trapped employees and provide first aid. Lack of familiarity with the building handicapped rescuers. Those who were mobile attempted to exit what was left of the embassy, a challenge given the destroyed stairs and darkness coupled with the rubble and smoke. In addition, many embassy staffers suffered from cuts, broken bones, and shock. Some coughed and stumbled. Others cried. Marine security guards in gas masks assisted. "People were walking like they were in a trance, like they were zombies," recalled Faith Lee. "Everybody was traumatized." Public affairs officer John Reid echoed her. "It was chaos," he said. "Glass and blood were everywhere."

The scene proved equally as frenetic outside. "From the top floors," wrote Herbert Denton of the *Washington Post*, "the screams and cries of trapped employees could be heard." Acrid black smoke from the embassy and at least eight burning cars filled the air. Concrete chunks along with license plates and hubcaps littered the ground. Flying debris had sliced one of the trees in half while the searing heat melted a nearby traffic light.

A Lebanese personnel carrier lay upside down in the surf where bodies and body parts bobbed in the water. An American security guard, who suffered from shock, paced out front.

"It's gonna blow," he repeatedly hollered. "It's gonna blow."

Ambulances and fire trucks converged on the diplomatic mission along with journalists, many of whom worked nearby. "Rescue workers and passersby began pulling limp and charred bodies out of the debris. Some carried out pieces of bodies on stretchers or wrapped in blankets," observed David Zucchino of the *Philadelphia Inquirer*. "A man's torso was brought out on one stretcher and a man's leg on another. Blood and body parts smeared the ground; some rescuers accidentally stepped on them." British journalist Robert Fisk with the *Times* watched a Red Cross worker use a bucket to scoop up remains. "We tripped over corpses," he wrote. "The roadway was slippery with water, glass and blood and other, more terrible objects which a team of Lebanese Red Cross men and women were shoveling onto stretchers."

American Marines, based four miles south at the airport, rolled up in jeeps twenty minutes after the blast. Colonel James Mead, commander of American peacekeeping forces, immediately sized up the damage. "It was," he noted, "a catastrophic event."

"One platoon is not enough," the colonel radioed. "Send two."

French troops turned over control to the Americans, who guarded the perimeter and began a sweep of the building. One Marine outside watched rescuers bring out bodies.

"Damn, damn, damn," he muttered.

Another paced the ruins.

"My buddy was in there," he said. "I can't find him."

Moments after the blast, an anonymous caller phoned the Beirut office of Agence France-Presse, the French wire service, claiming responsibility on behalf of the Islamic Jihad Organization. A similar call was made to the Beirut newspaper *Al Liwa*. Authorities assessed the Islamic Jihad Organization to be a pro-Iranian Shiite Muslim group. The terror organization had previously taken credit for the recent grenade attack that wounded five Marines. "This is part of the Iranian revolution's campaign against imperial targets throughout the world," the caller said. "We shall keep striking at any imperialist presence in Lebanon, including the multinational force."

Throughout the afternoon, rescuers dug out the wounded and the dead. Over them all dangled the body of a man in a tan suit coat, whose legs were pinned between the concrete slabs of the fourth and fifth floors. The employee's head and arms hung down, dripping blood on the slabs below. Around 5 p.m., rescuers pulled out what would prove to be the last survivor, who had spent four hours buried under the rubble and rebar. "He was," as one Red Cross worker told reporters, "very glad to see us." Hundreds of onlookers crowded around the perimeter to watch, including families of local employees. The Lebanese military struggled to hold back distraught relatives. "The more hysterical among them stood about screaming the names of their missing family members," noted Thomas Friedman of the *New York Times*, "while others leaned against a wall, gripping handkerchiefs or a purse and weeping silently."

Crews with Oger Liban, Lebanon's largest construction contractor, brought in portable lights, generators, and bulldozers, which would allow rescuers to work throughout the night. Jackhammers rattled as darkness settled over the capital. "With the giant floodlights," *Time* magazine observed, "it looked like a scene from an apocalyptic disaster movie."

Back in Washington, President Ronald Reagan was outraged by the attack, which he viewed as both "vicious" and "cowardly." At 11:50 a.m. in Washington—or 6:50 p.m. in Beirut—Reagan stepped out into the White House Rose Garden to address reporters, flanked by Vice President George H. W. Bush. "This criminal attack on a diplomatic establishment will not deter us from our goals of peace in the region. We will do what we know to be right," the president said. "The people of Lebanon must be given the chance to resume their efforts to lead a normal life free from violence without the presence of unauthorized foreign forces on their soil. And to this noble end, I rededicate the efforts of the United States."

At the American University of Beirut, the flood of injured and dead threatened to overwhelm the doctors, nurses, and attendants. Chaos enveloped the emergency room. An American diplomat, her head bandaged, surveyed the scene and turned to leave. "The ones who did this," she remarked, "I hope they die a slow death."

More than a hundred Lebanese men and women—relatives of those missing—swarmed the hospital entrance, desperate for information. The task of tabulating the dead and wounded fell to consular officer Diane Dillard, who had gone home to walk her dog over lunch when the bomb exploded. "I tried to get a fix," she recalled, "on who was there and who wasn't and where we stood." One of the doctors asked her to help identify the dead, whose crushed and burned bodies overflowed from the morgue drawers to the floor. Adding to the challenge, Dillard discovered, was the gray concrete dust that coated the remains. Another time a Red Cross volunteer asked her to examine a row of teeth detached from the skull.

"Now," the volunteer said, "I think this could be an American filling, don't you?"

"Well," Dillard stuttered, "it could be any filling."

That moment, though horrific, proved a revelation, one that ultimately allowed her to perform her difficult task. "I realized," Dillard later said, "that we weren't talking about people; we were talking about empty vessels. The people were no longer there."

The staff worked under tremendous pressure from the families and State Department, all anxious for information. "The attendant, a quiet man in white hospital robes, wrote his list of the dead Americans in Arabic on a brown washroom paper towel," one wire service reported. "Eventually, a nurse posted a list of 105 victims, those who were alive, on the window of the emergency ward. It heartened some relatives and distressed others."

Work continued at the embassy as Monday night rolled into Tuesday morning. Hours had passed since rescuers probing the rubble had pulled the previous body out at 6 p.m. In the meantime, bulldozers had worked to clear debris while laborers armed with jackhammers broke up large concrete slabs for easier removal. CIA economic analyst Susan Morgan, who was on temporary duty assignment to Beirut, hovered around the ruins. She had been at a lunch in the southern port city of Sidon when the bomb exploded. Morgan had rushed back to the capital, anxious to check on her office director and friend Robert Ames, who so far had not been located, either on the lists of wounded at the hospital or among the dead. The dropping temperatures prompted a Marine to wrap her in a blanket. Another offered her coffee.

At 2:30 a.m., Morgan sensed a change atop the debris pile, as rescuers suddenly converged around one spot. "A body has been found," she wrote in her diary. "My heart skips and I know." One of the officials waved her over and asked if she could identify the remains. "I look briefly. Yes," she wrote. "I am handed his passport and wallet."

An embassy officer reminded Morgan that she must retrieve all his papers, but she chose instead to accompany his body to the morgue. "The only thing that seems to matter," she wrote, "is that Bob not be left without the presence of someone who knows him."

When she reached the hospital at 3:30 a.m., Lebanese civil defense authorities guarding the entrance tried to dissuade her, arguing that it was too grisly.

But Morgan refused.

She climbed the rail and pushed inside the hospital. In the morgue, she counted five other victims on the floor alongside her friend Bob Ames. Before her lay the remains not only of America's top Middle East intelligence expert, but also a husband and a father. "I retrieve Bob's wedding ring," she wrote, "pray for his soul, and tell him goodbye."

CHAPTER 3

Lebanon, if it ever was a viable political entity, exists today in name only.
—LOREN JENKINS, *WASHINGTON POST*
October 10, 1982

L ebanon was a mess.

And the world knew it.

The attack on the American Embassy was only the latest blood spilled in an epic saga of violence that had dominated the recent history of this multifaith nation on the shores of the eastern Mediterranean. The seed of strife was planted in 1943, when Lebanon gained its independence from France. At that time, an unwritten agreement called the National Pact divided power between the three dominant faiths. According to a 1932 census—the only one then available—Christians comprised 51 percent of the population. As such, the pact mandated that Maronite Christians would hold both the presidency as well as a six-to-five ratio over Muslims in parliament. The prime minister would, in turn, be a Sunni Muslim, the second-largest group, while the role of speaker of the parliament would go to a Shiite. This arrangement, best described by a longtime Beirut reporter, amounted to a "social time bomb."

The intervening decades saw a reversal of Lebanon's demographics, leading Muslims to demand a larger share of control. An outbreak of hostilities in 1958 prompted President Dwight Eisenhower to briefly send in Marines to restore peace. To cling to power, the Christians formed militias, a move that triggered Muslims to do the same. Into this volatile mix landed the Palestine Liberation Organization, which was driven out of Jordan by the military in 1970 after igniting domestic violence and chaos. Palestinian leader Yasser Arafat set up operations in West Beirut—home to most of the capital's Muslims—effectively creating a state within a state. Lebanon's Muslims welcomed the new arrivals, hoping to incorporate Palestinian fighters into their own struggle. Over time Palestinian power grew to the point that guerrillas would stop local Lebanese and demand to see government identification cards. Such bullying behavior by foreign interlopers infuriated Christians. That, coupled with Arafat's attacks on Israel, which only invited retaliatory bombings and raids that wreaked havoc in the capital, led Christians to demand that the army follow Jordan's example and expel the Palestinians.

Those tensions climaxed on April 13, 1975.

On that spring morning in Beirut, unidentified gunmen killed four men outside a church in a drive-by shooting. Later that morning, Christian militiamen ambushed a busload of Palestinians, shooting and killing twenty-seven. Nineteen others were wounded. Those events sparked escalatory violence that led the Lebanese army to splinter along religious lines as the nation soon spiraled into civil war. The nineteen-month bloodletting would ultimately claim the lives of 60,000 men, women, and children, a staggering figure in a nation the size of Connecticut and home to just three million people. The fighting likewise ravaged Beirut, a once-beautiful coastal city hailed as the Paris of the Middle East. Neither side won. The conflict ended only after 30,000 Syrian troops, backed by Saudi Arabian cash, stepped in as a peacekeeping force. The war not only devastated block after block of apartments, hotels, and businesses, but wrecked the economy and eradicated government services, from law enforcement to the postal system.

The country fragmented along religious lines. The Christian-led government and supporting militias, weakened by the civil war, controlled only East Beirut and a few Christian pockets in the nearby mountains. Muslim militias and the Palestinians held West Beirut and areas south of the capital toward Israel. Syrian forces supported by the Shiites dominated the coastal city of Tripoli as well the eastern Bekaa Valley. Druze Muslims camped out in the Chouf Mountains, which peered down on the capital. "The sheer scope of the catastrophe which has hit Lebanon," the *Wall Street Journal* opined, "must be seen to be appreciated."

Over the next several years, the nation struggled, its tenuous peace interrupted by periodic artillery barrages, bombings, and gunfire. "Lebanon," as Defense Secretary Caspar Weinberger noted, "had become a killing ground where the conflicting interests of Syria, Israel and the Palestine Liberation Organization combined with local Lebanese antagonisms to produce a nightmare of epic proportions." Such fights were not always interfaith. Some of the worst violence involved rival Christian militias, who battled for power, money, and territory. These militiamen, *New York Times* reporter Thomas Friedman colorfully observed, shunned religious vestments, preferring instead cologne, gold chains, and armored Mercedes-Benzes. "They were Christians," the reporter quipped, "like the Godfather was a Christian."

By the summer of 1980, the Phalange emerged as the dominant Christian militia, run by thirty-two-year-old Bashir Gemayel, who had wiped out most of his rivals, including some who were tossed out of the upper-floor windows of a hotel. "Gemayel was something of an expert," Friedman added, "in gangland murders." In the struggle for Lebanon, Israel supported the Christians with money, weapons, and training since both sides shared the mutual goal of destroying the Palestine Liberation Organization. "The Israelis are terribly vulnerable to anyone who winks at them," Friedman wrote. "But Gemayel didn't just wink; he whispered the idea that the two of them could reshape Lebanon and forge a peace treaty."

Israel swooned.

But the Palestinians were not the only ones who threatened Christian dominance. Syria's role in Lebanon was not purely altruistic, but part of President Hafez Assad's hegemonic dream to bolster his nation's regional dominance. In addition to land, Syria wanted to install a puppet government in Beirut, one that would diffuse Israel's growing influence.

In the spring of 1981, Gemayel's Phalangist forces attempted to expand control to Zahle, a largely Christian city and the capital of the Syrian-controlled Bekaa Valley. In response, Syria besieged the city, lobbing artillery and torching crops. Anxious to undercut Syria, Israel threatened to jump into the fray in support of the Christians. "We won't let them perpetrate genocide in Lebanon," declared Israeli prime minister Menachem Begin.

On April 28, 1981, Israel shot down two Syrian helicopters. Assad responded by parking Soviet-made mobile surface-to-air missiles in Lebanon, which Israel threatened to destroy. Adding to this tension, Israeli jets pounded Palestinian positions in Beirut and southern Lebanon, triggering retaliatory rocket and artillery fire that paralyzed the economy of northern Israel. This mounting violence set off alarm bells in Washington, where officials feared a larger war. "Lebanon was a powder keg," Weinberger wrote, "a place where yet another Arab-Israeli conflict could ignite, placing in jeopardy Western interests throughout the region."

Reagan dispatched retired American diplomat Philip Habib, who famously helped then-president Richard Nixon negotiate the Vietnam peace talks that led to the 1973 Paris Peace Accords. The son of Lebanese immigrants, the bespectacled Habib flew to the Middle East, where he successfully brokered a cease-fire on July 24, 1981.

But that peace would prove short-lived.

Onto this stage waltzed Ariel Sharon. Israel's burly new defense minister hungered to destroy the Palestine Liberation Organization, whose mere existence he viewed as a threat to the Jewish state's survival. Sharon spent months secretly planning for war. All he needed was a provocation to break the cease-fire. That came on June 3, 1982, when an Arab terrorist shot and wounded Shlomo Argov, Israel's ambassador to the United Kingdom. Israel launched air strikes the next day before learning that the assailant was, in fact, not a member of Arafat's organization. Two days later, on June 6, Israeli troops invaded in Operation Peace for the Galilee. This ostensibly limited mission, Sharon assured his fellow cabinet members, was designed to capture twenty-five miles of southern Lebanon, so as to prevent future rocket attacks on Israeli settlements.

"Beirut," he promised, "is outside of the picture."

Prime Minister Begin told Reagan the same.

But Sharon had no intention of stopping in southern Lebanon. He instead ordered his troops to press all the way to Beirut, where his forces had numbered all 25,000 buildings on a large map to improve targeting. Syria objected, prompting Israel to destroy more than two dozen of Assad's surface-to-air missiles and shoot down scores of Arab warplanes—so many, in fact, that journalists labeled it the "Bekaa Valley Turkey Shoot."

Israel then sealed the capital and cut off power and water to the half-million residents, setting the stage for an urban siege designed to squeeze out the Palestinian guerrillas. Israel mercilessly bombed and shelled the city, hitting apartment buildings, hospitals, and public parks crowded with refugees who had poured in from devastated southern suburbs. "Even in Lebanon, a land inured to catastrophe, the bombardment of West Beirut was a horror beyond endurance," wrote syndicated columnist Jack Anderson. American military observers reported that some days Israel fired as many as 8,000 artillery rounds into the western half of the capital. "The siege," as Ambassador Dillon recounted, "was savage." Conditions in Beirut deteriorated. Feces littered the streets while the stench of burning garbage created a haze that hung over the city. "Walking the streets," observed *Guardian* reporter Colin Smith, "is like making a tour of a well-used ashtray." Hungry and shell-shocked residents picked through the rubble. "The entire fabric of life," added the *New York Times,* "is slowly unraveling in west Beirut."

As July rolled into August—and the intensity of the campaign increased—American nightly news programs broadcast images of flattened apartments and maimed civilians, which eroded public support for Israel, including among members of Congress. Republican senator Jesse Helms of North Carolina said Begin had done the impossible and made Arafat look sympathetic. Reagan's aides feared the blowback might hurt him politically, particularly after it emerged Israel had used American-made cluster bombs. "The United States was caught in the middle," Secretary of State George Shultz recalled. "The Arab world blamed us, as Israel's great ally and financial supporter, for all of Israel's deeds and looked to us to end the fighting in a responsible way. The Lebanese government particularly relied on us to save them from outside predators and to help them restore Lebanese central authority over their country."

The president's personal diary shows that he, too, grew increasingly incensed by the violence. "The slaughter," Reagan wrote on August 1, "must stop."

Yet it continued.

After Israel bombed Beirut for eleven hours on August 12, Deputy Chief of Staff Michael Deaver stormed into Reagan's office. "Mr. President," he began, "I have to leave."

"What do you mean?"

"I can't be a part of this anymore, the bombings, the killing of children. It's wrong," Deaver continued. "And you're the one person on the face of the earth right now who can stop it. All you have to do is tell Begin you want it stopped."

At 11:15 a.m., Reagan phoned the Israeli prime minister. If Begin didn't stop, the president warned, he risked the symbol of the war becoming the image of a seven-month-old infant with its arms blown off, a reference to a photograph that had appeared days earlier in the *Washington Post.* "Menachem," he continued, "this is a holocaust."

"Mr. President," the prime minister bristled, "I know all about a holocaust."

"It has gone too far," Reagan insisted. "You must stop it."

The president told him that the war now threatened Israel's relationship with the United States. "Twenty mins. later," Reagan wrote in his diary, "he called to tell me he'd ordered an end to the barrage and plead for our continued friendship."

"I didn't know I had that kind of power," the president confessed to Deaver.

The combination of Israel's attacks coupled with the failure of any Arab nations to intervene on his behalf convinced Arafat that at long last he needed to decamp from Lebanon. He refused to do so under the threat of Israeli guns, but agreed to leave with protection from a multinational force, which would include 800 leathernecks with the 32nd Marine Amphibious Unit plus another 800 troops from France and 400 from Italy.

The departure of some 15,000 guerrillas, who would soon scatter among a half dozen countries including Jordan, Syria, and Iraq, was predicated upon the assurance that Palestinian civilians left behind in refugee camps would be unmolested. Weinberger and the Joint Chiefs of Staff opposed the involvement of American troops. Lebanon was a distraction that risked creating a new front in the Cold War between America and the Soviet Union. Joint Chiefs Chairman General John Vessey, a World War II infantryman who fought in North Africa and Italy, argued that peacekeeping should be left to a lesser power. "Sticking Americans between Israel and Arab countries," the general warned, "was a bad idea."

But the commander in chief overruled the Pentagon.

With that decision, the United States, which had sat on the sidelines of the war for seven years, entered the arena. "The American debacle in Lebanon had begun," reporters David Martin and John Walcott observed, "dressed in good intentions and humanitarian motives."

On August 25, 1982, the Marines came ashore.

Over the coming days, the multinational force stood guard as Palestinian fighters—often firing celebratory guns skyward—flowed through the capital's port or departed overland. Arafat's exit on August 30 was like a scene from a rock concert, as a mob of admirers swarmed his entourage at the port. "Part of my heart," he told his supporters, "stays here."

The mission was a stunning success.

Rather than remain for a full month as initially planned, an anxious Weinberger ordered the Marines back aboard ship. Seventeen days after landing, American troops left without a single shot fired. Reagan celebrated by unveiling a proposed new peace plan for the Middle East, which called for a freeze on Israeli settlements in the occupied territories and for Palestinians to have full autonomy in the West Bank and Gaza with help from Jordan. The president hoped his ambitious plan would jumpstart stalled peace negotiations between Israel and its Arab neighbors. "The time has come," Reagan declared in a televised address to the nation on September 1, "for a new realism on the part of all the peoples of the Middle East."

But the president's honeymoon proved short-lived.

Israel hated his plan. "Begin," as one Israeli official later said, "looked at Reagan like a traitor." The outraged prime minister blasted Weinberger for almost four hours during a visit to Israel. He proved equally as hostile with Reagan. "A friend does not weaken his friend," he excoriated the president, "an ally does not put his ally in jeopardy."

Reagan's challenges, however, soon magnified.

On September 14 at 4 p.m., Bashir Gemayel's motorcade pulled up outside the Phalangist Party headquarters in Beirut, where he planned to deliver his weekly address to his followers. Over the years, the Christian warlord, who at times was on the CIA payroll, had grown more sophisticated as he shifted from guerrilla to politician, developing a close friendship with Ambassador Dillon. "I saw in Bashir," the ambassador said, "a potential leader for all of Lebanon." Gemayel had come to realize that it was wise to embrace the Shiites, who had become the largest of Lebanon's two dominant Muslim sects, but also the poorer and more marginalized. "All of us," Dillon said, "were guilty of underestimating the importance of the Shiites."

A few weeks earlier, Lebanon's parliament—with the help of generous bribes from Israel—had elected Gemayel president. His inauguration would take place in nine days. In exchange, Gemayel had promised to evict any remaining Palestinians and bring peace at last to the border. Israel's exuberance over his election prompted a rebuke from Shultz.

"You could crush him with your embrace," he warned.

But it was not the Israelis who crushed him.

Gemayel, who had survived two previous assassination attempts and had even lost his eighteen-month-old daughter in a remotely detonated car bomb attack, should have known to vary his routine. The day before Gemayel arrived for his weekly talk, twenty-six-year-old Habib Tanious Shartouni of the National Syrian Socialist Party—and operating on orders from a Syrian intelligence operative out of Rome—had left a suitcase bomb on the floor of his sister's third-floor apartment, directly over where Bashir held his weekly meeting.

"Let me tell you a story," Gemayel began that afternoon.

On an adjacent rooftop, Shartouni watched and waited.

"When the statue of the late president Bishara el-Kouri was sculpted,"

Gemayel continued, "his sons protested that its face bore no resemblance to their father's portrait. In time, though, they grew accustomed to the statue and forgot that it actually looked nothing like the photographs in their homes. The same thing will happen now. The opposition will grow accustomed to the portrait of the new president, even though it didn't want him."

At 4:10 p.m., Shartouni pressed the remote detonator, triggering a massive explosion that shook the city. The three-story building imploded, each floor pancaking upon the next while littering the streets with the arms and legs of the more than two dozen killed.

Rumors swirled that Gemayel had survived, but as the hours slipped past, efforts to find him in local hospitals diminished. At 9:45 p.m., a Mossad agent, checking corpses in the morgue at the Hotel Dieu Hospital, spotted a familiar wristwatch on a victim, whose battered face was unrecognizable. "The final proof of identification," Israeli historians Ze'ev Schiff and Ehud Ya'ari wrote, "was found in the pocket of the blue suit: Bashir's white-gold wedding ring."

Gemayel's assassination outraged Israel, who saw his death as a grievous blow to their efforts to shape Lebanon. His assassination likewise left unfinished Sharon's plan to eradicate the Palestine Liberation Organization's remaining political infrastructure in Lebanon. Within hours of Gemayel's death, Israeli troops again rolled into Beirut, this time as part of Operation Iron Mind. The public rationale was to prevent the capital from descending into chaos, but Sharon had ulterior motives. Israeli forces surrounded the Palestinian refugee camps at Sabra and Shatila. Sharon was convinced that the camps, despite the evacuation of the Palestinian guerrillas, still held as many as 3,000 fighters, a fact Dillon later refuted. "There were almost no adult males," the ambassador testified. "There were elderly men, women, and children." Sharon met with leaders of the Phalange militia, who were outraged over the assassination of Gemayel. He instructed them to go into the camps and root out terrorists.

"I don't want a single one of them left!" Sharon instructed.

On the night of September 16, Phalange militiamen crept into the camps. To assist in the operation, Israel fired 81mm illumination flares and later dropped others by plane. The militiamen then went door-to-door, massacring the inhabitants, a slaughter that would carry on for thirty-six hours. Word of the violence soon trickled out. On September 17, British reporter Robert Fisk ran into his *Washington Post* colleague Loren Jenkins, who was on the phone in the lobby of the Commodore Hotel, home to many foreign journalists.

"Fisky," he said, "something's going on in the camps."

Reporters arrived the next day only to be greeted by millions of flies. With handkerchiefs pressed over their mouths, the journalists navigated through the carnage. "When we had seen a hundred bodies, we stopped counting," Fisk recalled. "Down every alleyway, there were corpses—women, young men, babies, and grandparents—lying together in lazy and terrible profusion where they had been knifed or machinegunned to death."

Many of the dead had been shot, including men found lined up alongside walls with their hands and feet bound. Others bore signs of torture and trauma. Reporters observed women with their skirts hiked up and legs spread apart. One man had been castrated. Children populated the dead, including one infant still cradled in the arms of its deceased mother. "The bullet that had passed through her breast had killed the baby too," Fisk wrote. "Someone had slit open the woman's stomach, cutting sideways and then upwards, perhaps trying to kill her unborn child. Her eyes were wide open, her dark face frozen in horror."

"Jesus Christ!" Associated Press photojournalist Bill Foley repeated.

Friedman of the *New York Times* was horrified by the violence, which he observed had spared no creature, including horses so riddled by gunfire that their bellies had burst open. Friedman poured his anguish out into a four-page spread in the *New York Times* that would later earn him the Pulitzer Prize in international reporting. "Sabra and Shatila was something of a personal crisis for me," the Jewish reporter wrote. "This Israel I met on the outskirts of Beirut was not the heroic Israel I had been taught to identify with."

The murderers had made a hasty effort to bury some of the dead with bulldozers, but failed to finish the job, which Fisk discovered when he ascended what he thought was an earthen berm. "I could see a man's head, a woman's naked breast, the feet of a child," he recalled. "I was walking on dozens of corpses which were moving beneath my feet." Those efforts only complicated the challenge of tallying the dead, which Red Cross officials estimated ran between 800 and 1,000 people. "All of us wanted to vomit," Fisk concluded of his visit. "We were *breathing* death, inhaling the putrescence of the bloated corpses around us."

News of the massacre, which landed on the cover of *Time* magazine, horrified American leaders. Morris Draper, who served with Habib as special envoy to the Middle East, dictated a message to Sharon. "I have a representative in the camp counting the bodies. You should be ashamed," he said. "The situation is absolutely appalling. They're killing children! You have the field completely under your control and are therefore responsible for that area." Secretary of State Shultz agreed. "I was shaken and appalled," he said. So, too, was Reagan, who channeled his anger into a statement he released about the atrocities. "All people of decency must share our outrage and revulsion over the murders, which included women and children."

The massacre made a mockery of the United States—and led critics to blast Defense Secretary Weinberger for ordering the Marines out too soon. "We had promised to protect the Palestinian civilians," recalled National Security Council staffer Geoffrey Kemp. "It was our allies, the Israelis, who permitted the massacre to happen, and it was our boy Bashir Gemayel's troops that did the killing." Reagan was adamant that Israel immediately exit Beirut and all foreign forces subsequently leave Lebanon. To accomplish this, the president wanted to send the Marines back in as part of a reconstituted multinational force. Shultz supported the plan, but Weinberger and the Joint Chiefs of Staff once again objected.

"We shouldn't be the Beirut police department," Weinberger cautioned.

Reagan disagreed.

"I recognize your concerns," the president told those who opposed the mission, "but we have no choice now but to go back in and restore order."

In an address to the American people on September 20, the president declared that the time for talk had passed. The world now needed action. "The participation of American forces in Beirut will again be for a limited period," he said. "But I've concluded there is no alternative to their returning to Lebanon if that country is to have a chance to stand on its own feet."

The first mission of American military forces had been to oversee the withdrawal of the Palestine Liberation Organization, an operation that had a clear objective. But now, what precisely was the new mission? And without a defined goal, what would define success?

No one knew.

"We didn't have a solution to the problem," Ambassador Dillon admitted, "and we turned to the Marines."

CHAPTER 4

*The American public should not be surprised if this time,
there are some Marines who don't come back.*
—HAROLD SAUNDERS, FORMER ASSISTANT SECRETARY
OF STATE FOR THE MIDDLE EAST
September 22, 1982

The mission's ambiguous nature frustrated General Vessey. "American military forces are reared in the doctrine that says that if you are going to use the forces, you need to give them a task to perform. What is it that you want them to do?" Vessey said. "We never got a sufficiently defined task that either we or the forces on the ground really understood."

Weinberger echoed the general. "The multinational force had no mission, no rules of engagement. They weren't even allowed to protect themselves," the defense secretary recalled. "It was, I thought, a very wrong enterprise, from start to finish."

The only consolation was that most thought the mission would be of limited scope and duration. "We figured that once we got over our feeling of guilt and a little bit of law and order was established the Marines would be withdrawn," Vessey added. "That was the fundamental wrong assumption in Lebanon—that things were going to get better."

On September 29, 1982, the Marines returned.

The role of the leathernecks, officials spelled out in orders, would be one of "presence." The Marines would provide a stabilizing force, a buffer between warring factions.

"What is presence?" Colonel James Mead, commander of the Marine force, asked at the time. "They don't teach that at the War College." The colonel confided his confusion in Lieutenant General John Miller, commander of the Fleet Marine Force, Atlantic.

"Jim," the general replied, "the reason they didn't tell you what to do is because they didn't know what the hell to tell you to do."

Lebanon's instability and history of violence alarmed some members of Congress. "A lot of us are holding our breath," said Republican senator Ted Stevens of Alaska.

"We're going right into the fire on this one, where revenge, revenge, revenge is the order of the day," added Senator Henry "Scoop" Jackson, a Washington Democrat.

The same day Marines landed, Reagan fired off a letter to Congress, a requirement under the War Powers Resolution any time American troops deploy. In his vague two-page report, the president wrote that the Lebanese government had requested the presence of the Marines. Troops would serve as an "interposition force," so as to support the Lebanese government and military in restoring peace. Reagan could not specify how long the Marines would remain in Beirut, but he promised that it would be a limited operation. "In carrying out this mission, the American force will not engage in combat," the president assured lawmakers. "There is no intention or expectation that U.S. armed forces will become involved in hostilities."

On October 28, 1982—a month after the Marines returned—Reagan defined his twin objectives in National Security Decision Directive No. 64, a secret document titled "Next Steps in Lebanon." The president's primary goal was the withdrawal of Israeli, Syrian, and Palestinian forces. The second was to strengthen the Lebanese government, under the leadership of newly elected president Amin Gemayel, the older brother of the slain warlord. That would require rebuilding Lebanon's military so it could maintain peace and defend its borders. "I recognize that there are substantial risks in these undertakings which will confront our forces and those of our friends," Reagan wrote. "However, mindful of the recent tragic history of this traditionally friendly country and the opportunity which now clearly exists to further the cause of peace between Israel and all its neighbors, we cannot let this historic moment pass."

The president's new goals went far beyond providing just a "presence." America now planned to resurrect a country wrecked by years of war. "It was a wonder," Draper recalled, "that we had established for ourselves such an ambitious aim, which was nothing less than the removal of all foreign forces from Lebanon and the establishment of a stable country." It was a road filled with potential land mines, particularly since the central government controlled at best barely a third of the country, with the rest carved up between Israel, Syria, as well as various militias. Furthermore, in supporting the Christian-led government, America was, in essence, picking sides, a potentially dangerous proposition in a nation torn by religious strife.

The safety of the Marines depended upon American neutrality.

And how they fared would hinge on Amin Gemayel.

America had handcuffed its fate to the newly elected president, a forty-year-old political lightweight and playboy with perfect hair who was also a "corrupt" and "notorious womanizer." "He had all of Bashir's weaknesses," Friedman wrote, "and none of his strengths."

But American leaders looked past Gemayel to the Lebanese military, which was one of the few national institutions to have survived years of war and could serve as a vehicle for peace. "We saw the possibility of using the Army as a unifying force," Dillon said. "It was one of the places where all factions met and indeed in many cases worked together."

Though the idea of rebuilding the Paris of the Middle East that once graced postcards enraptured policymakers thousands of miles away in staid Washington offices, such lofty ambitions struck those in the rubble-strewn streets of Beirut as naive. Lebanon may have boasted a president and parliament, but it was a democracy in name only. "It is a tribal war," Friedman said, "on which a layer of Western diplomacy and constitutional language had been overlaid." Ancient hatreds and danger lurked beneath that veneer. "Lebanon was a kaleidoscope of different factions and groups," warned Draper, "not one of which could be trusted." Friedman agreed. "There are no good guys here," he added, "there are only bad guys and civilians." This was the perilous reality American troops would soon face. "If President Reagan really intends to keep the Marines in Lebanon until a stable government emerges here, he might consider building permanent housing for them," *Washington Post* reporter Loren Jenkins wryly observed. "Lebanese stability, like Lebanese unity, is mere wishful thinking."

This reconstituted multinational force would eventually triple the size of the original, totaling 6,000 troops from the United States, Italy, France, and later England. America's commitment would grow to 1,800 Marines, who staged out of the Beirut International Airport on the Mediterranean coast on the capital's southern end. The Italians would cover the zone just north of the Marines, including the Sabra and Shatila refugee camps, where the massacres had taken place, while the French would patrol the heart of Muslim West Beirut.

The Marines dug in at the airport, refurbishing war-scarred buildings, erecting large tents, and filling hundreds of thousands of sandbags. Jeep and foot patrols fanned out through the capital in November, and the following month Marines began training the Lebanese military.

"There is a feeling of rebirth and hope," Colonel Mead told reporters.

That feeling would not last long.

CHAPTER 5

We were fully conscious of being in the most dangerous city in the world.
—AMBASSADOR ROBERT DILLON
April 18, 2008

A t 6:30 p.m. on April 23, 1983, Marine One touched down on the tarmac at Andrews Air Force Base in the suburbs of Washington. The gray skies and drizzle that greeted President Reagan as he emerged from the helicopter reflected the somber occasion of his visit. The president and first lady were there that Saturday evening to honor and pay respect to the flag-draped caskets of the Americans killed six days earlier in the embassy bombing, an attack that had outraged the president. "Lord forgive me," Reagan wrote that week in his diary, "for the hatred I feel for the humans who can do such a cruel but cowardly deed."

It had been a difficult week. Marines and civilian rescuers had worked twenty-four hours a day digging through the rubble in a futile search for survivors. "Is anyone down there?" was a refrain often heard atop the pile. "If you can hear me, try to shout or move about."

No one ever replied.

Lebanese families had kept vigil as laborers deconstructed the ruins slab by slab, an arduous job set to the soundtrack of grumbling bulldozers and rattling jackhammers. A crane allowed rescuers to free the body pinned between the pancaked fourth and fifth floors. Ruptured tear gas canisters at times slowed progress. "Excavation teams," Thomas Friedman wrote, "had to use gas masks to fend off the stench of corpses rotting under the grotesque mound of concrete, steel reinforcement rods, broken furniture and torn clothing."

Two days after the attack, workers uncovered the remains of Lance Corporal Bobby McMaugh, the twenty-one-year-old Marine who had insisted on taking his little sister to her first high school dance and enjoyed handing out roses to female employees at the embassy. Fellow Marines elbowed

Lebanese rescuers aside before draping his body in an American flag and carrying him out of the wreckage as others stood in silence and saluted.

In their search for human remains, Marines also combed through the rubble for classified documents, a massive task since the bomb had destroyed the CIA substation. Troops loaded the debris onto trucks, hauled it to a secure dump, and then sifted through mounds of ripped and tattered paperwork under the glare of spotlights.

The recovery effort had ended only the day before. The final tally revealed that the attack had killed sixty-three people, including seventeen Americans. The remaining victims were Lebanese employees, visa applicants, and pedestrians. The blast wounded more than one hundred others. The United States had held a ceremony at 8:30 a.m. that Saturday at Beirut International Airport, where Marines, sailors, and soldiers formed an honor guard, joined by a platoon of Lebanese troops. Six military pallbearers carried each casket aboard a camouflaged C-141 Starlifter for the flight to Washington. "The ceremony was a sober and quiet one," a news reporter observed. "There was no band music or 21-gun salute."

The blast had vaporized the GMC, reducing the one-ton pickup to a piece of an axle and wheel frame, a couple of shock springs, and a mix of charred metal fragments. But those minuscule parts would allow investigators to trace the vehicle back to its original purchase in Texas, where it was then shipped to Dubai and eventually landed in Lebanon.

The search for a culprit, however, proved more elusive.

In the days since the attack, three groups had claimed credit: the Islamic Jihad Organization, the Arab Socialists Unionists, and the Vengeance Organization of the Sabra and Shatila Martyrs, which only muddied the investigatory waters. Without the perpetrator's identity, America could not determine the motive. "At this time," Secretary of State Shultz wrote in a cable, "it cannot be definitively ascertained exactly who perpetrated the bombing. As has been reported in the media, the suspects run the gamut from Syrians, Iranians, and/or Palestinians to perhaps even persons within the Lebanese political spectrum."

The terrorist's attack, even though it did not level the embassy, had rendered it structurally unsafe. The British would eventually invite the State Department to share quarters, but until then survivors relocated core offices to several nearby apartments. Diane Dillard turned her home into the consular office, while John Reid ran the public affairs operation from his apartment with additional diplomatic duties handled in his living room. The embassy's main hub of operations, however, was the home of Deputy Chief of Mission Bob Pugh, whose dining room functioned as a boardroom. The embassy's doctor converted one of the bathrooms into an exam suite, where he inspected wounds and changed bandages. Communications staff set up equipment salvaged from the embassy in the television room and on the sun-porch, while the embassy's cook whipped up soup and sandwiches in the kitchen. "His master bedroom," the State Department noted, "was the only room not commandeered by his colleagues."

Condolence messages from world leaders poured into the State Department and White House from Spain, Australia, and Japan to Turkey, Morocco, and Botswana. "Jordanians share with me our sense of outrage over this heinous crime," wrote King Hussein bin Talal. "It is an alien act to Islam, Arabism, and any form of human decency and morality."

"I and my ministers were horrified to hear of the ghastly attack on your Embassy in Beirut and send you sincere condolences," added the Sultan of Oman.

"We mourn the dead, express our profound condolences to the bereaved families, and pray for the speedy recovery of the injured," wrote Israel's Menachem Begin.

At the same time, the press and lawmakers questioned the embassy's meager security, given its location in the heart of what one reporter described as "the terror capital of the world." Guards at other embassies manned machine guns and towering walls.

Why did the United States, in contrast, depend only upon wooden sawhorses?

"Beirut is a war zone, yet the embassy stood unprotected by even a fence," argued the *Florida Today* newspaper. "It was child's play for a terrorist to drive a pickup truck packed with explosives to an entrance of the building and somehow detonate it."

"The embassy was a sitting duck," added the *Winston-Salem Journal*.

"Believe me," a former Lebanese army intelligence officer said, "it was always quite obvious that the Americans were just sitting there on the corniche, naked."

Undersecretary of State Lawrence Eagleburger, who had led the delegation to Beirut to escort the victims home, attempted to tamp down such charges. "An American embassy is in a country to deal with the people of the country. It's not a fort. It's not a vault. We don't hide behind steel doors and peek out through peepholes," Eagleburger said. "We have work to do and that happens to be dealing with the country in which we are assigned." Maybe so, but as reporter David Zucchino of the *Philadelphia Inquirer* noted, that came at a steep price. "In the end," he countered, "the openness the Americans so prized was literally blown to pieces."

Few beyond Senator Barry Goldwater, however, connected the attack on the embassy with the risk still faced by the Marines, who far outnumbered diplomats. "I think it's high time," the Arizona Republican announced, "we bring our Marines back."

His comments, however, drew scorn.

Like Reagan, many felt America needed to stay the course.

Columnists and editorial pages in towns and cities nationwide echoed the opinion of the *Arizona Republic*, one of the top newspapers in Goldwater's backyard. "If the Marines were to bug out now," the paper argued, "the result could be catastrophic."

Lost in the magnitude of the tragedy was the realization that a tectonic shift had occurred in domestic Lebanese politics in the last six months, one that would become clear in the months ahead. At the same time, dangerous foreign forces capable of extraordinary violence conspired to unleash terror. These dueling influences would soon haunt the United States.

While slain leader Bashir Gemayel had realized the importance of building bridges among the impoverished Shiites who made up roughly a third of Lebanon's population, his brother and successor did not. President Amin Gemayel viewed the Shiites, as Ambassador Dillon observed, "as low-class savages who could be ignored." He inflamed tensions by ordering the army to bulldoze Shiite shanties in southern Beirut, a move that alienated Nabih Berri, who commanded the powerful militia Amal. Berri was not a traditional thuggish warlord. He was an attorney by trade, a fan of John Wayne Westerns, a green card holder, and a frequent visitor to the United States, where his first wife and six children lived in Michigan.

The Shiites were not the only sect Gemayel offended. He likewise clashed with Walid Jumblatt, who headed the Druze Progressive Socialist Party, another Muslim militia. The balding and mustachioed Jumblatt, who in his youth wore blue jeans and leather jackets and raced motorcycles, occupied the Chouf Mountains, which overlooked the Marines at the airport. Similar to Berri, he, too, had been open to dialogue before Gemayel, like a political wrecking ball, obliterated any foundation on which to build national unity. Gemayel failed to realize that by destroying those potential relationships, he created an opportunity for Syria to exploit domestic divisions and doom any hope of national reconciliation. "If there were any in Lebanon's Muslim community whom Gemayel did not alienate, I didn't know of them," Friedman quipped. "Gemayel's pigheadedness soon became America's liability."

But rival factions were only one threat to Lebanese stability.

Ayatollah Ruhollah Khomeini, the Shiite religious leader who rose to power in Iran in 1979, saw an opportunity amid the chaos of Lebanon. He sent an army of 800 elite Revolutionary Guards into the Syrian-controlled Bekaa Valley, turning an old army base at the Sheik Abdullah Barracks into a terrorist incubator. Iranian guardsmen fanned out through the impoverished Shiite communities in southern Lebanon, attending mosque, giving speeches, and recruiting disenfranchised young men. These efforts had produced two homegrown Shiite terror organizations. The first was Islamic Amal, led by Hussein al-Musawi, a former chemistry teacher who had become frustrated with Berri and started his own more radical group. The second was the Islamic Jihad Organization—one of the three groups to claim credit for the embassy bombing—commanded by Imad Mugniyah, a Beirut University dropout who had fought with Yasser Arafat during the Lebanese Civil War. These two Iranian-backed organizations would soon be known simply as Hezbollah, or the Party of God.

The attacks in recent weeks on patrols of Italian, French, and American peacekeepers were the first clues of the violence ahead. The embassy, as it would later become clear, was the real wake-up call. "You could," Draper recalled, "smell the change in atmosphere all over Beirut." Even in a city known for bloodshed, the bombing had stunned locals, both for the choice of the target as well as the magnitude of the explosion. "The American Embassy," Red Cross volunteer Diyala Ezzedine lamented, "was always a symbol of security."

A sense of gloom and foreboding began to creep back into public life, as many sensed that the nation's newfound peace was slipping away. "It is unfortunate that whoever is the target, Lebanon is the victim," said Elie Salem, the nation's foreign minister.

"Sometimes," added popular arts promoter George Zeiny, "I feel we are doomed."

This was the stark new reality Reagan faced—though did not yet grasp—as he stepped down onto the tarmac at Andrews Air Force Base under gray skies and drizzle.

The evening's memorial marked the first of several scheduled tributes that would occur in the days ahead to honor America's slain diplomats and intelligence officers and staff. More than three thousand people would attend a public service at noon on April 26 at Washington's National Cathedral. Three days later, the CIA planned a private memorial at the agency's headquarters. The State Department, in turn, would host its own on May 6.

The president and first lady climbed into a black limousine, which spirited them to nearby Hangar Three. A large American flag hung on one wall of the cavernous building. Below it ran a single row of caskets, which had arrived from Beirut less than two hours earlier. Wreaths made of red and white chrysanthemums fronted each flag-draped coffin.

More than 150 wives, children, and parents of those killed in Beirut filled three rows of folding metal chairs, watching as the president exited the limousine followed by the first lady. The commander in chief slowly proceeded down the row of caskets before taking his seat in the front, joined by Secretary of State Shultz and his wife, Helena.

Following an opening invocation, the United States Air Force Band played the "Battle Hymn of the Republic." Fouad Turk, the secretary general of the Lebanese Foreign Ministry, spoke afterward about his nation's sorrow over the attack before turning the lectern over to the president. Reagan began with a deep breath, one picked up by the microphone. "There can be no sadder duty for one who holds the office I hold than to pay tribute to Americans who have given their lives in the service of their country," he said. "You here today, the families of these honored dead, I want you to know I speak for all Americans when I say that we share your sorrow and offer you our heartfelt sympathy. We are in your debt and theirs."

Silence settled over the hangar, interrupted only by the occasional click of a camera shutter or the shuffle of feet in the audience. Corralled in the back, news reporters focused on the families, noting that several wiped away tears. "These gallant Americans understood the danger they faced, and yet they went willingly into Beirut," the president continued. "And the dastardly deed, the act of unparalleled cowardice that took their lives, was an attack on all of us—on our way of life and on the values we hold dear. We would indeed fail them if we let that act deter us from carrying on their mission of brotherhood and peace."

Reagan reiterated his earlier statement that the attack would not deter America from its mission in Lebanon. "Let us here in their presence," he concluded, "serve notice to the cowardly, skulking barbarians in the world that they will not have their way. Let us dedicate ourselves to the cause of those loved ones, the cause they served so nobly and for which they sacrificed their lives, a cause of peace on earth and justice for all mankind."

The Air Force Band played the national anthem after which the president greeted the families, which overwhelmed him. At one point he pulled his pocket square from his suit jacket to wipe his nose. Nancy Reagan trailed a few steps behind, offering hugs and kisses. "It was a moving experience," the president confided in his diary. "We were both in tears—I know all I could do was grip their hands—I was too choked up to speak."

The experience haunted him afterward when he walked through the doors of the Washington Hilton hotel for the White House Correspondents Dinner, a normally jovial affair. When he approached the lectern and looked out across the ballroom filled with two thousand attendees, Reagan realized, he simply couldn't do it. The afternoon had depleted him. "Nancy and I had another sad journey that we had to make before coming here tonight," he said. "I just don't feel, coming as we did from Andrews Air Force Base, I could stand up here. If you'll forgive us, we'll just hold on to the script and take a raincheck, and I'll keep it for next year."

CHAPTER **6**

All our eggs seem to be in one fragile basket.
—Representative William Dickinson
October 18, 1983

Secretary of State Shultz returned the following afternoon to Andrews Air Force Base, where he boarded a thirteen-hour flight for the Middle East. The embassy bombing had highlighted the glacial pace of negotiations to remove foreign forces from Lebanon and jump-start the president's stalled peace plan for Israel. The process had become so bogged down that spring that National Security Advisor William Clark urged Reagan to bring in famed diplomat Henry Kissinger. Others in the intelligence community questioned whether it might be best to bypass a "fruitless mediation" and bring the Marines home. "A policy of quiet disengagement from a losing venture would enable the President to avoid being identified with Gemayel's fate," one analyst urged. "Amin's hold on 'power' is exceedingly precarious, and he is likely to be unseated or dispatched to his Maker well before the year's end."

But America welcomed a challenge.

Against such odds, senior diplomats Phil Habib and Morris Draper pinballed between Beirut and Jerusalem, eventually establishing a basic framework for a deal, though several difficult issues remained. The administration hoped sending Shultz would add the necessary gravitas to break the impasse and put a check in the win column.

Much was at stake for the White House.

After three years in office—and with an election on the horizon—the president had few accomplishments in the foreign policy arena. In contrast, Reagan's predecessor and one-term president Jimmy Carter—often chided in Republican circles as a foreign policy lightweight—negotiated the return of the Panama Canal, normalized relations with China, and brokered the Camp David Accords, which led to peace between Israel and Egypt.

Reagan was not the only one whose reputation was at stake. Critics had begun to target Shultz, who had taken over as secretary of state nine months earlier, accusing the sixty-two-year-old of being missing in action on the Middle East. In many ways, Shultz, who played football at Princeton and fought as a Marine in World War II, made an unlikely diplomat, having spent much of his career as an economist in academia. Armed with a doctorate in industrial economics from the Massachusetts Institute of Technology, Shultz had taught at his alma mater and later at the University of Chicago, where he served as the dean of the business school. He spent several years in the Richard Nixon White House as labor and later Treasury secretary before he took over as president of the Bechtel Corporation, an engineering and construction behemoth that built airports and hydroelectric and nuclear power plants around the globe. In a town like Washington, filled with large personalities, Shultz was soft-spoken and pragmatic. The only colorful flare in his otherwise humble personality was a Princeton tiger tattooed on his rump.

More than six months had passed since the Marines landed as part of the reconstituted multinational force. Many in Congress, the media, and even the White House feared the passage of so much time had cost Reagan his chance to secure the departure of Israeli and Syrian forces, the first step in the president's ambitious plan to bring peace to the region.

Newspaper headlines that week reflected the pressure as well as the pessimism. "Reagan Plan's Failure Began at Home," declared the *Wall Street Journal*.

"The Bungled Initiative," stated the *New York Times*.

"The Knives Have Come Out for Shultz," reported the *Washington Post*.

The secretary of state was particularly stung by a *Wall Street Journal* article, which blamed Reagan's failed peace initiative on Shultz's refusal to visit the Middle East until now. "Because the president isn't seen in the Middle East as a man versed in the issue, George Shultz's aloofness was particularly lethal," wrote correspondent Karen House. "His conspicuous absence spoke loudly of lack of interest." Shultz knew, on some levels, she was right. "I shared the frustration," America's top diplomat wrote, "and feared that the passage of time had both diminished our opportunities and compounded our difficulties."

Despite the frustration, Shultz soldiered on.

Syria remained the greatest challenge. President Hafez Assad took a long view, one best summarized by the *Guardian*'s James MacManus. "History as much as hegemony," the reporter observed, "accounts for Syria's think-ing on Lebanon." The fifty-two-year-old Assad, who had seized power in a bloodless coup, considered Lebanon a part of greater Syria, a hangover from the era before the breakup of the Ottoman Empire, which saw the region carved up into smaller nations. In addition, Assad distrusted Leba-non's Christian militias, who he believed were too pro-Israel. The 40,000 troops Syria maintained in Lebanon served as a check on the Jewish state's power. Assad's previous signals that he might support America's initiative had faded, a fact that coincided with the $2 billion Soviet resupply of 160 fighters, 800 tanks, and surface-to-air missiles. As many as 7,000 Soviet military personnel were now based in Syria. Assad felt emboldened. "He wanted Lebanon," Shultz said, "under his thumb."

But Israel proved just as difficult.

The Jewish state, which had suffered a black eye in world opinion follow-ing the brutal invasion of Lebanon, wanted to extract maximum benefit from the bloodshed. That came in the hopes of a peace treaty and full diplomatic relations. Such a move would be politically costly for Lebanon in the Arab world, where most countries refused to recognize the Jewish state. Israel had achieved that with Egypt via the Camp David Accords, but Egypt was a strong and independent country able to weather the fallout, a distinction Is-raeli leaders struggled to grasp. To aid Shultz, Reagan signed National Secu-rity Decision Directive No. 92, a secret one-page order titled "Accelerating the Withdrawal of Foreign Forces from Lebanon." The directive instructed Shultz to make clear that America had two courses of action in future deal-ings with Israel. "One is to restore and enhance the relationship," Reagan wrote. "The other course leads inevitably to a fundamental reappraisal of the entire U.S.-Israeli relationship. We clearly prefer the former course, but we are also committed to obtaining the withdrawal of foreign forces from Lebanon. U.S. leadership and our credibility as a world power is at stake."

Given Assad's intractability, the administration decided to sideline Syria and focus first on Israel, a snub that would ultimately prove to be a serious misstep. The secretary of state planned to keep Syria informed, but he also hoped that Saudi Arabia would later help put pressure on Assad to exit Leb-anon. Habib and his deputy, Morris Draper, had worked behind the scenes to create a framework of a deal, but many questions lingered. Those ranged from the security along Israel's northern border to what kind of relationship

Lebanon might accept with the Jewish state. Shultz benefited from more than just Reagan's cudgel. Sam Lewis, America's ambassador to Israel, confided in Shultz that Israel's continued bloodletting was taking a toll. "The mood in Israel," he told the secretary of state, "is turning sour about Lebanon."

Shultz arrived in the region with no plan in hand on how to bring the two sides together. His first stop was Cairo, where he met with Egyptian president Hosni Mubarak and America's ambassadors in the region. He flew to Israel for a listening session with Begin followed by one in Beirut with Gemayel, the latter of which afforded him a chance to visit the wrecked embassy. "It's simply incredible," he told reporters, "to see such enemies of peace."

The secretary of state shuttled back and forth between the two capitals, chipping away at each side's concerns with the skills acquired during his days as a labor negotiator. The conversations at times were difficult, particularly in Lebanon, where Gemayel had few allies. Not only did the Muslims distrust him, but so, too, did many of the Christians. Even though he was the brother of the martyred warlord Bashir, many in the Maronite community felt Amin was weak and too flexible. This meant that he feared not only the outrage of Syria and the Arab world, but also his constituencies at home. "We're not talking about the fall of a government," Foreign Minister Elie Salem warned Shultz at one point, "but the fall of a head."

The worries and the goals of each nation reflected in the unique style of negotiations. "The Lebanese, as much as possible, wanted to avoid putting anything down in writing," Shultz observed. "The Israelis, by contrast, wanted to put everything in writing."

"I feel like the broker between Talmudic lawyers and Levantine rug merchants," an exasperated secretary of state remarked.

"There are a lot of loose ends," said his executive assistant Ray Seitz.

"And they're getting looser," Shultz replied.

The drawn-out process and increasingly acrimonious talks only soured relations as the days ticked past. "The negotiations left an extremely bad taste with the Lebanese," said David Mack, director of the State Department's North Arab region. "Rather than gaining more trust in the Israelis, the Lebanese came to have less. That was also true for the Israelis."

Even with seemingly insurmountable challenges, an agreement eventually emerged, albeit one far less ambitious than Israel wanted. The proposed plan declared an end to the state of war between the two nations.

Israel would agree to withdraw its forces, but in a secret side deal with the United States was required to do so only if Syria also left. Security along the southern border, which was a major concern for Israeli leaders who feared attacks on northern settlements, would be handled by Lebanon, but there would be periodic joint patrols by both nations. Lebanon balked at full diplomatic relations with Israel, but agreed to allow liaison offices. On May 6—twelve days after Shultz had lifted off from Andrews Air Force Base—Israel's cabinet voted 17–2 to approve the deal. A formal signing was then set for May 17, 1983.

But Israel was only one half of the equation.

Shultz flew to Damascus to meet with President Assad. Backed by Moscow and marginalized by the United States, Assad had no incentive to help Washington, nor did Shultz offer any. Aside from America's earlier slight, a deal between Israel and Lebanon would undermine Assad's power in the region. The Syrian ruler, in fact, viewed Gemayel's signing as the "ultimate betrayal." "The real Syrian fear," as one observer noted, "is that peace between Lebanon and Israel would draw yet another Arab state into the Israeli orbit and leave Damascus further isolated and open to devastating attack by the Jewish state."

The state-run media in Syria left little doubt of Assad's scornful views of the deal. "Lebanon will become an Israeli protectorate and a base for spying on the Arab world," declared one such broadcast. "This agreement means Arab surrender."

Rather than cooperate with the United States, which was desperate for a deal, Assad realized it was more advantageous to play the role of spoiler. Shultz detected that subtle hint when he took a seat in the velvet green chairs of Assad's audience room. On the wall facing the secretary of state hung a painting immortalizing Saladin's victory over the Crusaders in the Battle of Hattin in 1187. The Arab autocrat who sat across from Shultz knew much of bloodshed. Only a year earlier his security forces had crushed an uprising in the city of Hama that killed an estimated 20,000 people. "Assad," as Moroccan King Hassan once warned Washington, "is intelligent but a devil." The violence showed that Assad, who may have outwardly shunned the lavish lifestyles of other dictators, could be just as brutal in his effort to hold on to power. "His manner was pleasant and engaging," Shultz recalled of the four-hour meeting, "even though his message was negative. He did not say no, and he invited me to return for further discussion. The discussion had gone as well as I could have expected. The real tests lay ahead."

On his way home, Shultz met with Defense Secretary Caspar Weinberger in Paris, who immediately seized on the critical failure of the secretary of state's deal. Israel's departure was predicated upon Syria's withdrawal, which Assad had no plans to do. In short, America was in no better position than it was before Shultz boarded the plane to the Middle East. "This agreement," Weinberger said, "gave President Assad of Syria veto power over any withdrawal and thus over Israel's ability to establish better relations with a key Arab neighbor."

CHAPTER 7

One of the things that protects us is the perception of neutrality.
If that should ever be lost, then we'll become targets.
—MAJOR GEORGE CONVERSE, LETTER TO HIS WIFE
June 10, 1983

Colonel Timothy Geraghty took over Marine operations in Beirut at 4 p.m. on May 30, 1983. The forty-five-year-old, who sported close-cropped hair, piercing blue eyes, and a chiseled jaw, looked as though he stepped right out of a Marine recruitment poster. A native of Saint Louis, the colonel stood five feet, ten inches tall and sported a lean and muscular physique with ripped forearms, the result of decades of push-ups. Geraghty had grown up in a tight-knit midwestern family, the fourth of seven children. His father had supported them by working in the same aluminum manufacturing plant as the colonel's grandfather. As a youth, Geraghty had attended a Franciscan parochial school, followed by the Christian Brothers College High School, a military school. Geraghty continued his Catholic education into college, enrolling at St. Louis University. Upon graduation in 1959, he signed up for officer candidate school. For Geraghty, the Marine Corps was his first and only choice. "We are," he said, "the best of the best."

Geraghty had fought in Vietnam, where he served as a company commander leading reconnaissance patrols into the sweltering jungles. He so enjoyed the experience that he twice extended his tour. In the wake of Vietnam, Geraghty rose up the ranks. He spent four years as the ground reconnaissance officer at the Development Center in Quantico, attended the Command and Staff College, earned a master's degree from Pepperdine University, and spent years with the Special Operations Group in Washington. Along the way, the married father of a ten-year-old son developed a strong reputation among officers and enlisted men. "He had a way of making you feel at ease with his friendly manner and an easy smile," recalled Glenn Dolphin. "The colonel was a team builder who wanted to include everyone in the process of making the unit work. I felt as if I had been given an opportunity to be part of his team."

Geraghty commanded the 24th Marine Amphibious Unit, or MAU, as it was commonly called. Such units are often referred to as the sharp end of the spear, a relatively small force of 1,800 Marines who are forward-deployed on ships and able to respond quickly to in extremis contingency operations. A typical amphibious unit consisted of four elements, including a command component, ground force, air arm, and a service support group. In Beirut, Geraghty's ground force—known as a Battalion Landing Team—was made up of the 1st Battalion, 8th Marine Regiment, under the command of Lieutenant Colonel Howard "Larry" Gerlach. Geraghty's air arm, led by Lieutenant Colonel Larry Medlin, consisted of the Marine Medium Helicopter Squadron-162 (HMM-162), which boasted four types of heavy-lift, transport, and attack helicopters. Major Douglas Redlich's MAU Service Support Group 24 (MSSG-24) provided everything from maintenance and motor transport to medical, dental, and military police. "But," as one Marine noted, "everyone thought their sole reason for existence and only worthwhile job was to make sure we received mail from home."

But the Marines were only one half of the American force in Lebanon. The rest consisted of Amphibious Squadron Eight (PHIBRON 8), a vital naval component under the command of Commodore Morgan "Rick" France. The forty-eight-year-old France lived aboard his flagship USS *Iwo Jima*, an amphibious assault vessel designed to transport Marines and helicopters into combat. The four other ships in France's squadron included the USS *Austin*, USS *Portland*, USS *Harlan County*, and USS *El Paso*. These warships would not only transport the Marines, helicopters, tanks, and howitzers to Lebanon, but would also remain offshore throughout the deployment, providing vital support with everything from expanded medical services to laundry.

Since the first troops landed to help remove the Palestine Liberation Organization the previous August, the Marines had maintained a continued presence in the war-battered capital. Geraghty's forces were the fourth Marine Amphibious Unit tasked to help maintain peace. Unlike previous units, which had cycled through every few months, Geraghty's troops were slated to remain in Beirut through the middle of November, the longest of any deployment so far. His forces likewise had arrived in the wake of the massive terrorist attack on the American Embassy, which most recognized had been a game changer. Colonel James Mead, who was Geraghty's predecessor, predicted the new arrivals had zero chance of making it through the deployment without a terrorist attack. "They will get hit," Mead concluded. "It's a question of where, when, and just how strongly they want to come after them." Mead's comments were not news to Geraghty. The colonel, who sat with a Marine Corps historian on the eve of taking command, was asked what he believed would be his biggest challenge. "Terrorism," he declared. "That's what I think is the biggest problem we're going to face."

The Marines had come over in Commodore France's flotilla, departing the North Carolina port at Morehead City on May 11, 1983. Geraghty had used the three weeks at sea to prepare his men, providing briefings on everything from Lebanon's history and culture to the latest intelligence and terrorist threats. A tape of those talks was then played on the shipboard television, which made an impression on many, including Second Lieutenant Maurice Hukill. "While we are here," the twenty-five-year-old wrote his family, "this thing is going to come to a head." Aside from lectures, troops cranked out push-ups and sit-ups and jogged laps around the deck. "I gave up smoking on ship," nineteen-year-old Lance Corporal Bill Stelpflug wrote his sister. "I still chew tobacco and cuss, so don't worry about me." Others listened to music, played cards, and watched movies, including *The Shining*, which was featured one night in the *Austin*'s wardroom. The Navy even hosted boxing tournaments. "I had never actually witnessed a boxing match," Dr. John Hudson, a lieutenant assigned to the Marines, wrote his wife. "These sailors and Marines are ferocious. They honestly love a good fight, too."

The prospect of foreign adventure excited many who were fresh out of high school and had seen little of the world beyond family vacations and boot camp. Stelpflug couldn't believe the Navy steamed right through the infamous Bermuda Triangle. "I never knew the ocean was so big and wild," he wrote in a letter. "I have seen waves 20 ft. high." The Atlantic's beauty drew his attention again in another letter. "The water is so blue it is incredible," he wrote. "Bluer than blue." Eighteen-year-old Private Henry Linkkila likewise marveled at the Rock of Gibraltar, which guarded the entrance to the Mediterranean. "Let me tell you," he wrote his mother, "that sucker's big." As the ships closed in on Lebanon, the realization of the danger ahead crystallized. Lance Corporal Bruce Hollingshead captured that in a letter, noting that many gathered a few days before arrival for a religious service on the flight deck complete with communion. "We are all nervous," he wrote. "I & everyone else did a lot of praying."

On May 28, the Marines reached Lebanon, the dark silhouette of the coastline visible along the eastern horizon. "Can you believe where I am!!! I can't get over it," Hudson wrote his wife. "Never in a million years did I think I would be in the Middle East." The leathernecks sloshed ashore the next day under the spotlight of news cameras and a barrage of questions from reporters. "I felt," Linkkila wrote, "like I was in a freak show." The troops settled in that day at Beirut International Airport, along the Mediterranean coast on the capital's southern end. The first Marines to occupy the airport in September 1982 had found the area littered with tens of thousands of pieces of unexploded ordnance left over from eight years of war. Explosives teams tasked to clear the area would later tally 125 types of munitions from nineteen countries. Beyond unexploded ordnance, the airport, as Geraghty and his predecessors all realized, was tactically unsound, consisting of low ground bordered on the south and east by the Chouf Mountains, an area occupied by various militias and the Israelis, who had pulled out of the capital. "We were," as one American general quipped, "in a goldfish bowl."

But the Marines were there not to fight; they were to serve only as peace-keepers.

The colonel's headquarters consisted of a two-story concrete building that had once housed the airport's firefighting school. A couple of old fire trucks sat rusting out back, riddled with gunfire and shrapnel holes, reminding operations officer Major George Converse of the ambushed vehicle in which outlaws Bonnie Parker and Clyde Barrow met their demise. Marines converted the half dozen truck bays into offices and living quarters, filling them with cots and mosquito nets. A former classroom with pink walls was adorned with maps and would serve as the Combat Operations Center, where service members would man phones and radios and track events in the city to build a common operating picture for senior leadership. Geraghty moved his personal quarters to a room upstairs connected by a spiral staircase, which he shared with his executive officer. On the wall of the first-floor officers club hung a plaque given by Major General Alfred Gray, the commander of the Second Marine Division. On it was printed a verse from the New Testament's book of Matthew, which would serve as a guiding principle for the Marines: "Blessed are the peacemakers," it read, "for they shall be called the children of God."

The Battalion Landing Team took over a four-story concrete building that once housed Lebanon's Aviation Administrative Bureau, though in more recent years it was controlled by the Palestine Liberation Organization, the Syrians, and the Israelis, who had used it as a field hospital. The bulk of Gerlach's forces—which consisted of Alpha, Bravo, Charlie, and Weapons companies—would man outposts around the airport while his headquarters and support staff moved into the building. Commonly referred to as the BLT, the building was located a few hundred yards southwest of Geraghty's headquarters. The battle-scarred structure featured a central atrium that ran from the ground floor to the roof—the type common in some hotels—encircled by balconied hallways that led to former offices that would serve as barracks for 350 troops. "I half-expected," one Marine joked, "to see a fountain bubbling in the large open center." That resemblance no doubt led to the creative plywood sign that dangled out front of the sandbagged entrance. "Welcome to the Beirut Hilton. Military Discounts Available."

Years of war had shattered all the windows, which Marines covered with plastic sheeting to keep out the blowing wind, rain, and sand. But drafts proved only one of the building's many problems. "It is infested by rats," Staff Sergeant William Pollard complained in a letter. "There is dirt everywhere." Linkkila echoed him in a note to his mother. "You ought to see where I live," the private wrote, "a big half burnt out building that smells like shit." Accommodations consisted of cots and salvaged or homemade furniture with portable toilets and showers set up in tents outside. "Everything here you have to jiggle—the lights, the radio, the whole nine yards," Sergeant Mecot Camara wrote in a letter to his family. "I shower out of a pail of cold water every morning. I've got wet clothes strung all over the room. It's great—really great." Few made out as well as Dr. Hudson, who moved into his fourth-floor room to find that the previous occupant had gifted him a desk, bookcase, two chairs, and a rug. "Most of the Marines are living in tents around the grounds of the airport," he wrote to his wife. "Their existence is pretty pitiful. Compared to them I have it great!!!"

The Mediterranean served as a natural western boundary for the airport. A string of outposts and checkpoints formed a perimeter that encircled the other three sides, enclosing an area of about eight square miles. One of Gerlach's infantry companies manned a position south of the airport near the tip of the runway. Another was stationed east of the tarmac along the perimeter road, while a third company occupied the library at the Lebanese Scientific and Technical University, northeast of the airport. Throughout deployment, Gerlach would periodically rotate the companies. The Marines set up Charlie Battery with its 155mm howitzers to the north along the main airport highway. Interspersed between the rifle companies were various outposts, including seven checkpoints jointly manned by Marines and members of the Lebanese Armed Forces. These were positioned at important intersections of nearby roads as well as along the main airport highway. Anywhere from four to fifteen Marines joined local forces, though the task of searching cars and questioning drivers fell to the Lebanese. "All in all," Converse observed, "I guess we're pretty secure."

Troops settled into a routine.

The cooks rose long before dawn to prepare the first of two hot meals of the day in the ground-floor mess hall of the Battalion Landing Team headquarters. Breakfast usually featured eggs, bacon, grits, and sausage patties, while dinners ranged from spaghetti and meat loaf to pork roasts and steaks. Lunch, in contrast, consisted of a field ration. Marines could enjoy two beers a night while dirty fatigues were sent out to the ships to be laundered.

The medical operation was run by Dr. Hudson, a twenty-eight-year-old physician who was aided by about fifty Navy corpsmen. A gifted musician and fan of Dixieland jazz, Hudson had worked his way through the University of Georgia by playing trombone at the Crystal Pistol, a thousand-seat theater at Atlanta's Six Flags Over Georgia amusement park. He was a colorful and at times irreverent personality—often compared to Alan Alda's character Hawkeye in the television show *M*A*S*H*—who once wore a gorilla suit to school and later waltzed into his anatomy final playing his horn. He had pulled a similar stunt on board the *Austin* during one of the boxing matches, when he wore a mop head as a wig and pretended to be the mother of one of his fighting hospital corpsmen, whom he cheered on while belting out notes from his trombone. "The whole ship," Hudson wrote his wife, "got a kick out of the scene."

The married father of a three-month-old son, Hudson had joined the Navy to help repay his medical school loans, but his long-term goal was to return home to the town of Milledgeville to be a country doctor. In Beirut, the physician and hospital corpsmen treated not only the Marines but also the British, Canadian, and American diplomats, as well as scores of journalists who showed up in the fourth-floor clinic. Sick call was offered daily from 8 to 10 a.m. and again from 1 to 3 p.m., but Hudson admitted those times meant little. "We really don't have any hours," the doctor said. "We see people whenever they show up."

Two Navy dentists cared for the oral health of the Marines. The senior of the pair was thirty-six-year-old Lieutenant Dr. Gilbert Bigelow, who previously had served in the Air Force during Vietnam. Bigelow had worked as an air traffic controller for forward units, calling in artillery and air strikes, a job in which he earned two Bronze Stars for valor. After the war, he had returned to school, earning a doctorate in dentistry from Howard University. With his degree in hand, he decided to climb back into uniform, only this time in the Navy, which offered him the promise of better duty stations—at least until Beirut. Bigelow's colleague was twenty-seven-year-old Lieutenant Dr. James Ware, a Savannah, Georgia, native who had followed his father's path into both the military and dentistry. Ware had attended Benedictine Military School before enrolling at Emory University and later the Medical College of Georgia, Hudson's alma mater. The doctor and dentist, in fact—both married Georgians just a year apart in age—had become fast friends on the voyage over to Lebanon, rooming together on board the *Austin*. The Beirut dental clinic featured two chairs, x-ray capability, and a pharmacy, which allowed Bigelow and Ware to perform everything from routine cleanings to root canals.

Protestant and Catholic chaplains tended to the spiritual care. Thirty-five-year-old Lieutenant Commander Father George Pucciarelli was the senior faith leader. A Massachusetts native, Pucciarelli—or "Pooch" as he was commonly called—had enlisted in the Navy Reserves in 1972 while still in seminary. He was joined by Lieutenant (j.g.) Chaplain Danny Wheeler, who was also thirty-five but from rural Wisconsin. Wheeler had spent a year in the Army during Vietnam before he enrolled at the University of Wisconsin and later Luther Seminary in Saint Paul. He had served as a parish minister before he decided to enlist in the Navy. In Beirut, the faith leaders would visit the rifle companies in the field on Saturdays and hold multiple services around the airport on Sundays, including one on the beach. But the center of religious life was a fourth-floor room in the Battalion Landing Team headquarters that Pucciarelli and Wheeler had converted into the Peacekeeping Chapel, complete with benches that resembled pews and an altar made from an old workbench.

To dress it up, the men draped a camouflage canopy from the ceiling, while Corporal John Olson painted a mural of a praying Marine that joined a list of the Ten Commandments. "Whenever you have a chance, stop in and make yourself at home," the chaplains wrote in the weekly base newspaper. "It belongs to you."

For many of the young Marines, Beirut was their first time overseas. The trimmed lawns and pristine infrastructure common in American towns and cities was gone, replaced by bombed and battered buildings, roadblocks, and unpaved roads that more closely resembled the set of an apocalyptic movie. "It's the pits," Staff Sergeant Pollard wrote home. "The worst place I have ever been." Many were stunned by the poverty and the filth, including the rancid stench of raw sewage that wafted through the area. The troops colorfully dubbed a feculent drainage stream near the airport "Shit River," a name that would later appear on Marine Corps maps. The piles of trash and debris shocked others. "Poor people in the U.S. have it good compared to this place," Private David Madaras wrote in a letter. "Everything here is blown to hell." Major Converse echoed him. "Some parts of the city are just shacks made out of tin and cardboard amid the rubble," he wrote. "No power or water with people living in squalor."

Despite the filth, Stelpflug marveled at the exotic markets, the palm trees, and the glorious sunsets over the Mediterranean. On the morning of June 3, an earthquake that measured 5.3 on the Richter scale shook him out of his rack at 4:07 a.m. "It was," he wrote his sister, "pretty wild." Another day, in a land littered with explosives, he found an arrowhead. "Hell, some people pay a lot of money to see the Mideast," he wrote. "I get paid for it."

The awful conditions only reinforced the desire of many to want to help. "We may or may not be successful," First Lieutenant Don Woollet wrote in a letter home. "But the undertaking, the quest itself, is noble. No other nation but the U.S. would ever attempt it." Others echoed him. "I'm excited about being here," said Staff Sergeant Robert Kline.

"To me," added Corporal Brad Trudell, "this is what the Marine Corps is all about."

In accordance with the peacekeeping mission, Marines were given a wallet-sized white card that spelled out strict rules of engagement, which, as investigators would later highlight, proved more prohibitive than the blue card issued to troops who guarded the embassy. The ten rules for Marines at the airport ranged from the need to protect civilians to requiring troops to use the minimum degree of force. "When on post, mobile or foot patrol, keep loaded magazine in weapon, bolt closed, weapons on safe. No round in the chamber," the rules mandated. "Do not chamber a round unless told to do so by a commissioned officer unless you must act in immediate self-defense where deadly force is authorized."

The leathernecks jumped into the job, conducting four to seven foot patrols a day through the adjacent Shiite slum of Hay es Salaam, which the troops dubbed "Hooterville." That was complemented by two jeep patrols through the greater Beirut area, all of which were designed to demonstrate the Marines' presence. "We try to let the American flag be seen by everyone," said Woollet, a 1980 graduate of the U.S. Naval Academy. Sergeant Stephen Russell agreed, pointing to the flag on his shoulder. "That patch is like a key to the city," he said. "It gives me a very safe feeling. People here respect us for what we're trying to do for their country."

But not everyone welcomed the Marines. The daily patrols likewise revealed a simmering hostility among Lebanon's Shiites. In Hooterville, Marines spotted posters of the Ayatollah Khomeini. Other times young men made jeering and degrading gestures or sent children out to harass the leathernecks, knowing that the Marines would refuse to engage. These actions prompted Geraghty to propose incorporating Lebanese troops on patrols. "The anti-American sentiment encountered," one report noted, "is a cause for concern."

In addition to patrols, Marines guarded the airport complex, the British Embassy, and the Duraffourd Building, the latter two home to America's displaced diplomatic operations, only now with enhanced security. "Barriers are being constructed in front of the embassy buildings to improve external security," one update noted. "Attempts to forcibly breach the barriers will be immediately responded to with fire." The Marines who took over guard duty at the embassy found it humbling. "It had a sobering effect on all of us and made us realize that this whole thing was for real," one said. "It makes us take our jobs more seriously."

Beyond patrols and guard duty, troops investigated and blocked tunnels under the airport as well as liaised with French, British, and Italian forces. The Marines demonstrated an amphibious assault on the beach for French noncoms and officers, offering tours of American landing craft. Others participated in familiar fire exercises and combined parachute operations with member forces and Navy SEALs. Marines instructed Lebanese mechanics in the fundamentals of diesel engines, troubleshooting fuel systems, and preventative maintenance. Embassy political officer Ryan Crocker, who survived the terrorist attack, briefed Marine officers. So, too, did Deputy Chief of Mission Robert Pugh, who stayed for dinner. Dr. Hudson delivered a lecture on snakebites and how to evaluate, identify, and treat them.

A group of 102 Marines and sailors left for Camp des Garrigues in France for training and liberty after the long ocean voyage. More would depart throughout the month for a little rest and relaxation in Greece, Turkey, and Sicily. Geraghty, meanwhile, briefed a revolving door of senior military and congressional visitors who cycled through Beirut.

The colonel wrestled with other unexpected challenges, including accidental weapons discharges that prompted him to further tighten the rules of engagement, barring any Marine on guard at an internal base post from inserting a magazine into his rifle. The worst of these events occurred at dusk on June 15 when a corporal on post scanned the horizon through the Starlight scope mounted atop his M16. The Marine noticed movement and centered his scope. The rifle roared. Two Lebanese privates jogged side by side south along the airport's perimeter road. The round tore through both legs of the first soldier. The bullet then ripped through the right thigh of the second soldier before coming to rest in his left leg. Fellow Lebanese joggers picked up the men, summoned a jeep, and brought them to Dr. Hudson's clinic, who made sure there were no life-threatening wounds before calling a Lebanese ambulance. To his surprise, the ambulance took an hour to arrive. When it finally did, Hudson was stunned to learn the paramedics did not have any stretchers. "The Lebanese expected us," he wrote to his wife, "to care for their wounded. You cannot imagine how pitiful their health care for soldiers is."

Geraghty feared the political blowback of an American Marine shooting two Lebanese soldiers. He hustled to visit General Ibrahim Tannous, commander of Lebanon's armed forces, who was quick to put the colonel at ease. Both soldiers, whom Geraghty would later visit, were expected to make a swift recovery. "What surprised me," Geraghty said, "was General's Tannous's amazement that a single M16 rifle round could penetrate four legs."

The Marines kept busy, even when not on duty.

Troops could lift weights in a makeshift exercise room in the lobby of the Battalion Landing Team headquarters. "The clang of Nautilus machines," Lance Corporal Michael Petit said, "was accompanied by the grunts of Marines working out at all hours." Afterward, many grabbed a cold drink from

Shuffles, the Lebanese man who ran a vending business from a closet under the staircase. "If you had ever watched Shuffles move you would have had no trouble figuring out how he got that nickname," wrote First Lieutenant Glenn Dolphin. "It didn't matter to anyone if he was a Muslim, Christian or Jew. He was just an old guy trying to support his family by selling soft drinks, candy, cigarettes and snuff to the Marines." Another favorite was General Billy, a black goat the previous amphibious unit had bought for thirty dollars to keep the grass trimmed. The general's preference, however, ran beyond weeds. "Within a short time," Dolphin added, "he had developed a taste for ponchos, poncho liners and sleeping bag covers."

Marines read books or leafed through the *Root Scoop*, the base newspaper, which was published on Fridays. The chaplains, who penned a column, encouraged troops to write letters and try to make new friends, a remedy for homesickness. "Yes, we're a long way from home, but let's not make it too miserable," the faith leaders urged. "Time always goes by!!!" For a taste of home, Marines could tune into the Armed Forces Radio and Television Service to watch episodes of *Magnum, P.I.*, *Buck Rogers*, and *Kung Fu*. Sitcoms ranged from *The Facts of Life* and *Happy Days* to *The Jeffersons* and *Laverne & Shirley*. One of the favorites, however, was *Soul Train*, which was broadcast on Saturdays. Troops crowded around the television, eager to watch scantily clad women dance. "It stopped traffic," recalled Navy Hospital Corpsman Third Class Don Howell. "We literally did nothing until *Soul Train* was over."

CHAPTER **8**

There are no sanctuaries in Beirut: that's the first
thing you learn there. Churches, mosques, hospitals, schools,
embassies—they are all fair game, all targets.
—ROGER SIMON, COLUMNIST FOR THE *LOS ANGELES TIMES* SYNDICATE
April 28, 1983

The ordered routine the Marines enjoyed behind the airport's gates differed greatly from life on the other side of the wire. Despite the presence of the multinational forces, which had offered the promise of peace, violence had crept back into daily life. Beirut once again resembled the Wild West with assassinations, shoot-outs, and car bombs.

Against this backdrop of daily violence, workers hustled to clear rubble, often bulldozing it into the sea. Others patched gaping shell holes and whitewashed the orange and yellow burns left from Israel's phosphorous shells. Even with such efforts, the once-grand city still bore innumerable scars from its violent civil war coupled with Israel's siege, the latter of which had damaged or destroyed nearly ten thousand homes. High-rise apartments and hotels with scorched interiors—and often filled with squatters—stood like tombstones over the flatlining nation. "This country," as one redevelopment official told a reporter, "has been mutilated."

Violence was woven throughout the fabric of daily life, as rival militias continued to target one another. "Life in this city is absurd not because people get killed, but because they get killed playing tennis or lying on the beach or shopping in the market or driving home from work," *New York Times* reporter Thomas Friedman wrote. "The city lives in that half-light between security and insecurity, war and truce, in which there is usually enough security to go about one's day but never enough to feel confident that it won't be your last."

Friedman had experienced the violence personally when his own home was destroyed by a bomb in June 1982 in an attack that killed nineteen of his neighbors. The reporter rushed home that afternoon to find the apartment building sliced open, resembling a dollhouse. He could see pots and pans dangling on the kitchen wall of one house while his own business cards littered the smoldering pile of broken concrete and rebar. "The pharmacist's wife who lived upstairs," he wrote, "a striking, tall, Lebanese blonde, was sandwiched with her son in her arms between two walls that had been blown together, forming a grotesque human fossil."

The violence proved so common that Coco, the pet parrot at the Commodore Hotel, could imitate the sound of incoming artillery shells. "It is a reflection of the macabre mood of this city," Judith Miller of the *New York Times* observed, "that longtime residents of the hotel find Coco's rendition hilarious." But Coco was only one way in which the Commodore served as a barometer of the city's violence. "The newcomer is routinely offered a choice of rooms," Miller added. "Would she prefer the shelling side of the hotel or the car-bomb side?"

Residents coped by popping prescription antianxiety medicines that were sold over the counter in Lebanon. "People ate Valium like candy," recalled CBS News correspondent Larry Pintak. "Fighters needed its calming effect on the front lines, businessmen needed it to help them face each day, students needed it to get through classes."

Children suffered the worst as the widespread violence prompted many to wet the bed or wrestle with chronic diarrhea. In a macabre sign of how warped life had become in Lebanon, youth often played games in the streets, pretending to plant car bombs. "Kids five or six years old talked about what they would do 'if' they grew up," Pintak added. "They quickly learned that dying of old age in their country was considered an accomplishment."

The insecurity of life in Beirut reflected in advertisements for shatterproof window coatings. "Any time, anyplace, an explosion can happen," companies warned.

Shopkeepers placed barrels or boulders—sometimes even box springs—outside stores to guard against car bombs. Locals learned to keep their windows open so that when a bomb exploded the glass was less likely to shatter. Grocery stores stocked bread, water, and canned food, along with snacks, like sweets and nuts. "Beirutis," Friedman observed, "talk about violence the way other people talk about the weather."

The headlines in the world's newspapers highlighted the steady stream of violence. "Beirut Hotel Torn by Blast," trumpeted the *Los Angeles Times*.

"Man Driving Bomb-Laden Car Kills 2," added the *Washington Post*.

"Sense of Doom Pervades Beirut," concluded the *Philadelphia Daily News*.

The car bomb proved the most terrifying for many. The kamikaze attack on the American Embassy was largely an anomaly. Most car bombs involved parked vehicles—a white Mercedes proved one of the most popular vehicles used in such attacks—left along busy roadsides. "Snipers and shelling never bothered me," said author Lina Mikdadi. "But booby-trapped cars, that is what really scares me. If I am in a traffic jam, I get hysterical."

Car bombs proved so pervasive that a pregnant woman was killed by one while being interviewed by Associated Press reporter Samuel Koo. On August 6, 1982, the journalist rushed to interview survivors of an Israeli air strike that had leveled an eight-story apartment building, killing the woman's husband and two children. "She was just starting to tell me her name through an English-speaking rescue worker when the massive blast came from the car just 25 yards away from us," Koo recalled. "Her chest was blown apart by shrapnel."

Friedman noted that he had seen so many attacks that he grew numb to them. "All car-bomb scenes," he wrote, "start to look the same after a while." Rather than focus on the bloodied victims or the scorched autos, his attention often drifted elsewhere. "After a while," the reporter wrote, "you find your mind focusing on the incongruities: the juicy roast chickens that were blown all over the street from an adjacent restaurant but somehow still look good enough to eat, or the smell of liquor from a shelf full of broken Johnnie Walker bottles."

The prevalence of such attacks had sparked a cottage industry of car bomb defusers. The nation's leading professional, Yosef Bitar, had sacrificed two fingers to the job. In the eight years since civil war broke out, he had defused 192 car bombs. He estimated as many as 500 others had exploded. "On any given day," a reporter wrote of Bitar, "he estimated there may be several cars or trucks moving around Beirut with bombs concealed in them."

The Marines were not blind to this violence.

The daily situation reports chronicled the parade of car bombs, explosions, and assassinations that played out day after day, week after week in the Lebanese capital. "A bomb was thrown from a white Mercedes car at the Bristol hotel," one such report said.

"The Libyan chargé d'affaires was shot 8 times and seriously injured by an unknown gunman in the Napoleon hotel," added another.

"A Datsun car exploded near the Pepsi Cola depot to the east of the airport," a third report noted. "Three people inside the car were killed."

In a letter home, Lance Corporal Bill Stelpflug wrote that car bombs exploded nearly every day around the university. Another time, he was scanning the cityscape with binoculars when he locked on to a building. "It blew up," he wrote, "before my very eyes." Fellow Marine Private David Madaras had one go off at 2:30 a.m. one morning near his post. "Boy I jumped off my butt and had my machine gun loaded in about 2 seconds," he later wrote his family. "That explosion helped me realize that keeping alert is very important."

Washington's stalled peace efforts did not help.

Israel had agreed to pull out as part of the May 17 deal, but only if Syria also left, which so far President Hafez Assad had no plans to do. The situation once again appeared intractable. "The White House," one journalist observed, "is desperately trying to convince itself that the past four years of American Middle East diplomacy are not about to go up in smoke."

CHAPTER 9

There is little about conflict in Lebanon that reflects
the traditional models of war.
—REPORT OF THE LONG COMMISSION
December 20, 1983

Undersecretary of State Lawrence Eagleburger hustled from Foggy Bottom over to Capitol Hill shortly before 10 a.m. on June 28, 1983. The fifty-two-year-old Milwaukee native, who wore rumpled suits and chain-smoked cigarettes between hits from his asthma inhaler, was joined this Tuesday morning by Ambassador Robert Dillon and Thomas Tracy, the assistant secretary for administration. The three statesmen climbed the granite stairs of the Rayburn House Office Building, a bureaucratic behemoth that had cost taxpayers a staggering $100 million. The four-story building, which spread across five acres, had required no less than seven million pounds of white marble. In addition to 169 congressional offices and dozens of committee and subcommittee rooms, the building boasted a barbershop, two gyms, a swimming pool, and a 750-seat cafeteria. Serviced by fifty-three escalators and elevators and 1,600 parking spaces, the architectural monstrosity—dubbed Edifice Rex—was universally panned for its resemblance to the colossal eyesores popular in autocratic countries. "It is quite possible that this is the worst building for the most money in the history of construction art," wrote *New York Times* architectural critic Ada Louise Huxtable. "It stuns by sheer mass and boring bulk."

The three statesmen navigated the building's labyrinth of hallways to room 2172—a cavernous committee room—to brief a joint hearing of two House Foreign Affairs subcommittees. Chairman Lee Hamilton, a bespectacled Indiana Democrat, gaveled the meeting to order at 10 a.m. The topic that morning was the embassy bombing seventy-one days earlier, a terrorist attack that had long since fallen off the nation's front pages, replaced by stories of the famine that gripped Ethiopia, the spread of AIDS, and Latin America's debt crisis. The Capitol Hill meeting that morning, in fact, would warrant only five paragraphs on page 9 in the following day's *New York Times*. That was more than the *Wall Street Journal* dedicated to the story, where coverage clocked in at a single paragraph totaling just two sentences. Before the committee was a request for $30 million to provide temporary space for America's diplomats as well as pay for a new permanent embassy in Beirut.

Hamilton turned the floor over to Eagleburger, who updated lawmakers on the attack that had killed sixty-three people, including seventeen Americans. "The United States is deeply committed to supporting the Lebanese government in its efforts to regain control over its national territory, restore its sovereignty, and to provide a stable, peaceful environment for its people," he began. "The terrorist attack did not shake this commitment."

The undersecretary added that the May 17 agreement that spelled out Israel's withdrawal from Lebanon represented a great first step. The attack on the embassy, Eagleburger continued, had rendered the building unusable, prompting the State Department to terminate the lease. The Lebanese government had found a new space that would serve in the interim, but the building needed rehabilitation because of damage from the war. In addition, the United States, which had stopped construction of a new embassy in 1976, planned to resume work on that building, but with design modifications for enhanced security. Eight million dollars of the money requested would cover the nine-month upfit of the embassy's temporary space, including new communications and office equipment, vehicles, and furniture. The remaining $22 million would go toward work on the new embassy. "The tragic events of the April 18 bombing only highlighted the lengths to which terrorists will go to accomplish senseless acts against those who do not share their beliefs," the undersecretary concluded. "We are continuing to study the Beirut incident to insure that we are doing all that we can to protect our officials abroad."

Eagleburger then called on his colleague Tracy, a forty-six-year-old career foreign service officer. Armed with before-and-after photographs of the embassy, Tracy walked lawmakers through the attack. He showed how the terrorist in a truck loaded with the equivalent of 2,000 pounds of TNT approached the embassy, entered the driveway exit, and gunned the accelerator. "The force of the explosion," he noted, "was enormous."

Lawmakers then peppered the duo with questions that would in a few months prove prophetic. "Given the type of attack you had here, with the car bomb," Hamilton asked, "is it possible to secure an embassy against that kind of attack?"

That all depends, Eagleburger replied, on how much space surrounds the building. The Beirut embassy fronted directly on the corniche. But space was only one variable. "I think it is virtually impossible ever to assure that you can defend against the type of attack that we saw in Beirut if the driver of the vehicle is prepared to committee suicide in the process."

"I would second that," Tracy added. "If a person is determined, as in this case, to give his life and is prepared to load a truck with more than 2,000 pounds of TNT, then the results are going to be quite devastating."

What was, Hamilton asked, the security like at the former embassy?

Tracy noted that the State Department had spent $1.5 million in recent years on security upgrades, but those were aimed at mob violence. "It is virtually impossible," he said, "to retrofit an existing building to protect against an explosion in excess of 2,000 pounds."

Short of stopping all traffic along the corniche, Eagleburger added, it was impossible to isolate the building from a suicide attack. "He could hit that building from any number of positions around its periphery," the undersecretary said. "And I think under those circumstances, it would be impossible to prevent the sort of attack that took place."

Hamilton asked about checkpoints, prompting Ambassador Dillon to speak up. The guards stationed out front of the embassy, he noted, were, unfortunately, dead, but he said that the distance from the checkpoint to the building was only about ten yards. Eagleburger then echoed the point he had made previously made in the press. "I think it is a fair statement that given what we are supposed to be doing in embassies around the world," he said, "it is never going to be possible for us to do our job and be totally secure at the same time."

Democratic representative Tom Lantos of California pulled back the lens from just Lebanon. "What is this administration doing currently to put the problem of terrorism on the front burner?" he asked. "How many more episodes will it require in different parts of the world to give this issue the top priority which I am convinced it merits, particularly in view of the fact that Americans have now become the prime targets of terrorism?"

Tracy said the United States had been tightening up security at embassies. "I think it is fair to say that our missions are about as strong as any in the world," he said. "Nonetheless, in areas where the government is less than in full control, or where there are problems of insurgency in the country and so forth, there will always be difficulties."

Eagleburger added that it was critical for friendly governments to exchange information needed to help track terrorists and determine how such networks operate. "But I think," he warned, "we are going to have to accept the fact that some degree of terrorism is a fact of life today that will not, I think, easily or quickly be done away with."

CHAPTER 10

You can't keep the peace, if you don't have the peace.
—LIEUTENANT COLONEL LARRY GERLACH
May 3, 1993

Marines continued to conduct jeep and foot patrols as June rolled into July. To improve security, Geraghty initiated joint foot patrols with the Lebanese Armed Forces, who provided one fire team to each of the three squad-sized Marine patrols.

The harassment of troops in the Shiite slum of Hooterville escalated. The daily reports showed that residents at times threw rocks, glass, and clothespins at the Marines. Others made derogatory gestures. One youth tried to ram a jeep with his bicycle, while another time a young man punched a Marine in the chest and then walked away.

"I hate Marines," one teenager yelled. "Me and my brother going to kill Marines."

"Americans no good," another hollered. "Marines go home."

Despite the harassment, Geraghty attempted to tamp down the concerns of his superiors, highlighting the positive interactions between his Marines and the locals. "Incidents of children throwing rocks and young men making derisive gestures are few and far between," he wrote in one of his weekly reports. "More typical are hundreds of unreported contacts which build good will and create an atmosphere of helpfulness and cooperation."

Beyond patrols, the Marines looked for positive ways to help the Lebanese and engender goodwill. Doctors Bigelow and Ware performed dental exams for children at a local orphanage. Other times villagers brought those in need of help to checkpoints, where hospital corpsmen assisted them. In early July, troops installed a playground in the Shiite village of Burj al Barajinah, just north of the airport. The Lebanese government donated the land. Villagers cleared the trash, built a fence, and installed lights. The Marines then erected the red-white-and-blue set, which included two swing sets, a merry-go-round, seesaw, and a monkey bar. "I loved doing this," said Corporal Maurice Colbert, the main welder on the project. "I love all the kids, so it was for a worthwhile cause. The result today was worth all the effort."

"I just wish we could put a playground at every corner," added Sergeant Kim McKinney.

Such moments of happiness served as an important counterbalance to the extreme deprivation the Marines experienced in the slums. A trash run to the dump would haunt Lance Corporal Michael Petit. Before the truck even stopped, a dozen children swarmed the trailer, picking through the garbage for scraps of food. "I felt sorry for the children," he wrote. "They were filthy. Ulcerated sores oozing pus dotted the legs of one boy who couldn't have been more than eight. Another was missing a hand. His bright eyes gleamed as he salvaged an unopened package of cocoa powder from the heap." In a column in the *Root Scoop*, First Lieutenant Miles Burdine encouraged any Marine who felt sorry for himself to visit Hooterville. "Look at the faces of the children and realize the death, destruction, and poverty many have experienced," he urged. "For some, it is all they know and possibly all they will ever know." Corporal William Gaines Jr. captured a similar sentiment in a letter. "Many people don't realize that these are people like you and me," he wrote. "They have families, husbands, wives, children. They feel fear, happiness, joy, and sadness. They are real—no better but no worse than us."

Geraghty continued to emphasize training, including inserting Marines by air for patrols, so as to practice helicopter operations. Troops conducted additional parachute jumps and cross-trained on weapons with other multinational forces. The French practiced amphibious operations on Green Beach in front of the airport, while the Italians welcomed the leathernecks on mobile patrol to drive through their live-fire range to simulate ambushes. "The men dismounted, returned fire at the dummy attackers, recovered a simulated casualty, and withdrew while maintaining covering fire," the monthly Command Chronology observed. "It is a realistic event and has provided the Marines with a good confidence building exercise."

Troops continued to help Lebanese soldiers with basic infantry skills and air assault techniques. Lebanese officer candidates enjoyed a tour of the Battalion Landing Team headquarters and the *Iwo Jima*. Geraghty presented certificates to the top thirty graduating soldiers out of a class of 280. Many of the Marines, however, privately scoffed at the poor skills of the Lebanese recruits. "If things got tough," Petit said, "we'd be on our own."

"Like the blind leading the blind," added John Dalziel.

The colonel liaised with fellow commanders of the other multinational forces to swap information. His July 9 meeting with Italian brigadier general Franco Angioni proved particularly instructive. Angioni, who had been in Beirut longer than any other multinational leader, oversaw one of Beirut's most volatile areas, home to Palestinian refugee camps at Sabra and Shatila. The typical Lebanese response, he noted, to any disturbance was brute force. Troops would descend upon an area, conduct mass arrests, and haul off scores of individuals with no concern for legal rights. Interrogations proved equally as harsh. "Rifle butts to the face were common, as were two or three policemen beating a suspect into unconsciousness," Geraghty recalled. "This was conducted on women and children as well as men."

Angioni convinced the Lebanese to dial back such tactics, which earned the respect of locals and was vital to the safety of his forces. "He feels that this balance has been maintained due to the high degree of neutrality evidenced by his soldiers," Geraghty said. "He feels that, should this trust be lost, his men will become targets in the inter-factional fighting."

Beyond meetings and training, the colonel sent Marines off on liberty trips to Turkey and Sicily. News reporters accompanied troops on patrols while Geraghty sat for media interviews. At the same time the colonel juggled the continual parade of American military and congressional leaders, including Secretary of State George Shultz and later in the month Joint Chiefs of Staff Chairman General John Vessey. "Too many VIPs!" Major George Converse complained in a letter. "All are going in a dozen different directions, seeing a dozen different things. All have to be briefed, protected, transported, and coddled too."

The lawmakers, who often donned brand-new starched fatigues, sparked private jeers from many of the Marines. "The congressmen loved to parade around the compound in their new uniforms," Petit recalled. "It was their chance to play Marine for a day." Officers rounded up Marines from each lawmaker's district to sit for a half-hour chat. "I wonder," Dolphin asked, "how many millions of dollars were spent on travel and per diem on something that a twenty-dollar telephone call could have accomplished just as well."

When not on duty, troops often filled sandbags or exercised, which was never easy in the brutal Middle Eastern summer. "It is hot as shit in Beirut," Bill Stelpflug complained in a letter to his family. "I mean at 7:30 in the morning you are sweating just standing still."

"You can lose as much as 5 or 10 pounds a day like this," added a fellow leatherneck. "But like they say, it is better to sweat in war than it is to bleed."

Despite the heat and humidity, American and French forces duked it out in volleyball while Marines and the sailors pummeled one another in a boxing match on deck of the *Austin*, with the leathernecks winning twenty-one of thirty-one bouts. On June 26, the Marines hosted a 5K and 10K race around the airport's perimeter road. More than three hundred Marines, sailors, French infantry, and Foreign Legionnaires competed. "Contestants," wrote the *Root Scoop*, "battled through the midmorning heat and humidity over a trail thick with dust." Corporal Charles Register charged across the 5K finish line with a time of seventeen minutes and thirty seconds, beating 133 challengers. First Lieutenant Ronald Baczkowski snatched victory over 174 others in the 10K with a time of thirty-three minutes and forty-four seconds. The Naval Academy graduate feared the SEALs would beat him, but he led the race at the halfway point. "I felt real good about a Marine finishing first, because the day before the French killed us in volleyball," he said. "But when they won, they were gracious winners and didn't rub it in."

That competition was followed on July 4 by the "Independence Day Run for Peace Marathon," an event created by the Battalion Landing Team's Weapons Company. Thirty-six Marines running in pairs logged 1.5 miles each, waving American and Lebanese flags, which represented the two countries working together. "In the end, it was not one marathon, but two, a total of 54 miles," the *Root Scoop* reported. "But the mileage wasn't important."

Corporal Dan Joy, who helped organize the run, said he wanted to show that the United States stood behind Lebanon. "We have a great opportunity here," Joy said of the mission. "We see it in the faces of the little kids when we drive through town."

Others celebrated the national holiday with a barbecue at the Beirut Hilton that featured hamburgers, hot dogs, cold melon, and cake. The Navy hosted its own celebration aboard the *Iwo Jima* for five hundred visitors, including American diplomats and fellow members of the multinational force who feasted on spareribs and beer and enjoyed a performance by Lebanese folk dancers. "Barbecues replaced helicopters on launch pads," one reporter wrote, "American flags hung from rails and seamen tested their skills in a regatta of cutters and landing craft."

Early one July morning amid the hustle of base activity, a staff sergeant sought out Captain Michael Ohler as he finished up breakfast, alerting him that Lieutenant Colonel Gerlach wanted to see him. The twenty-eight-year-old Naval Academy graduate feared he might be in some sort of trouble, a worry that was reinforced when he bumped into Gerlach's executive officer, who urged him to hurry up and go see the battalion commander.

Ohler knocked on Gerlach's office door.

The commander summoned him inside. Gerlach then held up a message and began to read aloud. "On June 29th," the lieutenant colonel began, "Captain Ohler's wife gave birth to a boy, Benjamin David. Both the baby and mother are doing well."

"I was dumbfounded. I didn't know what to say. It was such a shock," Ohler wrote in a letter that day to his wife, Gail. "All I could do was smile."

Gerlach congratulated Ohler, shook his hand, and told him he expected a cigar. Ohler ducked out of his office, excited to share the news with his friends. His newborn son would join his two-year-old daughter, Sarah. "God has blessed us beyond my comprehension. I've got a daughter and a son. I'm so happy," he wrote. "What a family we have."

On July 6, Hudson caught a flight out to the *Iwo Jima* to talk to the doctors. He could not get a helicopter back until that afternoon, so he went to the wardroom for lunch, which proved a bad idea since the pudgy physician was trying to shed a few pounds.

"How do you want your steak?" the cook asked.

"I couldn't believe it!" Hudson wrote. "I had an <u>air-conditioned environment</u>, tablecloth, silverware, <u>no flies</u>, decent company, and a delicious meal. I had a sirloin steak—tender and well done, <u>broccoli</u>! <u>Fried rice</u>, homemade bread, tea, <u>real Coke</u>, butter. I blew my diet and went back for seconds. I have not had that good a meal since I left the States."

Geraghty enjoyed his own escape one afternoon when he visited Lebanese troops learning to operate the 155mm howitzer. The training site was up in the mountains east of Beirut, an area under Christian control that boasted cooler temperatures and reminded him of southern France. While at the site, the colonel spotted what appeared to be a fortress perched atop a towering mountain peak. His Lebanese escort explained that it was a thirteenth-century abbey, one whose roots stretched back to the era of the Crusades. He offered to take the colonel on a visit, which Geraghty welcomed. The abbey's strategic location offered Geraghty a view east of the Syrian-controlled Bekaa Valley. To the west, he could see the blue of the Mediterranean. "The majestic scenery," the colonel recalled, "was breathtaking."

The abbot offered him a tour of the monastery. "I felt," Geraghty said, "like a student in a graduate course of the history of the Middle Ages taught by a scholar." The colonel soaked it up. He saw the stone beds covered with hay mattresses that the monks called home as well as the library filled with ancient texts in Latin, Arabic, and Hebrew. "On the return trip to Beirut," Geraghty wrote, "I had a strange feeling that I had spent part of the day in a Middle Eastern time capsule reflecting the beauty, turmoil, and tragedy of Lebanon today."

The colonel was not the only one to break away.

The Marines and sailors at times visited the destroyed former embassy along the corniche, including Hudson, who stopped by with dentists Jim Ware and Gil Bigelow. He mailed his wife a slide photo of him in front of the ruins. "It is unbelievable," he wrote, "how much destruction occurred in the building." Those brave enough ventured inside the battered building, climbing the dark and rubble-strewn staircases where terrified and bloodied diplomats had fled amid the smoke and tear gas. Troops peeked inside offices with toppled furniture or stared out through the gaping holes at the sea. First Lieutenant Neal Morris paused before a table still covered with food from lunch that day. Several noted the rust-colored stains that dotted the floor and walls, which resembled dried blood. First Lieutenant Mark Singleton swiped a stack of stationery with the logo of the United States Embassy. Others grabbed coffee cups and dishware emblazoned with the diplomatic logo. Lance Corporal Tim McCoskey used a sledgehammer to pound for half an hour on a safe he found, only to crack it open and discover it was empty. Lance Corporal Emanuel Simmons and several other Marines loaded up a truck with tables, chairs, and even a file cabinet to decorate their room. The experience, as many of them would later recall, was haunting. "It smelled," Simmons said, "like death."

At night, the troops watched the factional fighting that lit up the mountains as tracers painted the heavens. Singleton chowed down on hot dogs and Coke as one such battle unfolded. "It was," he remembered, "like watching the Super Bowl." The Marines sat on the sidelines of someone else's war, a fact highlighted by the volleyball games and footraces that took place behind the safety of the wire while car bombs and artillery duels thundered around them. Many tried to capture the experience. "The other night the fighting was incredible," Bill Stelpflug wrote. "Boom boom rat-tat-tat-tat-rat boom ker ker boom. Get the idea?" Jim Ware actually recorded sounds of the fighting. So, too, did Corporal Blaine Cosgro. Others climbed to the roof of the Battalion Landing Team headquarters for a better view. "We watch nightly fire fights then see the destruction in the daytime," Grant McIntosh, a special agent with Naval Investigative Services, wrote his family. "They put on one hell of a light show but you have to stop and remember that there are people on the receiving end of those tracer rounds."

As the weeks crawled past, homesickness infected some of the troops. Those who did not go on patrols felt like prisoners trapped behind the airport gates. The men worked six days a week only to escape into reruns of *Mork & Mindy* and *Hee Haw*. For many, mail served as the only tangible connection to home and the lives and loved ones left behind. Chaplain Danny Wheeler noticed the struggle his young flock faced. "My parish in Beirut was in flux," he said. "The men were having all the usual problems of growing up. They were unsure."

Wheeler spent his days driving around in a jeep to visit the rifle companies dug in along the airport perimeter. "How are you doing?" he would ask.

"We're making it," was a common refrain.

"Watch out for each other," the chaplain reminded them.

Hudson likewise struggled to assimilate. The battalion surgeon was a decade older than many of the Marines and had little in common with them. Unlike other officers, he had no interest in a professional military career. Beirut was a pit stop on his road home to Milledgeville, nestled along the winding Oconee River, where he planned to sew stitches, set broken arms, and treat colds as a country doctor. "This place is such a strain on people," he wrote his wife. "No wonder Marines are so weird." More than anything, however, Hudson missed his wife, Lisa, and infant son, Will, whose photos he stared at daily. "I cannot believe how adorable and precious he is," Hudson wrote of his son. "I love to look at his pictures and see all the joy he has." Lisa mailed him cassette tapes with recordings of Will cooing and giggling. Hearing their voices, he felt, was almost like being home. At the same time, Hudson felt guilty for leaving Lisa alone during the difficult first few months of nursing an infant. "I pray you are tolerating this situation graciously," he wrote in one letter. "I'm sorry that I ever got myself into this situation," he added in another. "Please don't hold it against me." In the top right-hand corner of each letter, Hudson kept a tally of how many days he had been on the beach versus how many he had left. "I love you and Will so much," he wrote. "We'll be a family again someday."

The repetitive nature of the work exacerbated the struggle. "Some people at night," Lance Corporal John Allman wrote his mother, "go off behind the trees and shout out all their feelings to keep from going crazy." Other Marines, like Lance Corporal Davin Green, tried to find the positive in the experience. "The Sea is pretty. We watch the sun come up and go down. We see whales and sharks. It seems like the Sea never ends," he wrote his sister, Sheria. "But I still miss home, I miss you too, Sis. I sure wish you were here with me, but I'm all right."

Private Henry Linkkila's letters revealed an eighteen-year-old who straddled the line between adolescence and adulthood, an experience made all the more difficult by being in Beirut. "I may be your 'kid,'" he protested in one letter, "but I'm also a goddamn man." Other letters, however, showed the hard-charging Connecticut youth, who liked to drink and fight, still missed the warmth of family. "As you can probably tell, I am depressed and thinking about home a lot!" he confessed. "I would give anything to be back home with you right now."

Linkkila's homesickness, like so many others, manifested itself in a disdain for the dust, the heat, and the boredom of Beirut. "I hate this place!" he wrote in one letter.

"This place really sucks!" Linkkila added in another.

"I wanna go home," he scrawled in big letters across an entire page.

The young Marines wrestled with distance not only from parents, but also from girlfriends and wives. To help, Wheeler and Father George Pucciarelli started a pre-marriage counseling class that would run Thursday nights for a month, beginning at 7:30 p.m. in the Peacekeeping Chapel. But that did little to ease the suffering of those who feared an unfaithful spouse. "Thank God I'm not married," Bill Stelpflug wrote home. "There are some pretty little 18/19-year-old wives in Jacksonville causing their own hate and discontent in Beirut. Some don't write and some write the wrong things. The N.C. Center for Abused Women may have some business."

Such concerns faded on the morning of July 22.

Marines manned checkpoints around the airport that Friday. The public affairs team passed out the latest issue of the *Root Scoop*, which included a rundown on promotions and courts-martial as well as a feature story on parachute practice and advice from the chaplains reminding troops not to worry too much. "Keep looking forward in hope," the faith leaders urged.

Up in his fourth-floor clinic, Dr. Hudson prepared to put a cast on the broken arm of an enlisted man while over in the Marine Amphibious Unit headquarters, Lieutenant Glenn Dolphin listened as a boom box blared Molly Hatchet's "Flirtin' with Disaster."

At 10:30 a.m., the first 122mm Katyusha rocket hit.

Up in his clinic, Hudson froze, wondering if the Lebanese might be undergoing explosives training. "When the second round hit," he wrote, "everyone knew we were being bombed. It was a very <u>humbling</u> experience." The doctor forgot about the cast, scooped up his helmet and flak jacket, and headed for the basement, which housed both a shelter and the enlisted men's club. "It sported several wooden picnic tables and a real bar with stools," Petit recalled. "There were even a couple of archaic video games in one corner."

Dolphin likewise grabbed his gear and rushed to the Combat Operations Center, where Geraghty and his senior aides hovered over the radio operators. More rounds rained down on the airport, a mix of Katyusha rockets and 120mm mortars. "The ground shook, and a hard shock wave passed upward through everything and everyone," Dolphin recalled. "The wave could be felt through the soles of your feet, up through the core of your body and into your head. I especially felt the vibrations from the shock wave in my chest and lungs."

"We're being shelled!" people hollered. "Get in the holes."

Hudson galloped down the five flights of stairs to the basement, where he encountered the first casualty, Lance Corporal Morris Dorsey Jr., who was headed up to the clinic to find him. Dorsey had been outside by the mess tent washing cookware when a half-dollar-sized piece of metal dug into the skin above his left shoulder blade. Hudson treated him right on the stairs. "I pulled the shrapnel out with my <u>bare</u> hands," he wrote. "The piece of metal was still <u>hot</u> and had also caused a burn on the Marine." The duo then headed down to the basement shelter, where Dorsey confided in the doctor that he was scared. "He wanted me to reassure him that he was okay, which he was," Hudson said. "I didn't even want to put a Band-Aid on."

After fifteen minutes, the attack ended.

The all-clear signal came forty-five minutes later. Marines emerged from foxholes, bunkers, and shelters. Eleven 122mm rockets and 120mm mortar shells had hit the airport. The attack killed one Lebanese civilian and wounded seven others along with three Lebanese soldiers. In addition to

Dorsey, Lance Corporal Donald Locke and Petty Officer First Class Kenneth Densmore suffered minor shrapnel wounds. Hudson treated the two leathernecks. "Both of these Marines," he said, "now have a new viewpoint on life." The doctor then headed back to the fourth floor to finish the cast, only this time he wore his helmet and flak jacket. "I definitely did not get depressed today," he later wrote his wife. "I was too scared."

The Marines determined that the attack came from an area controlled by Walid Jumblatt's Druze militia, which occupied the nearby Chouf Mountains. The mustachioed warlord, who was supported by Syria, despised President Amin Gemayel. The Druze, the Marines therefore assumed, had likely overshot a nearby Lebanese Armed Forces training camp and hit the airport. "Despite the close impacts and that it was well known that Walid Jumblatt hated our guts, the Druze were going to get the benefit of the doubt," Dolphin said. "Marines did not return fire." The attack reinforced for Geraghty the daily threats and challenges his force faced. "Caught between a multitude of factions and long-standing conflicts," the colonel wrote in his weekly situation report, "the Marines must maintain a fine balance."

CHAPTER 11

*The Lebanese, seeing the outside momentum toward a Lebanon
solution fade, seem to be turning to each other with guns in hand.*
—WASHINGTON POST EDITORIAL
July 31, 1983

Hours after rockets and mortars drove Marines into bunkers, Lebanese
president Amin Gemayel prepared to meet face-to-face with Ronald
Reagan in Washington. Secretary of State Shultz had recently returned from
his second trip to the Middle East, trying to salvage his May 17 deal for foreign
forces to leave Lebanon. Israel planned to pull back only from the suburbs of
Beirut and the nearby Chouf Mountains, a move that was not designed to help
Lebanon but rather to secure a more defensible position farther south and
decrease casualties. The Jewish state refused to vacate the Bekaa Valley in the
east unless Syria also exited. With its stockpile of new weapons, Syria still had
no intention of leaving. "Like a fisherman after a very bad day," one Western
diplomat noted, "Shultz tried one last cast and caught nothing."

The secretary of state made no effort to spin the situation. "I wish I
could report that somehow we see progress," he said, "but I can't give any
such report." One of his aides was even more blunt. "I'm not sure where
we go from here." Newspaper headlines trumpeted the fruitless results.
"Shultz Ends Tour with Message of Failure," heralded the *Guardian*.

"Miscalculations on Mideast Add Up to Near Zero for U.S.," added the
New York Times.

"Back to Square One in the Lebanon Quagmire," declared the *Observer*.

Even Reagan, despite his perpetual optimism, confided in his diary that
Lebanon was a fiasco. Absent the departure of foreign forces, the Marines
appeared stuck in Beirut. "It really is a can of worms," the president wrote.
"How to get Syria out is the problem."

Not only were Israel and Syria a challenge, but each day the violence
worsened, including a bomb-laden Honda station wagon that nearly killed

the prime minister. "The American and French Embassies are besieged by crowds of Lebanese seeking visas," reported Thomas Friedman, "and travel agents are doing brisk trade in one-way tickets."

The grace period of peace was clearly over.

The question, of course, was how much worse would it get?

Against this backdrop, Lebanon's president landed in Washington in search of help to clean up the mess he had helped make. It had taken only nine months for Israel—once enamored by slain leader Bashir Gemayel—to realize his brother and successor was a political deadbeat, best described by Friedman as a "sometime playboy, sometime businessman, all-time zero." Gemayel had so alienated various factions in Lebanon that he would never be able to deliver real peace for Israel. At the same time, Israeli forces in the Chouf Mountains, caught in the crossfire between Christian and Druze militias, continued to suffer casualties. The weekly return of dead and wounded soldiers to Israel wore on Prime Minister Menachem Begin, who faced antiwar protestors camped outside his home with signs that showed the body count.

"Was this disaster necessary?" Begin lamented.

In vacating the Chouf Mountains, Israel planned to dig in south of the Awali River, a natural boundary that would create a buffer zone to protect the nation's northern border. Along a seventy-mile stretch of the river, Israeli bulldozers plowed new roads and widened old ones. Workers dug trenches and constructed machine-gun nests, strung concertina wire, and installed floodlights. The Jewish state likewise planned to hang on to the port city of Sidon, an important banking and commercial center for southern Lebanon. Gemayel was smart enough to realize that Israel's withdrawal appeared more like a land grab, a move that could prove the first step toward the partitioning of Lebanon. His fear was that Israel would keep the south, Syria the north and the east, leaving Gemayel to preside over a Christian city-state in Beirut.

But partitioning was a long-term fear.

In the short term, Israel's withdrawal threatened to create a power vacuum in the Chouf Mountains, where Christian and Druze militias battled one another in what a reporter characterized as "one of the world's most vicious and least-known little civil wars." Israeli forces had provided the only stabilizing force in the region, brokering prisoner swaps, arranging cease-fires, and at times firing on one side or the other. Without Israel as a police force, many questioned whether Lebanon's fledgling armed services would be strong enough to wrest control of the region from the powerful

Druze militia. Syria exacerbated the tensions, aiding the Druze so as to inflame internal rivalries and undermine Lebanon's central government. Gemayel hoped American Marines might help fill the void after Israel's departure, but policymakers saw that as a bridge too far. If Israel was pulling out because it suffered too many dead and wounded, there was no way Congress would agree to replace them with Marines.

Gemayel's problems, however, ran even deeper.

Few political observers believed the attack on the airport the same day Gemayel planned to meet with Reagan was a coincidence. Most suspected it was a warning, one that Washington would be wise to heed. "Syria and its Lebanese allies," the *Guardian* quoted one observer, "are telling the President that he does not even control greater Beirut."

Despite the political bruising Shultz endured on his failed Middle East trip—coupled with Syria's obstinance and Gemayel's plummeting power, not to mention the terrorist bombing of the embassy just three months earlier—none of Reagan's declassified briefing papers raised the question of whether the United States should look for an exit.

America had made the decision to back Gemayel.

And that would continue. "Our support for him," Shultz advised the president on the eve of his meeting, "is absolutely essential in the rough days ahead."

The administration would invest America's full faith and credit to prop up a flawed politician who, one senior White House aide observed, "possessed none of the leadership qualities necessary for governing a stable country, much less one so riven by factional strife." This was the shaky foundation on which Lebanon's political house of cards now rested. National Security Advisor William Clark warned Reagan that Gemayel needed America's help to rid Lebanon of foreign forces or else his regime would likely collapse. "For better or worse," Clark warned, "we will be seen as largely responsible for events in Lebanon."

With that, Reagan welcomed Gemayel—dressed in a white suit and a tie that matched his perfectly coiffed jet-black hair—to the White House at 11:33 a.m. The two leaders posed for pictures in the Rose Garden, chatted in the Oval Office, and enjoyed lunch in the State Dining Room. That afternoon, despite the evidence of a brewing storm in Lebanon, Reagan publicly embraced Gemayel. "I'm impressed with the progress he and the government and people of Lebanon have made in rebuilding their country. It's my belief that energy and perseverance will triumph in the end," he concluded. "Lebanon can count on our support."

CHAPTER 12

The world must have been simpler in the days of gunboat diplomacy.
—President Ronald Reagan diary
August 10, 1983

To salvage the disaster in Lebanon—and on the same day he welcomed Gemayel to the White House—Reagan appointed Deputy National Security Advisor Robert McFarlane as his new special envoy for the Middle East. The forty-six-year-old McFarlane, who answered to the nickname Bud, would replace veteran diplomat Philip Habib, whom Syria had refused to work with after Shultz's failed first round of negotiations back in May. McFarlane came from a long line of public servants. His grandfather served as a Texas Ranger, while his father represented the Lone Star State in Congress and later worked as an attorney in the Justice Department's antitrust division. McFarlane graduated from the Naval Academy and joined the Marines, where he served two tours in Vietnam, a disillusioning experience that shaped his worldview. He blamed the media, pandering generals, and weak politicians for America's defeat in the jungles of Southeast Asia, lessons he would bring to Lebanon. "What was clear," he said, "was that because of political restrictions, we were not using our superior firepower to win the war."

After the war, and in what would prove another transformative experience, McFarlane served as a military aide to former national security advisor and secretary of state Henry Kissinger. McFarlane lionized the mercurial diplomat and political theorist, devouring all his books and articles. The experience, however, proved demanding as well as revelatory. Not only did he often work up to fifteen hours a day, but he also witnessed the bare-knuckle politics of Washington, where his boss frequently disparaged colleagues and wielded deceit as a political tool. "Working for such a complex, conspiratorial man, I found it hard, at times, to maintain my moral compass," McFarlane wrote. "It was a four-year course in political hardball." McFarlane unfortunately drew the wrong conclusions from his boss's behavior, which would later lead to his own downfall during the Iran-Contra affair. "Ultimately, what he sought to do, and frequently did achieve, transcended the dishonesty and cynicism of his methods," McFarlane said of Kissinger. "It was a classic case of the ends justifying the means."

Despite his idolization of his former boss, McFarlane was no Kissinger—and deep down he knew it. In a town like Washington, where pedigree mattered, McFarlane was plagued by insecurity, believing his middle-class upbringing and service academy education made him a lesser intellect than his Ivy League peers. It did not help that his own boss and role model had earned his undergraduate degree, master's, and doctorate from Harvard. "Following in Kissinger's wake," reporters Martin and Walcott observed, "was a little like living in the shadow of a brilliant, successful father." Even McFarlane's hobbies—he loved to tap-dance and play the banjo—seemed pedestrian and folksy in a town where power brokers wore black ties and gowns to the Kennedy Center for theater and the opera. His perfect salt-and-pepper hair and wardrobe of conservative dark blazers could not hide his self-doubt, which reflected in his demeanor. "He spoke in a monotone, which made him sound like a student who wasn't sure the answer he was giving was the right one," the two reporters added, "and he often lapsed into academic and military jargon which seemed more calculated to impress than inform the listener."

His personal ambition to rival, if not surpass, his former mentor, coupled with his hangover from Vietnam, guided his actions. McFarlane saw the military as an underutilized instrument in America's tool chest, a hammer that politicians had been too hesitant to swing since the defeat in Vietnam. The problem of Lebanon, he believed, demanded just such a solution. The former lieutenant colonel, whose refrigerator was emblazoned with a Semper Fi sticker, argued American leaders had blown the chance nine months earlier to expel all foreign fighters from Lebanon. Israel's drubbing had wiped out much of Syria's air force and surface-to-air missiles, providing the United States a perfect chance to follow the advice of W. C. Fields: "Never kick a man unless he's down." But American leaders had dallied, giving the Soviet Union valuable time to rearm Assad. McFarlane likewise had advocated that America skip the peacekeeping mission and send in a much larger force of several divisions, an idea that appalled Weinberger and the Joint Chiefs of Staff, who rejected the plan for fear it could devolve into a major war. "My arguments, and those of others who thought as I did, were overruled or ignored," McFarlane chafed. "As a result, a fragile but golden opportunity was lost."

In his score-settling memoir, the deputy national security advisor blamed anyone and everyone for the disaster in Lebanon, including the commander in chief. "Reagan," he wrote, "had no historical framework for dealing with what he was seeing."

That was tame compared to his view on Defense Secretary Weinberger, whom he despised and accused of being "criminally irresponsible" for initially pulling the Marines out after the departure of the Palestine Liberation Organization in 1982.

But McFarlane's biggest target was his predecessor, Philip Habib, whom he characterized as a dithering Middle East neophyte who had squandered America's chance to bring peace to the region. That was a harsh rebuke of a three-decade public servant, who had, in fact, created the framework for the Camp David Accords and successfully negotiated the departure of Yasser Arafat and the Palestine Liberation Organization a year earlier, a feat that prompted Reagan to award him the Presidential Medal of Freedom. "When it came to the Middle East," McFarlane wrote, "all Phil really knew was what he had learned growing up in a Lebanese-American family in Brooklyn. He had no depth in the Middle East. He had no experience dealing with Arabs or Israelis, nor had he ever been a man with strategic breadth, able to analyze American interests regionally, not just in Lebanon. As a consequence, he misread everything."

McFarlane's hubris and lack of self-awareness were stunning, particularly since many of the same criticisms he hurled at Habib could be made against him—and later were. Unlike Habib, McFarlane spoke no Arabic. Nor did he speak Hebrew. McFarlane likewise was neither a professional diplomat nor a negotiator. He had spent much of his White House career as a policy wonk and second chair to National Security Advisor William Clark.

Yet this was whom Reagan now depended on to resurrect America's flatlining peace initiative. And on whose success—or failure—rested the fate of the Marines.

On the eve of his appointment, the White House had dispatched McFarlane to the Middle East to test the waters over whether America might reengage following Shultz's failed second trip. On July 12—four days after the secretary of state had returned—McFarlane climbed aboard a Gulfstream III to London, where he met with Wadi Haddad, who served as Gemayel's national security advisor. He then flew to Saudi Arabia to see King Fahd, who agreed to try to help persuade Syria to exit Lebanon. From Riyadh, McFarlane traveled to Damascus, taking a perch on the same velvet green furniture where Shultz had recently sat. To his surprise, President Assad rambled on about the insignificance of human life in the cosmos.

One hour passed.

Then two.

Throughout the monologue, McFarlane's eyes drifted up to the painting of Saladin's men with curved and bloodied swords who towered over the defeated Crusaders.

"Tell me," Assad said through an interpreter as he leaned forward.

McFarlane perked up, anxious for a practical shift in the conversation.

"How do you account for the Bermuda Triangle?"

The president's absurd question stunned McFarlane. "My mind raced," he recalled, "trying to identify a strategy in this perplexing choice of subject and the Syrian leader's enigmatic manner. I had thought, listening to his existential rumination on the meaning of life, that perhaps his goal was to present an image of patience and of a sense of responsibility for his country and his people. But the Bermuda Triangle? I had to pinch myself."

McFarlane rattled off the various theories he had read over the years to explain the mysterious loss of ships in the waters between the North Carolina coast and the British island of Bermuda. Assad nodded. "But they are not satisfactory," the president replied. "I believe there is something more extraterrestrial to account for this."

After three hours of such meditations, the Syrian leader at last raised the issue of his history with previous negotiators. Assad announced that he had always liked Kissinger, whose diplomatic shuttles a decade earlier had brought him to Damascus, where he made time to visit museums and the marketplace and experience Syrian culture. The president hoped he could engage that way again with another American negotiator. McFarlane seized the opportunity to explain Reagan's goals for the Middle East, including his hope for a better relationship with Syria. Assad said he would welcome future conversations. "Six and a half hours after I had arrived at the Presidential Palace," McFarlane recalled, "I finally took my leave."

McFarlane had his work cut out for him.

After Reagan's July 22 announcement of his appointment, McFarlane spent the next week preparing his team before taking off again on August 1 for the Middle East. His first stop was Beirut, where he settled into Ambassador Robert Dillon's residence, which would serve as his headquarters. He met the following day with Gemayel. In addition to the removal of foreign forces, McFarlane recognized that internal rivalries were a major problem.

McFarlane's first priority was to urge Gemayel to embrace the idea of national reconciliation. Just like during the civil war, Lebanon once again threatened to violently splinter along religious lines. The latest crack to emerge was the creation of the National Salvation Front, a Syrian-backed political alliance that brought together the Druze, Shiites, Sunnis, and other Gemayel enemies. The goal of the organization, which was announced by Druze militia leader Walid Jumblatt, was to kill the May 17 deal with Israel. To head off such a schism, McFarlane urged Gemayel to publicly acknowledge his nation's historically unfair power structure and pledge his willingness to cede some political control to the other groups.

"We can take the Israeli option, the Syrian option, or the American option," the president countered. "I've chosen the American option, even though it poses risks for me."

McFarlane listened.

"Now it is up to the United States to deliver on its pledges."

Gemayel's response floored McFarlane.

The president was, in short, demanding that America solve his problems.

McFarlane realized in a flash what American diplomats, veteran journalists like Thomas Friedman, and, of course, the Israelis had all long since understood. "Amin is a fop," Dillon later explained to him, "a pretty boy without political vision, with no history of any relationship with counterparts in the Sunni, Shia, or Druze communities, and who enjoys no respect in any of these factions. He's a man with none of the courage of his brother Bashir."

McFarlane combined his work in Lebanon with visits to the capitals of Egypt, Jordan, and Saudi Arabia, where he unsuccessfully tried to convince leaders to cut off support for Assad. "Each head of government would pay lip service to our requests and promise to do his best," he said, "but it was clear that none of them would risk reprisals from Hafez al-Assad by taking unilateral measures to isolate him." Various Arab counselors at times leveled with him that none of the Arab states would dare cross Syria. "Assad respects power," was the message he often heard, "and unless you are prepared to use it against him, he will not yield."

Power was the one language McFarlane understood.

After meeting again with Assad, McFarlane realized that he faced the same challenge that had stymied Shultz on his earlier visits. Assad had no interest or need to help Washington—and McFarlane had no leverage to force him. Israel's plan to vacate the Chouf Mountains would only strengthen Syria's position in the region. All Assad had to do was wait. McFarlane's earlier hopes that he might somehow succeed where his predecessors failed now faded as he grappled with the reality of his challenge. "Assad," he wrote, "was determined to undermine our Lebanese policy and prevent a national reconciliation of any sort."

CHAPTER 13

The status quo in Beirut is violence.
—FATHER GEORGE PUCCIARELLI
January 1987

Tensions only escalated.

A group of Marines jogged along the perimeter road around 1:10 p.m. on the afternoon of July 31, when two gunmen armed with automatic weapons opened fire through the airport fence, unleashing ten to fifteen rounds before vanishing into nearby buildings. None of the joggers were wounded. A platoon of Marines passed nearby at the time of the attack. The leathernecks jumped out and gave chase, but found only 9mm shell casings. "Attack was definitely directed at U.S. personnel and could not be mistaken for stray rounds," one report noted. "Witnesses indicated that the gunmen fired from the hip and that the firing was over in seconds."

A Lebanese intelligence report days later stated that Shiite militiamen executed the attack as a warning to the Marines not to get involved in operations with the Lebanese military. "The number of Marines in the area and the firing position gave the attackers ample opportunity to injure Marines, no matter how poor a marksman they were," observed a follow-up analysis. "The vulnerability of U.S. Forces to attacks of this nature is highlighted by this incident."

Geraghty singled out the attack in his weekly situation report. "The danger in attacks of this nature is that the perpetrators may feel bold enough to try again," he speculated. "I have increased perimeter security during the day and have re-routed the jogging trail to reduce the number of targets. If given a good target, the Marines will respond in the future. It was only this lack of a clear target and the proximity of civilians that prevented any return fire."

At the start of August, Lieutenant Colonel Larry Gerlach, who commanded the Battalion Landing Team, rotated the rifle companies in the field. In the wake of the July rocket attack, the Army sent two AN/TPQ-36 Firefinder Radars, a sophisticated system designed to pinpoint enemy fire and direct countermeasures. A team of thirty-three soldiers from the Army Artillery School at Oklahoma's Fort Sill joined the Marines in Beirut to operate the system.

The recent attacks only confirmed Geraghty's initial concerns over the Marines' poor location at the airport. "Our tactical position," one of his officers quipped, "is possibly the worst since Custer at Little Big Horn." Not only did the Druze occupy the high ground, but the daily stream of cars, trucks, and equipment made defense difficult. "Tactically it is a terrible situation," the colonel said. "Because of the routine operation of an international airport, you don't have control, and where you don't have control, you don't have security."

But poor location was only one concern.

Daily intelligence reports revealed a change in the population. The Italians observed a dramatic increase of men pouring into the Sabra and Shatila refugee camps. Lebanese intelligence likewise reported Islamic fundamentalists moving into the impoverished Shiite suburbs in southern Beirut, including a disturbing number of armed militiamen near the airport. This was coupled with reports of ten stolen BMW and Mercedes-Benzes in Hooterville, vehicles favored for car bombs. These changes underscored the Lebanese military's lack of control. "There is every indication," one intel report stated, "of an increasing terrorist threat."

Geraghty and his Marines, who patrolled the streets and alleys of the slums each day, had already observed such changes. Posters of Khomeini multiplied and roadblocks mushroomed. Troops likewise reported a change not only in the tone of the population but also the demographics. There were fewer women and children on the streets and more young men, many in camouflaged utilities and armbands. "A new crowd," the colonel said, "had come to town."

These ominous changes were set against the backdrop of the continued fighting in the mountains above the Marines, which illuminated the skies with tracers as machine guns rattled and artillery thundered. "When I first arrived here in May I thought all this was beautiful," recalled Captain Chris Cowdrey. "Of course, it's not so pretty when it's right on top of you." Cowdrey wasn't the only one who felt the earlier novelty had vanished now that rockets and mortars had hit the airport, filling the air with scalding shrapnel and wounding fellow Marines. "It's a weird feeling just standing there watching people kill each other," Henry Linkkila wrote to his mother. "I hate this place with a passion." A 3 a.m. battle in early August proved so ferocious that it woke up John Hudson, who had been asleep atop his fourth-floor rack in the Battalion Landing Team headquarters. "This place is a <u>mad house</u>!!!!" the doctor wrote on August 8. "I just wonder what we are going to do if the fighting gets too close and heavy. I think we should get our butts out of Lebanon. We honestly have no business <u>here</u>."

As if to emphasize Hudson's point, two more rockets hit the airport that night in what Geraghty interpreted as a troubling sign. "These rounds indicated that the earlier attack two weeks prior was no longer an aberration and signaled more attacks were likely."

The colonel did not have long to wait.

At 5:23 a.m. on August 10, a Katyusha rocket crashed into the dirt outside the Battalion Landing Team headquarters. Nineteen-year-old Lance Corporal Michael Toma, who slept on the ground floor of the building, sat on his cot tying his boots when the round whistled overhead. "I heard it as it passed by," he recalled. "As I looked up towards my right, I saw the debris as it exploded." Toma dropped to the deck. "Shit hit the fan," he scribbled in his diary. "Scared the piss out of me." Unlike Toma, twenty-year-old Corporal John Dalziel was asleep in a building a couple hundred yards away when the rocket hit. "It did a better job," he wrote his parents, "of waking me up & getting me ready than any drill instructor ever did!"

The morning attack caught First Lieutenant Neal Morris out in the open. The twenty-six-year-old officer, who was up early that morning to lead a group of out-of-shape Marines through calisthenics and a run, had just stepped out of the head when the rocket zoomed overhead. "I heard it," Morris recalled. "Something about it did not sound right. As my brain was telling me to get down, it detonated inside our perimeter." Morris felt a sharp prick in his right thigh, followed by something wet running down his leg. In an effort to find cover, Morris hustled over to the sentry post. "Hey, Marine," he said to the guard. "Let me use your first-aid kit."

The guard looked down at his leg.

"Holy shit, sir," he exclaimed.

A corpsman arrived and applied pressure to his wound. Medics put him on a cart and ran him through an x-ray to make sure there was no shrapnel in his leg. Hospital corpsmen then took him down to the basement of the Battalion Landing Team headquarters. For the second time in less than three weeks, Hudson went to work patching up a Marine. The wound was six inches long and deep, slicing all the way down to the sarcolemma, the transparent membrane that covers muscle fiber. Hudson closed the wound in layers. "He is so lucky," the doctor wrote. "It could have easily killed him if it struck him somewhere else."

"This incident," Geraghty noted, "was just a prelude for the day's action."

The all-clear came about forty-five minutes later. Hudson had just enough time to shower the sweat off and change uniforms in his fourth-floor room before the rounds started coming in again, sending the physician back down to the basement bunker.

"Incoming rockets about every 30 seconds," one report stated.

Warships offshore sounded general quarters and moved into position to lend naval gunfire if needed. Two Marine Cobra gunships launched over Green Beach, ready to attack, while the Marines onshore huddled in foxholes and bunkers. "The rockets could be plainly heard as they flew over our heads," Dolphin recalled. "Some of those rounds fell short."

The Army's new fire-finding radar zeroed in on the attackers, who Geraghty suspected were aiming at the Lebanese Air Force's flight line and nearby camps. The 81mm mortar platoon dropped four illumination rounds atop the attackers, marking the first time the Marines used indirect fire. The attack ended at 7:35 a.m. Twenty-seven rockets had hit Marine positions. "This let the Druze know three things," Dolphin observed. "We know where you are. We know who you are. And finally, the next rounds we fire will be for keeps."

The attacks, as Geraghty wrote in his weekly situation report, not only underscored Beirut's deteriorating security, but also demonstrated how hard it had become for the Marines to remain neutral. "I feel," the colonel wrote of the Druze, "that if it serves their interest, they will directly attack the Marines position at the airport." Illumination rounds, while successful this time, might not stop the Druze in the future. "All of these deterrents are transitory," Geraghty wrote, "and once they feel they have the capability to deal with each threat, I believe they will become emboldened to take one more step. I am prepared to deal with each of their steps, and am confident that our response will be proper and restrained, yet send them the appropriate signals. If they fail to understand the signals, I am prepared to deal with that as well."

The Druze attacks on the airport revealed for the world the Lebanese president's impotence. Militia leader Walid Jumblatt had forced the shutdown of Beirut International Airport for the low cost of a few rockets and artillery rounds. The closure of the airport, which would remain shuttered for six days, had a tremendous impact on the capital, cutting off mail, foreign newspapers, and overseas imports, not to mention the loss of reputation and prestige. It likewise revealed the powerlessness of the Lebanese Armed Forces to keep this vital gateway open. To add insult to injury, Jumblatt's forces lobbed shells at the Lebanese Defense Ministry and the Presidential Palace. His forces also kidnapped three of Gemayel's government ministers, ultimately holding them hostage for several days. More importantly, the brazen attacks showed that Jumblatt—despite Gemayel's showboating in Washington—did not fear the United States. "We've got," Jumblatt told Beirut media, "nothing to lose."

Jumblatt's ferocity stemmed from his concern that Israel's departure from the Chouf Mountains would prompt the Lebanese military to team up with Christian militias against him. It was obvious to all that Israel's pullout was fast approaching. Large convoys of supplies, including corrugated sheet metal from dismantled firing bunkers, rumbled down mountain roads. Ammunition crates filled with mortars and .50-caliber rounds weighted down others. "The withdrawal," as one American intelligence report noted, "is in its final stages." Everyone knew it was only a matter of time before chaos erupted. "When the Israelis pull out," Hudson wrote his wife on August 12, "I'm afraid everything is going to go to <u>hell</u>!"

The Marines, who had so far been on the sidelines of the battle, found themselves caught in the crossfire. "We may not be the targets they want to hit. But what they are shooting is real ammo," one Marine told a reporter. "We can't stop them. If they end up killing a couple of Marines, what are they going to do then? Apologize and say they didn't mean it?" Rules of engagement barred the Marines from firing back except in self-defense, which irked many of the men. A few crafty troops in Alpha Company channeled that frustration into a sign outside a sandbagged mess tent that read: "The Can't Shoot Back Saloon."

"It's the story of our life over here," one Marine said when asked about it.

The attacks prompted Hudson to don his helmet and flak jacket any time he left the building. The night after the recent rocket attack, he slept in his clothes, boots, and war gear. "What I don't understand is what we are accomplishing by being here," he wrote. "We are not helping anyone keep the <u>peace</u>. These people are fighting as if we weren't even here." The escalating violence motivated Hudson to spend time preparing his hospital corpsmen for potential mass casualties. He likewise brought in dentists Gil Bigelow and Jim Ware. The bigger the team, Hudson reasoned, the better. Bigelow and Ware had begun to take x-rays and create full sets of dental records for each Marine, a task that would prove extraordinary valuable in the months ahead. Ware appreciated Hudson's efforts to include the dentists as equals. "He wasn't highfalutin," Ware said. "He recognized he needed us."

Geraghty attempted to explain the mission to reporters. "It's guard duty, and we do it well. This is a mission of constraint," he said. "We are showing our support of the Lebanese government and their sovereignty. The danger lies in the threatening environment—it's a country coming off of eight years of torment and tragedy. There are lots of people here committed to the failure of the peace-keeping effort and it doesn't take much to upset it."

On August 16, the new commandant of the Marine Corps, General Paul Kelley, arrived for a two-day visit. The fifty-four-year-old Bostonian, who sported thinning red hair and a barrel chest, had served two tours in Vietnam, earning a Silver Star, the Legion of Merit, and two Bronze Stars for valor. The commandant's visit warranted a little special treatment. "The best part of the whole day was dinner. Get this! Steak + Lobster," wrote Marine cook Henry Linkkila. "It was delicious! Of course, the cook got 2 lobsters." Lieutenant Glenn Dolphin added that Kelley's visit proved a morale booster for the troops, who had endured a tough few weeks. "The sight of their commandant standing there with them, in harm's way, wearing that same helmet and flak jacket, had a tremendous effect on the morale of our young enlisted Marines," he wrote. "His personality and obviously genuine concern for his Marines showed through."

The general met with reporters, telling them that the United States would not be intimidated by Druze attacks. "Marines have been used to danger for more than 200 years," Kelley said. "More of them are getting hurt driving automobiles in the United States than here in Lebanon." The general also chatted with the Marines. "A logical question is how long you're going to be here. I don't know how long you are going to be here," the four-star general leveled with his troops. "You're going to be here as long as it is required to be here."

Other dignitaries, including Secretary of the Navy John Lehman, cycled through Beirut. August saw the opening of a library in the basement of the Battalion Landing Team headquarters that boasted a whopping 5,500 titles donated as part of a program called "Books for Our Boys in Beirut." "There you will find books of every size and shape," the *Root Scoop* advertised, "from romance to mystery to drama; from fiction to academic textbooks." Alcoholics Anonymous began meetings every Sunday from 4:30 to

6 p.m. in the Peacekeeping Chapel. "The only requirement for membership," the notice said, "is the desire to stop drinking and using." The lull in attacks likewise allowed the Marines to hold an Ironman competition in August, which involved an obstacle course of logs, tires, a balance beam, and a cargo net followed by a two-mile run. Eighty Marines and sailors competed, though First Lieutenant Ronald Baczkowski, who won the 10K race back in June, once again snatched victory.

Liberty calls, which had been postponed because of the fighting, resumed. On August 18, nearly two hundred Marines and sailors departed Beirut aboard the *Portland* for a brief visit to Greece. Included among them was Dr. Hudson. At the last minute, the physician had arranged for his wife, Lisa, and six-month-old son, Will, to fly over from Georgia and visit him for a week. During that time, the couple toured the Acropolis, the ancient citadel that had towered over the heart of the Greek capital for more than three millennia. After months of Marine cooking and rations, Hudson savored moussaka and cold soft drinks and tea.

"I haven't had a drink with ice in it in months," he exclaimed.

Beyond exploring the winding streets and flower-filled alleys, Hudson welcomed the hours spent playing on the hotel bed with his son, whom he had not seen in three months. "It's so great to be together again," Lisa wrote in a postcard to her parents. "John is so skinny that I almost didn't recognize him at first but he's the same old bunny!"

Lisa did not ask him about Beirut, nor did he offer any details. "His personality was definitely different," she recalled. "He needed to get away from it all."

The days passed quickly until the time arrived for him to leave. The *Portland* would depart the evening of August 28 for the return to Beirut. Hudson said his farewells to his son and his wife. "Don't go downstairs with me," he said. "Stay up here with Will."

"We hugged," Lisa said, "for what felt like an eternity."

"I'll be back," Hudson repeatedly promised her. "I'll be back."

She hugged him again at the door as he departed. She stood and watched as he drifted down the hall toward the elevator. "John," she finally hollered. "Come back."

And he did.

"I have to hug you one more time," she said.

He wrapped his arms around her. "We held on to each other for dear life," she recalled. "That moment is frozen in my mind. Just like yesterday."

CHAPTER 14

The mission changed, but no one changed the mission.
—COLONEL TIMOTHY GERAGHTY
May 3, 1993

Israel's upcoming withdrawal from the Chouf Mountains prompted the Lebanese Armed Forces to launch an operation in southern Beirut on the afternoon of August 28 with the hopes of gaining a foothold to use in the pending fight over the mountains. Lebanese troops fanned out that Sunday through the Shiite slums, which were largely controlled by Nabih Berri's powerful Amal militia. That sweep, like kicking a hornet's nest, triggered an explosion in violence that once again shut down the commercial airport, cutting off Lebanon from the outside world. "The fighting," as Geraghty described, "was vicious and primitive."

The battle that afternoon, which involved mostly small-arms fire and was initially concentrated around the village of Burj al Barajinah, spread to nearby Hooterville. By 5:05 p.m., the intensifying fire moved closer to the airport and positions held by the Lebanese Armed Forces. The battle reached Checkpoint 69, a Marine combat outpost manned by thirty members of Bravo Company and a dozen Lebanese soldiers. "The outpost came under intense small arms fire," one reporter wrote. "The Marines and soldiers returned fire with M16 and M60 machineguns. The firefight lasted for about an hour and a half. It was the first direct attack on a Marine position."

Across the airport, Marines went on alert, slipping on helmets and flak jackets. Others jumped into bunkers as tracers zinged over the headquarters building. The fighting finally slowed around 7 p.m. and largely tapered off a half hour later. "Fighting continued in the distance," one report noted that night. "But it's quiet around the airport."

That peace would not last long.

The Lebanese military encircled Burj al Barajinah and Hooterville, triggering a renewed outbreak in fighting the following morning of August 29.

From 6 a.m. onward, Marine units across the airport came under fire, ranging from small arms and heavy machine guns to rocket-propelled grenades, mortars, rockets, and even howitzers. In accordance with the rules of engagement, Marines returned fire with the minimum level of force. The battle meanwhile migrated north into the French and Italian sectors of Beirut while the Druze militia joined the fight, raining artillery around the airport from positions up in the mountains.

"Fighting continues at heavy volume," one report stated.

"Groups of armed militia moving through area," read another.

At 9:40 a.m., Marines with the 81mm mortar platoon fired six illumination rounds over a suspected Druze artillery site as a warning to stop targeting the airport. Only minutes later Staff Sergeant Alexander Ortega Jr., who was with Alpha Company along the airport's eastern perimeter, ducked into a platoon command post tent in search of radio batteries for troops on the line. Second Lieutenant Donald Losey followed him, checking to make sure his Marines were under cover amid the attacks. At 9:44 a.m., a Druze mortar crashed into the command post tent, followed seconds later by another round. The scalding shrapnel killed Ortega instantly and mortally wounded Losey, who would survive only a few moments before he, too, succumbed to his injuries. The attack wounded three other Marines. Sergeant Donald Williams saw the fatal strike. "It just hit out of nowhere," he recalled. "I ran to check the sergeant and I saw he had been killed. The Navy corpsman was working on the lieutenant."

America had suffered its first combat deaths in Beirut.

First Lieutenant Mark Singleton, who was friends with Losey, was about three hundred yards away at the time of the attack. Shrapnel from another strike had wounded Singleton and several of his men. The lieutenant heard the tragic news crackle over the radio. "Staff Sergeant Ortega and Lieutenant Losey," someone announced, "are dead."

Marine amtracks rumbled up to Alpha Company's position to pick up the remains, which were transported to the landing zone and loaded aboard a helicopter at 10:16 a.m. for the flight out to the *Iwo Jima*. "Casualty section has coordinated with the Air Force for the return of the deceased," one message noted. "Aircraft standing by in Greece."

The Druze refused to stop, targeting the Lebanese Armed Forces outside the airport perimeter. The Marines meanwhile zeroed in on the attackers, using a mix of intelligence sources. That included the Army's fire-finding radar as well as Druze radio intercepts. Troops on the line used the flash-bang ranging method while visual observers on the roof of the Battalion Landing Team headquarters and in Huey and Cobra helicopters in the skies pinpointed the attackers. From this, Geraghty learned that the Druze were preparing another attack. The colonel ordered the 81mm mortar platoon to once again engage. Marines shot six illumination rounds over the Druze battery, which was firing a rocket every fifteen seconds. Charlie Battery joined the fight, hurling six 155mm howitzer illumination rounds.

But the Druze continued to fire.

The USS *Belknap*, a guided-missile cruiser that steamed offshore, fired two illumination rounds from its five-inch gun over the target area at 11:30 a.m. When those measures failed to stop the attacks, Charlie Battery swapped out illumination rounds for high explosives. At 11:45 a.m., the Marine howitzer roared, firing six 155mm point-detonating rounds. The attack, which marked the first time the Marines fired in anger, killed three Druze militiamen and wounded fifteen others. "The Druze battery immediately became silent," one after-action report noted. "The howitzer battery certainly reached out and touched someone."

A cease-fire soon followed, allowing troops to tally the dead and wounded. America had suffered two killed and another fourteen wounded. Over the span of twenty-four hours, Marines counted more than one hundred rounds of 82mm and 120mm mortars and 122mm rockets that had exploded in the airport area. "The small arms fire," one report noted, "was as great as that on a 200-yard rapid fire string of the Marine Corps rifle qualifications course."

While the Marines may not have been the intended target in many of the attacks, Geraghty determined that was a moot point. In at least eight small-arms-fire attacks, four rocket-propelled grenade strikes, and two mortar barrages, the Marines clearly were the designated target. Lebanese forces were nowhere near the location of those attacks. In each case, troops followed guidelines that specified preplanned levels of return fire. Small-arms fire, for example, was met only by small-arms fire. The Marines did not initiate any attacks and ceased firing as soon as the attackers' aim was no longer directed at the troops. "It was a very thoroughly thought out, gradual response. I was proud of the restraint shown by our men," Geraghty told reporters soon after the attacks. "We gave a clear message that we are here for peacekeeping and to support the government, but with an inherent right of self-defense."

Many of the troops, despite the deaths of two comrades, felt relieved that for the first time the Marines had fought back. Sergeant Mel Honeycutt, who helped line up the target as a member of Charlie Battery, felt a load lifted from his shoulders. "Our hands have been tied," he told a journalist. "It's been frustrating, but now we finally got to give back what we've been taking for months." To reflect this new reality, Alpha Company Marines amended the mess tent sign to read: "The Can Shoot Back Saloon" and later "The Did Shoot Back Saloon."

In the wake of the two Marine deaths, General Kelley fired off a personal message to Geraghty. "I know it is tough having the first combat casualties on your watch, but we have an outstanding commander on the scene and you and your Marines have my full confidence," the general wrote. "Please pass the word and continue the march."

Fighting throughout Beirut continued over the last few days of August. Marine positions around the airport occasionally came under fire, but nothing compared to the ferocity of the earlier fights. Some 150 reporters and guests at the Commodore Hotel, caught in the crossfire, crowded inside the basement, a wise move after a shell crashed into the fourth floor and destroyed several rooms. "The firing is so close," Associated Press reporter Terry Anderson said, "that you can hear the sound of the firing and then the explosion of the shell."

Newspaper headlines captured the outbreak in fighting, with many questioning whether Lebanon would again spiral into civil war and what that might mean for the Marines. "Beirut Battle Plunges Country Back into Chaos," announced the *Guardian*.

"Heavy Fighting Edges Lebanon Toward Civil War," added the *Fresno Bee*.

"Marines Now Caught in Beirut's Quagmire," declared the *Tampa Tribune*.

On the last day of August, some 10,000 Lebanese soldiers in M-48 tanks and armored personnel carriers rumbled through West Beirut, the city's predominantly Muslim area. Troops moved east to west, searching buildings for hiding militiamen and snipers while fighting block by block to clear the city. By nightfall, the fighting subsided. Only sporadic gunfire echoed through the capital. An uneasy calm soon settled over Beirut.

The question remained: How long would it last?

Geraghty reflected on the difficult few days his troops had endured. Not only had he lost his first Marines in combat in Lebanon, but he had been forced to fire shots in anger. "Keeping the peace became considerably more difficult this week as the ante was raised to the personal level. The Marines and sailors stood firm, did not flinch, and shipped home their dead with a quiet resolve to see the job through," Geraghty wrote in his weekly report. "Our support to the Lebanese people will continue and restraint will continue to determine the pace."

CHAPTER 15

We have given our Marines an impossible task.
—OTIS PIKE, FORMER U.S. REPRESENTATIVE FROM NEW YORK
September 2, 1983

President Reagan had escaped Washington for a little vacation at his California home. Nestled on 688 acres in the Santa Ynez Mountains overlooking the Pacific Ocean, Reagan's ranch offered him a retreat from the hustle of political life in the nation's capital. The century-old adobe home—dubbed the Western White House—was primitive compared to its Washington counterpart. The one-story home, which featured whitewashed walls and a red-tile roof, consisted of just five rooms that occupied barely 1,500 square feet. Two fireplaces served as the only source of heat, which the president provided via logs of oak and manzanita. Most days he liked to shed the mental stress of his day job by clearing brush, chopping wood, and riding horses with Nancy along the property's twelve miles of trails.

But Beirut now threatened that tranquility.

National Security Advisor William Clark woke Reagan at 1:55 a.m. Monday, one hour and ten minutes after the mortar attack killed Losey and Ortega. The president ordered his national security aides to gather in the White House at daybreak and prepare an update for him, which he received at 6 a.m. He then spoke with Defense Secretary Weinberger at 7:58 a.m. followed by Secretary of State Shultz at 8:24 a.m. That afternoon, the president jumped onto a fourteen-minute conference call at 1:14 p.m. with his national security counselors. Vice President George Bush, who had been on vacation in Maine, returned to Washington to lead the meeting. Based on those discussions, the president ordered no change in the size, scope, or mission of the Marines. "We condemn those who are responsible for the continuing violence which has claimed many victims, including our own Marines," White House spokesman Larry Speakes told reporters. "Once more, we call on all elements to end this senseless violence and unite behind the Lebanese government to restore national harmony."

The president then prepared to face the families.

When the news broke that morning, many Marine families braced for the worst. Staff Sergeant Ortega's wife, Robin, was home back in Jacksonville, North Carolina, near Camp Lejeune, where she cared for the couple's fifteen-month-old daughter, Heather. She was pregnant with the couple's second child, who was expected around Christmas. The staff sergeant had been thrilled. "Only 5 more months and I'll be a daddy again," he wrote his sister. "I really can't wait." Ortega's parents lived in the Rochester suburb of Henrietta, where he had grown up. The young Marine kept in touch with them through letters, filling them in on his life in Beirut. "We got bombed pretty good," Ortega wrote in what would prove to be his last letter. "The airport was closed for one week. When the bombs hit, all you could see was Lebanese people flying and dying. We had a couple of Marines hurt, but nothing serious. The best part is we got to fight back for the first time. So I guess I'm a combat veteran now (ha ha). I still feel the same though."

With so many troops in Beirut, Alexander Ortega assumed his son and namesake surely would be safe when he heard the news of the deaths that Monday morning. He left for work as a film finisher at Eastman Kodak. His wife, Helen, however, was overcome by dread. "I started having a terrible feeling," she said. "I knew my son was dead."

Colonel Michael Ferguson of the Marine Corps Reserve confirmed her worst fear with a knock on the door at 10:20 a.m. Throughout the day, the home filled up with loved ones and friends. "Members of the family had wandered the house during the afternoon asking the inevitable questions," one reporter observed. "Why our son? Why my brother?"

Those questions fell momentarily silent at 4:45 p.m. when the phone rang. On the other end of the line was the president. Friends and family gathered in the den fell silent. The Ortegas, locked in an embrace, shared the receiver. Reagan expressed his condolences. "Mr. President, I appreciate what you are saying very much," Alexander Ortega replied, "but you know, I'd hate to see any other parents going through what we're going through right now."

Reagan listened.

"You don't think there could be a chance of pulling those boys out of there?" he asked.

The president reiterated his public statements. The mission was necessary to help Lebanon grow strong enough to secure its own peace. "Mr. Reagan, I hope no other mother has to stand here talking to you—and hear what you're telling me," Helen Ortega said. "Please protect our American boys over there. Please, Mr. Reagan. Please."

"I want nothing more than that," the president replied.

"I loved him so much," she concluded. "Part of me died with him this morning."

A similar story unfolded more than six hundred miles south in the North Carolina town of Winston-Salem, where Lieutenant Losey had grown up. The six-foot-three Marine, who sported curly blond hair and answered to his middle name of George, was an avid practical jokester. He once hid a dead rat in his older sister Beth's car. On another occasion, Losey caught a snake and slipped it into his brother-in-law's bed as he slept. Losey had previously served four years in the Army, where he had helped guard former Nazi Rudolph Hess at Spandau Prison in Berlin. He later returned to school to earn a degree in anthropology from the University of North Carolina at Greensboro. Even in Beirut, he continued his studies, taking correspondence courses in psychology. People fascinated him. In his letters home, Losey wrote of the poverty he saw and the struggle faced by Beirut's children and refugees. "He thought if he did his duty in the service," his mother, Carol, later said, "he could help make this a peaceful world."

Unlike the married Ortega, Losey was single, though he was engaged to Gloria Isabel Angarita of Colombia, whom he had met while in college on a two-month summer travel program through South America. On that trip, like in Beirut, he had sympathized with the people. "He developed," his advisor Ramiro Lagos recalled, "a sincere and deep empathy for the poor and their struggle against the oppressors." Losey's father had died of a heart attack, but he was close with his mother and siblings. "George was a strong Christian man," his sister Kathryn remembered. "He was a blessing and a joy." His younger brother John had traveled to Camp Lejeune on the eve of his deployment to Lebanon. "I went there to see him," John Losey later said. "I picked up some of his stuff, brought it home. I mostly went to see him."

Three Marines had found Carol Losey at noon at Pilot Elementary School, where she served as the head librarian. "Neighbors and relatives came and went quietly all through the afternoon," a news reporter observed. "The telephone rang constantly."

One of those calls came from the Western White House.

Carol Losey said her conversation with the president was like talking to a good friend. "He was very warm-hearted," she said. "He offered his and Nancy's sincere sympathy."

Reagan assured Losey that he would make sure her son did not die in vain. "If there's anything I can do," the president concluded.

CHAPTER 16

Politics is the art of compromise. War is not.
—SENATOR ROBERT BYRD
September 29, 1983

The deaths of Losey and Ortega sparked protests from members of Congress. Arizona senator Barry Goldwater, the lone lawmaker who spoke out after the embassy bombing in April, reiterated his earlier view that the Marines should come home. "The United States," he argued, "has no business playing policeman with a handful of Marines." Democratic senator John Glenn of Ohio echoed him. "Our troops are clearly in a combat situation," he said. "We can no longer have the president denying that there is imminent danger in Lebanon."

Many lawmakers raised the War Powers Resolution, a 1973 law passed during the Vietnam War as a means to check a president's ability to wage war without congressional approval. The federal law mandates that a president notify Congress within forty-eight hours of troops entering combat and sets a sixty-day time limit for their withdrawal.

In his first report to Congress in September 1982, Reagan assured lawmakers that Marines would not be in harm's way. "I want to emphasize," he wrote, "there is no intention or expectation that U.S. Armed Forces will become involved in hostilities."

Much had since changed.

The president, who was loath to cede his constitutional authority over foreign policy to Congress, attempted to dance around that new reality in an August 30, 1983, update to lawmakers. Reagan acknowledged the recent fighting in Lebanon, including the tragic deaths of Losey and Ortega. But those deaths occurred, the president wrote, because of sporadic fighting between Lebanese Armed Forces and various militias, which spilled over into positions around the airport. In short, the Marines were not the targets, only innocent bystanders. "I believe that the continued presence of these U.S. forces in Lebanon is essential to the objective of helping to restore the territorial integrity, sovereignty, and political independence of Lebanon," the president added. "It is still not possible to predict the duration of the presence of these forces in Lebanon; we will continue to assess this question in light of progress toward this objective." Administration officials parroted that point in the press. "I believe," Shultz said, "there is no concerted effort to single out the Marines and target them."

Newspaper headlines trumpeted the administration's view, even as stories and photos about the deaths of Losey and Ortega at times appeared on the same page. "Reagan Insists," declared the *Miami Herald*, "Marines Not Involved in 'Combat.'"

"Marines Aren't Facing Imminent Hostilities in Beirut," added the *Ventura County Star.*

In private, however, some senior State and Defense Department officials raised fears over the administration's position, noting that attacks by the Druze and Shiite militias appeared aimed at both the Lebanese military and international forces. In addition, the violence only seemed to escalate—and no one had a road map of where it might lead. "This is a difficult situation, to say the least," one State Department official told the *New York Times.*

Members of Congress likewise challenged the White House's narrative. Refusing to label Marine engagements as "combat" or "hostilities" was a game of semantics. "We have people up in helicopters. We're shooting rockets and artillery," argued Illinois Republican senator Charles Percy. "If that isn't imminent hostilities, I don't know what it is."

"American forces are clearly involved in hostilities," added Senator Robert Byrd, a West Virginia Democrat, who feared a resumption of that nation's civil war.

Other leaders raised questions about America's continued role in Lebanon. Representative Henry Gonzalez wrote to the president that the Marines had been in Beirut for almost a year, during which time the situation had deteriorated. Neither Syria nor Israel showed any sign of real withdrawal. American mediation efforts had failed, while well-armed Lebanese factions demonstrated a renewed interest in slaughtering one another. "In these conditions, it is not only prudent, but absolutely necessary, to ask what the further risk of our young men can accomplish, what our interests are, and whether or not changes in policy are warranted," wrote the Texas Democrat. "It may well be that there is a case for continuing the mission of our forces in Lebanon; but that case has yet to be made, and the need for review is urgent."

Unlike when the troops first deployed, the deaths of the two Marines jump-started a far more robust public debate, sharpening the views of many on America's role in the region. A Gallup poll commissioned by *Newsweek* showed six out of ten Americans wanted the Marines home. The same poll revealed that Reagan's approval had dropped eight points since July, down to 44 percent. "It should be obvious by now," argued the *Asbury Park Press* of New Jersey, "if it wasn't earlier, that the Marines have been placed in a no-win situation in Beirut."

"Is America caught in a trap?" asked *U.S. News & World Report*.

"In bewilderment and desperation, the United States keeps trying to apply Band-aids to cancer," wrote *New York Times* columnist Flora Lewis.

Not all lawmakers and editorial pages advocated for a withdrawal. Some argued that while the Marine deaths were tragic, to pull out now would trigger the departure of other multinational forces. That power vacuum would doom Gemayel and launch Lebanon back into civil war. "Keeping the peace in Beirut is difficult," wrote the *Durham Sun* in North Carolina. "Perhaps it is futile. It certainly involves risks to American lives. But the attempt must be made."

A few reminded readers that the United States had landed in this mess because of Israel's disastrous war against Lebanon and the massacre of Palestinian refugees. Now, as Thomas Friedman noted, Israel had grown tired of the bloodshed and prepared to vacate the Chouf Mountains, "leaving the Marines to pick up the pieces in Beirut."

The questions and concerns raised by members of Congress and the press dovetailed with those of many Marines, who had spent recent days hunkered down in foxholes. "The only thing we do for fun here," Henry Linkkila wrote in a letter to his mother, "is count bullet holes in sandbags." The Marines, of course, followed the debate at home via the news. "No one wants to say we're in a hostile situation," said Corporal Richard McClain, "though it's pretty obvious to me that we are." Others challenged the administration's claims that the Marines were not the intended targets. "When the shelling starts, you figure that one, maybe two, rounds hitting us here is accidental," added a Marine. "More than that, it's just good aim."

Troops who months earlier had run a marathon waving the Lebanese flag now realized the depth of the country's sectarian hatred. America had little hope, many felt, of piecing the war-torn nation back together. "I don't think this country has a chance," Major George Converse wrote to his wife. "They just can't seem to stop fighting long enough to talk." Others agreed. "Lebanon is lost," a master sergeant confided to the *Chicago Tribune*'s Anne Keegan. "Everyone seems to think that now. We're seeing it every day as they fire on each other." This unfortunate realization dispirited many of the Marines, who had arrived in Lebanon hoping to make a difference. "Our troops," Grant McIntosh wrote his family, "feel so useless." Sergeant Robert Conley captured that sentiment in a letter to his dad. "I don't like the situation here. I don't respect the Lebanese Army or Government enough to risk my life for them. As far as I can see, no one can control the situation here," Conley wrote. "So that just leaves us sitting here, taking more chances each day of someone getting hit and accomplishing nothing."

CHAPTER 17

These past weeks have been tough on the Marines and
tough on the United States. I just trust that the politicians
will make decisions that are in our interest.
—CAPTAIN CHRIS COWDREY
September 11, 1983

At the start of September, Reagan summoned Bud McFarlane back to Washington. The deaths of two Marines had dramatically raised the stakes. The president, who did not want to make any more calls to bereaved families, was feeling pressure from the press and members of Congress. The special envoy had spent much of August shuttling between various Middle East capitals, with little success. He did manage to convince Gemayel to publicly call for a meeting of factional leaders to discuss the need for political unity, though he felt the Lebanese leader in the end did not go far enough. "Gemayel is just not a strong figure," a frustrated McFarlane conceded. "It was like pushing a noodle." A tireless worker, McFarlane had even met with Walid Jumblatt in Paris to press for a national reconciliation, only for the Druze militia leader to later slink away from such negotiations under threats from Syria. McFarlane's only tangible accomplishment, it seemed, was to alienate Ambassador Robert Dillon, whose residence he occupied in Beirut. Dillon, who would later describe McFarlane's team as "sons-of-bitches," chastised the overly ambitious special envoy for barring the embassy's experts from negotiations. "That situation," the ambassador later lamented, "became quite difficult for me."

The primary target of McFarlane's frustration remained Assad. The ruthless Syrian ruler, despite his willingness to meet with McFarlane, wanted to scuttle the May 17 deal and bend Lebanon's government to his will. "To these ends Assad is willing to run a high-risk policy using his considerable assets to physically intimidate Lebanese communal leaders as well as to employ military force in support of Syria's surrogates," one secret State Department memo explained. "Syria has become so implacably opposed to Amin Gemayel that it is willing to see him fall rather than attempt to reach some accommodation with him." To accomplish this, Assad tapped Druze and Shiite militias as proxies to wage war on Lebanon's central government and undermine Gemayel. He likewise welcomed the Iranians to set up terrorist training camps in the Bekaa Valley. The Syrian dictator no doubt felt emboldened by America's failure to retaliate in the wake of the embassy bombing, even after intelligence concluded Syria had likely played a role in the attack along with Iran. "Assad," as National Security Council staffer Howard Teicher wrote, "was able to slowly turn the screws on American diplomacy with a long-term campaign of escalating terror, subversion, and rocket and artillery attacks."

To counter this, McFarlane planned to pitch Washington on an idea to expand the multinational force's presence and mission. It was time to speak to Assad using the only language he understood—military might. The only way to drive Syria out of Lebanon, he believed, was to "use a massive amount of force." McFarlane knew it would be a tough sell for Defense Secretary Caspar Weinberger, who along with the Joint Chiefs of Staff had opposed America's military involvement in Lebanon from the beginning. In his memoir, McFarlane made no effort to hide his disdain for Weinberger, whom, like Habib, he accused of being out of his depth in his understanding of how to use the military as a tool of diplomacy. "This was," McFarlane wrote, "a reflection of his basic lack of historical knowledge of how force has been used in support of diplomacy through the centuries." The dislike, however, proved mutual. Weinberger, in his own scorched-earth account, characterized McFarlane as a want-to-be Kissinger, who was "strange" and "indrawn." In an insult that no doubt stung given McFarlane's reputation for insecurity, the Ivy League defense secretary labeled him an intellectual lightweight. "McFarlane," he concluded, "is a man of evident limitations."

Weinberger was not as two-dimensional as McFarlane characterized. In fact, the sixty-six-year-old San Francisco native, who had earned his undergraduate and law degrees at Harvard, had fought in the malarial jungles of New Guinea during World War II and later served on General Douglas MacArthur's intelligence staff. He was elected to the California Assembly and worked in the Nixon and Gerald Ford administrations, where his relentless cost-saving measures earned him the nickname "Cap the Knife." But he brought a different philosophy to the Defense Department, where he fought to grow the Pentagon's budget. A rabid Anglophile, Weinberger was fascinated by Winston Churchill, whose fight against Hitler he saw as a parallel to America's Cold War struggle against the Soviet Union. Just as Allied industrialization helped grind down the Axis powers, so, too, he felt could American deep pockets crush the Soviet Union. But despite his reputation as a hawk, Weinberger was reluctant to deploy troops. Power was a tool, he felt, best used sparingly. "I did not arm to attack," he said. "We armed so that we could negotiate from strength, defend freedom, and make war *less* likely."

The personal animosity between McFarlane and Weinberger highlighted the divide among Reagan's senior advisors over what, if any, role America should play in Lebanon. On an even deeper level it symbolized the fundamental differences between them over the question of when and if military power should be used. On one side stood McFarlane and Shultz, the latter of whom was anxious to see his May 17 deal succeed, a move that would no doubt burnish his reputation as secretary of state. The duo had spent months trying to secure a diplomatic victory, only to be frustrated by an intransigent and mischievous Syria. "For any Lebanese strategy to be successful," McFarlane now advocated, "it had to be founded on an effective political-military strategy." To compensate for failures at the negotiating table, McFarlane and Shultz now wanted to fall back on the military. Naval airpower and gunfire coupled with the Marines could play a vital role in applying pressure on Assad. This viewpoint reflected McFarlane's embrace of nineteenth-century Prussian military theorist Carl von Clausewitz. "War," as Clausewitz famously wrote, "is merely the continuation of policy by other means." Shultz laid out that argument in a previous battle with Weinberger. "The president wants teeth in whatever he does," he declared, "and it is up to the Department of Defense to provide the teeth."

On the opposite side of the debate stood Weinberger and the Joint Chiefs of Staff. "One has to think through very carefully," cautioned General Vessey, before "putting American troops in any kind of operation where we're using them as a political lever." Weinberger agreed. The defense secretary did not believe the State Department's May 17 agreement was worth the paper it was written on since Syria had no plan to leave. In addition, he saw no role for American Marines in Lebanon in what now amounted to a domestic struggle over political power. As the recent fighting showed, American troops no longer provided a stabilizing force. If anything, the

Marines now had a bull's-eye on them. He likewise challenged McFarlane's view of the need to meld diplomacy and power, which he felt was a slippery slope of military adventurousness that could spiral into a much larger conflict. "My own feeling," Weinberger said, "was that we should not commit American troops to any situation unless the objectives were so important to American interests that we had to fight, and that if those conditions were met, and all diplomatic efforts failed, then we had to commit, as a last resort, not just token forces to provide an American presence, but enough forces to win and win overwhelmingly."

Adding to the discord was the long-running rivalry between Weinberger and Shultz. In any administration, there is a natural competition between the State and Defense Departments, whose missions at times overlap. But the tensions between the two senior cabinet members proved far more personal. The men, of course, publicly downplayed the feud.

"That's nonsense," Shultz grumbled to a *Time* magazine reporter.

"I think that is overemphasized," added Weinberger.

But journalists from the *Washington Post* to the *New York Times* relished covering what one correspondent colorfully characterized as "one of the greatest cat-and-dog fights of the Reagan administration." The two sexagenarians had long worked together, first in the Office of Management and Budget under Nixon and later at the construction giant Bechtel. In both cases, Weinberger served in a lesser role than Shultz. But in the White House, seated in leather chairs around the cabinet room table, the men were at long last equals.

From a personality perspective, the two could not have appeared more different. A former academic, Shultz was a soft-spoken mediator who shunned the limelight. Weinberger, per his background as a litigator and politician, could be an aggressive debater, who, like his hero Churchill, embraced both confrontation and the spotlight. But the duo had more in common than many realized, including years of brawling in the Washington arena that had forged able adversaries. "Both were capable, intelligent, opinionated, energetic and turf conscious," historian Lou Cannon observed. "Both had tempers that could unexpectedly erupt when they felt slighted or betrayed. Both recognized that Reagan did not want to give offense to either of them and took advantage of their high standing with the president in different ways."

Reagan, a generally warm and affable leader who disliked controversy, responded to such bickering by seeking a compromise designed to end the fighting. "This trait," Cannon added, "inevitably invited middle-ground solutions aimed at mending differences, even in circumstances such as Lebanon where the middle ground courted catastrophe."

Other times, the president shut down, a move that led meetings to conclude without a decision. This proved to be one of Reagan's greatest deficiencies as a leader, particularly for a first-term president without extensive foreign policy experience. Such debate, as contentious and uncomfortable as it might have been, offered the commander in chief an important chance to ask questions, challenge various scenarios, educate himself, and ultimately develop a more informed solution. The questions over Lebanon, where 1,800 American Marines were caught in the crossfire of warring factions, warranted that kind of robust discussion. After a year of simmering tensions, the sudden escalation of violence furthermore demonstrated the urgency of rapidly processing intelligence and developing plans so the president could respond accordingly, whether that meant pulling the Marines out of Beirut, increasing troop levels, or something entirely different. Indecision could mean the difference between life and death, all of which was now held hostage by the interpersonal rivalries of a handful of Washington leaders.

This was the context that greeted members of the National Security Planning Group, who filed into the Situation Room at 11 a.m. on September 3, 1983. Around the wooden conference table that morning sat Vice President George Bush, National Security Advisor William Clark, Chief of Staff James Baker, Joint Chiefs of Staff Chairman General John Vessey, Weinberger, Shultz, Undersecretary of State Lawrence Eagleburger, and McFarlane, along with various other national security staffers. The Soviet shoot-down two days earlier of Korean Air Lines Flight 007 exacerbated worldwide tensions. The Seoul-bound plane, which had originally taken off from New York City, drifted into Soviet airspace, prompting the Soviet air force to shoot it down in a tragic decision that killed 269 passengers and crew. Among the dead were sixty-two Americans, including Representative Larry McDonald, a Democrat from Georgia. The back-to-back crises forced Reagan, who had planned to stay at his California ranch through Labor Day, to cut his vacation short and return to Washington only the day before. The president's calendar shows that he joined the session on Lebanon at 11:16 a.m.

"The purpose of this meeting," Clark wrote in an advance memo to all participants, "will not be to review all aspects of our Lebanon policy but rather to face this very tricky question of escalation and how we can use both diplomatic and military measures to deter the Syrians before we get to the point where it may be necessary to use military force. It is essential that we reach some tentative conclusion at the meeting or we may find ourselves in a situation where events are unfolding so quickly we will have little time to do anything except react."

There are no minutes of the meeting, but the declassified agenda and the discussion papers circulated in advance of the session help flesh out the intended conversation that Saturday morning. The agenda shows that the first of the two main discussion items centered on political and diplomatic strategies for Lebanon, including efforts to broaden domestic and international support for Gemayel's government, Israel's pending withdrawal from the Chouf Mountains, and policy options to discourage continued Syrian meddling. That discussion would be followed by one titled "Military Options to Complement Political/Diplomatic Strategies." This included how to deter or counter Syrian and Druze artillery attacks on Lebanese forces and the Marines as well as options for inserting a multinational buffer force along Syrian lines.

Israel's withdrawal—and the chaos it threatened to unleash—loomed large. "We are at a turning point," the State Department's advance paper warned. "Lebanon's future will very likely be determined in the next few days by what we, the Lebanese, the Israelis, and the Syrians do." Clark's assessment echoed his colleagues at State. "In the worse case," the national security advisor wrote, "we have to assume that fighting will break out following the Israeli withdrawal and that the Syrians may intervene with paramilitary forces, possibly disguised as Druze militiamen to engage the Lebanese Forces and the Lebanese Army." If that happened, he cautioned, America needed to be prepared for "large scale bloodshed" and "massacres," as well possible attacks on the Marines. "We have to be prepared," Clark wrote, "to take steps to deter and, if necessary, respond to direct or indirect Syrian military intervention."

To that end, the United States had warned Syria against attacks on the multinational forces. America would do what was necessary to protect the Marines. "If this demarche falls on deaf ears and Assad persists in playing brinksmanship," Clark advised, "we face a very critical situation. There may be no alternative but to consider the use of expanded military force." That could include airpower as well as placing multinational forces between the Lebanese military and Syrian forces, a move that would reduce how much pressure Assad could place on Gemayel's government. "Such actions," Clark cautioned, "would represent a dramatic escalation in our involvement in Lebanon which would have profound implications for our credibility as a world power, our relations with the Arab world and the Soviet Union, and our relations with the Congress." To buttress its warning to Syria, the United States planned to deploy another 2,000 Marines offshore on ships as well as leave the aircraft carrier USS *Eisenhower* in the area. "The line," as the State Department memo declared, "has been drawn."

Despite the fears outlined by the State Department and members of the National Security Council, Reagan's advisors once again deadlocked during the hourlong session. "The meeting," as National Security Council staffer Teicher recalled, "proved to be an exercise in tough rhetoric and divided results." On one side fell McFarlane, Shultz, Eagleburger, Clark, and the National Security Council staff, who wanted to expand America's mission to balance out Israel's withdrawal and buy more time for a political solution. Opposite them stood Weinberger, Vessey, Bush, and Baker, who opposed any change in the role or mission of the Marines short of withdrawal. The status quo prevailed. "No new decisions were made. The rules of engagement were not changed. The United States would continue to act only in self-defense, if fired upon directly," wrote a frustrated Teicher, who sided with his National Security Council colleagues. "We did not have the power in place or the will to win, and the Syrians knew it."

CHAPTER 18

The war is definitely escalating right in front of my eyes.
—DR. JOHN HUDSON, LETTER TO HIS WIFE
September 4, 1983

The *Eisenhower* carrier battle group steamed closer toward shore at the start of September, joined by the French flattop *Foch* and several Italian naval gunfire ships. The Joint Chiefs of Staff ordered an additional 2,000 leathernecks with the 31st Marine Amphibious Unit to redeploy from the Pacific to Lebanon, though the troops would not arrive until September 12 and would remain aboard ship unless needed. In the battered Lebanese capital, the embassy began organizing for the possible evacuation of American citizens. That included reviewing and updating emergency plans, examining evacuation sites, and establishing radio communications between the diplomatic missions in Beirut and Tel Aviv and all naval task force commanders. Despite a lull in fighting, the Marines suspended all patrols and hunkered down in flak vests and helmets. "An eerie silence settled over the city," Geraghty recalled. "The fighting during this period had been the most explosive that had occurred since our arrival."

News correspondents poured into the capital, lured by the recent fighting that had turned Lebanon into one of the world's biggest stories. International reporters arrived from a diverse range of countries, including Turkey, Spain, Belgium, and Denmark. Local American television stations sent crews to do stories on hometown Marines while small-town papers requested phone interviews. Colonel Geraghty was in high demand for interviews ranging from the *Baltimore Sun* and *Miami Herald* to Tom Brokaw and Ted Koppel. The public affairs office escorted an average of thirty to forty reporters a day, overwhelming the staff of two officers and six enlisted men. "The Beirut press corps," recalled Major Bob Jordan, head of public affairs, "had now swelled to more than 300 correspondents—about one for every four Marines on the line."

Amid this increased media attention, the Joint Chiefs ordered Geraghty to resupply a Lebanese Armed Forces base north of Beirut with 500,000 rounds of ammunition from his force's contingency stockpile. The colonel, whose troops accomplished the job with helicopters and landing craft, felt such a move jeopardized America's precious neutrality. "The peacekeeping mission," Geraghty wrote, "was indeed getting foggy."

On September 2, the Marines held a memorial service for Lieutenant Losey and Staff Sergeant Ortega, whose deaths four days earlier still reverberated through the ranks. Two M60 tanks stood guard with barrels aimed toward the mountainous battlefields that rimmed the horizon. At the late-day service, as the sun eased down the western sky over the Mediterranean, Father Pucciarelli addressed his flock, his white vestments contrasted against his black combat boots. Behind him fluttered three flags, two American and one Lebanese, all at half-staff. "We come together this evening as the sun goes down to give honor to our two friends," the Catholic priest said. "They died so as to give time and space to the Lebanese army to get themselves in shape so they can bring peace, honor and integrity here to Lebanon."

The Marines read from the Twenty-Third Psalm, a passage often chosen for funerals for its reassuring message. "Though I walk through the valley of the shadow of death, I will fear no evil: for thou art with me; thy rod and thy staff they comfort me." Troops recited the Lord's Prayer and sang "Amazing Grace." Amid the somber ceremony, as Chaplain Danny Wheeler read a passage from the Bible, a single rifle shot echoed to the east.

Lieutenant Colonel Larry Gerlach, who commanded the Battalion Landing Team, eulogized Losey and Ortega. "Our country, our way of life can only survive as long as we have strong young men who are willing to pay the ultimate price if it is called for," Gerlach reminded his Marines. "They died in a very difficult mission. They died in a mission of peace-keeping. It calls for dedication, it calls for discipline and it calls for restraint."

Back in the United States, families and friends prepared to bury the fallen Marines. First Lieutenant Mark Singleton, who was wounded by shrapnel the same day Losey died, escorted his friend's body home, a journey that had taken him from Beirut through Cyprus, Germany, Delaware, and Philadelphia before landing in North Carolina. Singleton had made the first leg of the trip with his helmet pulled low over his eyes so no one would see his emotions. The two Marines, both from small southern towns, had been close. "We were both brought up in the country so we hit it off right away," he said. "We knew what it was like to go out in a tobacco patch. We knew about hunting and fishing. We could relate to the simple things."

When Singleton reached Losey's home, family members pulled him into a room.

"Tell us what happened?" Carol Losey asked.

Singleton walked the family through that day, describing the mortar attack that had killed the two young Marines inside the platoon command post.

"George said you have a family," Losey continued.

Singleton confirmed, telling her that his wife and infant daughter were over at Camp Lejeune. To his surprise, Carol Losey insisted that he leave them and go home to Jacksonville and visit his family. After that, she said, Singleton could come back and help them with the funeral. "You haven't seen your family," she insisted. "You need to go see them."

On September 4, more than three hundred people overflowed the wooden pews at New Friendship Baptist Church in Winston-Salem, spilling outside onto the lawn, all for a chance to say goodbye to George Losey. It was in this redbrick church, adorned with white columns and a matching steeple, that Losey was baptized nineteen years earlier. On May 1, the last Sunday before he shipped out to Beirut, the young lieutenant had asked his Sunday school class to pray for him. Losey now returned four months later in a flag-draped coffin that stood alone before the altar in the center of the sanctuary. In the audience with his mother and siblings that Sunday sat his fiancée, Gloria, who had flown in from Colombia. Carol Losey had asked his college advisor and friend, Ramiro Lagos, to phone her with the news of his death.

"Lord," she had cried, "why did it have to be him?"

The Reverend Warren Kerr fought back tears as he eulogized Losey. "He made the greatest sacrifice," Kerr told those gathered, "that of his own life for his country, for the people of Lebanon, and maybe that will say something to the people for the world."

At the conclusion of the forty-minute service, six Marine pallbearers carried his remains down the front steps of the church to a white hearse as the organ played. "The precision of their pace," one reporter observed, "made a dull, reverberating thud." Six additional Marines escorted Losey's family into matching white limousines. Officers on motorcycles led the procession to Oaklawn Memorial Gardens. Additional police blocked traffic at intersections, where officers stood with bowed heads and white helmets pressed against their hearts.

At the grave site, cooled by a late-summer breeze, Reverend Kerr read aloud from the Old Testament before turning the procession over to a Marine honor guard.

"Fire the volley," a Marine cried out.

The seven assembled leathernecks each fired three rounds as part of a twenty-one-gun salute. A lone bugler played "Taps," whose sad notes drifted across the cemetery. Losey's bespectacled mother, who for most of the service sat with her hands clenched in her lap, wiped away tears and sobbed. Behind her stood Lieutenant Singleton, who had returned after visiting his family. He placed his arm around her shoulder as she wept.

Major General Alfred Gray, commander of the Second Marine Division, took the folded American flag that had covered his casket and offered it to Losey's mother. The general presented a second flag, the one that had covered his remains when he arrived in the United States, to his grandfather. After the service, Gray reminded reporters that Losey had died protecting his men. "There is," he said, "no higher calling than that."

Ortega's funeral followed two days later at St. Richard's Roman Catholic Church in the tiny Pennsylvania community of Barnesville, near where his wife, Robin, was raised. Dozens of Marines, whom Ortega had worked with as a recruiter on Long Island, had boarded a bus at 4 a.m. that morning just to make the 10 a.m. service. Only four years earlier, in the same redbrick church nestled amid the rolling landscape where mourners now gathered, Ortega was married. "The Bible reminds us that you do not know what will happen tomorrow," the Reverend Joseph Walen told those gathered. "We are here today to attest to that truth."

Ortega's burial followed at Sky-View Memorial Park, a lush cemetery filled with trees, flowers, and sun-faded flags where the young Marine had once enjoyed jogging. A green canopy shaded the family and the casket from the ninety-degree heat. Ortega's fifteen-month-old daughter, Heather, who clutched a cloth doll, wriggled in the arms of a relative. Reporters noted that his wife sat stoically throughout the service, even as rifles roared and taps echoed. After the service, Ortega's uncle James Knopp read a statement from the family. "Alex loved the Marines," he said. "He died for what he's always believed in—peace."

Brigadier General James Joy, assistant commanding officer of the Second Marine Division, stood in for General Gray, who had departed for Beirut. Joy lauded Ortega's sacrifice. "Staff Sergeant Ortega died a hero," he said. "We're very proud of him."

News coverage of the funerals circulated among the troops in Beirut, where Hudson was heartbroken to learn Ortega's widow was pregnant. An article he read on Losey made him weep. The unexpected deaths of the two Marines forced him to reflect on his own mortality. "Years ago I used to think about dying and the thought didn't bother me much. In fact, I used to look forward to dying," Hudson wrote to his wife, "but now I'm not ready for it and especially now that I have such a wonderful family. I so want to see Will grow up and spend my life with you. You have certainly made my life worth living. I just hope I get back home."

The deaths likewise brought into sharper focus the rapidly deteriorating landscape in Lebanon. Even before the suspension of patrols, troops could sense that change in the slums around the base, where the Shiites had become more hostile toward the Marines. Young men carried AK-47 rifles. Others shouted Khomeini's name. The rise in aggression, Glenn Dolphin feared, paralleled a decline in the perception of American neutrality. "It was getting harder and harder to imagine how we were going to be successful in our role as peacekeepers when no one in this country seemed to want peace," Dolphin wrote. "None of the parties involved seemed to be the least bit interested in building a strong, self-supporting Lebanon. They were only interested in settling old scores and defending their own little fiefdoms."

Political struggles between Congress and the White House over the War Powers Resolution, which the Marines followed in news reports, only exacerbated the frustration. Hudson, who had to pluck out shrapnel and stitch up wounds after each attack, was furious about the administration's efforts to argue that the troops were not in combat. "The President is lying when he says Marines have not been the target," he wrote to his wife. "The Marines have been fired on intentionally and they've been firing back—rifles, helos, artillery, and an aircraft carrier is waiting off the coast. This is what makes me so mad. I will never trust my government again! So much has happened here that has not been reported—it's incredible."

Dolphin feared that Democrats would use the recent Marine deaths to sabotage the president. In an effort to protect Reagan, Republican allies would spin the conflict into a story totally divorced from the reality of what the Marines actually faced, all of which would only confuse the American public. Frontline bureaucrats like McFarlane, Dolphin added, failed to inspire confidence. Compounding this challenge was the perpetual threat that the fragile Lebanese government would collapse and trigger a relapse of civil war.

Into this volatile mix, Israel lobbed a grenade.

The Jewish state announced the time had arrived to vacate the Chouf Mountains. The Israelis, who had spent a year pushing Gemayel for a peace deal, were done. "At this stage in time," an Israeli spokesman told reporters in defense of the withdrawal, "we have no reason to believe that if we gave them any more time, that anything will change."

Though American officials had known of Israel's intent to withdraw, the announcement of when caught Washington off guard. The sudden departure likewise gave no time for the multinational force or Lebanese military to coordinate how to cover the 240-square-mile area Israel planned to surrender. American officials pleaded with Israel to delay the withdrawal. Reagan even phoned Prime Minister Begin, who put him in touch with Defense Minister Moshe Arens. At a minimum, he asked Israel to wait at least until the Lebanese Armed Forces could occupy those areas before leaving, but it was not to be. "No soap," the president wrote in his diary on September 3. "It was too late—the Israelis are already on the move."

Journalists and Marines anxiously awaited the fallout as Israel's forces descended from the mountains. "In the Commodore Hotel," reporter Robert Fisk wrote, "there was a dark mood among the television crews and correspondents. The scale and ferocity of the fighting frightened all of us." A similar tension hung over the Marines. "That night," Geraghty said, "all could hear the rumble of Israeli tanks, personnel carriers, and heavy vehicles heading south."

The bull's-eye, as history would show, would soon fall on the United States Marines.

Israel's departure triggered an immediate outbreak in fighting between the Christian and Druze militias, as the nearby mountains once again lit up with gunfire. "For the entire day and into the evening," Richard Bernstein wrote in the *New York Times*, "the dull thud of artillery resounded throughout the greater Beirut area." At the Marine compound, troops slipped on helmets and flak jackets. Hudson watched from his fourth-floor balcony as artillery shells chewed up the mountainside. "Being here is such an unusual experience," he wrote to his wife. "I'm afraid before this day is over, we'll be involved in direct fire again, and I'll be confined to the life of a mole down in the basement." The physician had recently acquired a room in the base-ment, which he converted into a battle dressing station. That morning, as machine guns rattled in the distance and artillery thundered, he listened to John Lennon's "Give Peace a Chance" on the radio. "What irony," Hudson remarked. "This place is <u>crazy</u>!"

This fire soon turned to Marine positions at the airport. That escalated on September 6. Eleven rockets came shortly before 1 a.m. "The time of flight," the monthly Command Chronology reported, "was only two to three seconds." More rockets started again at 3:45 a.m. Over the course of almost two hours, twenty-one rockets hit the airport. One such strike instantly killed Corporal Pedro J. Valle and mortally wounded Lance Corporal Randy Clark. Fellow platoon mate Lance Corporal Bradley McLaughlin, who saw the rocket explode in front of Valle, described the attack in a letter to his wife. "Babe it was real bad," he wrote. "It tore his legs and arms off his body. We ran up to help them. Clark had two broken legs and a broken arm and half his face was gone. He was still alive but we knew he was dying."

The howitzer battery fired 155mm illumination rounds while Cobras launched at dawn to find rocket-launcher locations. "The massive amount of launcher positions and impacts in the hills through the previous night," one report stated, "made it impossible to determine which position was firing on the airport." The attacks continued throughout the day, with more than 120 rounds landing around the airport by 4 p.m. The fire finally died down that evening, leaving Geraghty once again to tally his casualties. "Stakes are being raised weekly," he wrote. "Our contribution to peace in Lebanon since 22 July stands at 4 killed and 28 wounded."

CHAPTER 19

The only thing these people understand is responding muzzle
flashes and barking iron. Poor Lebanon.
—LANCE CORPORAL BILL STELPFLUG, LETTER TO HIS FAMILY
September 18, 1983

Hours after a rocket killed two Marines—and on the same day Alexander Ortega was buried in the rolling hills of rural Pennsylvania—Reagan again prepared to call bereaved parents. Earlier that morning, casualty notification teams had visited the families of Pedro Valle in Puerto Rico and Randy Clark in Wisconsin to deliver the tragic news.

Amelia Ramos had spotted the two Marines in dress uniforms that Tuesday morning walking down her street in Old San Juan. The olive skin and mustache of one made her think it was her son, back home in Puerto Rico for a surprise visit. She let out a laugh as her heart raced with excitement. "When the Marines didn't smile," her sister Emma Quinones told a reporter that day, "she knew it wasn't her son. She knew something was wrong."

The Marines next visited the home of his father, Santos Valle, who though divorced lived just a few blocks away from his ex-wife along the cobblestone streets. The retired Army sergeant, who had served for twenty-eight years, including tours in Korea and Vietnam, cried at the news. The twenty-five-year-old Valle, one of three sons, had followed his father into the military, joining the Marines right out of high school and serving for seven years. On the walls of Santos Valle's home, mixed in with his own framed military decorations, dangled a photo of his son's platoon. Pedro stood at the front, a bazooka clutched in his hands. "Ever since he was a boy," his father recalled, "he wanted to be in the Marines."

At 5:49 p.m. on September 6, Reagan spoke for a few minutes with Santos, the first of two calls he would make that evening from the White House to Puerto Rico. The president offered him his condolences. "Be calm," he assured him. "Be strong."

Santos Valle, a military man, understood. "Pedro sacrificed his life for the ideals of his country," he said. "I am proud because he was defending democracy."

A similar story unfolded in the tiny Wisconsin village of Minong, nearly two thousand miles north. Unlike Valle, who was an older career Marine, nineteen-year-old Clark had served barely a year. The six-foot-two Clark had been a high school superstar, a football lineman who helped lead his team to an undefeated season and conference title his senior year. Upon graduation in May 1982, he enlisted in the Marines. There were no jobs in his home-town of 557 residents. His father, James, a construction superintendent, had been out of work for a year. His mother, Norma, supported the family labor-ing in a jacket factory. In letters from Beirut, Clark wrote that he was scared, but he assured his family he would be fine. "Don't worry about me," he wrote in his final letter. "I'll be all right, and I'll come home in one piece."

Reagan reached the family at 5:58 p.m. Unlike Santos Valle, who was proud of his son's sacrifice, James Clark was mad at the wasted life of his son. When the first Marines died, he said, America should have pulled out. The situation had devolved into a fiasco with Marines functioning as police officers, getting picked off two or three at a time.

"Why," he asked throughout the day, "do we have our boys over there?"

Clark shared that view—and much more—with the president, including a stern warning if things didn't change. "I'm sure as hell," he said, "not going to vote for you next year."

The ten-minute conversation upset Reagan, who wrote about it that night in his diary. The calls that Tuesday evening—coupled with the ones he had made eight days earlier to the parents of Losey and Ortega—served as a reminder of the danger men faced because of his orders. These painful con-versations were the gritty by-product of decisions made around a conference room table, far removed from the thunder of artillery and rockets, the flying shrapnel, and the terror that hung over the Marines. "I called the parents of the 2 Marines—not easy," he wrote. "One father asked if they were in Leba-non for anything that was worth his son's life."

In Beirut, the deaths of Valle and Clark rattled the troops.

"The reality has hit," said Private First Class Tom McCaleb. "Now we know there is a definite chance we could be killed at any time. We do a lot of praying."

Alpha Company commander Captain Paul Roy, who had lost four men in the span of barely a week, struggled to adjust to this violent reality. "We didn't expect this kind of action. Things will never be the same,"

Roy said. "You don't know when the next shell is coming in. It could be quiet now, but in five seconds one could land right here."

Efforts to memorialize Valle and Clark had to be delayed twice because of continued attacks on the airport. Finally on September 13, Father George Pucciarelli and Chaplain Danny Wheeler organized a service at the Battalion Landing Team headquarters. The priest, dressed in his white vestments, stood behind a waist-high altar, where two candles flanked a cross mounted in the center. Behind him stood the American and Marine Corps flags.

Two hundred tired Marines in dusty fatigues and helmets crowded around. Others stared down from the torched mezzanine above. Artillery grumbled in the distance throughout the twenty-minute service, which included the singing of "Amazing Grace" followed by a twenty-one-gun salute. "Both were highly motivated," recalled Lieutenant Colonel Gerlach, commander of the Battalion Landing Team, "hard-charging Marines."

Roy memorialized his men. The thirty-four-year-old captain, who grew up in the small town of Winslow, Maine, tried to remain positive. In a recent letter to his parents, he focused on his company's successes. "The Marines are defending themselves and fighting back," he wrote. "The Marines are great. I'm real proud of the company and how it is performing." But fellow officers could see the toll the losses had taken on him, including Glenn Dolphin. "The strain he was under was beginning to show. He looked exhausted," Dolphin recalled. "The skipper's face was drawn, and flecks of gray were just beginning to show in his dark hair."

Roy pushed his own stress aside as he remembered his men. He knew Valle particularly well, since the youth had once served as his driver. "It was evident from my conversations with both of them in times past, they cared deeply for their families and loved ones back home and that they themselves came from loving homes," Roy said. "It showed in their performance and attitude. I am confident they are beside us now, giving us courage to march on."

The assembled Marines listened.

"By their ultimate sacrifice," the company commander continued, "they have given this land a chance to find its own destiny."

But had they?

That question and others would be asked the following day six thousand miles to the west in Clark's tiny hometown of Minong. In the gymnasium at Northwood High School, workers set up one thousand folding chairs in anticipation that the beloved teenager's funeral would double the town's population for the day. The high school announced plans to start a scholarship in Clark's honor as well as retire his No. 74 football jersey, which his younger brother Kelly had worn the previous Friday night in a 20–6 victory over rival Prairie Farm. Before the game, players from the opposing team had presented a check for the new scholarship.

During the service, Pastor Arvid Sundet of Calvary Lutheran Church echoed many of the concerns raised by the Clark family. "We are confused and hurt," he said. "We don't even know if his death has served a purpose." The parishioners nodded. "And so we ask questions," he continued. "We question our national policies. We question our president, and we join the Clark family in asking why. What for? Peacekeeping is not a satisfactory answer."

James Clark spoke again with reporters following his son's burial at Greenwood Cemetery, where his high school classmates served as his pallbearers. He wished the president would come to Minong without any of his advisors and just walk the field with him where his son once played. Then he could ask him the questions on his mind, questions that no doubt many Americans would be hard-pressed to understand, given the complicated sectarian and political rivalries that dominated Lebanon. "Who are we defending?" Clark would ask. "Who are the Druze? Who are the Christians? Who are the good people? I would like for him to answer me that question."

CHAPTER 20

It's really hard to write a letter home now because we're
all concentrating on staying alive.
—LANCE CORPORAL BRADLEY MCLAUGHLIN, LETTER TO HIS WIFE
September 9, 1983

I n Beirut, the Marines started digging.

The primitive foxholes the men built back in May soon evolved into underground fortresses, connected by a network of trenches that resembled a World War I battlefield. "The most popular item, besides mail," said Major Bob Jordan, "became the sandbag."

Throughout the month of September, the Marines operated like an assembly line, shoveling sand into one bag after another after another. Troops filled so many—approximately 100,000 that month—that headquarters struggled to keep this precious commodity in stock. This brought the total used to more than a half million. In addition, Marines rolled out 10,000 feet of concertina wire and hammered in 1,000 engineering stakes for a total of twenty tons of materials. "If the filling of sandbags had been an Olympic sport," Glenn Dolphin quipped, "there would have been several gold medals handed out during the deployment."

Troops likewise picked through the rubble of shelled buildings for lumber and scrap metal that could be used to shore up shelters. "Bunkers were dug deeper, and sides were reinforced with stakes and pallets," noted the *Root Scoop*. "Windows and air vents were added by packing sandbags around wooden frames and covering them with screen to keep the mosquitos out." Once the bunkers were completed, the men linked them to others via trenches, creating bunker complexes that troops colorfully dubbed "Sandominiums."

Life in the dank shelters was arduous. Temperatures soared and the humid air stagnated. The men lived off rations. "Sometimes we go a couple of days without showers and hot chow. The chow I can live without," John Dalziel wrote his father, "but the showers are a must here. After a couple of days or so, everybody gets an odor. Kinda gross. But I guess that is war!" The Marines had little to do but think, as the hours crawled past and the artillery thundered. Sergeant Michael Massman, who at thirty was one of the older Marines, slipped on headphones to drown out the shelling. "I can honestly say," he wrote home, "that I know what the human heart tastes like, because mine has been up in my throat quite a few times."

Lance Corporal Bradley McLaughlin, who had seen the violent deaths of Clark and Valle, felt exhausted. "I have no emotional feelings any more. I can't cry, I can't laugh. It's like I'm just existing. Our days are spent in a dirty, sand-filled trench with a sand-bag roof that ain't going to stop anything if we get hit," he wrote his wife. "All we hear all day long, day after day is constant shelling and machine gun fire all around us. We just sit here wondering when the next shell will land on top of us, and who will be the next victim."

Hospital Corpsman Third Class Joseph Milano likewise struggled with the recent deaths, a fact he shared in a letter home. "I can't help thinking of those parents of the Marines killed, how they feel. I wish I could tell them we tried to help. I know there was nothing we could have done but I can't help feeling helpless," Milano wrote. "I wonder how long it will take before people forget about these Marines. Their faces burn in my memory. I'll never forget. How could I?" Hudson, in contrast, felt bitter. The deaths of Losey and Ortega, Valle and Clark underscored for him the pointlessness of the entire mission in Lebanon. "It is so sad," the physician wrote to his wife, "that four Marines have died for absolutely nothing."

The deaths reinforced for others a desire to be home. "This whole thing is crazy," Private Henry Linkkila wrote his mother. "I won't be happy until I am out of this God forsaken country." He wasn't the only one who felt that way. "Can't wait to split this shit-hole," Lance Corporal Bill Stelpflug wrote. Despite being tired, filthy, and a bit shell-shocked, the nineteen-year-old never lost his empathy for those who had it worse. "I saw the most sad sight—a bunch of civilians whose houses had been hit. They didn't know where to go and were all dusty," he wrote. "If only they would stop fucking fighting and start building."

"Beirut is not hell," became a common phrase, "but you can see it from here."

The increased danger exacerbated the emotional distance some felt from loved ones back home. Captain Michael Ohler, who gazed at a new photo he received of his wife and children, wrestled with the fact that he had not yet met his newborn son, Ben. "No matter how I wish it or try he still is a stranger and that bothers me terribly," he wrote his wife, Gail. "My son, whom I have wanted for so long, and I don't even know him." Ohler likewise was troubled by how much his two-year-old daughter, Sarah, had changed in his absence. "She looks completely different from what I remember. I feel so detached. I feel like you're the only person I know in the picture," he confessed. "I wish I could just come home now. I feel so far away lately."

In between lulls in the shelling, Chaplain Danny Wheeler visited the rifle companies dug in around the airport. The soft-spoken pastor understood that the troops at times needed someone to comfort and assure them. "Is it okay to be afraid?" one Marine asked him.

"Fear," he replied, "helps keep you alive, sharp and alert."

The young Marine listened.

"I'm frightened too," Wheeler assured him.

Like many others, Ohler placed his faith in the Lord. A devout Christian who often peppered his letters home with references to the Bible, Ohler sought to assure his wife of his safety. "Don't dwell on my danger," he urged. "Dwell on God's power."

"God is in control!" he added in another. "Rest assured I'll be home in one piece."

Long days in the bunkers exhausted the men, who soon nicknamed the nefarious mountain assailant "Ollie the Mad Mortarman." "Everyone reacted to the artillery barrages differently," Michael Petit said. "Some of the troops seemed unconcerned; others, their nerves worn raw, jumped at every sound." The volley of fire taught some a valuable new skill. "My hearing had developed the ability to discern the difference between incoming and outgoing fire," recalled Dolphin. "I could plainly hear the trademark *thunk* of a Soviet 82mm mortar clearing its tube and the roar of a 122mm rocket *wooshing* its way toward us."

The Marines, unable to fight back, kept their heads down. "You feel helpless," said Private First Class Sidney Decker. "We're guinea pigs. What are we doing here?" Private Thomas McCaffrey echoed him. "We are sitting ducks," the nineteen-year-old said. "We are supposed to be peacekeepers here, and we are not supposed to fire back. But how are we supposed to keep the peace if we are just sitting here getting fired on?" The men drew little comfort from the Pentagon's decision to at least award them hostile-fire pay. "Sixty-five dollars a month," Petit scoffed, "hardly seemed just compensation for getting shot at."

Geraghty was sympathetic to his men. No one likes to take a punch and not strike back. "Essentially, we're an offense-oriented unit," the colonel told reporters. "We like to take the fight to the enemy. This mission does call for restraint. That causes frustration."

On September 7, Major General Alfred Gray, commander of the Second Marine Division, arrived for a two-day visit. He was accompanied by Lieutenant General John Miller, head of the Fleet Marine Forces, Atlantic. Amid sporadic shellfire, the colonel briefed the generals. Inside the Combat Operations Center during one such attack, Dolphin could not help but notice that Gray sat calmly reading a book. "The old warhorse did not appear to be taking any special notice of the mortars zooming over our heads," Dolphin said. "I remember at one point the noise and concussion of an exploding round was particularly sharp. I know I jumped. I again looked over at Gray. He must have noticed my response. He looked up from his reading, looked me dead in the eye, and winked. Gray then went back to his reading."

"This son of a bitch isn't even concerned," a stunned Dolphin thought. *"What am I getting so jumpy about?"*

Gray had imparted a vital lesson to the young lieutenant. "That one small gesture had an immediate calming effect on me, which the general intended. The whole incident lasted just a few seconds, but it was another lesson in leadership that I've never forgotten."

The following day, Geraghty escorted Generals Gray and Miller to the battered Ministry of Defense building to meet with General Ibrahim Tannous, commander of the Lebanese Armed Forces. During the briefing, one of the Marines on the security detail entered and whispered into Geraghty's ear that he had a phone call. "Who is it?" the colonel asked.

"Silver Screen Six, sir," came the reply.

"Who is that?"

"Sir," the Marine insisted, "you have to take this call."

Under the glare of his bosses, the colonel excused himself. He stepped outside the briefing and picked up the phone. "Colonel Geraghty," he announced.

"Colonel," came the reply, "this is the White House. Stand by for the president."

The conversation, according to Reagan's daily calendar, lasted just three minutes, during which time the president assured the colonel that he would provide any support needed to stop the attacks on his troops. "Tell the Marines," Reagan concluded, "the entire nation is proud of you and the outstanding job you are doing against difficult odds."

"Semper Fi, Mr. President," Geraghty concluded.

CHAPTER 21

The fact that the Marines are in Lebanon as part of an international
peace-keeping force does not require them to be sitting ducks.
—*MIAMI HERALD* EDITORIAL
September 8, 1983

McFarlane and his colleagues on the National Security Council staff refused to back down. Assad needed to feel military pressure to force
his withdrawal from Lebanon. After his unsuccessful trip to Washington,
the special envoy jetted back to the Middle East. With McFarlane in Beirut,
his National Security Council colleagues Philip Dur and Howard Teicher
worked on incremental military measures that might put heat on the Syrian
dictator but without risking a brawl with Weinberger or the Joint Chiefs of
Staff. Dur was a thirty-eight-year-old Navy commander, while Teicher was
his junior by a decade and a Middle East analyst who had jumped right from
graduate school into government. Like McFarlane, the duo shared the view
that military might was the necessary key to unlock a solution for Lebanon.

The process produced a proposed draft of a new national security directive for the president to consider. The secret two-page order called for
the United States to provide "accelerated and expanded" training and resources to the Lebanese military. A tally showed that America had already
provided a generous stockpile of weapons, ranging from thirty-four tanks
and eighteen howitzers to more than twenty-nine million rounds of small-
arms ammunition. The directive likewise mandated that the military share
"tactical intelligence and reconnaissance support." Beyond aid and intel,
the proposed order instructed American forces to use "aggressive self-
defense against hostile or provocative acts from any quarter" in the form
of naval gunfire and air support. Lastly, the directive called for the deployment of the USS *New Jersey*, a World War II–era battleship whose sixteen-
inch guns would provide a menacing silhouette on the Mediterranean
horizon. Weinberger and Vessey opposed the idea as being too escalatory,

but Reagan overruled them, signing National Security Decision Directive No. 103, titled "Strategy for Lebanon." "The situation is worsening," the president wrote in his diary on September 10. "We may be facing a choice of getting out or enlarging our mission."

The directive increased America's military commitment, but still did not go as far as McFarlane or his National Security Council colleagues wanted in order to truly step on Assad's neck. That same night in Beirut, McFarlane watched the fighting in the hills from the ambassador's residence. Since Israel's departure a week earlier, Lebanese forces had duked it out in the Chouf Mountains. The battle now centered on the village of Suk al-Gharb, which was held by the Lebanese 8th Brigade under the leadership of Colonel Michel Aoun, a commander Ambassador Dillon characterized as a "tough little son of a bitch." The strategic village not only overlooked the airport and the Marines, but also offered a direct line of fire into the capital, as opposed to lobbing shells over the mountains. The Druze, joined by Syrian-controlled Palestinians and other Muslim militias, fought to seize this vital perch.

As the battle raged, mortar and artillery rounds chewed up the mountainside. A few rounds even hit the ambassador's compound, including one that splashed in the swimming pool and sent McFarlane and his team scurrying inside for cover. Huddled inside a room reminiscent of a closet, McFarlane felt that if Suk al-Gharb fell, so, too, would Beirut. The fall of the capital would topple Gemayel's government and bring an inglorious end to America's efforts. "It was the moment of truth," he said, "for our entire Lebanese strategy."

McFarlane crafted a dramatic message to Washington the following day, one his critics would later deride as the "sky-is-falling" cable. "This is," the special envoy began, "an action message." McFarlane predicted that without American intervention, the Lebanese military likely would be defeated and the Gemayel government brought down within twenty-four hours. Artillery supplies were nearly gone, he wrote, and military morale was shot. "In short, tonight we could be behind enemy lines. Faced with this threat," he wrote, "we must decide whether the US will, by withholding direct support, allow the fall of the government."

This was no longer a civil war. Palestinians and Iranians had joined the fight, he wrote, battling hand to hand with axes. "For the first time the threat appears unambiguously foreign," McFarlane continued. "If true this represents foreign aggression against Lebanon." Suk al-Gharb's strategic location, once controlled by hostile forces, posed a direct threat to American Marines. "To wait until an attack is at our doorstep before responding would be too late," he wrote. "It is within our current rules of engagement, in my judgment, to take action to prevent such a loss from occurring." He was aware this might be a tough sell for Congress and the American public, given the overall ignorance of the complex realities of Lebanon, but time was imperative. "The fact is," he concluded, "that we may be at a turning point which will lead in a matter of days to a Syrian takeover of this country north of the Awali. It is requested that this situation be considered by the NSC and guidance provided within the next four hours."

McFarlane advocated that the United States change the rules of engagement to allow direct military support of the Lebanese Armed Forces. This would, without any doubt, end American neutrality. "It was time," McFarlane bluntly said, "for the Marines to fire back."

McFarlane showed his proposed cable to Dillon, whose staff he had kept in the dark for weeks. The veteran diplomat doubted the situation was as dire as McFarlane said, nor did he think any harm would come to the Americans if the Druze prevailed. McFarlane needed to wait. "I wanted some time to consult with my staff, but McFarlane said there was no time," he said. "In later years, I wished of course that I had stopped the message, but I didn't."

The special envoy fired off his flash cable.

Back in Washington, the National Security Planning Group assembled at 6 p.m. One hour and fifteen minutes later, Reagan signed off on McFarlane's request. The one-page order, which became an addendum to National Security Decision Directive No. 103, declared that Suk al-Gharb was vital to the safety of American Marines. As a result, if the American ground commander determined that the area was in danger of falling to non-Lebanese forces, and the host government requested help, then the United States could intervene. "Assistance for this specific objective," the president's order stated, "may include naval gun fire support and, if deemed necessary, tactical air strikes, but shall exclude ground forces."

The next day, the Joint Chiefs of Staff instructed Geraghty that he could unleash his massive firepower to support the Lebanese Armed Forces under the outlined conditions. The order marked a significant escalation in the role of the Marines, who were now being tasked with going on the offensive in support of the Lebanese military. "I understood, all too well, the consequences of this decision," the colonel said. "For all practical purposes, it would eliminate whatever appearance of neutrality and impartiality we had left."

Geraghty had doubts about McFarlane's interpretation of the battle. His own intel showed that the Lebanese were managing. But the authorization of American force opened a Pandora's box. McFarlane was ready to fight. "What followed was a rancorous week of requests by McFarlane and members of his staff to allow the use of naval gunfire and air strikes," Geraghty recalled. "To their great consternation, I blocked these requests. I thought that they were overreacting and not considering the implication of their demands."

McFarlane's representatives hounded Geraghty to fire, including Brigadier General Carl Stiner, who was the special envoy's Joint Chiefs of Staff liaison officer in Beirut.

"General," the colonel hollered back, "don't you realize we'll pay the price down here? We'll get slaughtered! We're totally vulnerable!"

At one point, McFarlane reached out directly to Geraghty.

"Sir, I can't do that. This will cost us our neutrality," the colonel protested. "Don't you realize that we'll get slaughtered down here? We're sitting ducks!"

Geraghty's frustration mounted. No one appreciated his dire circumstances. The colonel needed only to step outside his command center to glimpse his vulnerability. The airport was tactically unsound. All the factional groups in the mountains above the capital had his coordinates. Four Marines, in fact, had already been killed, another twenty-nine wounded while the rest lived like moles in bunkers. Intelligence estimated that 600 mortar tubes could be aimed at them. Each day—each hour—his security diminished. Despite myriad challenges, Geraghty had guarded America's neutrality like the Holy Grail, knowing that was all that kept his men safe. "President Reagan's national security advisers were not thinking through the implications of their decisions, particularly the repercussions against the multinational force," he wrote. "I wondered if anyone else realized where this fucking train was headed."

Beyond the vulnerability, what infuriated Geraghty was the total breakdown in the chain of the command. Why was he, as the on-scene commander, expected to take orders from the deputy national security advisor and special envoy to the Middle East?

It made no sense.

Geraghty spelled out his concerns in a lengthy report to Vice Admiral Edward Martin, commander of the Sixth Fleet, arguing that his forces were being pulled ever deeper into direct military action. "Our increasing number of casualties has removed any semblance of neutrality and has put us into direct retaliation against those who have fired on us," the colonel wrote. "It is relatively immaterial who has pulled the trigger." Since July, he wrote, his troops had lived in a constant state of alert, which threatened to exhaust his men and his resources. "I am concerned," Geraghty added, "that the end does not appear to be in sight and I perceive that the involvement in the Lebanese internal struggle has exceeded our original mandate. We have, in fact, changed the rules and are now an active participant." The Lebanese military requested everything from targeting data and intel to training and ammunition. "We are actively their allies," he wrote. "Our credibility as an effective deterrent is becoming suspect with the opposition."

Geraghty felt not only that his efforts were being taken for granted, but that there were some who believed his forces should be doing even more—and that he was to blame for holding back. Even more alarming, he had exhausted his means to deter attacks on the airport. "In effect," he concluded, "I have reached my limit of response given the capabilities of the weapons within my force and the constraints of the current rules of engagement."

No sooner had Geraghty fired off his report than a new order arrived for him to once again dip into his reserve stockpile to resupply the Lebanese military, this time with 1,345,050 rounds of ammunition. The September 14 request, which was delivered by Marine helicopters, reflected the fierce fighting. Two days later, artillery struck the Ministry of Defense and the ambassador's residence. The hit on the latter prompted self-defense fire from the *Bowen* and *John Rodgers*, which hurled seventy-two rounds at six separate targets.

The battle continued to rage in the mountains and in southern Beirut, where the Amal militia maintained pressure on the Lebanese military to prevent any troop reinforcements in the Chouf. To counter this, the Lebanese army declared martial law. "Anyone on the street not on government business," one report noted, "will be shot, day or night."

Shells rained down around the airport while sniper fire pinged checkpoints manned by Marines. In the mountains overhead, the battle for Suk al-Gharb built toward a violent climax. In addition to the Druze and Palestinian fighters, American radio intercepts detected Farsi, which pointed to the Iranian Revolutionary Guard. At daybreak on September 19, those forces launched a brutal artillery barrage, one so violent it stunned even the grizzled Geraghty. "Military observers nearby, like those of us farther away," the colonel recalled, "had never viewed such an expenditure of ammunition at so great a blistering rate."

A ground assault on Suk al-Gharb followed. General Tannous, who was in the Ministry of Defense's Operations Center, received a desperate radio call from Colonel Aoun, who was low on ammunition. He feared the enemy would overrun his position. Tannous reached out to Geraghty for help. Geraghty conferred with his boss, Commodore Rick France, aboard his flagship, the *Iwo Jima*. The two agreed that all the president's conditions had been met. Suk al-Gharb was in danger of falling to foreign fighters, prompting the Lebanese government to officially ask for help. Geraghty, who for months had steered the course of neutrality, had run out of ways to protest. Washington had backed him into a corner.

All his work with the Lebanese to date—training, manning checking points, and executing patrols—was defensive in nature. Naval gunfire was offensive.

There was, he realized, no turning back.

"I gave the orders," the colonel said.

The *Virginia*, *John Rogers*, *Bowen*, and *Radford* steamed in close as gun crews prepared to engage. Navy F-14s and A-6s streaked through the skies in preparation to identify targets and radio results. At 10:04 a.m., the guns thundered, one after the other. Over the next five hours, the Navy hurled 360 five-inch rounds into the mountains over Beirut. Geraghty monitored it from his Combat Operations Center until the last shot was fired at 3 p.m. The gunfire worked. The Ministry of Defense reported that the attackers fled. Suk al-Gharb was saved. "It was a dilemma wherein we were obliged to provide support," Geraghty said, "but in doing so we terminated our peacekeeping mission while opening ourselves to unknown retribution."

The Rubicon had been crossed.

"My gut instinct," the colonel leveled with his staff, "tells me the Corps is going to pay in blood for this decision."

CHAPTER 22

This country doesn't know what to do without wars.
—CAPTAIN MICHAEL OHLER, LETTER TO HIS WIFE
September 28, 1983

Shelling was not the only trouble the Marines faced.

A larger and more deadly threat loomed.

Up in the mountains in the Syrian-controlled Bekaa Valley, Iranian Revolutionary Guards continued to nurture and develop an army of homegrown Lebanese terrorists. Iran's presence in the region was an outgrowth of the 1979 revolution that had toppled the pro-Western monarchy of Shah Mohammed Reza Pahlavi and led to the installment of Khomeini as the head of a new Islamic theocracy. With that upheaval had come massive societal crackdowns on everything from women's rights to the press, movies, and music.

Saddam Hussein, who was the secular ruler of neighboring Iraq, seized on Iran's turmoil to invade, kicking off what would prove to be a bloody eight-year war that would lead to more than one million dead and wounded. Iraq's invasion prompted Iran to seek to spread the seeds of its religious revolution to other Middle Eastern nations.

Lebanon was the perfect choice.

The war-ravaged nation, held together as one historian colorfully noted with "chewing gum and bailing wire," offered a remote place to train and develop militant followers. Syrian ruler Assad had initially proven hesitant to allow Iran to set up in the Bekaa Valley, but like Khomeini, he, too, despised his neighbor Saddam Hussein.

What began with two dozen Iranian Revolutionary Guards in the summer of 1982 had since ballooned into more than eight hundred. Much of the Iranian activity was centered on Baalbek, which boasted some of ancient Rome's greatest ruins, including a complex of temples dedicated to Jupiter, Venus, Mercury, and Bacchus. Iran's forces took over the Sheik Abdullah Barracks and the Al Shas Hotel. The arrival of the Revolutionary Guard had dramatically changed the town. Stores no longer sold booze, while women strolled the streets dressed in black shrouds known as chadors. Posters and murals of Khomeini adorned the walls of buildings. "Baalbek," as historian Robin Wright observed, "resembled a little Tehran."

Iranian forces tapped into the undercurrent of frustration felt by many in Lebanon's downtrodden Shiite community. To recruit followers, Iranian leaders fanned out through the Shiite slums around Beirut, visiting mosques and making speeches. Others helped pay for schools and organize much-needed social services, including sewage and trash pickup. Many had grown frustrated with Amal leader Nabih Berri, who was considered too secular and moderate. Not only did Berri resist Iran's overtures, but he had refused to fight Israel during its invasion and had since demonstrated a willingness to deal with the United States. The fact that he held a green card and had family in America likewise made him suspect.

Resentment of Berri, who preached a policy of nonviolence, had led young firebrand Hussein al-Musawi to leave the organization in June 1982, starting a far more radical group known as Islamic Amal. A former chemistry teacher, al-Musawi settled in Baalbek and trained with the Revolutionary Guard. "We are," he once declared, "the children of Iran."

Another individual pulled into Iran's orbit was Imad Mugniyah, a Beirut University dropout who had fought alongside Yasser Arafat during the Lebanese Civil War. Mugniyah started the Islamic Jihad Organization, which, like al-Musawi's group, embraced violence as a political tool. "Imad Mugniyah was a masterful organizer and operator," recalled former CIA director of operations Charles Allen. "Few of his lieutenants were as capable."

Iran welcomed the destructive desires of al-Musawi and Mugniyah, bringing their organizations under its control on June 27, 1983. These two groups would soon become known as Hezbollah, and their signature attack became the suicide car bomb, best characterized by historian David Crist as the "poor man's smart bomb."

"If Hezbollah had GPS-guided bombs dropped from thirty thousand feet," remarked one Lebanese member of the group, "they would not need martyrs."

The organization's first such attack occurred in the southern city of Tyre on November 11, 1982. The group recruited seventeen-year-old Ahmed Qassir, who sought revenge for the loss of several family members killed during Israel's 1978 invasion of southern Lebanon. At 7 a.m. that Thursday, Qassir rammed a car loaded with explosives and gas canisters into a seven-story Israeli army headquarters. The explosion, which leveled the building, killed ninety people, including seventy-six Israelis and fourteen Arab prisoners.

The bombing of the American Embassy followed.

And now al-Musawi wanted a new mission.

The terror leader met with a Revolutionary Guard officer at the Sheik Abdullah Barracks on September 1, 1983. He wanted "special targets." His first instincts were to attack the Christian Phalange, who dominated the politics of Lebanon. The officer reported the conversation to Hojjat ol-Eslam Ali Akbar Mohtashemi, Iran's ambassador in Damascus. Mohtashemi served as the middleman in the chain of command who relayed orders from Iran's foreign minister in Tehran to the Revolutionary Guards in Baalbek.

Al-Musawi grew impatient as the days turned to weeks and the battle raged at Suk al-Gharb. He followed up, this time with a request for thirty tons of explosives. His eagerness resulted in an invitation to Damascus to outline his plan. On September 22—three days after America intervened on behalf of the Lebanese—al-Musawi sent his relative and confidant Sayed to meet with Mohtashemi at the embassy in the Syrian capital.

"Yes," the Iranian ambassador agreed, "you should certainly concentrate your operations as much as possible on the U.S. forces, Phalange, or the Lebanese army."

But the Iranian had another suggestion, which Sayed liked even better.

"You should," Mohtashemi offered, "undertake an extraordinary operation against the U.S. Marines."

CHAPTER 23

How many Marines are going to have to be killed
before we start a shooting war?
—SENATOR BARRY GOLDWATER
September 11, 1983

George Shultz traveled over to Capitol Hill shortly before 10 a.m. on September 21, 1983. The secretary of state, who was joined that Wednesday by General Paul Kelley, planned to brief the House Committee on Foreign Affairs on a proposed compromise announced the day before between the White House and Congress in the battle over the War Powers Resolution. Much had happened since the first Marine deaths three weeks earlier, which had triggered the tug-of-war between the two branches of government. The casualty count now stood at four dead and more than two dozen wounded. The president had since authorized the use of naval gunfire and tactical air support, making it hard to buy the administration's earlier insistence that American forces sat on the sidelines of the fight.

The 1973 War Powers Resolution muddied what already was a constitutionally murky question. The president served as the commander in chief, according to the Constitution, yet lawmakers had the power to raise armies and declare war. Despite that, Reagan feared that bowing to congressional demands would create a terrible precedent. Did the commander in chief need the approval of a majority of 435 lawmakers to deploy a small number of troops anywhere in the world? Administration officials feared such an interpretation would open a Pandora's box. "What that means," one White House official told the press, "is that some foreign party, merely by shooting at your troops, can force you to withdraw them within sixty days if Congress fails to act, and there are lots of way in which Congress can fail to act. If that's true, then we've put a gun to our head in a whole host of difficult negotiating situations abroad."

Many lawmakers, in contrast, worried that failure to invoke the War Powers Resolution would likewise set a precedent, one that would ultimately weaken Congress. The 1973 debate near the end of the Vietnam War to pass the federal law had proven incredibly divisive, requiring Congress to override President Richard Nixon's veto. "What is at stake here," argued Democratic representative Stephen Solarz of New York, "is the ability of Congress to exercise any control over the dispatch of American forces into combat situations."

The fight increasingly had little to do with the Marines hunkered down in Beirut bunkers, boiling down instead to a struggle over raw political power. "There are few issues of greater importance than the issue confronting us— the balance of powers between the legislative and executive branches," declared Senator Robert Byrd. "This issue is bigger than political parties, bigger than personalities, bigger than any particular office of the United States."

Despite the bluster, many privately believed America could not simply pull out. Such a move might damage the nation's reputation and embolden Syria and the Soviets. That did not stop Senate Democrats, who hoped to regain the majority in the next election, from capitalizing on the crisis and demanding Reagan acknowledge troops faced hostilities.

Recognizing that the fight would not go away—and fearing a political bruising—Reagan's aides had worked with senior lawmakers on a compromise that would spare the nation a constitutional crisis. The proposed deal allowed Reagan to keep troops in Lebanon for another eighteen months, but it handcuffed the size of the force, restricted the Marines to Beirut, and barred any expansion of the mission. The timetable was believed to be long enough that antagonists would not want to simply wait out America's departure. It was also thought that eighteen months would provide the administration time to work out a solution in Lebanon and punt the issue beyond the next presidential election, where it might otherwise be politicized. "I am especially pleased," Reagan said, "that this proposed resolution not only supports our policy in Lebanon but now enables us to advance United States peacekeeping interests on the solid bipartisan basis that has been the traditional hallmark of American foreign policy."

This was the political backdrop as Shultz took his seat in room 2172 of the Rayburn House Office Building, the same spot where Undersecretary of State Eagleburger and Ambassador Dillon had appeared less than three months earlier in the wake of the embassy bombing. Shultz would brief lawmakers and answer questions this morning and then appear that afternoon before the Senate Committee on Foreign Relations. The House and Senate would then vote on whether to pass the compromise resolution in the days ahead.

Chairman Clement Zablocki, a seventy-year-old Wisconsin Democrat, gaveled the meeting to order at 10 a.m., announcing that the proposed compromise had the support of both Democratic and Republican House leaders as well as the president.

Zablocki turned the meeting over to Shultz, who read a statement that outlined Lebanon's tumultuous history. Peace in the region, including among Israel and its neighbors, depended upon success in Lebanon. America's goals remained the removal of foreign forces, a stable Lebanon able to provide its own security, and peace along Israel's northern border. "These objectives are not changing," Shultz said. "They are, and have been, a constant of our policy. The latest outbreak of fighting should not cause us to lose sight of them."

Gemayel's election in the wake of the bloodshed in the summer of 1982 had provided Lebanon a second chance. America had stepped in to assist, brokering the May 17 agreement between Israel and Lebanon. More recently, Shultz noted, Gemayel had called for a national dialogue on reconciliation among the various rival factions, a policy America pushed for and supported. "The problem," the secretary of state said, "has been Syria." Lebanon's neighbor, which fielded the largest army in the war-torn nation, had so far refused to negotiate. Syria had welcomed Palestinian fighters into the Chouf Mountains and armed groups fighting the Lebanese government. At the same time, Syria wielded its political leverage over various internal factions to obstruct national reconciliation. "The question arises," Shultz said, "whether Syria's aim is to assure its security or assure its domination of Lebanon."

America now focused on brokering a cease-fire between the myriad factions that would allow a chance to resolve internal rivalries. Once secured, the United States would rally international support behind the Lebanese government. The multinational force, Shultz warned, was being targeted by those who hoped to block any political reconciliation, which had forced American troops to defend themselves. The political uproar in Washington over the War Powers Resolution had only weakened America's effectiveness by raising doubts about the nation's staying power. Such rhetoric likewise could lead to additional attacks by aggressors to further erode American resolve and hasten a departure. Reagan therefore had agreed to the proposed compromise despite his reservations. "What we are doing in Lebanon is right," Shultz concluded. "There are risks involved, but any important undertaking involves risks."

Lawmakers peppered Shultz with questions, ranging from the timeline of the compromise to the extent of the Soviet backing of Syria. Others inquired about the progress of training the Lebanese military. Outside of the questions on the proposed compromise, a few lawmakers drilled down on important areas that exposed the spiraling violence in Lebanon and the increased threat faced by American troops. Those occasionally testy exchanges during the two-hour-and-thirty-three-minute hearing exposed a disconnect in how the administration viewed America's role in Beirut versus how it was perceived by the various fighting factions. General Kelley, who did not speak often, likewise revealed how his own views differed from Colonel Geraghty and many of the Marines. More than anything, the hearing demonstrated that events on the ground in Beirut moved far faster than officials in Washington could comprehend.

One such example of the disconnect came when Republican representative William Broomfield of Michigan asked if the job of the Marines had changed in any way, particularly given the recent use of naval gunfire. "The role of the Marines," Kelley assured lawmakers, "has not changed. That mission was a peacekeeping mission and has remained a peacekeeping mission." Naval gunfire was aimed at the high ground above the Marines, which was critical to self-defense. The general's views, however, stood in sharp contrast to those of Colonel Geraghty, who feared that the use of naval gunfire had "terminated" America's peacekeeping status. "I don't see that the mission has changed at all," Kelley concluded. "It is the same mission."

Representative Jim Leach argued that the United States, which had hoped to bring the Marines home by Christmas 1982, now appeared bogged down in a complicated civil war. The Iowa Republican zeroed in on Geraghty's greatest fear—that America had stumbled into the fight and had picked sides. "It would appear in the eyes of many, whether we like it or not, we are involved in one side of the civil war as well as one side of the religious strife."

Shultz pushed back, arguing that America backed the elected government of Lebanon. The reality, of course, was that while the United States viewed President Amin Gemayel as the nation's legitimate leader, none of his adversaries did. "As far as involvement in a civil war is concerned, of course we do not believe we are so involved, we don't want to be involved. We have it as a point of principle in our policy that we are not taking sides and we aren't," Shultz said. "We are supporting the legitimate government of Lebanon."

Representative Toby Roth echoed Leach, arguing that America had landed in a tar pit. "When our Marines went ashore, they didn't have ammunition in their guns, they didn't have Navy air strikes. Today they have ammunition in their guns, they do have air strikes, they do have artillery from naval bombardment. So, it is a different situation," the Wisconsin Republican stated. "What I am afraid of is that we're getting into a tremendous trap and quagmire and I think many members of Congress that I have talked to feel the same way."

Kelley jumped in to answer. Unloaded rifles was the call of the on-scene commander. "It was as much for the safety of the Marines in the area as for anyone else. It had no political connotations whatsoever," the general said. "When the Marines went ashore a year ago, they had immediately available to them every single weapon system that is ashore today. There is no change in that. Those naval gunfire ships have been on the gun line for one year. All this is in total defense of our Marine positions and has no offensive connotation."

"General, in all due candor, we do have a civil war over there," Roth countered. "We have the Druze, Muslim sects, Phalangists. There is no way we can solve that problem. It is a political problem. We should send the politicians over there, not the Marines."

"This situation needs a strong viable military background," Kelley fired back.

"Well, General, let me say this," Roth continued. "There is no light at the end of this tunnel. This resolution is going to be one that will come back to haunt us."

"I do not agree with you, sir," Kelley argued. "I think there is some hope there. I think as long as there is hope in that country to find a reasonable solution to a long-lasting problem, I think that we should persevere. That is the American way."

Shultz interrupted, pointing out that the Marines were not tasked to solve factional fighting. "That is not their mission," the secretary of state said. "They can't perform that mission. That is the job for the political structure of Lebanon to solve. That is their problem." Furthermore, Shultz added, much of the violence was the result of Syrian involvement. "This is not a civil war," he declared. "Those are non-Lebanese forces."

"I don't care how you phrase it, I don't care what you say, this is a civil war," an obviously irritated Roth countered. "As long as you have all these foreign factions, as long as you have the factions in Lebanon, you are never going to have a strong central government there. The Marines and the multinational forces cannot solve that problem."

"We want the politicians to solve it," the secretary of state argued. "Politicians, with all due deference, cannot solve problems absolutely alone. They sometimes need some help and the stability that can be provided by the multinational forces."

Democratic representative Howard Wolpe of Michigan brought up an important point, one that until now had seemed to evade lawmakers. Congress, as a result of its power struggle with the White House, was now being asked to legitimize America's involvement in Lebanon. Congress was like the dog who had caught the car. Passage of the compromise meant the credit or the blame would no longer be just the president's burden. "I can only say," Shultz told lawmakers, "you started it. This whole process is the result of a congressional initiative."

Representative Olympia Snowe grappled with what lawmakers might expect in the future, given how America's military role had increased from an initial reluctance to use self-defense to the introduction of naval gunfire and airpower. "We now support the Lebanese Army position because we extended the self-defense of the Marines to the fortunes of the Lebanese Army. My question is: What could we expect over the next eighteen months militarily?" the Maine Republican asked. "Our combat role could change dramatically if the Gemayel government is threatened. What could we anticipate in the next eighteen months that would prevent us from getting involved in a full-scale military conflict in Lebanon?"

"We have a mission. We don't have any plans to change that mission," Shultz insisted. "The right to self-defense is something that is always present. It is not something new. What is new is that our forces have been fired upon so that they are exercising that right."

"I understand the concept of self-defense," Snowe countered, adding that it was necessary to protect the lives of American Marines. "Nevertheless, concerning the Lebanese Army, we came to their aid in defense of Suk al-Gharb because it was vital to American interests. What we appear to be saying now is that the defense of the Marines is extended to whatever happens to the Lebanese Army. It seems to me that is broadening the military role."

"It is not extended to what happens to the Lebanese Army. It is extended to this particular place. That is because at that place, as the Commandant of the Marine Corps said in typical Marine language, they would be looking down our throat."

New York Democratic representative Robert Garcia shared with the committee a letter given to him by a constituent whose son was a Marine in Beirut. In the letter to his parents, the Marine recounted the first attack on American forces on the morning of July 22. "In two minutes everyone had their gear and was huddled in a bunker. Rounds were coming in at twenty-second intervals. In my foxhole there were five of us," Garcia read aloud from the letter. "Here comes another one, bang, bomb. The looks on the guys faces were indescribable."

Garcia noted that the first news many received of attacks against American forces came at the end of August, when the first two Marines were killed. But American troops, he noted, had been taking fire as far back as July. "I think the mother of the Marine makes the case that most of us have tried to describe to you, Mr. Secretary, and there are many other mothers who do not understand why we are there, why their children are there," Garcia said. "That is why at this moment we are not sure we are doing the right thing in Lebanon, Mr. Secretary. Nothing I have heard today has convinced me that what we are doing there is correct. As an American I have a responsibility. We should not place these Marines in a helpless situation where they have no chance to defend themselves, where they are sitting ducks."

"The Marines are not sitting ducks. They are on an important mission. They are performing well and they are defending themselves," the secretary countered. "We do have an armed force in this country, spend a lot of money on it. I don't think it is inconceivable that we should occasionally be willing to use it."

Kelley spoke up, reminding the committee that he had recently visited Beirut. The general described a Christmas card from the previous year that depicted Marines emulating the famous flag-raising on Iwo Jima during World War II. Instead of a flag, the card showed Marines lifting a cedar of Lebanon beneath a caption that read "Helping make it right."

"That is the way," he said, "I think the bulk of our Marines feel, sir."

Representative Douglas Bereuter ended the morning's questions, stating that from the beginning he had opposed the deployment of the Marines. "I can see no reason for optimism in the Middle East. It seems to me that there is no new light at the end of that tunnel. We are finding ourselves in a new situation, a trap, and the executive and legislative are about to come together and close the door." The Nebraska Republican doubted the efforts Shultz outlined would ever come to fruition. "I don't see the likelihood of a

Lebanon national consensus on the direction for that country. I don't see the likelihood for the kind of national unity or identity now that is necessary for a modern nation-state. That country is at civil war," he said. "Can you say anything to give me any sense of optimism about that situation?"

"I tried," Shultz concluded, "and I hope I have given some reason to feel we should be there. I can tell by your statement that there is no way I could give you any."

The committee adjourned at 12:33 p.m. Shultz headed to the White House, where he met with Reagan at 1:46 p.m. During the half-hour meeting, Shultz found the president preoccupied by the deteriorating situation in Lebanon. "Are we going to let the Syrians and the Soviets take over?" the president asked. "Are we just going to let it happen?"

Despite the increased doubts over the possibility of success—from lawmakers, the press, and even many of the Marines—Shultz doubled down on America's position. "I was, if anything," the secretary of state wrote, "even more convinced than the president that we must stand firm in Lebanon, for worldwide as well as for Lebanese considerations."

The questions raised by members of the House Foreign Affairs Committee dovetailed with the views of ten members of Congress who just that week visited the troops in Beirut. During that time, Representative Larry Hopkins, a Republican of Kentucky, said he had to duck attacks. The visit convinced him that America needed to find an exit.

"I don't want this country," he said, "going into the body bag business."

Representative Sam Stratton, the New York Democrat who led the House Armed Services Committee delegation to Beirut, was equally as blunt in his comments afterward to Weinberger. "You're going to have a massacre on your hands."

Others raised similar concerns, though most believed that an American withdrawal would doom Lebanon to violence and civil war. In short, America was trapped.

Representative John Spratt, a South Carolina Democrat, interviewed a Marine who told him about preparing the obliterated body of a friend for transport out to the carrier. "My God," the Marine said. "What are people back home talking about? This is war, man."

Georgia Democratic representative Richard Ray likewise talked with several Marines, including a couple who confided in him that they wanted to go home and asked if Americans understood what was really going on in Beirut.

Both Spratt and Ray observed that the violence had brought an end to the daily patrols and checkpoints. The leathernecks passed the hours in helmets and flak jackets hunkered down in bunkers, raising the question of what was the point of the mission. "Marines are trained to fight, to be aggressive," Ray said. "And there they are filling sandbags under hostile conditions day and night." Spratt echoed him. "It was perfectly clear to all of us," the South Carolinian added, "that this is not a peace-keeping mission."

What was clear was the massive military buildup in the region. In addition to the Marines on the beach, another 2,000 leathernecks sat aboard ships just off the Lebanese coast. Some fifteen American warships—crewed by more than 10,000 sailors—prowled those waters, including the nuclear-powered carrier *Eisenhower* and the recently arrived battleship *New Jersey*, capable of hurling a 2,000-pound shell up to twenty-three miles. "Standing in the ship's bridge and looking at all the naval ships in sight," said Republican representative William Dickinson of Alabama, "it looks like we are getting ready for World War III."

The concerns raised by members of Congress reflected those of many Americans. A *Washington Post*/ABC News poll in late September showed seven out of ten people felt another eighteen months in Beirut was too long. A majority favored six months or less. Sixty-seven percent likewise felt Lebanon was not important enough to risk a war.

The public's patience was running out.

So, too, was the willingness of the other multinational forces to blindly follow America's path of military escalation, which many feared risked pulling them all into a wider conflict. With the exception of England, each nation had suffered casualties. The United States so far had four killed and thirty-seven wounded. The French had lost eight with another twenty wounded, while the Italians counted twelve wounded. British prime minister Margaret Thatcher, who visited the White House that month, pressed for a visible de-escalation of the Navy's presence. "The Thatcher government's objective," one memo to Reagan stated, "is to restrain Western involvement in what the British characterize as an internecine struggle."

Those frustrations extended beyond the prime minister's office and were shared by the foreign service officers in Lebanon. "The arms of my men are sore from shaking hands; their faces hurt from smiling, they would not point a gun at anyone and now the bloody Americans want to drag us into a war with these people," complained one British diplomat.

On September 28, 1983, in spite of the growing opposition, the Democratic-led House voted 270–161 to keep the Marines in Lebanon for another eighteen months. The Republican-controlled Senate followed the next day with a vote of 54–46. The House then signed off on the Senate version with a vote of 253–156. "The vote was of immense importance," Shultz later wrote. "It let everyone know that the United States had staying power."

The president and congressional leaders championed the resolution's passage. "Today's vote," Reagan said in a statement, "sends a strong signal to the world: America stands united, we speak with one voice, and we fulfill our responsibilities as a trustee of freedom, peace and self-determination." Despite efforts by the president and congressional leaders to put a positive spin on the vote, many lawmakers realized America was in a no-win situation. "We're all troubled," said Representative Daniel Mica, a Florida Democrat. "No one wants eighteen months. No one wants us even to be in Lebanon. But no one has a better solution."

"Staying is bad," added a fellow House Democrat, "but leaving is worse."

"We all agree it's a quagmire," stated Senator Nancy Kassebaum, a Kansas Republican.

The vote reinforced for some the lack of a clear objective, a handicap that had plagued the mission from the start, but one that had now grown exponentially more dire with the escalation of violence. "What is our mission, other than being shot at?" asked Democratic representative Elliott Levitas of Georgia. Florida Democratic representative Sam Gibbon agreed. "If we are there to fight, we are too few," he said. "If we are there to die, we are far too many."

CHAPTER 24

Basically everything around here is back to normal. Whatever normal is.
—CORPORAL JOHN DALZIEL, LETTER TO HIS FAMILY
October 3, 1983

In the wake of the battle of Suk al-Gharb, McFarlane flew to Damascus on September 23 to meet with Assad. As he had for months, the Syrian ruler continued to resist. One hour turned to two, then three and four. McFarlane's frustration soared. As the conversation wound down, he felt he had to demonstrate to Assad America's resolve. Enough was enough. "By the way," McFarlane announced as he stood up to leave. "The president has ordered the battleship *New Jersey* to Mediterranean waters. I expect it to arrive tomorrow."

His veiled threat marked yet another significant escalation in a week that had seen many. Gone was any semblance of American neutrality. But McFarlane felt he had no other option. Missing from his recollection of the encounter is any discussion about whether McFarlane considered how such a threat might be received by a brutal dictator. "It was a final gambit," he admitted. "I had pretty well reached the end of my rope with Assad."

McFarlane flew back to Beirut, where shellfire continued to rain down around the mountains and the capital. Two days later, the frustrated special envoy, who paced the ambassador's residence, phoned his pastor, Dr. James Macdonnell, at St. Mark Presbyterian Church in Washington. "I really need your help," he said, asking for prayers.

"We're with you," came the response. "Hang in there."

McFarlane hung up and turned to his wife, who had accompanied him to Lebanon and stayed at the ambassador's compound. Despite the shellfire, he made a curious suggestion. "Let's go for a swim," McFarlane said. "I think it's going to be all right."

The next day, September 26, the Syrian and Lebanese leaders agreed at last to a cease-fire. The various religious groups later announced plans to meet in Geneva on October 30 for a conference on national reconciliation. In his quest to rival Kissinger, McFarlane no doubt felt vindicated. For months he had pinballed between various Middle Eastern capitals, prodding world leaders while battling his rivals in the Defense Department. He had even managed to bend the rules of engagement to allow America's military intervention. "The cease-fire was a watershed," he wrote. "We left Beirut in October on a high note, feeling that we had carried the day and that the situation in the Middle East was at least temporarily stabilized."

But others had doubts.

"'Cease-fire,'" Geraghty wryly observed, "is a relative term in Lebanon."

Despite his skepticism, the colonel welcomed a reprieve for his exhausted Marines, who after living in dank bunkers were anxious for a hot meal, shower, and a cot. Geraghty gave his troops a pep talk via the *Root Scoop*: "We have just come through a difficult trial where we lost good friends and comrades," he wrote. "We have survived heavy shelling and endured the deprivation of many creature comforts, but the real challenge lies ahead." He reminded his men to remain alert and not lose sight of their mission as peacekeepers. The mission would be over soon enough. "We must be mindful that our role is supportive of all Lebanese people," he concluded. "Let us go home with our heads held high in the knowledge that we have completed a most difficult mission; and completed it in an outstanding way."

In the wake of the battle over Suk al-Gharb, additional intelligence emerged, which Geraghty studied. Some observers reported that the Lebanese military exaggerated how dire the situation was for them. "It was another occasion," the colonel said, "when I wondered if we had been had." But others reported that American involvement truly was decisive. What stood out to Geraghty, however, were the light casualties. For such a consequential battle, the Lebanese had suffered only eight killed and twelve wounded. That said, Geraghty concluded American intervention was, in fact, warranted. "I was also convinced," he said, "that the rules of the game had changed forever with that decision, with its consequences unknown."

The airport reopened for the first time in thirty-two days, welcoming a Middle East Airlines flight from Saudi Arabia that touched down at 4:45 p.m. on September 29. "The pilot circled Beirut four times before landing," Thomas Friedman observed. "The sound of the plane coming into the city brought traffic to a near standstill. People craned their necks and rushed out to their balconies to watch as their air link with the outside world was finally restored." That afternoon arrival would soon lead to an average of three dozen flights per day, carrying 2,400 passengers. A thousand employees headed back to work at the airport, while as many as three times that many cars and trucks cruised daily past the Marine compound. The return of commercial jets, which roared over the Marines, proved a far better annoyance than the previous month's artillery and rockets. "All things," Geraghty quipped, "are relative."

As September ended, the broiling heat subsided. The days grew shorter. "All was quiet again today," Major George Converse wrote. "We take it one day at a time." An American intel report echoed him. "Beirut appeared almost back to normal today," it stated. "Traffic was heavy, people were out in the streets and most shops and businesses were open."

The leathernecks likewise adjusted to this uneasy new calm, though the occasional dropped helmet made them all flinch. "Things are so tenuous here that all hell could break out in a minute," Hudson wrote his wife. "It is nonetheless a very pleasant change to have peace, normal routine, and running water!" Others agreed. "I can't believe how quiet it is. It's like a regular big city," Bill Stelpflug wrote his family. "Now I have to deal with boredom and worry about looking like a regular Marine again. I put polish on my boots for the first time in a month and got a haircut." Henry Linkkila took a few moments to jot a note of thanks to his mom and stepfather for all their recent support. Their steady stream of correspondence, he confessed, was the only thing that kept him from escaping over the wire. "All your letters of love + support really make me feel great inside," he professed. "I love you both very much!"

The situation remained too unstable to resume patrols, but Lieutenant Colonel Gerlach took advantage of the lull in fighting to rotate the line companies, the last time troops would do so before the deployment concluded. Supply staff passed out space heaters and new canvas for tents in preparation for the coming rainy season. "When the shelling stops," Corporal John Dalziel wrote in a letter home, "time goes fast." In their downtime, the Marines lifted weights and watched movies. Others joined a new touch football league. Games were held in the parking lot behind the Battalion Landing Team headquarters. In the first official game, the Headquarters and Supply company trounced the Communications Platoon, 39–24. "Our major concern, since we're playing on asphalt, is safety," explained Captain Peter Scialabba, the league coordinator. "There is no contact; emphasis is put on pass patterns and play execution."

Robin Ortega, the wife of Staff Sergeant Alexander Ortega, who was killed on August 29, mailed the men a care package of candy, which the Marines appreciated. "I wanted to do some small thing to make your daily life there easier," she wrote. "You are in my thoughts daily." Beyond work and downtime, the leathernecks began to envision the return to the United States in November. Captain Michael Ohler sketched floor plans for the home he wanted to build for his growing family, which included a cathedral ceiling in the living room. To help visualize the rooflines, he went so far as to construct a cardboard mock-up. Ohler even designed an accompanying playhouse for his daughter, Sarah, one that resembled a southern plantation. "To be together with you again," he wrote his wife, "will be great."

The long deployment to the Middle East was at long last winding down. The worst, it seemed, was behind them. Hudson couldn't help but notice how happy everyone around him was again. "People are starting to <u>sing</u> in the showers—a first for Beirut," he wrote. "Everyone, including yours truly, is getting more and more excited about going home."

October 1983

Terrorists can attack anything, anywhere, anytime. Governments cannot protect everything, everywhere, all the time. It is a certainty that terrorists will attack the least defended target. It is a virtual certainty that there will always be a vulnerable target.

—Brian Michael Jenkins, testimony before the Long Commission
November 17, 1983

A Marine sits on the bumper of a car that was destroyed when a huge bomb explosion wrecked the American Embassy in Beirut. Rescue workers continued to search the rubble for those missing.
AP Photo

CHAPTER **25**

The Lebanese people turned completely against us.
—MORRIS DRAPER
February 27, 1991

Peace proved elusive.

Despite the late September cease-fire, by early October gunfire once again rattled across the capital. Daily situation reports read like a crime blotter filled with kidnappings, car bombings, and shootings. "Sniper fired at a civilian pickup and injured one and seriously wounded another," one such report stated.

"A white Peugeot 505 car exploded in West Beirut," added another.

"Armed men and barricades throughout southern suburbs."

Beirut, in short, had returned to chaos.

Such violence alarmed Geraghty. Though his troops were not on patrol, men still had to run resupply convoys to the embassy and the line companies as well as trash to the dump. A message went out to the troops, reminding them to be on guard. While the cease-fire had given the Marines a breather, the message warned, it had likewise provided the same for any adversary, who could now travel about freely and plan attacks. "During the shelling it was easy to dive into bunkers for protection," the message stated. "It is not so easy now, when we must move about and conduct the day-to-day activities." Do not, officials cautioned, take any security shortcuts. Wear flak jackets and helmets, and, if needed, take an extra shotgun. "Since they do not have the authority to shell us at will, those who would do us harm will have to use other means to strike at Marines," the message warned. "Ambushes along the narrow streets, car bombs in the perimeter and snipers are all ways to kill Marines with very little retribution."

Much of the violence now centered on the Shiite slums that ringed the airport, where the Marines had long noticed a change among the local population. "The cease-fire," as Michael Petit observed, "meant nothing to the militias; it was merely an opportunity to dig in deeper before beginning the war anew." The dense area of cinder-block shanties the troops had once patrolled with the hopes of engendering goodwill turned hostile. "Positions and buildings were sandbagged and stocked with ammunition," the Marines reported. "Militiamen were visible on a daily basis carrying weapons while manning checkpoints and bunkers."

Amid this escalation, two soldiers who operated the fire-finding radar broke regulations and took a jeep off base without security. In the center of Beirut, a green Mercedes suddenly blocked the soldiers. "The driver," one report stated, "pointed a pistol at them and told them to get out." A second vehicle arrived with four Amal militiamen armed with AK-47 rifles. The gunmen disarmed the soldiers, including flak jackets, and drove them first to a school building and then to the home of Nabih Berri, who commanded the powerful Shiite militia. "I figured," Lance Corporal Petit said, "the Army soldiers would be dead by the end of the day."

A livid Geraghty worked with Gerlach to assemble a quick reaction force when the duo learned that Berri had released the soldiers to the French, stating that he had no animosity toward the Marines. The soldiers arrived back on base followed by the jeep. Though the crisis was averted, Petit recalled witnessing Geraghty's stress as it unfolded. "His face was a mixture of anxiety and concern," he wrote. "The kidnapping was the culmination of weeks of life-and-death decisions, and for the first time I saw the colonel without a look of self-assurance. He was approaching his limit, and the sleepless, agonizing nights had taken their toll."

But more trouble was still to come.

At 2:41 p.m. on October 5, a helicopter carrying an aide to McFarlane came under fire. "A single round," one report stated, "passed through the aircraft cockpit causing the pilot to take evasive action." The following day another round tore into the aft rotor blade of another helicopter, which caused a shudder and loss of airspeed, forcing the pilot to abort. The back-to-back attacks prompted Geraghty to make changes. "The vulnerability of aircraft," the Command Chronology observed, "using standard transit patterns over the city was reevaluated and actions were taken to protect the aircraft which included staggered flight times and routes, terrain flying, and limiting nonessential help orientation flights over Beirut."

Day by day, the attacks escalated. On October 9, a sniper hit a Marine in the right shoulder. Four days later, an assailant in a speeding car hurled a grenade at the sentry post in front of the Duraffourd Building, wounding a Marine in the left thigh and ankle. In his room up on the fourth floor of the Battalion Landing Team headquarters, Hudson could hear the crack of gunfire. Others reported the same. "I don't know," Private David Madaras wrote his family, "if this country will ever see peace." Unlike before, when rounds aimed at the Lebanese at times hit the airport, this was clearly different. The Marines were the target. Troops returned to high alert, with flak jackets and helmets once again the daily wardrobe. "The direct threat against Marines," the colonel wrote in his weekly report, "has increased significantly."

At 10:03 a.m. on October 14, a jeep zoomed along the airport's perimeter road when a sniper fired in the distance. A round ripped through the right and left thigh of driver Lance Corporal William Riddle. Less than forty minutes later, a second sniper targeted Sergeant Allen Soifert, who was a member of the Explosive Ordnance Disposal team. The bullet struck Soifert in the chest, prompting him to crash and roll his jeep. Under fire, rescuers retrieved the Marines and brought them to Hudson. Riddle had no pulse in his right leg, but he still had movement. The doctor stabilized him for evacuation to the *Iwo Jima*. Soifert, in contrast, was in far worse shape. "He was still alive when he arrived," Hudson noted, "but he was close to death."

The doctor and hospital corpsmen attempted to give him intravenous fluids, since he had lost so much blood. Chaplain Danny Wheeler comforted the young Marine, reciting the Lord's Prayer. "Our Father, who art in Heaven, hallowed be thy name."

Soon after, Soifert quit breathing. The doctor bagged and then intubated him, inserting a tube into his mouth and down his trachea. "He looked like he was improving," Hudson recalled, "but then he quickly went worse." Hospital corpsmen administered intravenous fluids while Hudson injected him with epinephrine and began cardiopulmonary resuscitation.

"I can't do any more," Hudson finally said. "There is too much damage."

"You could hear the frustration and the hurt in his voice," Wheeler said.

Soifert was gone. "I pronounced him shortly thereafter," a distraught Hudson wrote his wife. "It's kind of hard to accept the needless murder of a fellow American."

Eighteen-year-old Lance Corporal Craig Stockton watched hospital corpsmen load Riddle, who had an intravenous line in his arm, into a helicopter for the flight out to the *Iwo Jima*. Five minutes later, a second helicopter arrived for Soifert, whose face was covered by a blanket. "I can't tell you what I felt at that moment," Stockton wrote to his family back home near Rochester. "There were quite a few things running through my mind—hate, compassion, so many things." The Marine had been shot along a road Stockton traveled almost daily on trash runs. "It could've been me so easily. It's scary as hell. I'm sick of being scared just sitting here. I'd rather be in the full offensive being scared & *doing* something about it," he added. "A lot of things happen around here and I can handle them just fine. I'll handle this too, but I don't think I'll be able to forget seeing them take that dead Marine right in front of me."

Soifert would not be the last.

Two days later, on October 16, Marines at the university library came under fierce fire, including hits from five rocket-propelled grenades. Three Marines were wounded. The Marines returned fire, but the firefight proved too heavy for a medevac helicopter. The British sent in armored scout cars to help evacuate two of the more seriously wounded Marines. The fighting continued. At 10:03 p.m., a sniper shot Captain Michael Ohler in the head, instantly killing the twenty-eight-year-old father of two. "Being shot at is a novelty, but it grows old," Ohler had written to his family only a few days earlier. "You put it out of your mind."

Three days prior, Ohler had officially submitted his resignation from the Marine Corps. His plan was to open a boat-rescue business with his brother. "We've taken the big step," he wrote to his wife, Gail. "It's kind of scary, but it's done." His focus was on coming home. "Always remember," he concluded his last letter, "that I love you."

Ohler's death haunted Hudson, who considered him one of his few friends in Beirut. The two officers had much in common, including infant children. The fact that Ohler never had a chance to cradle Ben in his arms upset Hudson, who thought often of how much he missed his own son, Will, back home in Georgia. "It is so sad that he lost his life for Lebanon," Hudson wrote his wife. "I want to come home so badly; pray that I make it safely."

The back-to-back deaths triggered a free fall in morale. Hudson, who manned the Battalion Aid Station, witnessed the evolving war with each wounded Marine who landed atop his surgical table. "It's a different kind of environment now—these Marines are being picked off by snipers who are aiming at them," he wrote his wife. "I expect our losses of 6 dead Marines will increase again soon. I just hope I'm not one of the statistics or casualties." Others agreed. "One hell of a ceasefire were having here, huh?" Henry

Linkkila wrote his mother. Unlike with artillery, where the Marines had radar to pinpoint and respond to attacks, snipers could fire and then vanish into the slums. "You never know where or when they will attack next," Corporal John Dalziel wrote his family. "So we take every day as it comes."

The Marines finally had enough.

"If fired upon," Major Jordan told reporters, "we're going to fire back."

Marine snipers, separated by a football-field-sized no-man's-land that divided the airport from the neighboring slums, scanned the windows, walls, and crevices in search of the snipers. Armed with a M40A1 bolt-action rifle, Corporal Frank Roberts started hunting. "It is strange at first," he admitted. "You see them through your scope and the cross hairs are on them and you know you are going to blow them away. But then, after a while, you see your buddies getting killed and it doesn't make any difference to you anymore."

But the violence continued.

At 4:22 p.m. on October 19, a car bomb hidden in a blue Mercedes detonated alongside a resupply convoy returning from the embassy, wounding five Marines. Lance Corporal Michael Toma was in one of the follow vehicles. "Shit man," he wrote in his diary. "I almost bought the farm today." A six-by-six truck absorbed the brunt of the blast, though shrapnel peppered three jeeps and blew out the windshield of one. The experience left Toma shaking for several hours. "I hope," he added in his journal, "I never come this close to dying again."

First Lieutenant Mark Singleton led the quick reaction force that rescued the ambushed convoy. The wounded Marines all landed before Hudson in the Battalion Aid Station. "It is amazing," the doctor wrote, "how lucky these Marines are." He removed glass from one Marine's eyes. Four had ruptured eardrums, and all had cuts from flying glass. "One had an anxiety attack—he just couldn't get over how close to death he'd come. All are doing well right now," the physician concluded. "I however still remained unharmed & lucky."

CHAPTER 26

War is hell and so is Beirut.
—DR. JOHN HUDSON, POSTCARD TO HIS IN-LAWS
September 1, 1983

The only bright spot in this otherwise dark time was the marriage of Hospital Corpsman Bryan Earle to Lebanese local Micheline Abi Ghanem. The twenty-one-year-old Ohioan had served on a previous deployment in Beirut, where he often conducted patrols through Hooterville, helping treat and care for the locals. During that time, he befriended Micheline, a teenager whom he recruited to serve as a volunteer medical translator.

"It was," she recalled, "love at first sight."

The two could not have come from more different worlds. With bright blue eyes and sandy brown hair, Earle had grown up in the tiny town of Painesville, where he had played football and wrestled at Harvey High School. Micheline, in contrast, sported curly dark hair and matching eyes. Raised Christian in a largely Shiite area, she knew little of life without war. "I never really had a childhood," she said. "You grow up so fast."

Day after day, as Earle made his rounds through Hooterville, the two grew closer. "They fell in love," one newspaper reporter observed, "amid the kind of tragedy and conflict of which Hemingway novels are made." Earle met Micheline's mother and befriended her brothers, often enjoying home-cooked meals with her family. Locals he treated at times left dried fruit and other goodies for Earle and his fellow Marines at her home. "The days together with Earle were everything in my life," Micheline said, "everything I lived for."

With his first deployment winding down, he asked her to marry him on February 13, 1983. Micheline encouraged him to return home and visit his family, friends, and even his high school girlfriend—to make certain he wanted to marry her.

No sooner had he left in February than letters started arriving from him. Earle volunteered to return in May with the 24th Marine Amphibious Unit. "I found somebody," he told his fellow Marines, "who I want to spend the rest of my life with."

Earle taped sixteen pictures of her above his rack on the fourth floor of the Battalion Landing Team headquarters. "He was infatuated with her," recalled friend and fellow hospital corpsman Darius Eichler. "His main goal was to get her out of Lebanon."

Arranging a marriage in the war-torn capital proved difficult, but the American Embassy helped facilitate it and the Navy allowed him leave. The couple, meanwhile, attended the chaplain's pre-marriage counseling course and had bloodwork drawn in the base clinic while his colleagues took up a collection, presenting them with a gift of fifty dollars and a bottle of wine.

The sniper attacks, coupled with the wealth of roadblocks and checkpoints, mandated a small wedding ceremony in a Catholic church on Hamra Street in West Beirut. About twenty people attended, mostly Micheline's family members as well as a Navy chaplain. "Our hearts were full of happiness to be getting married and be united for life!" she remembered. "Being at the church that day felt as if it was almost a dream. We were like two old souls who found each other and nothing was going to separate us from that day forward!"

The embassy had arranged for the couple to honeymoon in a nearby hotel. On the afternoon of October 16—less than six hours before a sniper would kill Michael Ohler—Micheline watched her sister and mother walk through the church. Though excited to start her new life with Earle, she knew it meant leaving behind her country and family, which was a lot for a teenager to process. As though he could sense her thoughts, Earle whispered in her ear. "You'll be visiting them once a year," he said. "I promise."

She looked up at him.

"I love you today and always," he declared. "Now let's go and get married."

CHAPTER 27

Things will have to get better over here. I don't see how they could get worse.
—HOSPITAL CORPSMAN JIMMY RAY CAIN, LETTER TO HIS MOTHER
October 7, 1983

Back in Washington, Reagan phoned Allen Soifert's family on October 14. Three days later, he spoke with the father and widow of Michael Ohler, where he learned the Marine captain left behind two small children, including a son he had never met. In the wake of the call, which left the president in tears, Reagan sent a letter to Gail Ohler. "In the days ahead, Sarah and Benjamin will ask you many questions about their father," he wrote. "Let them know that their father died trying to restore peace in a troubled land. As they study the history of our nation, let them know that their father was one of the few in his generation whose life made a difference—and one of the few who made the ultimate sacrifice so that others might live. As they grow up in a land of freedom and security and in a world that is at peace, let them know that it was their mother who caused the President to weep, with sorrow and appreciation."

National Security Advisor William Clark resigned to become secretary of the interior, prompting Reagan to replace him with Bud McFarlane on October 17. McFarlane no doubt felt vindicated in his quest to rival Kissinger. "It was a moment of great pride for me," he wrote. "I had reached the pinnacle of a long public service career, a position of special trust and authority that represented the culmination of all my efforts and aspirations."

The Lebanese cease-fire had proven tenuous, as the recent uptick in violence showed. But it wasn't only the Marines who suffered. Patricia Nakhel, a fifteen-year-old Lebanese civilian, wrote to Reagan that month, imploring him to do more. "You are the last hope," she wrote, "for the salvation of our country." The youth recounted huddling for weeks in a bomb shelter. "Do I really deserve to live like this, just because I am Lebanese?" she asked. "Maybe I am too young to understand why the world is so unjust but I sure know one thing, no person deserves death, no matter what the circumstances are." Reagan agreed, writing that he wished more of the world knew of stories like hers. "I promise you," the president concluded, "we will do everything we can to end the bloodshed and terror that presently devastate your country."

To that end, Secretary of State Shultz outlined his views on America's road ahead in a ten-page paper to the president. "The ceasefire in Lebanon, a major achievement of our diplomacy, means that the struggle in Lebanon now shifts to the political arena." The secretary of state acknowledged that America had committed its prestige to back Gemayel, a position made all the more challenging since Israel's departure from the Chouf Mountains. "This has created a vacuum," he wrote, "which we have been drawn into to sustain."

Syria remained the central problem. Assad wanted to kill the May 17 deal, drive the Marines out of Lebanon, and install a more friendly government. A Syrian success would not only humiliate the United States but would strengthen Assad's position in the Middle East, boost regional radicals, and undermine moderate nations. To counter that threat, Gemayel needed to use the political process to broaden his base and pull the Druze and the Shiites out of Syria's embrace. "A satisfactory outcome to the Lebanese political negotiations should be our priority objective," Shultz wrote, "since so much depends on it—our standing in the Middle East and our prospects for bringing the Marines home in honorable circumstances."

To accomplish this, Shultz once again fell back on the military. "To ensure a tolerable outcome," he wrote, "it will be more important than ever to maintain the balance of forces so that Syria cannot intimidate the other parties and steamroll the conference." A breakdown in the cease-fire, which Assad would welcome, would undermine any national reconciliation and create complications with Congress. To prevent that, the United States needed to keep the battleship *New Jersey* parked off the coast as a symbol of might as well as shun any suggestion that the time had arrived to reduce forces. "Now is an appropriate time to consider broadening the Rules of Engagement for our forces," Shultz urged, "so that there will be more of a sense that we are still there to be reckoned with if the ceasefire should break down."

Weinberger, of course, disagreed. In a three-page rebuttal, the defense secretary highlighted the "fragility" of Lebanon, arguing that it was time to consider alternative options for the deployment of the multinational force. "The static position of the Marines ashore," he wrote, "presents an extremely difficult defensive situation." The recent sniper attacks illustrated how American forces had been drawn into the factional fighting. Any change in the rules of engagement risked undermining the national reconciliation because it would remove any incentive for Gemayel to make concessions. If anything, Weinberger argued, it was time for the Marines to pack up. "It might be necessary and desirable," he argued, "to reduce or eliminate US ground presence in Beirut and keep our forces offshore, perhaps bolstered by additional naval gunfire support. Thus, we would not be weakening our commitment to help secure peace in the Mid East, but would actually strengthen it in terms of fire power."

What to do with the Marines was one of the top issues on the agenda when the National Security Planning Group sat down in the Situation Room at 11:01 a.m. on October 18. Reagan once again faced two diametrically opposed viewpoints from his two senior cabinet members. On the one hand, Shultz wanted to keep the Marines in-country and expand the rules of engagement so as to keep political pressure on Syria. Opposite him stood Weinberger, who advocated that it was time to pull the Marines back aboard ship before any more of them were killed. As events would soon show, this was the last real opportunity for the president to divert a coming tragedy of a magnitude few could imagine. No minutes exist from the sixty-three-minute meeting, but Reagan described it that evening in his personal diary. "All the options on how to keep trying for peace, avoid murder of our Marines, not suffer a disastrous pol. defeat etc.," he wrote. "No decisions, but option papers being drawn up for my decision."

That delay would soon prove deadly.

As a reminder of the high stakes involved, family and friends of Allen Soifert gathered that same day at Temple Beth Abraham in the small New Hampshire city of Nashua to say goodbye to the twenty-five-year-old Marine. Ohler's funeral would follow on October 24. Police then escorted the family to the cemetery west of downtown. Residents lined the sidewalks and watched from the front steps of homes as the limousine passed. Once again, a Marine rifleman fired a twenty-one-gun salute before the bugler blew "Taps." "We too are casualties," Rabbi Gerald Weiss reminded attendees. "We too today are hurt and wounded."

CHAPTER 28

In Beirut, the enemy is unseen. He is the chaos and instability that rides
with the whirlwind of civil war, invasion and political strife.
—Warrant Officer Charles Rowe, *Root Scoop*
August 12, 1983

Hussein al-Musawi, founder of the Islamic Amal terrorist group and now a
leader in Hezbollah, had taken Iranian ambassador Mohtashemi's advice.

A strike against the Marines, if successful, would prove even more extraordinary than an attack on the embassy. The Marines were, after all, a symbol of American might.

For the operation, he brought in Abu Haydar Musawi, who commanded a
martyrdom group known as the Husayni Suicide Forces. On October 18—
the same day Reagan's advisors argued in the Situation Room over whether
to withdraw the Marines—Abu Haydar Musawi arrived in Beirut. He was
joined by twenty members of his suicide squad.

Several trucks arrived the following day, which were parked outside the office of Islamic Amal. At the last minute, the French were added as an additional
target, payback for the recent sale of Super Étendard fighters to Iraq. The plan
mirrored the one used against the Israelis in Tyre and the American Embassy in
Beirut. Technicians loaded two trucks with thousands of pounds of explosives.
To magnify the blast, workers added tanks of compressed gas. "The detonators,"
as historian David Crist noted, "were connected near the steering wheel for easy
access by drivers, enabling them to ignite their cargo even if wounded."

Accounts vary as to the identity of the driver, who has alternately been
identified as either Lebanese Shiite Assi Zeineddine or Iranian national Is-
mail Ascari, though as Crist wisely notes, the latter seems less likely given
Iran's desire not to leave its fingerprints on the mission. The date selected for
the operation proved easier. Al-Musawi needed a day in which the Marines
would be relaxed, their guard down. For that, there was only one option.

Sunday.

CHAPTER 29

Please don't worry cause it's almost over. God bless you all.
See you when I get home.
—CORPORAL EDWARD JOHNSTON, LETTER TO HIS FAMILY
October 13, 1983

The rising violence against the Marines coupled with near-constant alerts had left many of the troops exhausted and frustrated. Some sought refuge in the countdown until the deployment ended. "We will be leaving this god forsaken place in one month," Henry Linkkila wrote to his mother. "That's the best news I've heard all day."

The end was close.

So close.

Chaplain Danny Wheeler tried to prepare his young flock for that reality, cautioning them in his weekly *Root Scoop* column on how best to ease back into society. The Marines had experienced a lot since arriving in Beirut, including much destruction and death. It would take time to process and heal. "We have something to share with the people back home," the chaplain wrote. "Don't blow it by immature acts of trying to prove yourself as the Beirut Vet who thinks he can punch out everybody or drink more than everybody."

Linkkila could have benefited from that advice. The cook and a few of his friends drank too much one night and picked a fight with several other Marines over which music to play—rock or disco. Words escalated into punches. As a result, Linkkila was banned from the enlisted men's club, ordered to stand guard duty, and forced to attend Alcoholics Anonymous classes. "Real good, huh?" he wrote to his mother. "I already know what you're going to stay, 'Dumb,' right? 'You'd better lay off the booze!' Right? Etc. etc. etc. Well, I've already got the message, ok? I can't afford any more fines and I was starting to get the shakes."

Fears continued to grip many of the Marines and sailors, particularly as the time wound down and the violence escalated. Few felt those emotions as strongly as Hudson, who time and again had been called upon to patch up the wounds of war. The unlikely battle surgeon had plucked scorched shrapnel from arms, legs, and torsos. He had stitched up gashes from rockets and car bombs. He had beat on men's chests to bring them back to life, and when he proved unable to save them, he had the tragic responsibility of pronouncing them dead. He had, in short, been the arbiter between life and death. In many of his more than six hundred pages of letters, Hudson wrote of his fear that he, too, would fall victim to the violence in Lebanon. The twenty-eight-year-old wanted only to return to his wife and eight-month-old son, to the small-town life he so loved on the banks of the Oconee River, where he could play Dixieland jazz on his trombone. "I so want to see Will grow up," he wrote, "and spend my life with you."

"I say a prayer every night that the Lord will return me to your arms," he said in another.

"Enclosed with this letter is my hope for our long future together."

Hudson was not alone in his fear. A certain fatalism crept into the outlook of many who put pen to paper while stretched out atop cots in the Battalion Landing Team headquarters or scattered amid the sea of bunkers and tents. "I have never been so scared in my life," twenty-one-year-old Corporal Douglas Held said on an audiotape he mailed to his family. "I just hate it." Nineteen-year-old Lance Corporal Johnnie Copeland agreed. "I know everyone has to go sooner or later, but I just hope it's not here," he wrote. "This is a terrible place to die."

Those fears led Sergeant Richard Blankenship to put his relations in order. "I'm writing this letter to let you know I love you guys. I'm so proud to have you as my family, and I'm proud to be your son. I hope everything works out for you all. You deserve the best," he wrote. "Just pray for me over here because we need it every day. Dad, all you told me when I was growing up, I'll always remember. You're a super dad. And mom—well I hope I have never disappointed you in any way. I wouldn't trade you for any other mom. Donnie—take care bro. I love you man. You take care of mom and dad for me. You're a man now. Shelley—my lovely sister, take care of yourself. You have always been my favorite. Your boyfriend better take care of you. I love you a lot and I know you will go far, and Beck, I love you too. You've been a good sister to me. Be good to mom and dad, for they need it. Don't take this letter wrong. I'll do my best to return to you guys. Remember I'm a crazy jarhead. I just wanted you to know how I feel."

Exhaustion was a theme in many other letters. "I just can't wait to get home," Private First Class Rui Relvas wrote, "to get some sleep, some peace." Bill Stelpflug likewise dreamed of his return to Alabama, where he missed hunting, fishing, and drives through the countryside. He had been gone so long he joked that maybe he had lost his southern accent. One thing was certain—he had had enough of war. "I think I've lost my thirst for danger & excitement," he wrote. "My war hungry soul is quenched." Stelpflug spent his days envisioning his return for the holidays. "I think I'll take a bus back just to see what it is like to come home so slow and happy instead of leaving so fast and sad," he wrote. "I think I'll have them drop me off 10 miles from home, so I can savor every pasture, pond and familiar sight."

Similar concerns weighed upon thirty-nine-year-old First Sergeant David Battle, whose wife had long urged him to get baptized, a rite he had so far refused.

"I'll know," Battle assured her, "when I need to be baptized."

That premonition hit him on October 21, leading him to knock on Chaplain Wheeler's door. The two men, both Vietnam veterans who lived in neighboring rooms on the fourth floor of the Battalion Landing Team headquarters, had developed a deep friendship over the many months in Beirut, swapping stories each night over glasses of Baileys and coffee.

"Chaplain," Battle asked, "is there any reason I can't be baptized?"

"No," Wheeler exclaimed. "Let's do it."

Wheeler arranged to do it the following day in Battle's room, which featured a sofa, lounger, and two racks. The chaplain snagged a cushion from the Peacekeeping Chapel for Battle to kneel upon. His washbowl, which he used for shaving, held the holy water. Against the backdrop of distant artillery and gunfire, Wheeler read from the book of John; chapter three, verse sixteen. "For God so loved the world," he began, "that he gave his only begotten Son, that whosoever believeth in him should not perish but have everlasting life."

"David Lee Battle, I baptize you in the name of the father," Wheeler said, repeatedly sprinkling him with holy water, "the son, and of the holy spirit."

Wheeler used the water to make the sign of the cross on Battle's forehead. "David," he concluded, "you are now a child of God. Now you are part of the family."

Battle rose to his feet and the two friends embraced.

Elsewhere that Saturday many of the Marines looked forward to a United Service Organizations concert by the six-piece country-western group

Megaband. The group performed two shows, an earlier one near the Service Support Group building and a follow-up one later in the afternoon outside the Battalion Landing Team headquarters. "Marines greatly enjoyed the band," one report stated, "as well as pizza from the world-famous *Iwo* Hut."

Not everyone, of course, could go. Lance Corporal Burnham Matthews and others in his reconnaissance unit had to head out on an all-night security patrol around the airport's perimeter. Dr. Jim Ware popped over for a few minutes, but he didn't love the music, so he left. First Lieutenant Glenn Dolphin didn't even know of the concert until he heard the tunes. He drifted outside and found a spot to watch. "It occurred to me that, compared to us, the members of the band looked so clean," he said. "To me, the contrast was striking. It caused me to take a hard look at the Marines surrounding me. Our uniforms were threadbare and sweat-stained. We looked dusty, faded and weather-beaten. It was not only our clothing, but our hair and skin also looked washed out. We looked aged and older than we actually were."

That evening those Marines not on duty fanned out for bed. Some drifted back to tents. Others headed to quarters in other buildings. The rest marched up the headquarters stairs, including Hudson, Stelpflug, Wheeler, and Earle, whose honeymoon had ended that day. Earle needed to complete the residency application for Micheline, whom he planned to send to Ohio to stay with his parents as he wrapped up deployment. Chaplain Wheeler reached his fourth-floor room and collapsed on his rack by the wall, where all the previous chaplains who had served had signed their names and added a prayer, prompting Wheeler to dub it the "Blessing Wall." His roommate Corporal John Olson stretched out atop his own cot by the window.

"Good night, Johnny," Wheeler said.

"See you tomorrow, Chaplain," came the response.

Hospital Corpsman Third Class Don Howell readied for bed, when fellow sailor James Jones appeared alongside his cot. "What up?" Howell asked.

"I just got finished reading the Bible," Jones replied.

"Let me say a prayer before going to bed," Howell said.

He closed his eyes.

"Our Father, who art in Heaven," he began, "hallowed be thy name."

CHAPTER 30

Is the glorious dream of a peaceful Lebanon worth American lives?
—LARS-ERIK NELSON, NEW YORK *DAILY NEWS* COLUMNIST
October 19, 1983

Half a world away, President Reagan hoped to unwind with a weekend getaway to Augusta National Golf Course in Georgia, home to the prestigious Masters Tournament. The president and first lady were joined by Secretary of State Schultz, Treasury Secretary Don Regan, and former New Jersey senator Nicholas Brady and their wives. "I was looking forward to a couple of days of relaxation," Reagan recalled, "although I hadn't played golf in quite a while and didn't have high hopes for my performance on the links."

Lebanon was not the only world hot spot the president faced.

Tensions had long simmered on the island of Grenada, which, like Cuba, functioned as a Soviet satellite in the Caribbean. Construction of a new 10,000-foot runway—the type used by military planes, not commercial airliners—had previously drawn American scrutiny.

But those fears paled compared to the eruption days earlier of domestic political violence. On October 13, a military coup overthrew the regime of Prime Minister Maurice Bishop, a Marxist acolyte of Cuban leader Fidel Castro. The military junta, which proved even more radical than Bishop, initially arrested the political leader before murdering him five days later. The military then instated a curfew with orders to shoot anyone caught in violation.

The White House's concerns centered on St. George's University School of Medicine, a private institution owned by American investors and headquartered in New York. About eight hundred Americans studied medicine on the Caribbean island, triggering fears of a potential repeat of the Iran hostage crisis that had doomed Jimmy Carter's presidency.

Grenada's neighbors likewise felt on edge, fearing that the unrest might leap to other islands. The day after Bishop's assassination, the president ordered the aircraft carrier *Independence* and its task force along with Marine replacements headed for Lebanon redirected toward the Caribbean. The Joint Chiefs of Staff, meanwhile, had begun putting together a plan for how to land forces, if necessary, to extract the American students.

Amid this tension, Reagan had escaped to Augusta, leaving Vice President George Bush at the helm of the Special Situation Group tasked to monitor Grenada. The first family had settled Friday night into the Eisenhower Cottage, a six-bedroom white brick home near the tenth tee that was built in 1953 to house the D-Day commander and former president. The group enjoyed dinner at the clubhouse and then retired for the night.

The phone on Bud McFarlane's bedside table rang at 3 a.m. The national security advisor, who had accompanied the president's entourage to Georgia, picked up the receiver to find the vice president on the line. The Organization of Eastern Caribbean States, made up of a half dozen of Grenada's neighbors, had requested the United States invade.

"The operative issue," Bush said, "is how do we respond?"

McFarlane relayed the news to Shultz before the men decided to wake the president. A little past 4 a.m., the trio gathered in the cottage's living room, Reagan dressed in his pajamas, robe, and slippers. "The United States is seen as responsible for providing leadership in defense of Western interests wherever they may be threatened," McFarlane advised. "For us to be asked to help and to refuse would have a very damaging effect on the credibility of the United States and your own commitment to the defense of freedom and democracy."

"You're dead right," the president agreed.

How long, Reagan asked, would it take to plan a rescue of the American students?

Forty-eight hours, McFarlane replied.

"Do it," the president instructed.

Reagan then went back to bed.

At 9:31 a.m., Reagan joined a National Security Council meeting by speakerphone. An invasion of a small island, one staffer warned, could trigger political blowback.

"I know," the president said. "I accept that."

Reagan then hit the links on a cloudy Saturday, playing the first nine holes with Shultz, Brady, and Regan. After lunch in the clubhouse, the foursome started on Augusta's back nine. On the sixteenth fairway, however, the Secret Service swarmed the group, halting the game. Agents rushed Reagan into an armored White House limousine, where the president who had nearly been killed by an assassin's bullet two and a half years earlier learned that a gunman had crashed a blue Dodge pickup truck through one of Augusta's gates. Charles Harris, a forty-five-year-old unemployed pipefitter dressed in jeans, a flannel shirt, and a hat that read "Dixie—The Closest Thing to Heaven," had then used a .38-caliber pistol to take seven hostages in the pro shop, including a couple of White House staffers. Harris made two demands: whiskey and a meeting with the president. "Normally," Reagan recalled, "I wouldn't have made any response to demands by a terrorist. That only encourages more terrorism. But I was told that the gunman was very unbalanced and the lives of the hostages were in imminent danger."

At 3:01 p.m., the president phoned the pro shop from the limousine. "This is Ronald Reagan," he began. "I understand you want to talk with me."

Silence greeted him. "The man hung up without saying a word," Reagan said. "We dialed the pro shop again—in fact, four more times—but every time he hung up on me." The Secret Service nixed the gunman's insistence on a face-to-face meeting. Agents instead recommended Reagan return to Washington, which the president refused, settling instead for a trip back to the Eisenhower Cottage, where he spent the remainder of the afternoon and evening. "One by one the hostages got away one way or another. The gunman was then taken into custody," the president wrote in his diary. "And so to bed—after a pleasant dinner."

CHAPTER 31

It felt just like an earthquake.
—STAFF SERGEANT ALPHONSO HERNANDEZ
October 23, 1983

The first light of dawn stretched across the Beirut sky at 5:24 a.m. that Sunday, October 23, 1983. Colonel Geraghty climbed out of his bunk a few minutes later, pulled on his uniform and boots, and washed his face with cold water. The Marine commander lived on the second deck of what had once been the airport's firefighting school, a two-story concrete structure in the shadow of the much larger building that now housed the Battalion Landing Team headquarters. Geraghty walked downstairs to the Command Operations Center, where he checked in with the watch officer and thumbed through the latest communications. "Saturday night," he recalled, "had been, by Lebanese standards, relatively quiet."

The colonel stepped outside, where the morning temperature hovered around seventy-seven degrees. A few Marines returned from patrol while a handful of others prepared for physical training. It was almost tranquil. Reveille, which normally blared at 5:30 a.m., would sound at 6:30 a.m., giving troops an extra hour of shut-eye. "Sunday is my favorite day," Hudson once declared, "because I get to sleep as late as I want." Brunch would follow from 8 a.m. until 10 a.m., a treat that included omelets. The Navy Broadcasting Service planned a 1:55 p.m. showing of the Los Angeles Raiders versus the Washington Redskins—a game that had played live twenty-one days earlier—followed that evening by the 1960 Western *The Magnificent Seven*, starring Yul Brenner and Steven McQueen. "Sunday was normally the day people could anticipate reading a book, writing a letter, or passing a football around," remembered Staff Sergeant Randy Gaddo. "Later in the afternoon, everyone would normally enjoy a cookout, featuring hamburgers and hot dogs with all the trimmings."

Gaddo was one of the few up early. Even though it was Sunday, the *Root Scoop* editor had eight rolls of film he wanted to develop in his photo lab up on the third floor of the Battalion Landing Team headquarters. The previous eight-page newspaper, which had landed among the troops just three days earlier, featured a roundup of the escalating sniper attacks against American forces, including the recent killing of Soifert and Ohler and the wounding of eight others. In the weekly "Chaplain's Corner" column, Father George Pucciarelli drew from the Old Testament book of Ecclesiastes to offer comfort for the Marines in these dangerous times. "Life is dear," the priest reminded readers, "but eternal life is dearer."

Gaddo left his tent for the headquarters building, a route he had done so many times that he knew it took him just fifty-one seconds. Like Geraghty, he noted the quiet; absent was the normal soundtrack of artillery and gunfire. At the last moment, Gaddo decided to slow down. It was, after all, Sunday morning. Why rush? Besides, he could use a cup of coffee. He diverted to the Combat Operations Center, where he poured a mug of dark brew, sweetening it with a couple of scoops of sugar. Coffee in hand, he returned to his tent, where he sat at his small field desk and began to jot down notes. "The birds were singing louder than I've ever heard birds sing," Gaddo recalled. "It was like a symphony."

Lance Corporal Burnham Matthews had just returned from an all-night security patrol around the south side of the airport, where the Marines had fanned out along the perimeter to intercept anyone who might infiltrate the compound. The towering Texan climbed three flights of stairs and turned left toward the third-floor room he shared with five other Marines on the building's north side, anxious to collapse on his cot. Once inside, Corporal Kenny Farnan, who was headed downstairs to shave, pointed to Burnham's M16. "Your rifle is filthy," he advised him. "You need to clean your rifle before you go to bed."

"Okay, Corporal," Matthews replied, sitting down at the wooden desk by the window, where he began to field-strip his M16, beginning with the rifle's sling.

Followed by the handguards.

Then the bolt assembly.

In the room next door, Sergeant Pablo Arroyo was also up cleaning his rifle. "You don't know," the native Puerto Rican said, "what the day is going to bring."

Unlike Matthews and Arroyo, most of the 350 Marines, sailors, and soldiers crowded inside the towering Beirut Hilton still slumbered. The men dozing in military-issued sleeping bags came from a wide range of cultural and religious backgrounds. Troops hailed from big cities like New York, Philadelphia, and Dallas as well as small towns, from Michigan's Fire Lake to Little Mountain, South Carolina, home to just 282 residents. Some had grown up on sprawling farms while others came from congested inner-city public housing projects. Education ranged from high school to medical school. The building, and the men dreaming in it, represented a cross section of America. Traces of the men's lives were captured in photographs of wives, girlfriends, and children taped to concrete walls and tucked inside worn wallets.

Chaplain Wheeler, who had baptized First Sergeant David Battle the day before, snoozed in his fourth-floor bunk in the northeast corner of the building. Steps away on the same floor, Hudson slept as he always did, with his right hand over his face, palm facing upward. Down on the second floor dozed Lance Corporal Emanuel Simmons, who had gone to bed the night before dressed in his boots and flak jacket. When he woke up in the middle of the night to use the head, he opted to strip down to just his long underwear. Up on the building's roof, Corporal Joseph Martucci and others stretched out in sleeping bags, while five stories below in the building's basement, Hospital Corpsman Third Class Don Howell resisted the urge to find a urinal as he tried to grab just a few more minutes of quiet atop a cot in the Battalion Aid Station. A late-night alert had sent Howell to the basement, where upon the all-clear he had decided to remain where he was instead of hiking back up to his fourth-floor bunk. Throughout the building many of the Marines, who disliked sleeping in uncomfortable dog tags, had slipped them off, depositing them on bedside tables, dangling them from the edge of their cots, or lacing them up in the front of their dusty boots.

Security that morning fell to a handful of guards stationed at seven outposts that encircled the compound. Lance Corporal Eddie DiFranco manned post six, one of two sandbagged positions that protected the south side of the building. Linkkila, recently promoted to a lance corporal, guarded neighboring post seven approximately forty feet away. A row of concertina wire divided the Marine compound from an adjacent airport parking lot, which was often used by delivery trucks and civilians, including kids who played soccer and families who occasionally picnicked. On the weekends, many Marines liked to strip off their shirts and toss the football alongside the barbed wire, hoping to impress the attractive Lebanese women who gathered on the opposite side. Dressed in helmets and flak vests, the Marines, who had been on duty since 4 a.m., carried night-vision goggles and M16s. To prevent accidental discharges, Colonel Geraghty had ordered his men to keep their rifles unloaded.

It had been an uneventful morning for the guards. The only activity was the brief appearance of a lone stake-bed truck. It had entered the parking lot with its lights off around 5 a.m. The truck looked like a delivery vehicle and was a common sight in Beirut, particularly near the airport. It circled the lot and departed, continuing south down the perimeter road toward the terminal.

The guards relaxed.

Thirty more minutes passed.

Then an hour.

Corporal Farnan emerged from the building. Dirty and sweaty after being out all night, he walked over to the water buffalo, a portable trailer where he could brush his teeth and shave. "That's the first time," Farnan recalled, "that I ever left my rifle behind."

Shortly past 6:15 a.m., a second truck pulled into the lot, which the morning light revealed to be a yellow Mercedes. It appeared to be a similar vehicle, if not the same truck that had entered and then departed the lot an hour earlier. The truck turned west, paralleling the concertina wire, as the driver, like before, looped the lot. Unlike earlier, DiFranco heard the rev of the Mercedes's engine as the operator shifted into a higher gear and increased speed. The driver then executed a sharp turn north and aimed his five-ton truck straight toward the wire barrier. Something felt wrong.

DiFranco rammed a magazine into his rifle and chambered a round as the truck crashed through the barbed wire, producing a popping noise that survivors would later tell investigators resembled gunfire. The Mercedes accelerated, charging across the 450 feet that separated the concertina wire from the building. Before DiFranco could shoulder his M16, the truck blew past him, the operator gripping the wheel with both hands. "I caught only a glimpse of the driver as he passed by," DiFranco wrote in a handwritten memo for investigators. "He was wearing a blue shirt and had the smile of a crazy person on his face when he looked at me."

In nearby post seven, Linkkila had only briefly served as a guard, his punishment for getting into a fight. His first sign of trouble came when the truck tore through the wire, but like DiFranco, he simply couldn't load his rifle fast enough. "I would have emptied the magazine into the truck," he later testified to Congress, "but there wasn't any time."

Sergeant of the Guard Stephen Russell manned the building's entrance in a plywood shack reminiscent of a ticket booth, though reinforced with a double wall of sandbags. The twenty-eight-year-old Massachusetts native, who had followed his two older brothers into the Marine Corps, had been on duty since 8 p.m. the night before. His M16 was propped against the wall of his guard shack. He wore a 1911A1 .45-caliber pistol on his web belt. Russell faced the inside of the building as he chatted with a fellow Marine who was about to head out for a jog when he heard the commotion behind him. He wheeled around as the truck threaded a path between guard posts six and seven and then swerved around several metal sewer pipes that had been strategically placed in an attempt to prevent just such an attack. The Mercedes, now traveling in excess of thirty-five miles per hour, bore down on him.

"What is that truck doing inside the perimeter?" he thought.

Then he realized.

"Get the fuck outta here!" he hollered at the Marine next to him.

Russell served as the last line of an impossible defense—one man armed with a handgun standing between a terrorist in a five-ton truck bomb and hundreds of sleeping Marines and sailors. There was nothing he could do.

"Hit the deck!" Russell shouted as he charged out of his guardhouse and raced north across the building's atrium. "Hit the deck!"

Farnan, who seconds earlier had washed his face, darted toward the building but instinctively stopped. "I just watched it go in," he remembered. "Went right in the lobby."

Russell looked back over his shoulder as he ran to see the Mercedes obliterate the guard shack and penetrate the building's atrium, spraying sand across the floor of the lobby. The truck came to a sudden stop, snagged on the atrium's overhang. Silence followed. One second turned to two. "Son of a bitch," Russell said of the terrorist. "He did it."

The clock in the basement recorded the precise moment of detonation: 6:21:26 a.m.

The entire attack had taken just ten seconds.

The blast, which investigators later determined exceeded 12,000 tons of TNT, proved more than six times as powerful as the one used against the American Embassy in April. "The FBI Forensic Laboratory," a Pentagon report later noted, "described the bomb as the largest conventional blast ever seen by the explosive experts community." For those on the ground, the split-second detonation, which would kill and maim hundreds, proved unimaginable. "It was," as one survivor later recounted, "like every atom in the universe blew apart."

The destruction was immediate and catastrophic. The building's open internal architecture, capped by a roof that functioned like the cork on a champagne bottle, trapped and magnified the devastating violence. The explosion blew out the bottom of the building, driving the concrete slab eight feet into the earth. At the same time, the blast tore the upper three floors off the concrete support columns, each with a fifteen-foot circumference and supported by 1¾-inch iron rebar. "The building," one report concluded, "then imploded upon itself and collapsed toward its weakest point—its sheared undergirding."

Up on the roof, Corporal Martucci, who had heard the initial furor far below, started to sit up in his sleeping bag just as the bomb exploded. "We saw the center of the roof actually lift, blow out," the corporal recalled. "We had wrapped ourselves in our sleeping bags; I guess it was instinct due to the noise, but we rode the roof down after that."

Sergeant Arroyo, cleaning his rifle on the third deck, heard what he thought was gunfire, a common sound in the Lebanese capital. "It's Beirut," he said to himself, "that's like a rooster croaking in Puerto Rico in the morning." Next door, Lance Corporal Matthews caught the commotion as he reassembled his M16. "There is something going on," Matthews hollered to another Marine in his room. "Wake everybody up."

Matthews never heard the bomb's explosion, but he saw a bright orange flash as the escaping rush of pressure tore the door off its hinges, lifted him out of his chair, and hurtled him through the window. Matthews flipped over once in the air and then landed on his feet three stories below where he collapsed and rolled to a stop. He climbed back up onto his feet. "I turned around and looked," Matthews remembered, "and the building was gone."

Matthews was one of the lucky ones.

The explosion had thrown him clear of the building, where, like an accordion, the fourth floor had collapsed upon the third, followed by the second, and then the ground floor. Corporal Farnan was one of the few to witness the building's disintegration. The blast pressure had ripped his shirt off, knocked the wind out of him, and tossed him against a nearby curb. He struggled to breathe as concrete fragments rained down on him and a cloud of dust rose into the sky. "I was in the eye of a hurricane," Farnan said. "I can't believe I wasn't killed." Hundreds of Marines and sailors lay buried beneath the rubble of a building that seconds earlier had been their home. Many were dead, crushed under tons of pancaked concrete and rebar; men who had gone to sleep, never to wake up. Others, however, had survived, trapped beneath cots, desks, and toppled walls that for the moment shielded them from the onerous weight of the wreckage.

Hospital Corpsman Don Howell, on a cot in the basement, heard what sounded like the roar of a freight train as the building came down on top of him. A piece of concrete struck him in the right eye. "It felt like a boulder," he said. "That's when I turned around and tried to cover my head." Lance Corporal Simmons, who had been asleep on the second floor, struggled to understand what happened. "I never heard the blast, never felt myself falling," he said. "I couldn't see anything and all I felt was dirt." Chaplain Wheeler, who had been asleep on the fourth floor, experienced the same. "I didn't hear anything," he remembered. "Next thing I knew I woke up below the floor and below the debris—buried. That's when I first realized things weren't right. I was pinned. I couldn't move. I didn't know what happened."

The clock now ticked on their survival.

CHAPTER 32

Bodies—and pieces of bodies—were everywhere.
—RABBI ARNOLD RESNICOFF

Colonel Geraghty had returned to his office and quarters on the second floor of the nearby Marine Amphibious Unit headquarters building, which he shared with his executive officer, Lieutenant Colonel Harry Slacum. The colonel had planned to review daily reports and schedules with Slacum, who was still stretched out in his bunk when the bomb exploded. "Shards of glass from blown-out windows, equipment, manuals, and papers flew across my office," Geraghty said. "The entry door to my office, which was on the far side aways from the explosion, had been blown off its hinges."

"What the hell was that?" the colonel shouted, his ears ringing.

Glass blanketed Slacum's bed and dust flooded the room. Geraghty grabbed his helmet, flak jacket, and .45-caliber pistol as Slacum slipped on his shower shoes. The officers charged down the spiral stairs to the Combat Operations Center to find that the explosion had hurled radios, communications equipment, as well as people across the room. "There were long vertical cracks in the back wall," observed First Lieutenant Glenn Dolphin. "Papers, logbooks, batteries, desks, chairs, anything that would move, had been thrown onto the floor."

"Is everybody okay?" Slacum shouted.

"Everybody is okay down here," confirmed First Lieutenant Joseph Jacobs, the watch officer, as he massaged his own injured shoulder.

Geraghty rushed outside to investigate.

"God, you have been cut," Jacobs said to Slacum. "I'll get a corpsman."

Slacum looked down, realizing then that he had slashes on his leg and back.

Geraghty emerged from the building into a thick fog of dust and ash, which blocked his view in every direction. Major Robert Melton, his logistics officer, joined him. The acrid stench of destroyed concrete mixed with explosives filled the air. Geraghty felt a sickening knot tighten in his stomach, convinced the base had taken a direct hit from artillery or a Scud missile. "I knew," the colonel recalled, "that whatever had happened spelled big trouble for us."

The fog dissipated.

"My God," Melton exclaimed. "The BLT building is gone!"

Geraghty wheeled around and faced south, stunned to find only a pile of concrete and twisted rebar where the four-story Battalion Landing Team headquarters once stood, a scene he struggled to process. The colonel, who on the eve of his arrival in Beirut had told a Marine historian that terrorism was his greatest fear, now stared at the wreckage of what was the largest terrorist attack on American forces to date. "I can't explain to you my feelings there," Geraghty would confide in that same historian just weeks later. "It was just unbelievable."

There was, he realized, one certainty.

Casualties would be massive.

The colonel rushed back inside the Combat Operations Center and jumped onto a secure voice satellite with Sixth Fleet Commander Vice Admiral Edward Martin, who was aboard his flagship just offshore in the Mediterranean. Geraghty alerted him of the building's destruction and the expectation of heavy casualties. More reports, he concluded, would follow.

Slacum had retreated upstairs, where he pulled on trousers and boots, when Geraghty appeared. "The BLT is gone!" he exclaimed to his executive officer.

A shocked Slacum listened.

"You won't believe it," Geraghty continued. "The building is gone!"

Slacum had to see this for himself.

He finished dressing and raced outside, navigating through calf-deep chunks of concrete. "It was deathly silent," the executive officer recalled. "There was a gray dust over everything you could see as far as you could see." That fine powder was a mixture of pulverized concrete and glass, doorframes, filing cabinets and paper, as well as skin, fingernails, and hair. The dust now settled on the ground, like snowflakes. Slacum swiveled his head to survey the area. That's when he saw it. The first bodies. "I heard no one," he said. "I saw no one move."

The executive officer ran back to the Combat Operations Center and ordered the radio operator to get in touch with the other members of the multinational force and alert them of the attack. He likewise instructed the radioman to request immediate medical help from the Italians, whose forces were the closest. The destruction of the battalion headquarters had wiped out communications with all the line companies in the field that provided defense, a dangerous dilemma if the bomb was only the first wave of a larger assault. The Marines effectively were blind. Those concerns intensified when news came over the liaison radio at 6:25 a.m. that French forces two miles north at Ramlet el-Baida had suffered a near-simultaneous attack, collapsing an eight-story building and killing and wounding dozens of paratroopers. "My mind raced to absorb all the details about exactly what was coming down," Geraghty recalled. "What about the Italians and British? Were these coordinated attacks a prelude to a ground assault?"

The colonel believed so.

Geraghty demanded security be reinforced and changed the rules of engagement, allowing Marines to shoot any vehicle that failed to stop when ordered. Slacum instructed Captain Timothy Tanner and First Lieutenant Stephen Mikolaski to establish communications with the line companies. Geraghty and Slacum then drafted a flash message to the National Military Command Center in Washington, requesting that the Second Marine Division's Air Alert Force be flown in immediately from Camp Lejeune to replace Battalion Landing Team headquarters. "To buttress support," Geraghty said, "I requested an additional rifle company to augment security for the rescue operation and the anticipated follow-on attacks."

Marines struggled to process the gravity of the assault, even as Major Melton relayed the first report that a truck bomb was likely used in the attack. Many had sipped beer and enjoyed a concert only hours earlier in the shadow of a building that now smoldered in ruins.

"There must be hundreds dead down there," Melton added.

"Everything and everyone," Dolphin recalled, "seemed to stop for a second as the weight of Major Melton's words hit us."

As though to reinforce that message, a winded staff sergeant burst into the Combat Operations Center. "The BLT is gone," he declared. "It's fucking gone!"

I couldn't get up. I couldn't get out. All I could do was holler, scream for help.
—CHAPLAIN DANNY WHEELER
January 19, 2023

Pablo Arroyo, who moments earlier had cleaned his M16 in his third-floor room on a beautiful Sunday morning, woke up in the dark, buried under rubble and in pain. Arroyo moved his arms, then his hands, followed by his legs and feet. "You have a choice," the sergeant realized. "You can die or you can live. It's up to you to make the choice."

"I did not come here to die," he told himself.

Arroyo pushed forward with his feet as he dug his fingers into the debris ahead of him. Like a worm, he wriggled around concrete slabs and through the rock, clawing his way forward as he ground down his fingernails. "When I made it to the surface," he recalled, "I couldn't recognize where I was." The entire landscape had changed. Not only was the building gone, but the explosion had denuded the nearby cedar trees, which bent away from the blast. "When I looked up," he said, "I saw limbs in the trees, arms and legs in the rubble around me."

Arroyo surveyed his own body. The explosion had stripped him naked minus his military-issued Seiko Turtle Dive Automatic Date 6309-7049, which was still strapped to his left wrist. He had a hole about the size of a Liberty silver dollar in the left side of his head, which he didn't realize at the moment had exposed his brain. He suffered ruptured eardrums and a broken jaw while his mouth felt like it was full of gravel. Arroyo opened his mouth only to watch as his teeth tumbled to the ground around him. He reached up to find a tooth in front, hanging by a piece of gum. "I was so frustrated," he said, "I just pulled it out and threw it on the ground with the other ones." A later count would reveal Arroyo had lost eight upper teeth and five lower ones. "I looked at my legs and I started counting the holes. At twenty one, I stopped counting on my right leg," he said, "and at eleven, I stopped counting on my left leg."

Burnham Matthews, who had been in the neighboring third-floor room, found him amid the debris. "Dude," Matthews hollered to him. "You look like shit."

Arroyo stared back, noticing the big gash across his friend's nose.

"You don't look so hot either, cunt face."

Corporal Farnan, who had been blown against a curb on the southeast side of the building, struggled just to breathe. "It sucked the wind out of my chest," he said of the blast. "I thought I was dying there." Large and small pieces of concrete continued to rain down around him as he caught his breath. "It probably took a good five minutes," he recalled, "for all the debris to come down." Farnan stumbled to his feet. Bodies and body parts littered the area. The corporal instinctively moved north around the rubble, heading toward where he knew his troops lived. On the north side of the building, he felt relieved to find Matthews and Arroyo. "I had to go to the rubble," he recalled. "I had to make sure my men were safe."

CHAPTER 34

This isn't combat, it's murder.
—MAJOR ROBERT JORDAN
October 23, 1983

Navy dentists Lieutenants Gil Bigelow and Jim Ware lived in the Marines' Service Support Group building, which was located a few hundred yards north of the explosion. Bigelow had just woken up and was sitting on his rack, pulling on his boots when the bomb went off. The door blew off the hinges and dust flew into the room. "It was just unbelievable," Bigelow said. "I thought we had taken a direct hit on our building."

"God, what was that?" Ware said.

The dentist assumed it was an artillery strike and fished his camera out of his pocket to take a picture of the door. The mass-casualty plan called for two aid stations. The main one—staffed by Hudson and a team of nineteen corpsmen—would be located in the Battalion Landing Team headquarters. The second would operate out of the basement of the Service Support Group building. The goal was to stabilize the wounded and prepare them for helicopter transport to the *Iwo Jima*, which had two operating rooms, an x-ray suite, and a mobile surgical team. Bigelow left to investigate while Ware headed to the basement to prepare the aid station.

"Is anybody hurt in the building?" he asked en route.

"No," came the response. "Does anybody know what's going on?"

No one did.

Ware pulled a radioman aside. "What's the walkie-talkie saying? What's the headquarters saying?" the dentist prodded. "Can we go back to sleep?"

The radios were strangely silent. There was no communication with either the Battalion Landing Team or the Marine Amphibious Unit headquarters.

"We think the BLT has been hit," Bigelow announced upon his return.

"What is going on over there?" Ware asked. "Have you talked to John Hudson?"

"No," he replied, "but I'm going to ride over there."

Bigelow jumped into the driver's seat of a jeep accompanied by Major Douglas Redlich, his commanding officer. The men navigated south through the dense fog of dust, passing a handful of wounded Marines, who trudged, like zombies, away from the destruction. When the officers reached the ruins Bigelow didn't even stop. He immediately circled back, arriving at 6:35 a.m., just twelve minutes after the blast. He hustled down to the basement to find Ware spreading peanut butter on a cracker for breakfast.

"Jim," Bigelow said, his voice quivering. "Prepare for mass casualties."

"I'll set things up here," Ware said. "Just start sending them over."

Bigelow grabbed emergency medical supplies along with five hospital corpsmen and rushed back. The dust at times forced him to cough, spit, and blow his nose. With the building destroyed, there was no aid station to operate. Gone, too, he realized, was the on-site medical team, headed by Hudson and his team of corpsmen. All were asleep in the building when the bomb exploded, their fate below the rubble now uncertain. "I knew," Bigelow said, "we were on our own." The dentist and his few hospital corpsmen served as the front line of medical rescue, as broken and blood-ied Marines crawled out of the rubble. He needed to stop bleeding, make sure patients were breathing, and then move them back to the aid station for stabilization and transport to the *Iwo Jima*. "Some of these guys," Bigelow recalled, "died in your hands."

Back at the Service Support Group building, Ware still had no idea of what to expect. Bigelow had told him only to prepare for mass casualties, but failed to mention that the entire building was leveled. Ware assumed that Hudson, as the battalion surgeon, was leading the medical response. The scope of the disaster evaded him. So, too, did the realization that the emergency relief for scores of wounded Marines now fell to two dentists, who on any given day would fill cavities, yank out wisdom teeth, or per-form root canals. Ware and a team of ten hospital corpsmen and two den-tal technicians set up cots, grabbed stretchers, and unpacked intravenous tubes and fluids, splints, bandages, and scissors. The first eight wounded Marines, those who were able to walk, arrived at 6:36 a.m., covered in white dust as though dipped in flour. "All patients," Ware's after-action report stated, were "dazed and could not hear."

The medics began primary and secondary body surveys, which included checking vital signs and tagging patients. Hospital corpsmen next began applying pressure dressings and tourniquets, administering oxygen and intravenous fluids, and splinting wounds.

"Are you okay?" Ware asked one lance corporal.

"I don't know what happened," replied the stunned Marine, who had been on the roof. "All I know is the building started to move and I began to roll and roll and roll."

Ware listened.

"You've got to help those people," the Marine cried. "You've got to help those people."

Ware next turned to Burnham Matthews, who had survived his three-story fall but suffered multiple shrapnel wounds. The explosion had ripped out his nasal septum, the bone and cartilage that divided his nostrils. His back, which had absorbed the brunt of the blast, was peppered with pieces of concrete and metal. The lance corporal narrated a rundown of what he had witnessed, a stream-of-consciousness account of the human carnage. "At this point," Ware observed in his report, I "began to realize magnitude of situation."

"*I wonder what John Hudson's seeing,*" he thought to himself.

At 6:45 a.m. a six-ton truck rolled up with critically injured Marines. Ware looked in the back and saw the first survivors pulled from the rubble. Unlike the walking wounded, the men fished from under the concrete suffered compound fractures and crush wounds.

"*Holy shit,*" Ware thought. "*What are we going to do?*"

The dentist grabbed a half dozen men and started off-loading the wounded, carrying them down to the basement aid station, which he realized served as a poor location. The narrow stairs made it too difficult to maneuver with a stretcher. "My main concern at this time," he wrote in his report, "was to establish different areas of treatment to differentiate the degree of wounded for triage purposes and patient care and eventual priorities for medevac."

Ware directed the walking wounded to the basement. The critically injured would be divided between the front hall, back hall, and the Senior Noncommissioned Officers Club. A chief would supervise each area while an outside tent would serve as the morgue. "I had sectioned out four areas of medical care at my site to identify the most critical people who were going to be put on the helicopter," he recalled. "I had immediate care, delayed care, expectant, and the dead." Ware ordered morphine and Tubex syringes distributed and sent a runner to deliver narcotics to Bigelow. Hospital corpsmen moved through the wounded, checking the airway, breathing, and circulation of each new arrival before taking pulse rate and blood pressure, a task handicapped by a shortage of stethoscopes. "I jumped around a great deal," Ware said. "Our biggest problem was communication. We had to rely upon runners."

Ware assigned a Marine to each patient—or in some cases, every two to three patients—to monitor their status, keep them awake, and provide moral support. "All morphine and tourniquet patients were labeled on forehead as of time of procedure," Ware noted in his report. "Critically wounded patients had vital signs taken as often as possible."

The wounded continued to arrive by truck and on foot as uninjured Marines converged on the bomb site to help. Glenn Dolphin found a wounded Marine whom the blast had left naked minus the waistband of his red athletic shorts. He was covered in dust and shivering, the likely result of shock. "His left arm was badly broken above the elbow," Dolphin observed. "It dangled loosely at his side. The fingers on his hand were dark blue and very swollen."

Dolphin covered the Marine with his jacket and escorted him toward Ware's aid station. "I don't want to lose my arm," he pleaded. "Please don't let me lose my arm."

The lieutenant tried to reassure him, but the youth grew unresponsive and tried to sit. "I was convinced," Dolphin said, "that if he stopped moving he would just lay down and die. He seemed totally out of it. Nothing I said seemed to penetrate his daze."

Desperate to save him—and unable to carry him—Dolphin had no choice but to get in the Marine's face. "If you want to keep that arm, you'll keep moving," he hollered. "The doctor is not coming to you. You have to go to the doctor." Dolphin's tough love worked. "His vacant, listless eyes sprung back to life," he said. "He rallied and started walking again."

Corporal Brad Ulick likewise assisted, including one Marine who had his hand pressed over his left eye. "They're dead," the injured man said. "Everybody's dead."

Ulick helped him into a jeep.

"My eye hurts," the Marine repeated. "My eye hurts."

"He took his hand down," Ulick recalled, "and his eye was missing."

The injuries the medics saw often proved horrific, ranging from broken bones and burns to crushed limbs. "Some of these guys were blown into bits," Bigelow said. "I was recovering arms and legs." First Sergeant David Battle, whose fears of just such an attack had led him to be baptized only the day before, reached the aid station via truck. Ware assumed he was close to the explosion given the violence of his injuries. "His whole body was burned," he said. "His life was over." Another Marine arrived with his torso ripped open. "I could see his rib cage," the dentist recalled. "It was like an animal on the side of the road after being hit by a car."

And the trucks kept coming.

More wounded and more dead.

Within an hour, the initial eight patients had jumped to sixty-five wounded and fifteen killed. Those who initially appeared to be in rough shape, Ware soon realized, were actually far better off than the latter patients who cycled through his station. Marines rushed into nearby rooms, dragging more cots out into the corridors. The floors soon turned tacky with blood while men walked around crying. "It was," Ware recalled, "a multi-ring circus."

CHAPTER 35

*We just got on top of that rubble and listened
for people. We would see an arm sticking out or a leg sticking
out and we started digging and pulling them out.*
—MARK SINGLETON
December 21, 2022

Commodore France ordered a medical team ashore from the *Iwo Jima* and activated two additional ones from the battleship *New Jersey* and the guided-missile cruiser *Virginia*. Sailors from the tank landing ship *Harlan County* and the dock landing ship *Portland* would likewise help dig out survivors. France recalled the *Austin* from a port visit to Alexandria, Egypt, and requested medical evacuations to hospitals in Cyprus and Germany. "Extent of casualties," he concluded in a message to Washington, "unknown."

First Lieutenant Anthony Pais, who flew with the Marine Medium Helicopter Squadron 162, was asleep on the *Iwo Jima* that Sunday when the sound of chains being dragged across the flight deck roused him. The Baltimore native and graduate of the Virginia Military Institute, whose father served as a guard in the Nuremberg Trials, was still in his rack when the squadron duty officer burst into his stateroom. "Get up!" he said. "The BLT's been hit!"

"So what's new?" Pais quipped, noting that the building always drew fire.

"No, this time they've really been hit!"

The twenty-six-year-old jumped out of his bunk, pulled on his flight suit, and rushed to the ready room, where the flight duty officer briefed Pais and copilot Captain Michael Hagemeyer on that day's frequencies and call signs. Pais then signed for the aircraft before heading topside toward his CH-46 Sea Knight, a tandem-rotor helicopter designed to transport Marines into combat. Medics armed with everything from intravenous fluids and catheters to bandages, dressings, and peroxide climbed aboard as Pais circled the helicopter on inspection before jumping into the cockpit's right seat and firing up both engines.

He then dropped the rotor brake and pushed the condition levers forward. "You are clear for takeoff," the air boss crackled over the radio.

Hagemeyer gave the signal for the aircraft handlers to pull the chocks seconds before Pais lifted off the *Iwo Jima*'s deck at 6:45 a.m., aiming east toward Beirut as he ascended to an altitude of three hundred feet. The trip, which Pais had done countless times, normally took about fifteen minutes. Visibility that morning was about four miles. Land-based units were oddly silent. "There was nobody to talk to," Pais recalled, "nobody on the radio." Five miles from shore, the pilot began to step down his altitude. He crossed the Lebanese coastline and headed toward the Marine compound. "All I saw," Pais said, "was a pillar of smoke."

On the ground, Marines set up a perimeter, rolling out heavy vehicles along with fifty-five-gallon drums filled with sand to control access, allowing guards to screen any potential threats amid the rush of Lebanese fire trucks and ambulances. Others attacked the rubble before the cloud of dust even settled, using their bare hands and Marine-issued Ka-Bar knives until shovels, axes, and sledgehammers arrived. Fueled by adrenaline, the Marines clawed at the rock pile, shredding their fingers and knuckles. The explosion had not only pulverized the structure but obliterated human bodies, littering the wreckage with arms and legs as well as torsos and heads. Flesh likewise dangled from the limbs of nearby trees, many denuded of foliage. Scattered amid the debris, rescuers discovered dead birds, killed in flight. The abundance of human remains, blood, and entrails overwhelmed the senses. "You could smell guts," recalled David Madaras. "Bodies were lying all over," added Gunnery Sergeant Herman Lange, another of the initial rescuers. "People were trapped under the concrete. I could hear them screaming."

"Get us out," Marines hollered. "Don't leave us."

Rescuers followed those voices down into the rubble. Each person who dug on the pile emerged with a horror story. Michael Petit stumbled over a squishy object at his feet. "I glanced down," he recalled. "A severed hand, palm up, lay next to my boot. It wore a wedding ring. I swallowed hard, forcing down the bile that had risen to the back of my throat."

Glenn Dolphin, who left the Combat Operations Center to assist, spotted an overturned jeep. "There was a leg," he noticed, "complete with boot and sock, sticking out from under the vehicle." Hoping the Marine might be alive, Dolphin reached down, grabbed the boot, and yanked. To his horror, he discovered, the leg was severed from the rest of the dead

Marine's body. Like Petit, he fought the urge to be sick. "I immediately dropped the leg," Dolphin remembered. "It was as if I was having a nightmare. This couldn't be really happening. I prayed that I'd wake up any minute and it would all be over."

An equally emotional battle played out underground for those survivors who woke up disoriented and in pain, buried under tons of rubble. Navy corpsman Don Howell struggled just to breathe, choking on the thick dust in the basement of the destroyed building. The darkness robbed the twenty-one-year-old of a view of his surroundings, but he could hear the muffled voices of others trapped in the wreckage around him, letting him know he was not alone. "What the hell happened?" one Marine hollered. "Where the fuck am I?"

"You're in the basement," Howell replied.

"What?" came a stunned answer.

"Where were you?" Howell shouted.

"On the fourth fucking deck."

That Marine had fallen the equivalent of five stories yet miraculously survived.

Howell's eye hurt from his injury, prompting him to strip off his T-shirt and press it against his battered face. The last words the corpsman spoke before he drifted off to sleep the night before were the Lord's Prayer. Howell closed his eyes again in grace.

"God," he whispered, "please get me out of here."

Howell blinked to find a beam of light penetrating his underground prison. The single ray not only illuminated the dust in the air around him but revealed a path toward his salvation. "It was so radiant," he recalled, "and so obvious that it wasn't there before."

Elsewhere in the darkened wreckage, Emanuel Simmons fought the urge to panic. The twenty-three-year-old New Yorker, who had been on the second floor almost directly above where the truck crashed through the guard shack, used his right arm to push against his surroundings. "All I felt," he said, "was rock." At that moment, Simmons realized he had no sensation in his left arm. Had the explosion severed it? Pinned down on his stomach, Simmons moved his right hand around the front of his body, searching the rubble. Amid the rocks and concrete, he found a hand, one with a distinct piece of jewelry on the fourth finger: a gold ring engraved with the emblem of a cobra. A girlfriend in New York had given him that ring long before he joined the Marines. "I knew then," he said, "it was my hand."

Simmons seized the wrist, hoping that if he could only hang on to it, doctors might be able to reattach it. He focused then on calming himself. There were several other Marines in the room with him when he went to sleep. Where were they?

Why was he now alone?

Simmons felt his breathing deteriorate. Fear seized him. Like his friend Howell, he turned to the Lord. "God," Simmons prayed. "Please don't let me die here."

He then relaxed and his breathing improved. At the same time, Simmons began to hear muffled voices above him. "Get me out of here," he hollered. "Get me out of here."

"Quiet, quiet," he heard someone above shout.

"Get me out of here," Simmons continued to yell.

"We hear you," someone assured him. "We hear you, bud."

Simmons held on as the workers removed a concrete slab. He felt rocks and gravel slide down on his neck. "That's when I realized," he said, "I'm going to be okay."

Danny Wheeler was not so fortunate.

The chaplain had been asleep in his quarters on the fourth floor of the building's north side. The blessing wall next to his bunk had collapsed against another, forming an A-frame that helped protect him. Alone in the dark, the chaplain realized he likely would not survive, that he would die buried in the rubble. "I was angry," Wheeler recalled. "I was very angry."

"God," he said, "so this is what you plan to do? Kill me?"

That opening salvo, uttered in a moment of frustration, helplessness, and anger, began a conversation that Sunday between Wheeler and God. Amid the horror—the blood, the dust, and the debris—he confided his fears in the Lord. If he died, what would happen to his wife and three young children back home in Jacksonville, ages two, five, and seven?

Who would take care of them?

"It's going to be all right," God assured him. "I'll take care of them."

"We got closer and closer," Wheeler said of his relationship with God. "I wasn't angry anymore." Everything, the chaplain realized, one way or another, would be all right. He could feel the comforting presence not only of God, but of those previously departed souls. "It was a moment in which I was between death and this life," he said. "I was at peace."

Up above, the chaplain's faith colleagues rushed to pull survivors from the wreckage. Thirty-seven-year-old Rabbi Arnold Resnicoff was normally stationed aboard the USS *Puget Sound*, part of the Navy's Sixth Fleet that covered the Mediterranean. The rabbi had arrived in Beirut on Friday to conduct a memorial service for slain Marine Allen Soifert. Religious custom forbade unnecessary travel on Saturday—the Jewish sabbath—so Resnicoff had stayed an extra night, crashing with Father George Pucciarelli. The duo were two of the first rescuers on the scene after the explosion. Pucciarelli had paused only long enough to slip on his flak jacket and helmet before he grabbed his stole—a cloth religious vestment similar to a scarf—and vial of oils and rushed out the door. "Follow me," he had instructed Resnicoff.

The two religious leaders had reached the ruins within minutes of the collapse, struggling to process the scene as the dust enveloped them like a sandstorm. Neither wasted a minute to jump in and help. "I started giving last rites," Pucciarelli said, "to those that I found were dead and those who were seriously wounded." Resnicoff wiped the blood from the faces of the injured and covered their mouths to prevent them from inhaling the acrid dust. The rabbi peeled off his undershirt and began ripping it into pieces that he could use as wipes and bandages. "There were bodies all over," Resnicoff recalled. "It was like being in a horror movie."

"Over here," Pucciarelli hollered. "There's a man hurt over here. Get a stretcher."

The priest moved on to the next Marine.

Then another.

Pucciarelli would tell a Marine Corps historian several weeks later that he tended to more than 150 dead and wounded that Sunday, including three he pulled from the rubble. The Catholic priest was no stranger to such violence, having once worked as a chaplain for a police department and later in an emergency room. But none of those experiences compared to the scope of the carnage here. This was personal. Before him that morning flashed the faces of young men he knew, Marines who over the many months in a war-torn land had confided in him their fears and struggles as he helped provide spiritual counsel and guidance. A terrorist's explosion had now left these young men dead, disfigured, and broken. "I have never seen so many cuts and gashes," Pucciarelli said, "huge cuts that were just torn open."

Resnicoff used up every last fiber of his undershirt. He then removed his yarmulke, the traditional headgear worn by rabbis, and wiped the brow of an injured Marine. The words of the Old Testament prophet Malachi, who wrote of the cruelty and suffering he witnessed more than two and a half millennia earlier, echoed in Resnicoff's mind.

"Have we not all one Father?" the prophet had asked. "Has not one God created us all?"

The morning's attack revealed that the answer to that question still escaped so many, but not Pucciarelli and Resnicoff. At one point the priest noticed that his friend's yarmulke was missing. He tore the camouflage fabric from his helmet and fashioned a new one.

"Well," Resnicoff said, "we have a Christian and a Jew taking care of our men—a priest and a rabbi working side by side."

Pucciarelli agreed. "In the midst of desolation and death," the priest recalled, "I was reminded of the brotherhood of man."

The dust slowly dissipated and the morning sun climbed into the sky. Gasoline from overturned jeeps and destroyed diesel generators seeped down into the wreckage. Heat from the fires ignited small-arms ammunition stored in the basement, which cooked off only to be muffled by the tons of debris. British, Italian, and Lebanese rescuers arrived to help, including army commander General Ibrahim Tannous, who met with Geraghty. "Whatever you need, you've got," the general assured him. "We'll bring every emergency crew in Lebanon to bear on this, and I'll get you heavy construction equipment in here immediately to lift some of these layers off these people."

Cranes soon appeared courtesy of Oger Liban, Lebanon's largest construction company, which had provided equipment after the terrorist bombing of the American Embassy six months earlier. Geraghty moved his command post to his jeep. Armed with a PRC-77 radio and aided by his driver, Corporal Michael Cavallaro, the colonel set out for the bomb site, which reminded him of newsreel footage of wrecked European cities at the end of World War II. "I felt strongly that it was important that I be visible to my men and the rescue teams to offer encouragement and support while they carried out the heart-wrenching, gruesome task," he said. "It was surreal. Mangled, dismembered bodies were strewed throughout the area in a grotesque fashion. One Marine's body, still within his sleeping bag, was impaled on a tree limb."

The arrival of construction equipment allowed crews to lasso large slabs of concrete and hoist them off the pile. Workers used blowtorches to burn through rebar and sledgehammers to break up rock. Survivors at times emerged from beneath concrete slabs, moaning and covered in dust. Other times Marines tunneled down in search of them.

"There's someone alive in there!" a rescuer shouted at one point.

Others on the pile perked up.

"I can hear him calling for help," the Marine continued.

Petit watched as the leathernecks clawed at the rocks with their hands to widen the entrance. A Marine then wriggled down into the rubble. He popped out moments later followed by another Marine, blanketed in filth and blinking at the bright sun.

"Oh, God," the rescued man wailed. "I'm alive!"

Petit sized him up as he slid down the pile toward the others. "He didn't have a scratch on him," he marveled. "Barefooted, he wore the lime-green surgeon's top and trousers in which he had slept. He rubbed the back of his head. Dust peppered his dark skin and hair."

"I'm alive!" he continued to cry. "I'm alive."

Another Marine embraced him as others encircled them.

"It's okay," the rescuers assured him.

Randy Gaddo had a similar experience when he heard a muffled cry for help from under the rubble. "I hear you, but I can't find you," he hollered. "Keep yelling." To his surprise, the leatherneck responded with a familiar tune. "'From the Halls of Montezuma, to the shores of Tripoli,'" he sang. "'We fight our country's battles, in the air, on land and sea.'"

"Keep it up," Gaddo shouted. "Keep it up!"

As the trapped man belted out the Marines' Hymn, Gaddo and several rescuers managed to dig him out unharmed from a crevice beneath a collapsed wall.

But not all stories ended as well.

Rescuers at times could hear wounded men trapped below, separated by a few feet or even inches. But the immovable weight of tons of concrete and rebar made it impossible to save them; their blood bubbled out beneath the rocks and shock shut down their organs.

"It was literally a race against time," Geraghty acknowledged, "and we were losing."

When possible, hospital corpsmen passed morphine to them to ease their suffering. Other times troops reached down to hold their hands. "There was a dying Marine just feet below us," Dolphin recalled. "We could see, touch and talk to him, but we couldn't save him. All we could do for him was to make sure he knew that he wasn't dying alone."

A similar nightmare confronted Corporal Brad Ulick, who along with several other rescuers was unable to lift concrete slabs off a trapped comrade. "By the time we got to him, he was dead," Ulick recalled. "But the worst part was his fingers were raw down to the bone where he tried to dig himself out through the concrete."

Others endured similar tragedies, including Gaddo, who managed to free one Marine with the help of three others. "All of a sudden," he recalled, "his stomach opened up and his innards started coming out. I grabbed them and tried to push them back inside."

In another instance, Gaddo and Pucciarelli spotted a Marine, still alive in his sleeping bag, sandwiched between two collapsed floors with only his feet protruding. "We tried to pull and pull, but he was in there. We couldn't do anything. We couldn't move tons of concrete," Gaddo said. "We stood there and watched him shake, shake, shake, and then he was still."

Such events added to Geraghty's increasing anger. "Many bodies and portions of bodies were totally burned," he said. "I had a tough time keeping my psychological balance." He was particularly disturbed when he came upon medics attending to Lieutenant Colonel Gerlach, commander of the Battalion Landing Team. Gerlach, who had earned a Purple Heart in Vietnam, had been in his office on the second floor. The blast had thrown him clear of the building. "To put it bluntly," Geraghty said, "he looked a mess." In addition to a crushed face, he suffered a broken neck, left arm, and right leg. "My first impression was that he was dead," the colonel said. "As I knelt down for a closer look, I came very close to getting sick. I was surprised that he was still living but frankly didn't give him much of a chance for survival."

"*Here lie the fucking unintended consequences*," Geraghty thought, "*of getting sucked into an eight-sided civil war while trying to carry out a peacekeeping mission.*"

Buried under the rubble on the building's north side, Chaplain Wheeler continued to fight to stay calm. "I was trying to keep myself oriented without going crazy," he said.

"You can't lose it," he told himself. "You have to keep it together."

Wheeler's eyes adjusted, and even though he had lost his glasses, he could make out shapes in the dark. "I'm Danny G. Wheeler," he hollered to alert rescuers, "and I'm alive!"

But no one came.

One hour passed.

Then two.

Wheeler's voice went hoarse. Alone in his concrete crypt, he tried to distract himself. His wife, Brenda, had mailed him a collection of Louis L'Amour paperbacks, classic Western adventure stories. In each book, characters confronted impossible challenges, from battles with outlaws and kidnappers to cave-ins, yet managed to survive. Wheeler replayed those novels in his head. "I was imagining myself," he said, "as one of his characters."

Major Doug Redlich, who commanded the Marines' Service Support Group, divided rescuers into teams. Given the language barriers, volunteers from each nation were assigned a corner of the destroyed building on which to dig. Communication was primitive, consisting of hand and arm signals and sketch pads. Rescuers then fanned out with an ear to the ground, listening for any sounds of survivors. "The groans were everywhere," recalled First Lieutenant Mark Singleton, who helped Redlich with the rescue efforts and led the quick reaction force that provided overall security. "You could hear them and so you just went to where you heard the noise and started digging." At times, one voice in the rubble might reveal two or even three buried survivors. With so many dead and wounded, rescuers ran out of stretchers, forcing them to improvise with cots, ponchos, and plywood fished from the rubble. "Every five minutes you looked, there was somebody coming out," Singleton added. "He was half naked on a stretcher. He was black and blue, or his head was gone, and his arms were gone."

Elsewhere in the wreckage, Marines turned over debris in search of telltale bloodstains. "Once a blood trail was located, the digging effort followed that trail until a body, or more often a body part, could be recovered," Dolphin said. "This was not the funeral-home type of death with which all of us eventually have to deal. It was an indescribably gruesome, raw and visceral crime scene. This was murder, plain and simple." To Dolphin fell the grim task of helping remove the Marine who was impaled in a tree. "I grasped an end of the bloody sleeping bag. Blood ran down and stained the inside of my fingers. As gently as we could, we pulled the bag through the tree's branches and down to the ground," the lieutenant said. "I purposely did not look at the captain. I felt that in the interest of my own sanity, I needed to start filtering out as many horrific images from being planted into my memory as I could."

In such cases, Marines often sought the help of the chaplains. "As the dead were dug out, Marines would come up to me to ask that the bodies of their buddies be blessed," Pucciarelli remembered. "A small group of Marines would gather around and watch solemnly as I anointed the forehead of the lifeless form before me. They had found a way to show respect for their dead comrades, and I was touched by how mindful the Marines were to provide services for their fallen brothers and by the strength they drew from prayer."

As the hours ticked past, the rows of the dead grew longer, men covered by ponchos and poncho liners. "We ran out of body bags quickly and requested an emergency resupply," Geraghty said. "The bloody bodies, along with the rising temperatures, caused a repugnant odor of death and drew flies, which added to the mayhem." Staff Sergeant Calvin Openshaw, whose father was a coroner, stood watch until rescuers hauled them to the morgue. Even for Openshaw, who had worked as a medical lab technician, the scene was gruesome. "I saw one man blown in half," he said. "I did not know such things could be done to human bodies."

Dolphin endured a similar experience when he fetched a poncho liner from one of the bodies that was needed to cover a wounded man suffering from shock. As he did so, Dolphin glimpsed the dead youth, dressed only in red Marine athletic shorts. "He was just a kid," he said. "There was blood seeping from his nose and mouth. A crushing blow to the chest had killed him. His entire body seemed to be swollen around this huge dent in the center of his chest." Such scenes replayed over and over again exhausted the rescuers. "There were a lot of guys standing around," Openshaw said, "not really hurt bad, just in shock, just wiped out."

Resnicoff and Pucciarelli lost faith that their colleague Chaplain Wheeler would be found. "Pooch and I were so sure that he was dead," Resnicoff said, "that we had promised each other that, when the day came to return to the States, we would visit his wife together."

Wheeler's Advent stole fluttered in the wind like a pennant, marking the spot where he was buried. "What is that purple cloth?" a Marine asked.

Pucciarelli overheard the question. In a Marine compound, where camouflage fatigues were the daily wardrobe, the color purple was rare. The priest immediately recognized the bright cloth as the same one his friend wore around his neck during service.

"That's Danny's stole," he exclaimed. Pucciarelli snatched the cloth and peered down into the rubble. "Who's there?" the priest hollered. "Who's down there?"

Wheeler, who had lost his voice from his hours of earlier shouting, now struggled to respond. "This is Chaplain Wheeler," he cried. "Come get me!"

"We'll be right there," Pucciarelli replied. "Hang on!"

Marines started digging down. Wheeler banged his ration box and his watch to make noise. "The next thing I knew, I felt a hand on my hand," Wheeler said. "I held it."

"Hang on, buddy," someone above shouted. "We're coming for you."

Sand fell down the back of Wheeler's shirt. The tunneling forced the walls to shift, increasing pressure on him, particularly on his wedged head. Pain shot through his skull. "*How much pressure,*" he thought, "*can a human being take before the head bursts?*"

"Hurry up," he cried. "Hurry up!"

The walls likewise pushed on his chest and diaphragm. Struggling to breathe, he thought of Jesus crucified on the cross, desperate for air as his diaphragm collapsed.

"*I can't die this way,*" Wheeler thought.

Suddenly the pressure miraculously vanished. Crews hoisted the wall that seconds earlier had threatened to crush him. Charlie Company commanding officer Captain Chris Cowdrey climbed down next to Wheeler. "Chaplain," he said. "What can we do for you?"

"I'm thirsty. Can I get some water?"

Wheeler watched a canteen passed hand to hand down a line of Marines. The dusty and dehydrated chaplain lifted the canteen and pressed it to his lips, gulping the chemically purified water. "It tasted," Wheeler recalled, "like nectar." Marines cleared the rubble that pinned one of his legs and then yanked. "My foot," he said, "came out like a cork in a bottle."

Rescuers hoisted Wheeler atop a stretcher. He felt the warmth of the sunlight and felt the cool air that he imagined blew down from the ancient and cedar-lined mountains of Lebanon. "It was heaven," he said. "It felt so good." Rabbi Resnicoff hovered over his friend like a parent, counting all ten fingers and toes. "I didn't realize that I was so obvious," Resnicoff later said, "but the truth was that we could not believe that he was in one piece."

Alone in the dark in the wreckage of the destroyed building, surrounded by hundreds of dead and the dying, Wheeler had, like the biblical figures of

Jacob and Job, argued, questioned, and wrestled with God, before in the end he made peace with his Lord. More than five hours after a terrorist's bomb imprisoned him in the bowels of the building, Wheeler was finally free. The chaplain would prove the last soul God delivered alive from the wreckage.

Rescuers gently carried Wheeler down off the rubble pile and toward the aid station. "Racked with pain, still unsure of his own condition," Resnicoff said, "he asked how his clerk was. Like so many of the men we would save that day, he asked first about others." Wheeler's spirit soared as he watched the parade of faces and smiles float past him, men who had gathered for a glimpse of their chaplain. "My Marines," Wheeler said. "These were my people."

Bigelow made his way back to the Battalion Aid Station to check on Ware as the wounded cycled through en route to the *Iwo Jima*.

"How many patients do you have over there?" Ware asked his friend.

"We don't have any more patients," Bigelow replied. "Everybody's here."

"Oh, okay," Ware said. "Where's John?"

Bigelow had no choice but to level with his friend. The irreverent doctor the men loved, the trombone-playing father of an eight-month-old son back home in Georgia, had vanished. "We haven't found John," Bigelow said. "He must have been in the building."

Ware had spent the morning focused on his own lifesaving work, convinced Hudson was leading medical efforts at the bomb site. Not only did the full scope of the tragedy still evade Ware, but until that moment it never occurred to him that Hudson might not be a rescuer, but a victim. The gravity of that realization now settled upon him.

"Well," Ware finally stammered, "how many people were hurt?"

"Everybody," Bigelow replied.

CHAPTER 36

If you saw the blast, you know why they can't find some guys.
—LANCE CORPORAL STEVEN DIAZ
October 29, 1983

At 12:30 a.m. in Washington—barely eight minutes after the blast—word of the attack first sounded inside the National Military Command Center, a cavernous room spread across portions of the Pentagon's second and third floors. The two-story command center, which had been expanded and updated in 1976 at a cost of $15.4 million, featured one wall filled with six screens, allowing participants to view anything from routine capital weather to bomber strikes. Another wall boasted an alphanumeric display of the position and readiness of all American missiles aimed at the Soviet Union, while elsewhere a half dozen digital clocks showed the time in various regions around the globe. At the center of the room stood a twenty-five-foot-long table with a tan chair at the center reserved for the secretary of defense. "Dr. Strangelove," a newspaper reporter once marveled, "would feel right at home."

"Explosion at BLT ⅛ Hq," the flash message read. "A large explosion at BLT ⅛ Hq Bldg collapsed the roof and leveled the building. Large numbers of dead and wounded."

At the same time, alarms sounded inside the White House Situation Room and over at the State Department, less than a mile away. Staffers at all three agencies pored over the sudden flurry of message traffic between military forces in the Middle East and Europe—reports of heavy casualties, requests for medical evacuation flights—and jumped onto two conference calls to pool information. "As it became more clear what was happening, more people were made aware of it," one official said. "You obviously don't awaken the principals of the department until you're sure you have something that merits their attention."

That time had arrived.

A staffer at the National Military Command Center phoned Army Major General Colin Powell. The forty-six-year-old general, who served as Weinberger's senior military aide, knew immediately he had to alert his boss. At 1:30 a.m., he woke Weinberger. "The news came out in dribbles," recalled Powell, who continued to phone in updates. "Each time, I had to convey the mounting horror to a Defense Secretary who I knew was squeamish about death."

Forty-five minutes later, the Situation Room's watch officer rang Bud McFarlane at Augusta National Golf Course in Georgia. "I felt," the national security advisor later wrote, "as though I had been stabbed in the heart." McFarlane called the president at 2:39 a.m., informing him of the attack, which so far had a confirmed death count of approximately forty-five. McFarlane then hustled over to the Eisenhower Cottage and woke up Shultz, who along with his wife shared the quarters with the president and first lady. Six minutes later, Reagan, dressed in his yellow pajamas and a blue robe with matching slippers, emerged from his bedroom and took a seat on the couch with McFarlane and Shultz.

"How could this happen?" the president asked. "How bad is it? Who did it?"

The White House, which had battled Congress to keep Marines in Lebanon, had downplayed violence against them as isolated incidents. "The role there," an administration official had assured the press in September, "is as a peacekeeping force."

A terrorist bomb had shattered that illusion.

The president questioned whether he should order the Marines brought home. "McFarlane," as one account noted, "argued strongly against a recall." Reagan authorized officials in Washington to alert senior congressional leaders as well as Italian and French officials with the multinational force. The president phoned Marine Corps Commandant General Paul Kelley, asking him to find out more details on the extent of the casualties. Other issues the trio discussed included how to better protect the Marines, who could be held responsible for the attack, and what America's response should be. Most already suspected Iran. "Those sons of bitches," the president growled. "Let's find a way to go after them."

The politics of the attack likewise hung over Reagan, particularly how to deal with Congress. But none of those issues, he realized, could be handled from Augusta.

"Let's go back to Washington," the president announced.

Air Force One, McFarlane advised, could be ready at first light. "There was to be no more sleep for us that night," Reagan recalled as he settled in with McFarlane and Schulz. "As dawn approached, the news from Beirut became grimmer and grimmer."

At 6:34 a.m., the president and first lady departed the Eisenhower Cottage in the dark in a motorcade bound for the Augusta Municipal Airport. The plane roared down the runway and lifted off. Reagan, as he always did aboard Air Force One, slipped into sweatpants.

Air Force One reached Andrews Air Force Base less than two hours later, where the president climbed aboard a Marine helicopter at 8:25 a.m. for the ten-minute flight to the White House. The dark green Sikorsky VH-3D settled on the soggy South Lawn with the Washington Monument visible in the distance despite the fog and clouds that hung over the nation's capital on a day in which temperatures would top out in the upper fifties. Dressed in a tan overcoat and slacks, Reagan ducked his head as he exited.

"A somber President Reagan arrived at the White House," one aide recalled, "his face etched with every one of his seventy-two years."

The president and first lady paused at the south portico. Armed with an umbrella to fend off the drizzle, Reagan told the reporters he would not take any questions as he headed toward the Situation Room. "I know there are no words that can express our sorrow and grief over the loss of those splendid young men and the injury to so many others," he began. "I know there are no words also that can ease the burden of grief for the families of those young men."

Camera shutters rattled as the president spoke to the assembled journalists. Nancy stood to his left, her hand grasped in his. Shultz hovered in the background.

"Likewise, there are no words to properly express our outrage and, I think, the outrage of all Americans at the despicable act, following as it does on the one perpetrated several months ago in the spring that took the lives of scores of people at our Embassy." But the president refused to be deterred. "We should all recognize that these deeds make so evident the bestial nature of those who would assume power, if they could have their way and drive us out of that area, that we must be more determined than ever that they cannot take over that vital and strategic area of the earth or, for that matter, any other part of the earth."

Reagan briefly stopped by the residence before heading down to the Situation Room in the basement of the West Wing at 8:57 a.m. "Remind me to never go away again," he said to Weinberger as he took his seat at the head of the wooden table. "Look what happens."

Around the table and in chairs along the wall sat sixteen members of his cabinet and senior staff, including Vice President George Bush to his right and Shultz to his left. Others included Joint Chiefs Chairman General John Vessey and General Kelley. A map of Lebanon sat perched atop an easel. The seven items on the agenda were designed to provide the president with intelligence, military, and diplomatic updates prior to a discussion of how to handle the press and lawmakers. "He was in a white rage," recalled National Security Council staffer Major Oliver North, "but he was also as alert and as purposeful as I'd ever seen him."

"We'll make them pay," the president declared.

CHAPTER 37

*Pro-Iranian Lebanese elements are, for the moment,
considered prime suspects for the attacks.*
—DEFENSE INTELLIGENCE AGENCY
October 23, 1983

I n the offices of the Time & Life Building, which towered forty-eight
stories over the Avenue of the Americas, editor Jacalyn McConnell monitored the wire services and CNN. It had been an otherwise quiet night in the
midtown Manhattan offices of *Time* magazine. That week's issue was done.
Reporters based around the nation and globe had filed their stories. Editors
had then marked them up as designers assembled the photos and laid out the
pages. Elephantine presses rolled, spitting out millions of copies of the glossy
newsweekly that would hit the nation's newsstands that Monday.

Beirut wrecked that calm.

CBS claimed to be first with the breaking news shortly before 2:30
a.m., followed ten minutes later by CNN. Bulletins then moved on the
wire services. "Such late breaking news," *Time*'s publisher later noted, "is
the raison d'être of McConnell's job."

McConnell grabbed the phone and dialed the magazine's world senior editor, Henry Muller, followed by the deputy chief of correspondents, William
Mader. At 3:15 a.m., Muller in turn rang Ray Cave, the magazine's managing editor, who dressed and hustled into the headquarters forty-five minutes
later. "By 5:30 a.m.," one report noted, "all the beat reporters, principal writers, and support staff were filing into the New York office."

On the ground in Beirut, Middle East Bureau Chief William Stewart
reached the scene, phoning in the first eyewitness report. "In almost four
years of covering the Middle East," he dictated, "I have never seen a more
appalling or sickening sight than I saw this morning."

Stewart's report coupled with the mounting casualties testified to the
gravity of the tragedy unfolding six time zones away. At 7:30 a.m.—while the

ABOVE: Rescuers carry a victim of a terrorist bomb that wrecked the American Embassy in Beirut on April 18, 1983. The entire front of the building collapsed. *AP Photo*

BELOW: Workers pick through the debris of the American Embassy in Beirut, which was destroyed by a car bomb on April 18, 1983. *AP Photo*

President Ronald Reagan
and First Lady Nancy Reagan
honor the victims of the
embassy bombing during a
ceremony at Andrews Air Force
Base on April 23, 1983.
National Archives

ABOVE: Marines with the 24th MAU come ashore in Beirut on May 29, 1983.
National Archives

BELOW: The Battalion Landing Team headquarters building, known by the troops as the Beirut Hilton, was home to as many as 350 Marines, sailors, and soldiers.
National Archives

A Marine waves at a Lebanese youth while on a mobile patrol through Beirut on October 1, 1982, during a time when the troops were largely welcomed by the locals. *National Archives*

Marines jog past the ruins of a tank during their daily physical training on July 1, 1983. *National Archives*

ABOVE: A Marine stands near the wreckage of a car bomb—a frequent peril amid the chaos of Beirut—in November 1982. *Marine Corps*

OPPOSITE TOP: Defense Secretary Caspar Weinberger, pictured during a press conference in Beirut on December 1, 1982, urged President Reagan to end America's involvement in Lebanon. *National Archives*

OPPOSITE BOTTOM: Secretary of State George Shultz, pictured on a visit to Beirut on July 1, 1983, clashed with Weinberger over the use of Marines in Lebanon. *National Archives*

Marine frustration over the limited rules of engagement is reflected in the establishment of the Can't Shoot Back Saloon, pictured here on July 1, 1983. *National Archives*

CAN'T

T BACK

OON'

OPPOSITE TOP: Marines display a collection of questionable "stray rounds" that impacted around the Beirut International Airport in September 1983. *Marine Corps*

OPPOSITE BOTTOM: Navy Dr. John Hudson, pictured here with his infant son, Will, feared the violence would only escalate. He made sure dentists James Ware and Gilbert Bigelow were prepared for a possible mass casualty event. *Photo provided by Lisa Hudson*

ABOVE: Navy dentists James Ware (left) and Gilbert Bigelow spearheaded the medical rescue efforts after a terrorist bomb killed Dr. John Hudson. *Photo provided by James Ware*

A Marine sniper peers through the scope of the M-40A1 rifle as tensions increase on October 1, 1983. *National Archives*

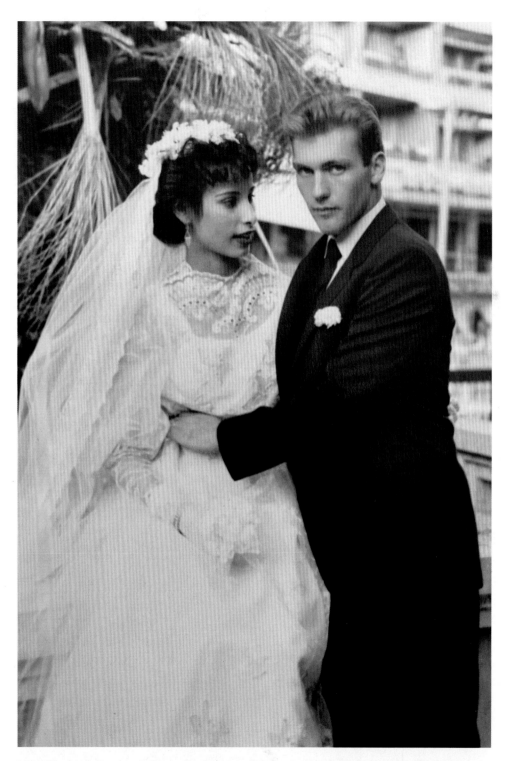

Navy Hospital Corpsman Bryan Earle married Lebanese local Micheline Abi Ghanem days before a terrorist bomb would claim Earle's life. *Photo provided by Micheline Thompson*

president was still aboard Air Force One returning to Washington—Cave made the extraordinary decision to trash the previously printed covers of that week's issue. *Time* would instead lead with the terrorist bombing in Beirut, a decision that would cost the magazine $300,000—a figure that would equal nearly $900,000 in today's figures. The hastily designed new cover featured a black-and-white photo of Marines carrying bloodied and shirtless Sergeant Armando Ybarra on a stretcher. "Carnage in Beirut," trumpeted the headline. "Mideast Madness Hits the Marines."

A similar story played out a few blocks away in the Madison Avenue offices of *Newsweek*, which likewise stopped the press run on its original cover story on the big business of medicine, but not before one million copies were printed. The remaining 2.5 million copies—or about 70 percent of its weekly circulation—would carry the new cover, making the magazine's loss about half that of its rival. "This is the latest cover story that *Newsweek* has ever put together from scratch on a Sunday," editor Maynard Parker said. "The last time *Newsweek* changed a cover on a Sunday was when Ford pardoned Nixon."

In a sign of how few photos were available in the aftermath, both *Time* and *Newsweek* used the same image for the cover. *Newsweek*'s international edition decried the "Slaughter in Beirut," while the domestic issues ran with the headline "The Marine Massacre."

U.S. News & World Report, the nation's other newsweekly, had gone to the printers at midnight Friday, forcing the magazine's 2.2 million readers to wait a week.

The CBS News desk called anchor Dan Rather at 3 a.m. He had issued standing orders to be notified in the event of any urgent news story. As the picture of the tragedy in Beirut crystallized, the desk phoned the *Evening News* anchor again at 6 a.m. By then the veteran newsman was already up and making tea.

"This is big," Rather was told.

Word likewise reached senior congressional leaders, many of whom had recently battled Reagan over the presence of Marines in Beirut. At 3 a.m. the State Department's congressional relations office phoned Senator Charles Percy, an Illinois Republican and chairman of the Senate Foreign Relations Committee. An hour later, the same office woke Senate Majority Leader Howard Baker, a Tennessee Republican, followed by Speaker of the House Thomas P. "Tip" O'Neill Jr., a Massachusetts Democrat. Many lawmakers, like Reagan, doubled down on America's position. "We should not leave," Baker said, "at the point of a gun."

CHAPTER 38

We are no longer a deterrent force in Lebanon.
We are a target. Our Marines are targets.
—Senator Sam Nunn
October 23, 1983

eputy Press Secretary Larry Speakes greeted reporters at 9:15 a.m. in the White House Briefing Room. The forty-four-year-old had assumed the role as the administration's lead spokesman on March 30, 1981, the day a deranged John Hinckley Jr. had shot his boss, James Brady, in the head above the left eye. Speakes had grown up in the Mississippi Delta town of Merigold, home to just 714 residents, a place so minuscule, in fact, it lacked a movie theater, barbershop, or even street signs. The sandy-haired southerner later enrolled at Ole Miss, though he dropped out to pursue journalism in the civil rights era. A love of politics led him to become the press secretary for his home state senator James Eastland, which proved a springboard to similar roles in the administrations of Richard Nixon, Gerald Ford, and now Ronald Reagan. Known to friends as "the Mississippi Catfish," Speakes adored Elvis and Merle Haggard, though the job's stress often prompted him to turn to Mozart to quiet his nerves.

Since the days of Teddy Roosevelt, reporters had roamed the halls of the West Wing, hunting for stories while working out of offices that had grown increasingly congested as the number of White House reporters climbed. Understanding the importance of television in politics, Nixon had undertaken a $574,000 renovation thirteen years earlier, converting Franklin Roosevelt's pool into a plush new press office featuring a dozen broadcast booths, forty desks, and a built-in stage for briefings. Reporters could hammer out stories against the backdrop of the gentle tunes of Muzak or simply unwind atop the beige suede Chesterfield sofas. "This," Nixon declared on a tour upon completion, "is better looking than the Hilton."

Much of Washington had been awake for hours, buzzing about the terrorist attack as Speakes approached the lectern. "The information I'm going to run through here is simply to probably give you information you have already received from Beirut, seen on the wires, and so forth," he began. "But at least it will establish where we are and everything."

Speakes gave a brief account of the attack, from the time of the blast to the Marine units involved. At the moment, casualties stood at 76 killed and 112 wounded. The French, he added, so far counted 18 confirmed dead. Lebanese foreign minister Elie Salem had phoned American ambassador Reginald Bartholomew to convey his nation's regret and horror. Red Cross and local disaster relief agencies meanwhile provided aid while workers used construction equipment to clear rubble and search for survivors. At the moment, the president was in the Situation Room for a briefing he anticipated would run about an hour.

As soon as Speakes wrapped up his remarks, journalists opened fire with questions. "Do you plan to send more troops?" one reporter asked.

"Were there any movements ordered earlier today?" added another. "Any diversion of naval units?"

Speakes answered as best he could with the limited information then available in Washington. The president's meeting that morning, he explained, would address contingencies, including whether additional troops would be sent to the Middle East. Only fifteen minutes earlier, he added, the Pentagon reported no major movement of forces. "Now, whether tactical movements are taking place, I think that would be better to come from Beirut."

Questions then turned to who might have executed the attack.

"Certainly, we do have, as we've had all along, some suspicions, but we're not in a position to go into what we may suspect," the press secretary said.

Reporters proved quick to connect that morning's truck bombing of the Marine headquarters with the similar suicide strike on the American Embassy just 188 days earlier. "Do you think," one reporter asked, "the same group is responsible for both?"

Speakes chose to answer that question on background, meaning reporters could not use his name in print and he would be listed simply as a "Senior Administration Official" in the White House transcript. "It's much too early for us to draw those conclusions," Speakes cautioned. "As I say, we have suspicions. We are looking closely at that."

Another reporter chimed in that other officials already blamed Iran.

"Some people in the government do have that suspicion," Speakes confirmed. "But I don't even want to, on background, pinpoint it that much, because honestly I don't think we can—we don't have conclusive evidence that we can state to you now."

"Who blew up the American Embassy?" a journalist asked.

"Has there been any claim by any group?" another added.

"Not that I'm aware of," Speakes said.

"Who blew up the American Embassy?" a reporter pressed.

"I don't think we ever came to a public determination on that," Speakes said. "There have been a lot of suspicions, a lot of intelligence, but nothing that we ever have stated publicly."

"So does that mean we are still trying to find out who did it?"

"Certainly," the press secretary said.

"We don't know who conclusively did it?"

"I don't think we ever really said firmly," Speakes replied.

"But do you know?" a reporter asked.

"What's the holdup?" added another.

The press secretary tried to shut down that line of questioning. "I think you've gone far afield here," he argued. "When we're prepared to state it publicly, we will do so. Meanwhile, we continue to assess information beginning with the embassy bombing right on through terrorist acts that have taken place up until 12:20 a.m. this morning."

CHAPTER 39

We have put these Marines in an impossible position.
—Representative John Murtha
November 8, 1983

At the same time Speakes tangled with the press, veteran journalist Lesley Stahl fought her own battle for information with the administration. The forty-one-year-old White House correspondent and new host of CBS's *Face the Nation* had, like others across the capital, received word of the attack via a 3 a.m. phone call. She got up, dressed, and hustled to the studio. Her weekly news program, which had held public officials accountable in Washington since it first aired in November 1954, had previously booked Weinberger to appear that Sunday morning to talk about the escalating violence against Marines in Lebanon.

Would the attack prompt him to cancel?

Stahl jumped onto a call with David Gergen, the forty-one-year-old White House communications director. A former journalist, Gergen, like many others in the capital, had migrated over to public service, serving in the Nixon and Ford administrations before landing a job with Reagan. "We're awfully sorry," Gergen leveled with Stahl. "But Cap's in a national security meeting in the Situation Room which we think could go on for several hours."

"But David," Stahl pressed, "don't you think the American people are going to want some word from the administration? We're talking about the wanton murder of who knows how many Americans."

Gergen listened.

"Let us set up a camera crew in the White House," she continued. "All Cap would have to do is leave the meeting for ten minutes max."

The communications director assured her he would ask. He phoned back soon after, informing Stahl that Weinberger was, in fact, considering the interview.

"We'll send our crew right over," she said.

In the CBS studio Stahl prepared an updated list of questions. No one knew for certain if Weinberger would show up. Gergen loitered in the

Roosevelt Room as the CBS crew ran power cords and set up lights, a tripod, and a camera. Stahl anxiously stared into the camera.

"No guarantees," Gergen reminded her.

Downstairs in the Situation Room, the president and his national security advisors reviewed the details of the attack followed by the latest intel, which pointed to Iran.

"Can't we do anything to Iran?" Reagan asked.

"It might make us all feel better," Weinberger cautioned, "but that would not punish those responsible." The defense secretary advocated pulling the Marines back aboard ship, a suggestion that drew pushback from Shultz. "To withdraw now would undermine our entire policy," he warned. "It would be a disaster for American prestige."

At 10:30 a.m.—and as the National Security Planning Group meeting neared its conclusion—Weinberger slipped out and headed upstairs to the Roosevelt Room, situated right across the hall from the Oval Office. Stahl felt an incredible sense of relief wash over her when she saw the defense secretary slip into the chair. "I almost wept," she later confessed. The nation, which had woken up that Sunday morning to the horrible news of the terrorist attack, hungered for answers. Unlike Speakes, who had fumbled through his briefing and talked largely only on background, Weinberger was America's top defense official and a household name.

His word mattered.

And he knew it.

More importantly, Weinberger had to mask his personal opinions, which differed from those of his boss. "I was very well aware," he wrote, "that today, one inadvertence or awkward answer on my part could cause a very great deal of damage."

The red light flashed on; the show was live. "Mr. Secretary," Stahl began, "you have just left a meeting of the National Security Council. What response is the Reagan administration planning in light of the deaths of all of these Marines this morning?"

"The immediate reaction here is one of enormous sadness and great outrage at this act of senseless terrorism, which is very similar, perhaps perpetrated by the same people to the attack on our embassy some months ago," he began. "There's also, of course, a full-scale attempt to find out just who is responsible, and that investigation is underway."

"But what about the response?" Stahl pressed, reminding him that Reagan previously said we would not stand by and let Marines be brutalized.

"That is certainly true," he said, though he cautioned that America, despite circumstantial evidence and suspicions, needed to first confirm who ordered the attack.

"Am I to assume that no reprisal action has been planned as of this point?" she pressed.

"No, you can't assume anything," he shot back. "The meeting is not over and there is a great deal of discussion about what would be suitable and the best things that should be done."

"When the president spoke on the lawn this morning, he made a veiled reference to whom he thought might be responsible. It sounded a little bit as though he might be blaming the Syrians or even the Soviets. Is that what's in your mind?"

"There is a lot of circumstantial evidence and a certain amount of it points toward Iran," he said, adding that there are many groups in that area that have made threats. "Obviously we're looking at everything and looking at it very carefully."

"Is there any possibility that we will be beefing up the Marine contingent there?"

The Marines were in Beirut, he noted, to provide a secure environment for a peace deal. That was not going to change by adding more Marines. The important action, Weinberger said, was to decrease the vulnerability and risks faced by the Marines.

"There's no talk of pulling them out, then?" Stahl asked.

"No," he said. "Our commitment to the cause of securing a peaceful Mideast of course remains because it's absolutely vital to our national interest and it's absolutely vital to the interest of the free world. We can't simply leave the area to terrorism."

"The administration will obviously come under enormous pressure to pull the Marines out. There's already considerable public opinion in support of pulling them out. You have been quoted as saying you think they should come out. Have you changed your mind personally and are you now fully committed to keeping this contingent of 1,600 Marines in Beirut?"

"The goal remains the same and the commitment is unchanged despite this horrible tragedy," he said, "and it's just a further reminder of the kind of world in which we live and how dangerous it is and how much risk there is in everything we do."

CHAPTER 40

The volume of casualties was incredible.
—DR. PATRICK HUTTON
January 27, 2023

O n board the *Iwo Jima*, doctors, nurses, and hospital corpsmen hustled to prepare for scores of casualties. The 18,000-ton warship, which carried twenty-two helicopters and was designed to transport Marines into combat, would serve this Sunday as a mobile emergency room. With a deck that stretched 602 feet in length—a distance comparable to almost two football fields—the *Iwo Jima* sported a crew of 650 sailors and could accommodate an additional 2,000 Marines in air-conditioned berths. An onboard utility plant generated enough power to light a small town as well as distill up to 100,000 gallons of fresh water each day for use by galley cooks and sailors in need of a hot shower and a shave. The *Iwo Jima* boasted a bakery, post office, and library, not to mention a barbershop and store, which sold everything from magazines and greeting cards to radios and even jewelry. Sailors looking for a deal could pick up tax-free cigarettes on Mondays, Wednesdays, and Fridays, or unwind nightly with an 8 p.m. movie shown in the hangar bay. "It is," as the ship's welcoming brochure bragged, "virtually a city in itself."

Like any city, the *Iwo Jima* featured a hospital, complete with two fully equipped operating rooms, an x-ray suite, and a two-bed intensive care unit. The ship's seven-bed general ward could be expanded to care for up to one hundred injured sailors and Marines. A general medical officer ran the *Iwo Jima*'s small hospital with the help of a dozen corpsmen. In case of just such a crisis, the Navy had deployed Surgical Team Fourteen aboard the ship. This nineteen-person mobile unit—one of fifteen such rapid-response teams in the Navy—featured a general and orthopedic surgeon as well as an anesthesiologist and nurse anesthetist. Other members included an operating room nurse, administrative officer, plus another thirteen corpsmen, all trained to work in the operating room. "The wisdom of this deployment," the team's three doctors later observed in a report, "was to prove itself on this day."

The dual medical organizations had worked in tandem since arrival off the coast of Beirut in May, tackling routine medical procedures, from twisted knees to the occasional hernia or hemorrhoid surgery. Dr. Fraser Henderson, the twenty-nine-year-old head of the *Iwo Jima*'s medical department, had spent part of his youth on a cattle farm in the Australian Outback. That rugged experience had taught him a vital lesson. "You always," he said, "have to plan for the worst." To do just that, Henderson had ordered thousands of bags of intravenous fluids, enough to handle more than a hundred patients. He likewise secured additional antibiotics, bandages, and test tubes. Henderson and the others then created an emergency plan to convert the sprawling hangar bay into a triage center. A locker stored on deck held intravenous fluids and sets of tubing and needles and catheters. The doctors recruited volunteers from the ship's crew to help. Each patient would have a designated attendant armed with a clipboard and pen to jot down notes dictated by the doctor, but more importantly these volunteers would offer comfort to the wounded. "My mission," Henderson recalled, "was to plan for mass casualties."

That plan was put into action Sunday morning as the first helicopters loaded with the wounded touched down on the *Iwo Jima* at 7:40 a.m., one hour and nineteen minutes after the explosion. Stretcher bearers rushed them down the aircraft elevator to the hangar bay, which the air boss had cleared of all helicopters, as hospital corpsmen readied racks to hold stretchers. "Everyone knew their place," Henderson said. "Everyone was in position."

Similar to what Bigelow and Ware did onshore, medics on the *Iwo Jima* performed an initial survey, checking airways, blood pressure, and pulse rates. "Each of the wounded was inspected for the presence of arms and explosive devices," one report added. "The master-at-arms was available in case of infiltration among the wounded by a terrorist." Hospital corpsmen administered fluids to maximize circulation and combat shock while doctors armed with stethoscopes listened to each patient's heart and lungs. Neurological exams followed to confirm whether a patient could feel his arms and legs, feet and hands. When needed, medics inserted catheters and splinted fractures. Others gave injections of antibiotics and tetanus. "Identification was a critical thing, knowing exactly who we had on board," Henderson said. "That's not medical care, but it turned out to be one of the most important things we did, identifying every single patient."

Despite the organization and resources, doctors could not provide in-depth or definitive care to a vast number of wounded. Medical evacuation planes, which the Navy had requested three minutes after the blast, were inbound from Turkey, Italy, and Cyprus. The job of those on the *Iwo Jima* that Sunday morning was to stabilize patients for transport to shore-based hospitals, either at an American base four hours away in Germany or Italy or at the British Royal Air Force hospital in Cyprus, less than an hour's flight from Beirut. Those planes, however, would not arrive for hours, prompting doctors to transfer patients in need of immediate surgery up to the operating room. The rest would be ranked for priority of evacuation.

The volume of wounded soon skyrocketed.

Within ninety minutes, sixty-five of the worst-injured Marines and sailors crowded the hangar bay, organized into two long lines, one dedicated to the more seriously wounded. Men arrived with cracked skulls and crush injuries. Others suffered broken bones, contusions, and ruptured eardrums. Many had inhaled dust and smoke or suffered intra-abdominal injuries. "There were," as one medical report stated, "no walking wounded." Doctors had to insert chest tubes and irrigate eyes. Medics observed that the dust often was caked on so thick that it made it impossible to discern a patient's ethnicity. "All of them," Henderson noted, "were in shock."

The sixty-five injured sent to the *Iwo Jima* that morning, a post-attack analysis revealed, amounted to almost half of the 112 wounded in the terrorist attack. Of that total, twenty-six were treated for minor injuries by the Battalion Aid Station and returned to duty. Fourteen others landed in Lebanese hospitals, while the rest would go directly from the rubble to medical evacuation flights. Seven died during treatment, including two that Sunday.

Thirty-seven of the wounded suffered from various and often multiple head injuries, including thirteen with skull fractures. Nearly half of those were either depressed or compound fractures. Six others had broken facial bones, while twenty more had split scalps that required debridement and sutures. One out of every four suffered a concussion.

Dr. Patrick Hutton, the orthopedist with Surgical Team Fourteen, witnessed some of the worst, including a Marine whose brain was visible through an open skull fracture.

"Am I going to die?" the young man asked.

Hutton knew he would.

Hospital corpsmen carried the Marine forward of the operating room to the general medical ward. "The idea," Hutton said, "was to have a quiet space for him." The thirty-five-year-old doctor then took a break from his work and sat with the Marine, wanting to comfort him and make sure he was not alone when he passed. "I talked," Hutton said, "did some prayers."

The Marine held on for fifteen minutes before he slipped away.

The pressure on the doctors, nurses, and hospital corpsmen proved intense. "Keep your head down, keep working," Henderson told himself. "It's going to work out."

Despite that tension, the medical teams remained organized and professional. Doctors circulated among the wounded while every ten minutes hospital corpsmen rechecked each patient's vital signs. Volunteers perched alongside the injured, holding their hands and whispering words of comfort. Henderson looked up to spot one of the ship's bakers helping out, still dressed in his white hat. "Everyone was just doing what they had to do," the doctor said. "It was extraordinary." Lieutenant Commander Mauricio Aparicio, the head nurse for Surgical Team Fourteen and the one who conceived of using volunteers to comfort the wounded, agreed. "Nobody was yelling. Nobody was screaming," he said. "Every patient had somebody with them. That was phenomenal to me."

Some of the wounded, like Lance Corporal John L'Heureux, who was impaled by debris, would never even remember being on board the *Iwo Jima*. The nineteen-year-old Massachusetts native had climbed into his sleeping bag on the roof of the Battalion Landing Team headquarters and closed his eyes at 4 a.m. for a nap. "I woke up," he said, "in Germany." Others who drifted in and out of consciousness would recall only snippets, including Lance Corporal Michael Toma, who had been asleep on the ground floor when the bomb exploded. "While I was in the ship's infirmary I vomited blood," the Pennsylvanian said. "A catheter was inserted and I observed blood in my urine. At this point I began to question whether I would survive my injuries." Lance Corporal Emanuel Simmons, who had clung to his left wrist since he found it below the rubble, did not realize until he was on a helicopter inbound to the *Iwo Jima* that his arm was, in fact, still attached, albeit broken. "Tell the guys," he begged sailors, "I'm okay."

Starting at 12:30 p.m., helicopters began transporting stabilized patients back to the Lebanese capital, where the wounded would soon board medical evacuation flights for hospitals in Europe. The first such plane, an Air Force C-9 from Turkey, touched down at Beirut International Airport ten minutes later. A C-130 from the British Royal Air Force arrived at 1:10 p.m., followed a half hour later by a Navy C-9 out of Sigonella, Italy. The fourth and final plane of the day was an Air Force C-141, which would not arrive until 7:40 p.m.

Hospital corpsmen hustled to load the wounded onto medevac planes that featured metal racks along each side that allowed stretchers to be stacked four high, leaving a narrow central corridor for doctors and hospital corpsmen to maneuver. Bags of intravenous fluids dangled from overhead hooks. During this time, a wounded Marine, just pulled from the rubble, arrived at the landing zone with a massive head injury. "Patient was judged terminal," one cable stated, "senior medical officers on scene elected to take patient for humanitarian reasons in that medication could start immediately and medical team would do all they could till death."

At 2:21 p.m.—exactly eight hours after the terrorist attack—the first plane roared down the runway and climbed into the skies, the Royal Air Force's C-130 bound for Cyprus. An Air Force C-9 followed at 3:12 p.m., headed for Germany, while a Navy C-9 lifted off at 3:51 p.m. for Naples. Those first three planes carried a total of fifty-six wounded Marines and sailors. The final C-141 with thirteen patients would not leave for Germany until 10:49 p.m.

Sergeant Pablo Arroyo, whose body was riddled with dozens of holes and who had lost almost a third of his teeth, was strapped down on a stretcher on the C-9 bound for Germany. The New Yorker stared up at the bottom of the stretcher above, where he watched blood from his fellow wounded Marine spread across and saturate the canvas. "Pablo, I thought to myself, no matter how bad you are, you are better off than the guy above you."

Steps away rested Navy corpsman Don Howell, who had followed a beam of light out of the basement of the destroyed building. Medics had since bandaged both of his eyes, forcing him to interpret his surroundings via sound. He could hear the familiar beep of heart monitors as well as Marines calling out to one another, asking who was on board, who had survived. "Did he make it?" was a question repeated over and over again. "Did he make it?"

"I don't know," was sadly the common refrain.

Twenty minutes into the flight, Howell heard the terminal patient with a head injury begin to code. He sensed the movement of the onboard medical staff as each converged on the dying Marine. From his days as a corpsman in the Charleston Naval Hospital, Howell could envision the frantic yet fruitless effort to save him: chest compressions, intravenous push of medications, and fluids. "Then," Howell recalled, "it was over."

CHAPTER 41

Beirut was just destruction, absolute total destruction.
—Dr. Gilbert Bigelow
January 25, 2023

Work continued Sunday afternoon in Beirut as the job evolved from rescue to recovery. Men used jackhammers to break up the concrete and blowtorches and hacksaws to slice through the sinuous veins of rebar that held the building's skeletal remains together. "All of the rescuers looked like ants on an anthill, but no one slowed down or vacillated," Geraghty said. "The more I surveyed this heinous scene of absolute madness, a seething rage again rose within me toward those who committed this despicable act of war against peacekeepers. The rows of dead bodies and body parts and the shattered, burned bodies of the severely wounded all added to my disgust to this act of pure terrorism." Geraghty wasn't alone. "During the day," Glenn Dolphin added, "my mood went from shock and terror to anger and thoughts of revenge."

Sporadic sniper fire slowed recovery efforts.

So, too, did Lebanese looters.

Through it all, the Marines worked. "This energy comes from somewhere," Bigelow said. "I don't know where it comes from but you just keep going until you can't go anymore."

Situation reports charted the steadily rising tally of the dead. The 30 reported killed that morning jumped to 57, then 76, 111, 135, and 146, a number that would continue to rise in the hours ahead as rescuers stripped back layer after layer of the wreckage. With the critically wounded patients airlifted to the *Iwo Jima*, the frenetic pace of medical efforts at Battalion Aid Station slowed, giving Ware a moment to breathe.

"I've got to go over there and figure out what's going on," he announced.

The dentist, who had yet to glimpse the bomb site, made his way to the ruins of the Battalion Landing Team headquarters. "When I saw the building, it was unimaginable," he recalled, "even with the patients I had seen, it was still unimaginable."

Rounds continued to cook off underground, prompting Geraghty to worry that the smoldering fires beneath the rubble might ignite the large antitank missiles stored in the basement. Rescuers hauled the deceased to a makeshift morgue set up in a Lebanese Air Force maintenance hangar near the helicopter landing zone. The mortuary plan called for remains to be flown to Germany, where identification would be confirmed through fingerprints and dental records. Workers placed bodies—many caked in dust and blood—atop cots and on the floor until the deceased could be secured in metal transfer cases, which the medevac planes had delivered. Others created piles of arms, legs, and heads. Over it all hung the stench of burned flesh, vomit, and excrement. "Mom, I put four of my very best friends in body bags," wrote an anguished Brad Ulick, who worked in the morgue. "I hurt so bad and I want to cry, but I cannot. I can't even accept the fact it happened. I am mad, hurt, crushed, empty and much more. What do I do? I could always rely on you for wisdom. Mom, what in Christ's name do I do?"

Since that morning, news media had swarmed the area. The terrorist attack was one of the largest stories in the world, one whose carnage stunned even veteran reporters in the war-torn capital of Beirut. *New York Times* reporter Thomas Friedman, shaken from his bed ten miles away, had rushed to the scene. That morning's paper carried Friedman's latest article on how Washington's actions had transformed the Marines into combatants. "Elusive Targets," the prophetic headline stated. "Peacekeepers Become Another Warring Faction."

"This is incredible," Friedman confided in his colleague Robert Fisk as the journalists surveyed the destruction. "It is the most brilliant act of terrorism."

Fisk, who reported for the British daily the *Times*, couldn't help but agree. "This was," he observed, "the most professional massacre ever perpetrated in Lebanon."

Major Bob Jordan, the lead public affairs officer, accommodated the reporters, many of them noticing his bloodstained forearms, a by-product of digging dead and wounded Marines from the rubble. From that day forward, as many as 160 print, radio, and broadcast journalists would visit each day. The only ground rules were that reporters could not photograph identifiable bodies or body parts. "We let them shoot, let them do their jobs," Randy Gaddo added. "We wanted the American public to know what happened."

But tensions still flared.

Emotionally and physically exhausted Marines, who had spent hours pulling friends from the ruins, resented the media's presence. At one point, Marines confronted a photographer as he snapped a photo of a body being hauled from the wreckage. "The men are very sensitive right now," Jordan cautioned the journalists. "They have a lot of grief today. You guys are voyeurs to them. They think it's obscene for you to come looking around."

Gaddo, who worked daily with the press, felt that conflict personally. "How does this make you feel seeing this?" one reporter asked him on a tour.

He later acknowledged that it was a legitimate question, one designed to elicit an emotional response, but at that moment he was too raw. "That is the stupidest damn question I've ever heard," Gaddo barked at the reporter. "How do you think it makes me feel?"

Throughout the day, journalists interviewed Marines willing to talk. Some of them questioned what the attack might mean for the mission. "I only wish now that President Reagan would pull us out," Lance Corporal Walter Maxey, who guarded the main gate, told a reporter. Private First Class Albert Burton nodded in agreement. "We're speaking for everyone out here."

Along with bodies, workers recovered M16s and .45s from the wreckage, many with bent barrels and splintered stocks, stacking them in piles. "Some of the .45s," Dolphin said, "had been smashed by the weight of the concrete and exposed to the heat of the fires in such a way that the frames and slides of the weapons were effectively welded together."

Classified documents surfaced amid the debris along with the pages of military manuals. Mixed in with official files were personal items, what one reporter hauntingly described as the "loose ends of men's lives." Cassette tapes and athletic shorts. Photos, letters, and cash. The crushed carton of a Monopoly game and a box of raisins. A *Playboy* centerfold. The wind blew pages of a Bible across the airport highway while a journalist found the ripped-out page of a hymnal featuring the funeral song "Be Not Afraid."

Marines paused at times, holding items that reflected the shattered lives of friends and brothers. "When you picked up a picture and it was some guy's kid or it was him with his wife," recalled Mark Singleton, "that would tear your guts out."

"Bastards," one Marine said as he sorted through such belongings.

A similar story unfolded several miles to the north, where rescuers dug through the remains of the French headquarters, using five bulldozers, two cranes, and scores of Lebanese volunteers. Rescuers pumped oxygen into the rubble to help anyone who might still be alive. Littered amid the rubble, reporters observed sleeping bags, mess kits, toothpaste tubes, novels, and a photo of a French soldier twirling his red beret on a beach.

"What beasts!" one soldier hollered. "What an insane country."

Periodic sniper fire continued to harass the Marines that afternoon, forcing them to break and take cover. Amid the strain, one gunnery sergeant snapped. "You motherfuckers," he shouted. "You dirty motherfuckers. Come and get some, you bastards."

Lebanese looters proved another frustration. Father Pucciarelli caught one rescue worker trying on a pair of boots next to a dead Marine. John Dalziel observed an arm protruding from two slabs of concrete. As the day passed, he noted, the watch and the ring vanished. So, too, did other items. "It's like salt in the wound," he remembered. "It's just shitty."

Navy dental technician Paul Dziadon, who was based aboard the *Iwo Jima*, had flown ashore to help. The twenty-five-year-old had spent much of the morning helping dig out the wounded and administering first aid. He approached Dr. Ware that afternoon.

"Lieutenant," he asked. "What do you need me to do?"

Ware had a big job for him, one that would prove vital in the days ahead, as technicians in Germany struggled to identify the remains of the deceased. "I've got to get the dental records out," Ware told him, "so we've got some identification."

Those records had been stored in the basement of the Battalion Landing Team headquarters. If the files even survived the bombing and subsequent fires, finding them would require tunneling down through the unstable rubble. Dziadon jumped on it.

Armed with a flashlight, the dental technician wormed his way through the large slabs of rubble down into the basement. Once inside, he discovered several more dead bodies along with boxes of dental records, which were still largely intact. He dragged the boxes out. Workers loaded them on a plane to Germany the next morning. "He was a hero," Ware said of Dziadon. "He probably never received credit for how brave and courageous and selfless he was."

The afternoon faded to evening. Floodlights illuminated the pile, giving it the familiar glow of a Friday night football game as workers settled in to dig through the night.

Inside the logistics office, others began the painful task of sorting confidential materials from personal items, a job that fell to Michael Petit. The corporal opened the first of dozens of plastic bags. "The smell of the bombing—the smell of dirt and blood—assaulted my nostrils," he said. "It was as if I was back at the building. I battled with my stomach, trying not to gag."

Inside a torn and bloodied leather satchel, Petit found a stack of letters, including a handmade birthday card covered in hearts drawn by a little girl.

"I love you Daddy," the card read.

Petit's heart sank.

He thumbed through other torn and bloodstained letters, carefully putting aside personal items to be saved. "I miss you and am very worried," one note stated.

"I don't have to tell you how proud we are," added another.

"It's a boy!" announced yet another.

Petit could stomach it for only so long. He felt like a grave robber, sifting through the intimate lives of the dead. The corporal headed for the exit. The awful stench of death hit him again as he wiped tears from his eyes. "It was ground into my hands and clothes," he recalled. "There was no way I could escape it. I doubled over, vomiting onto the dark red earth."

Petit wasn't the only one to struggle that night. Rabbi Resnicoff, who had spent the day ministering to the dead and dying, found a few moments to pen a letter to his wife and mother. "I am all right, but things here are beyond description," he wrote. "There are bodies—and pieces of bodies—all over." In closing, he assured his family he would see them soon. "This is one time I'm needed," he concluded. "I'm all right. It's just a terrible, terrible tragedy."

The day's adrenaline was replaced by exhaustion.

Some would work through the night, while others would find a spot on a cot or in a corner to grab a few minutes or hours of sleep, though at times even that proved difficult for many. "Every time you closed your eyes," Brad Ulick recalled, "you had nightmares." Dziadon returned to the *Iwo Jima*, where he sat down for a late-night meal that had been put out for them. To his surprise, the Navy had prepared ribs, which killed his appetite. "I saw," he recalled, "enough ribs that day." The dental technician instead stripped down and took a shower. "I couldn't get that smell off of me," he said. "I threw up and then I broke down."

Dziadon wasn't alone. The horror of what they had endured and seen caught up with them. Petit stretched out near midnight on the floor of the basement. Even as he closed his eyes, he could hear the rhythmic pounding of jackhammers breaking up concrete.

"Are you okay?" a friend on the floor nearby asked.

"I don't think I'm ever going to be okay," he answered.

CHAPTER 42

Jesus, why? I don't blame you, but why does Satan have the power to do this?
—CORPORAL BRAD ULICK, DIARY ENTRY
October 24, 1983

At 11:13 a.m. that Sunday in Washington, Larry Speakes approached the lectern for the second time to face reporters. The president had just concluded an hour-and-forty-minute meeting with his national security advisors to assess the tragedy in Beirut. Reagan had asked for additional information, Speakes noted, which he would receive when the group reconvened at 4 p.m. In addition, Weinberger had spoken by phone to his French counterpart, while State Department and White House officials briefed members of Congress starting at 5:20 a.m. "The assessment," Speakes assured the press, "is that the mission of the United States and the multinational force has not changed. There is no change in our commitment, and we are exploring ways to reduce the vulnerability of our forces in Lebanon."

"The Marines will stay in present numbers?" a reporter asked.

"There's no change in our commitment," the press secretary repeated. "There's no change in our mission."

"Do you have any new casualty figures?"

The Pentagon, Speakes said, would soon announce those numbers.

Has the president ordered any retaliation?

"Not at the moment," he added.

"What's the circumstantial evidence that's pointing to Iran?" another asked.

Evidence gathered since the embassy attack in April, Speakes said, coupled with more recent intelligence involving the sniper attacks against the Marines.

"Secretary Weinberger did not rule out an act of reprisal," a reporter observed, circling back to the question of American retaliation. "What do you say about this?"

There have been no decisions yet, he said, or even recommendations.

"What is the circumstantial evidence that the Iranians are involved?" another asked again.

"Intelligence," Speakes said.

"Was there any surprise and has there been any study of how a truck could crash through a gate and get all the way into the headquarters without being stopped?"

"That's exactly what they're looking at on the ground," the press secretary replied. "That's what we would like answers to, also."

Did the president plan to visit the wounded? Would the Marines be repositioned? Had the administration reached out to Iran? The transcript shows that Speakes had few answers during the nineteen-minute briefing, given that the attack had occurred less than twelve hours earlier and half a world away, where the focus remained on rescue operations.

"I don't know the answer to that," he confessed at one point.

"I honestly do not know," he responded another time.

"I do not know specifically."

That did not stop reporters, who continued to holler questions. "Can you tell us what information the president is looking for?" a reporter asked.

"Any and all," Speakes concluded. "We'd like to find out who did this."

CHAPTER 43

No reason exists for troops in Lebanon. Provide Security.
Define Purpose. And bring the troops home now.
—MOLLY MARKERT, TELEGRAM TO THE WHITE HOUSE
October 25, 1983

The absence of concrete information did not prevent many on Capitol Hill from sounding off about the tragedy, which threatened to rip open the wounds from the administration's recent battle over the War Powers Resolution. To ease the anxiety, White House officials reached out to senior congressional leaders, including arranging for Secretary of State Shultz to brief the Senate Foreign Relations Committee. "If there was any central theme," *Washington Post* reporter Helen Dewar observed, "it involved horror, frustration and complaints that the administration needs to clarify, and perhaps redefine, the purpose of the Marine deployment."

That was evident in the comments of many lawmakers.

"The role of our Marines has not been clearly defined," argued Senate Minority Leader Robert Byrd, a West Virginia Democrat. "At present, our people are just sitting ducks in a defenseless situation where they don't even know who is attacking them."

"What are the Marines doing there?" asked Senator Sam Nunn, a Georgia Democrat.

Despite the outcry, few called for the immediate removal of U.S. forces. The attack once again underscored America's challenge. A pullout, many believed, would not only doom Lebanon but send a message to the world that terrorism works. "People say we ought to get the Marines out of there; that is an easy thing to say," House Speaker Tip O'Neill commented. "But what are the circumstances ultimately? It would be a complete victory for the Russians."

After finishing up in the Situation Room that morning, the president stopped by the Oval Office before heading upstairs to the residence, no doubt tired after the early start to what had proven a stressful day. He had lunch with the first lady at 12:10 p.m., after which he spoke for several minutes on the phone with Gemayel, who expressed his condolences.

At 3:57 p.m., Reagan returned to the Situation Room to meet with the National Security Planning Group. The two-page declassified agenda shows that the meeting would begin with an intelligence briefing by CIA deputy director John McMahon, who would address "issues bearing on decisions to retaliate." That included a review of the intel prior to the bombing as well as the "location and vulnerability of factions implicated in planning and execution of Beirut attacks." Shultz and Weinberger would argue the pros and cons of a counterstrike, while McFarlane would review the "need for additional intelligence" and "planning for retaliatory measures." Other agenda items included a proposed press statement, how to reduce the vulnerability of the Marines, and the need to send a delegation to Beirut.

Even after more than four decades, the thirteen-page meeting minutes remain classified. The declassified portions of the five-page intelligence talking points prepared for McMahon, however, blame Iran for the bombing. "Our best judgment," the memo stated, "is that Iranian-supported radical Shia groups were responsible for the attacks." Those same groups, the document continued, were "principally responsible" for the recent sniper attacks, which killed two Marines. American intelligence specifically pointed to Islamic Amal, the terror group led by Hussein al-Musawi, which operated out of the Bekaa Valley and formed part of Hezbollah, as the perpetrators. "There is also a possibility of Syrian involvement," the memo continued. "At a minimum we believe Damascus has turned a blind eye to the activities of its Iranian allies and provided indirect support by allowing them to move through Syria into Lebanon. Syrian intelligence officials in Lebanon may be providing additional assistance." A spot report that day from the Defense Intelligence Agency echoed the CIA, accusing Hezbollah of both the embassy bombing and recent sniper attacks. "The French are a logical target of Iranian sympathizers vengeance," the report added, "since they are a primary arms supplier of Iraq."

Few in Washington doubted the intelligence community's assessment, including Reagan, who vented his frustration that night in his personal diary. "We all believe Iranians did this bombing," the president wrote, "just as they did with our embassy last April."

Reports from participants show that debate during the three-hour meeting largely mirrored the morning session with the secretaries of state and defense arguing over whether America should retaliate. "We need to show resolve," Shultz said. "We need to take action against those who committed this atrocity and strengthen the Lebanese government."

"It must be directed at those who perpetrated the act," Weinberger warned.

"We must show," Reagan interjected, "that the cause was worth dying for."

Based on the meeting, the president signed National Security Decision Directive No. 109, titled "Responding to the Crisis in Lebanon." The two-page document—of which two lines still remain classified—provides a window into Sunday's secretive discussions. "The Director of Central Intelligence will prepare an urgent summary of all source intelligence detailing what we know about the elements which planned, perpetrated, supported, or otherwise facilitated these attacks," the order stated. "That assessment should include the best information we have about the location of line units and headquarters for these elements." The possibility of Syria's involvement likewise needed to be determined. "Based upon the above assessments, the Department of Defense will submit options for overt military retaliation against identifiable sources of terrorist activity against our forces," the directive read. "The Department of State will provide a policy review of the costs and benefits of such retaliation."

The president ordered General Kelley to lead a delegation to Beirut to conduct a comprehensive review and prepare a report on how to modify the deployment and improve security for the Marines. The general also would discuss the need to tighten security in southern Beirut with Lebanese leaders and meet with the commanders of the other multinational forces on reducing overall exposure. America's new ambassador to Lebanon, Reginald Bartholomew, who had just arrived to replace Dillon, would sit down with Gemayel. "He should," the directive stated, "formally request that the government of Lebanon sever all diplomatic relations with the Islamic Republic of Iran." In addition, he needed to push national reconciliation. America's patience was done. "He should stress," the president's order concluded, "that while we are committed to the process of reconciliation, the U.S. government cannot tolerate interminable delays in the process."

As the meeting broke up that night at 6:57 p.m., Reagan put his arms around General Kelley, who would leave first thing in the morning for Beirut.

"Vaya con Dios," Reagan told him. "Go with God."

CHAPTER 44

What is Mr. Reagan going to do with all the blood on his hands?
—ROBIN POZONITZ, LETTER TO THE EDITOR
October 28, 1983

E lsewhere in the White House, it had been a hectic day.

The phones rang.

Telegrams arrived.

Just like in the wake of the embassy bombing, condolences from world leaders flooded Washington from as far away as New Zealand, the Philippines, and Zambia to the Dominican Republic, Barbados, and Senegal. The African nation of Togo declared twenty-four hours of mourning, while Pope John Paul II condemned the attack as an "act of war" in his sermon to eighty thousand worshippers in Saint Peter's Square. "A feeling of great pain, of horror and of execration surges in the soul," the pope preached, his voice at times emotional. "They were young lives cruelly cut off while they were carrying out a mission of peace."

A few leaders advocated American restraint, including British prime minister Margaret Thatcher and Egyptian president Hosni Mubarak, both of whom understood the tremendous domestic pressure on Reagan to punch back. "We should not only apply maximum self-restraint in the face of such acts of cowardice, but it is also our duty to defeat the purpose of their perpetrators by not playing into their hands," Mubarak cautioned. "The most effective answer to this unholy challenge is to push harder for peace." German chancellor Helmet Kohl likewise reminded Reagan that the answer would not be found in violence. "Only a political solution," he wrote, "can lead to a reconciliation of the various Lebanese religious denominations and to a full restoration of Lebanon's sovereignty, territorial integrity, and independence."

Staff and volunteers dutifully logged the names and comments from members of the public who took time to reach out to the administration.

As of 4 p.m. the White House had received 870 phone calls and telegrams related to the attack.

Anne Higgins, who ran the office of communication, assembled a sampling of those comments for the president. In her one-page memo to Reagan, Higgins singled out a message from Dr. Kenneth Morrison, whose son, Lance Corporal Ross Morrison, remained unaccounted for in Beirut. "My son has chosen the acceptance of responsibility for the privilege of living in this country. As I look out my window this morning across the fields of New Hampshire, I wonder if at any moment I will see two Marines coming up my driveway. My thoughts at this time go to you, Mr. President, in recognizing the tremendous responsibility that you carry," Morrison wrote. "I stand firmly with you in this moment, not from a political standpoint but from a standpoint of an American. I know my son does also."

Others echoed those sentiments, including Mr. and Mrs. Thomas O'Hara, whose son was a Marine headed to Grenada. "The tragedy in Lebanon is truly beyond comprehension," the Massachusetts couple wrote. "Our faith, confidence and trust in you is complete."

Not all the correspondence was so warm. Former Marine James Cobb of Baltimore, whose son was also headed to Grenada, wrote that his disgust with the administration prevented him from remaining silent any longer. "Don't you think it is time for us to take a stand or get the hell out?" he cabled. "Someone must pay for this tragic act of war."

Several messages agreed with Cobb. "Stop the politics," wrote Navy veteran Ron Rackley of South Carolina. "Let our men fight or get them the hell out." Others urged the president to exit Lebanon. The mission was no longer worth it. "Please bring the Marines home now," wrote the mother of two leathernecks. "We don't want any more killed."

It is plain that the United States can't pull out under fire without rewarding terrorism and weakening its credibility in the region.
—Buffalo News EDITORIAL
October 24, 1983

The messages and telegrams that poured into the White House reflected the anguish facing Marine families, all desperate for news as images of the carnage flooded television screens. For many, the first word of the attack came when anchor Charles Kuralt began his CBS News *Sunday Morning* program. "If you're just waking up and joining us," he announced, "I'm sorry to have to tell you that at least seventy six U.S. Marines were killed in an explosion this morning. At least 118 were wounded, and those numbers may rise higher."

That was the case in the small Georgia town of Milledgeville, where Lisa Hudson had returned to stay with her parents while her husband finished his deployment in Beirut. She had settled into her childhood bedroom on the family's farm, raising the couple's eight-month-old son, Will, with the help of her parents. Lisa's daily routine started with the morning news, which most days included a brief update on Beirut. On this Sunday, she had time enough to pick Will up from his crib before her mother appeared in her room. Lisa reached for the television knob, when her mother stopped her. "Don't turn it on," she warned her.

"What do you mean?" Lisa asked. "Mama, what's going on?"

"There's been a terrible bombing in Beirut."

"How do you know?" Lisa asked.

"Because I've seen it."

"Mama, I have to see," Lisa pleaded. "I have to see."

Lisa turned on the television. Images of the destruction flooded the screen. She could see rescuers atop the rubble pile. Others rushing with stretchers. Reporters talked of the climbing casualties. "I can't look," she said, turning off the television. "I know he's gone."

"You don't know," her mother cautioned. "He's the doctor. You know he's busy."

From California and Kentucky to New York and Florida, that same story played out for hundreds upon hundreds of families. Mothers and fathers, wives and children agonized as they waited for information. Minutes felt like hours. Stomachs churned. Many perched before televisions with radios blaring in the background. Others hovered over the phone or called Marine recruiting offices, the Pentagon, Red Cross, Camp Lejeune, and even the American Embassy in Beirut. "I couldn't watch the television," said Virginia Murphy of Pennsylvania, whose son Michael Murphy was a lieutenant. "I was just praying and waiting for the phone to ring." A similar story unfolded in the New Jersey home of Lois Prince, desperate for news of her son, Gregory. "I'm nuts. Every time our phone rings, I grab it," she said. "He's our only son."

Friends showed up at the homes of families to comfort them, often bearing plates of cold cuts and casseroles. So, too, did local news reporters, anxious to capture the unfolding story. "Every time I hear a car door slam or the phone ring, I think this is it," said Charlotte Drennen of Pennsylvania, whose son Richard was a corporal. "I think they're coming to tell me."

"You're afraid to answer the phone, you're afraid to answer the knock at the door," added Carol Collins, who worried over the fate of her twenty-year-old son, Stephen. Rose Nash of Michigan, whose nineteen-year-old son, John, was in Beirut, agreed. "I know I won't sleep tonight," she declared. "I won't sleep until I hear from him."

Throughout that Sunday—a day in which many people would attend church, enjoy lunch with family, and watch football—the casualty numbers climbed. NBC interrupted football games eleven times that afternoon with updates, three more than rival CBS. ABC periodically broke away from live coverage of the New York Marathon to report on Beirut.

Families scanned the faces of the Marines on the screen who picked through the rubble. Pennsylvanian Joan Galt, who had just mailed her son Robert a letter filled with colorful fall leaves as a reminder of home, studied the Marines on her television as she chewed her fingernails and dabbed her eyes with a tissue. "It's those kinds of shots we all watched hoping we could get a glimpse of him," she said. "We have been glued to the television."

For some, like Margaret Martinez of Denver, hostility trumped fear. "Just send some of us mothers over there who are angry and hurt, just give us a few hours," declared Martinez, whose son Eugene was in Beirut. "Those men won't know how to handle it."

The parents of Lance Corporal Morris Dorsey were fortunate. A photograph of their son atop a stretcher was one of the first images transmitted by the Associated Press. Editors at the *Poughkeepsie Journal* recognized his image from when he was wounded in the July 22 rocket attack, an injury that required Hudson to pluck a piece of still-scalding shrapnel from his back. The journalists printed the latest image from the wires and visited the family.

"That's my son!" his mother hollered. "He's alive. He's alive. At least he's alive."

The reporter scribbled down her comments.

"That's Morris," she continued. "I know his head. I know his feet. This is my son."

As the afternoon faded into evening, many families began to relax. Some contemplated sleep and the return to work on Monday. "Every hour that goes by and nobody comes knocking at my door, it's just that much more relief to me," one mother said.

"No news is good news," added William Conrad, a Maryland father.

The violence of the attack—and the immediate need to rescue survivors and render care—slowed the ability of the Marines to tally the names of the dead and wounded. Once collected, officials in Beirut sent the information to the Marine Corps headquarters at the Pentagon, where it was disseminated to district offices for family notification. "Not since the Vietnam War," one press report noted, "have so many officers been mobilized at one time to inform relatives of the deaths of loved ones." The first casualty notification teams moved out Sunday evening. "The initial reactions of survivors are unpredictable," a Pentagon spokesperson said. "Some go into shock and faint. Others have questions about details: How did he die? When will the remains arrive? How much will the government pay towards the funeral?"

At the same time that casualty notification teams prepared for their heartbreaking duty, more than three hundred Marines began leaving Camp Lejeune for Cherry Point Marine Air Station, along the North Carolina coast, flying in shifts aboard large Huey helicopters. At Cherry Point, the Marines—each carrying an eighty-pound pack, an M16, and a helmet—boarded the first of thirteen C-141 transport planes for the trip to Rhein-Main Air Base and then on to Lebanon to replace those killed and wounded. "We have a mission to do," said Lieutenant Colonel Edwin Kelley, the commander of the Beirut-bound troops. "We are going with a level head and do the job we were assigned to do. We are ready."

Major General Alfred Gray, commander of the Second Marine Division, said morale had reached a fever pitch among the Marines. "If we were barbaric, we could defend against this sort of thing, but we are not," the general told reporters. "It is possible to train and defend against any type of terrorist attack, but it is difficult to counter this kind of attack when our honor, training and Western civilization and our respect for human life is involved."

CHAPTER 46

We are dealing with madmen.
—SENATOR THOMAS EAGLETON
October 23, 1983

S peakes met with reporters at 7:06 p.m. for his third and final briefing of the day. The press secretary began by reading a two-paragraph
statement drafted by the State Department, which senior leaders had just
vetted in the Situation Room. That message confirmed America's commitment to Lebanon. The Marines would remain. "One thing is clear," Speakes
declared, "those who sponsor these outrages believe that they can intimidate
the government of Lebanon, its people, and their friends in the international
community. They are wrong. We will not yield to international terrorism
because we know that if we do, the civilized world will suffer and our values
will be fair game for those who seek to destroy all we stand for."

During the thirty-six-minute briefing, Speakes informed reporters that
America planned to respond to this criminal act as soon as the perpetrators
were positively identified. In the meantime, General Kelley would visit Beirut while additional troops would fly in to replace those killed and wounded
so that the force would remain at full strength.

"Can you tell us what kind of responses you're talking about?" a reporter asked.

"That is for those who brought about this act to be worried about," the
press secretary replied. "All I can say to them is wait and see."

"Are you any closer to determining who they are?"

"We are assessing our intelligence," he said. "We are cooperating with
foreign intelligence services to try to come to some conclusion."

"Making progress?"

"I think so, yes," Speakes replied.

"Is the circumstantial evidence still pointing toward the Iranians?"

"This is part of our assessment."

"Should we believe them to be guilty?"

"That's up to you," the press secretary said.

"Oh, no, no. It's not up to me," the reporter pushed back. "I'm asking you if the United States believes that."

"We are assessing the situation and when we're prepared to have some conclusions, we will then take the action that we—"

"You said that there were no decisions made on changing the force," another reporter interrupted. "Were any decisions made?"

A number of decisions were made, which the public would see in the days ahead.

"Is Syria involved in any way?" another reporter asked.

"We are looking into that, yes."

What motivation, another asked, would the Iranians have?

"Two reasons. They want to run us out. And the second thing is they want to disrupt the peace process," he said. "They don't want the government of Lebanon to be able to restore its sovereignty. Now, anybody who would do an act like this, clearly that's their intention."

Another reporter brought up the embassy bombing in April. "We still haven't figured out who did that, at least we haven't publicly announced it," the correspondent stated. "Are we going to make a larger effort to figure out who did this?"

"We will leave no stone unturned in an effort to pin the blame on someone," he said. "You can rest assured that there's every impetus on our part, on the president's part, to get to the bottom of this and do what is necessary to assure it doesn't happen again."

"First the embassy bombing, then sniper attacks, now this. Any word on how far the United States is going to go, how much they're going to take?"

"We believe that our presence there is an essential ingredient to this peace process," Speakes replied. "Our commitment is firm, solid, and will remain so."

"But you're also saying that, considering the nature of things there, this could happen again on the same scale. There's no way to stop it."

"Anything can happen," he replied. "There's no denying that."

The reporters jotted notes.

"But," he concluded, "we will take every step to see that it doesn't happen again."

CHAPTER 47

It was total devastation. It was the worst thing I've ever seen.
—Representative John Murtha
October 30, 1983

Work continued in Beirut on Monday.

Marines armed with oxyacetylene torches sliced through bent and twisted rebar that held together large concrete slabs. Workers broke them up with sledge- and jackhammers while others hauled the debris to a growing pile at the unused end of one of the runways. "It is a long and tedious task," Major Jordan told reporters. "We have an entire building compressed into a very small space." Geraghty echoed him in his own situation report that day. "Marines are performing the grim task of searching through the excavated portions for survivors," he wrote. "The going is slow and there is much work to be done. It is impossible to estimate how long complete excavation will take. All hands are performing superbly."

Twenty-four hours after the blast, the pace of operations had noticeably changed. Gone was the frantic tempo of rescuers fueled by adrenaline who attacked the mound with bare hands and shovels desperate to find friends. In its place was a more deliberate effort as laborers used cranes, bulldozers, and dump trucks to deconstruct the pile slab by slab so as not to further destroy the remains of Marines still buried in the rubble. In areas of the pile that were stable, workers tunneled through the debris. "Many of the bodies are in pieces and will never be identified," Jordan said. "Survivors? If there are any in there, it would be a miracle."

Rescuers often located bodies by smell. When one was found, work momentarily paused to prepare for the removal of a dead comrade in arms. One such recovery occurred shortly before noon. Rescuers on top of the mound called out for a stretcher, which others soon fetched only to trade out moments later for an olive-green body bag. "One of them gingerly pulled out a Marine fatigue shirt and went through the pockets looking for identification," observed *Philadelphia Inquirer* reporter David Zucchino. "He found a cigarette lighter."

Workers bagged the lighter and the shirt. "At 12:03 p.m. the men up top pulled out the newly found body—a young man with dark blond hair and skin the color of ash," Zucchino added. "He wore only a pair of red Marine-issue shorts. His hands were folded across his chest." Around the body, rescuers discovered a leather shaving kit and several letters, which the men zipped inside the body bag before carrying the remains down to an ambulance. As men hauled the body, another worker dug out a blue nylon wallet, which he tossed below.

"Give that to the body that just left," he said.

One of the men picked it up and wiped it clean.

"It belongs to that guy right there."

Another such discovery would haunt Father Pucciarelli. Workers uncovered a Marine who had initially survived the blast but was trapped in a pocket far beneath the rubble. The building's collapse had cut his left arm badly while debris pinned his legs. The Marine could still move his right arm, which he used to try to stop his bleeding. "It was hopeless," the priest said. "He next reached into his wallet and withdrew photographs of his wife and children. He placed them on a ledge in front of him—and in this way, remembering his family, he died."

Troops with the Italian and British forces joined the efforts. So, too, did Anthony Pais, one of the pilots who volunteered to help dig when he was not needed in the skies. Pais learned that since the majority of the men had been killed in their cots, when he uncovered the top of a mosquito net, he was likely to next find the body of a slain Marine. "You knew then you were pretty close," he recalled, "so you would call the corpsmen over."

On another occasion, Pais sifted through the debris only to make a traumatic discovery. "I came across this large piece of human gore," he said. "It was someone's intestines." The pilot froze in shock, staring at the guts in his hands as a corpsman approached.

"Put it in the bag, sir," the medic instructed him. "Put it in the bag."

The hospital corpsman opened a plastic bag and Pais deposited the intestines. The medic sealed the bag, marked it, and handed the pilot several fresh bags. "Sir," the corpsman concluded, "if you come across something, you put it in the bag and give it to me."

ABOVE: Marines on the roof of a Lebanese University building watch as artillery rounds hit near the Beirut International Airport in September 1983. *Marine Corps*

BELOW: A terrorist bomb levels the Battalion Landing Team headquarters at 6:21 a.m. on October 23, 1983. *Marine Corps*

OPPOSITE: A Marine, his leg deeply torn from the explosion that destroyed the Battalion Landing Team headquarters, is carried by comrades for emergency medical treatment in Beirut on October 23, 1983. *AP Photo*

ABOVE: President Reagan, at Augusta National, makes an early morning phone call on October 22, 1983. *National Archives*

ABOVE: Marines carry their dead comrades away from the four-story command center that was destroyed in a bomb blast on October 23, 1983. *AP Photo*

OPPOSITE TOP: Rabbi Arnold Resnicoff, who helped the wounded and dying in the aftermath of the terrorist attack, is pictured here with his homemade yarmulke. *National Archives*

OPPOSITE BOTTOM: Rescuers armed with picks and sledgehammers dig through the concrete and tangled rebar of the former Battalion Landing Team headquarters on October 23, 1983. *Marine Corps*

Rescue workers recover a body from the wreckage.
Marine Corps

OPPOSITE TOP: Workers dig through the rubble. *Marine Corps*

OPPOSITE BOTTOM: President Reagan speaks to reporters on the south lawn of the White House about the terrorist attack in Beirut upon his return from Augusta National on the morning of October 23, 1983. *National Archives*

RIGHT: Marine Commandant General Paul Kelley presents Navy Hospital Corpsman Third Class Don Howell, who was blinded in his right eye, with a Purple Heart in Germany on October 24, 1983. *National Archives*

BELOW: A wounded Marine undergoes emergency medical treatment at a local hospital in Beirut on October 23, 1983. *AP Photo*

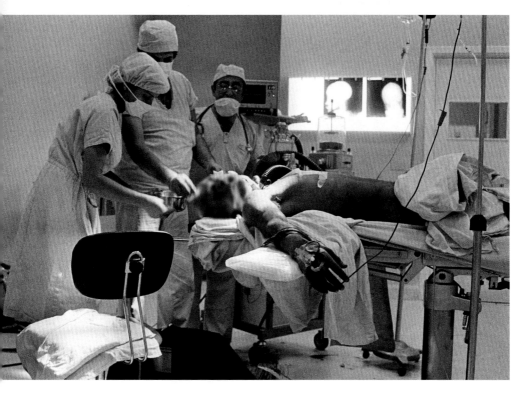

OPPOSITE TOP: Burnham Matthews (left), who was blown out of the building, and James Dudney talk to reporters on October 29, 1983. *Marine Corps*

OPPOSITE BOTTOM: President Reagan gives a speech to the nation about the terrorist attack in Beirut on October 27, 1983. *National Archives*

ABOVE: Vice President George H. W. Bush, pictured here with Colonel Timothy Geraghty and General Paul Kelly, inspects the damage done by a terrorist bomb. *Marine Corps*

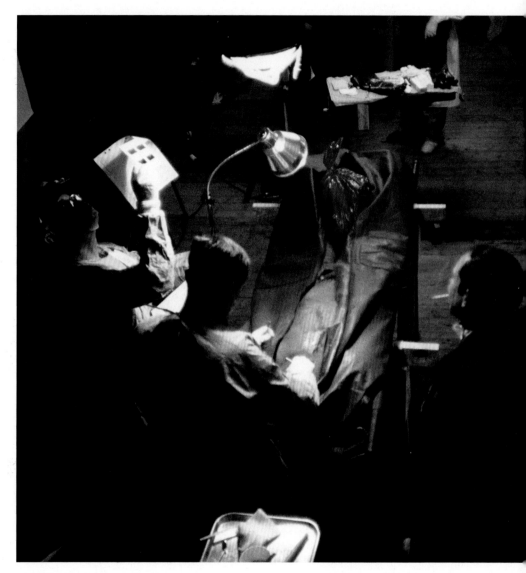

ABOVE: A dental identification is performed on a deceased Marine at the casualty processing center in Germany. *National Archives*

OPPOSITE TOP: Aluminum transfer cases filled with the remains of Marines killed in the terrorist attack in Lebanon are stacked inside the casualty processing center in Germany. *National Archives*

OPPOSITE BOTTOM: In Germany, medical personnel confer over the identification of a Marine inside the casualty processing center. *National Archives*

President Reagan and the First Lady greet wounded Marines during a memorial at Camp Lejeune on November 4, 1983. *National Archives*

ABOVE: The USS *New Jersey* fires a salvo from her 16/50 guns during a deployment off the coast of Beirut, Lebanon, on January 9, 1984.
National Archives

LEFT: Marines wait to depart on the beach in Beirut on February 26, 1984.
Marine Corps

Navy Seabees in flak jackets and helmets joined the leathernecks in the hunt for classified papers and personal effects as artillery thundered and automatic weapons rattled in the distance. "Marines on their hands and knees," one journalist noted, "combed the rubble for identification cards, tags, clothes and anything else that might identify their dead comrades." Michael Petit found a pair of camouflage trousers with the owner's name still legible in the waistband. "*How ironic*," he thought, "*that the trousers had survived but not the man.*" Rabbi Resnicoff, who still wore his makeshift yarmulke, watched the Marines sift through the rubble, pausing at times to gaze at found photos. "Today, it's slowed down and it has finally hit them," he said. "I've seen a lot more crying today than yesterday. They've had time to think."

Troops separated the recovered weapons, ordnance, communications gear, and documents into piles. Inside the Marine Amphibious Unit headquarters, others worked to tabulate the lists of dead and wounded, a tough job since the Battalion Landing Team headquarters had been destroyed. Marines had to build lists from partial rosters. Over them hung the fear of accidentally listing a Marine as dead, an error that would devastate a family. "The task was monumental," Petit said. "We checked and double-checked our work."

As Petit worked, another Marine entered the office. "I don't know how they'll ever identify some of the bodies," he declared. "We lifted a slab off one. He was crushed and burned. There wasn't much more than a blackened shadow left."

Marines increased security at the airport. A two-and-a-half-ton supply truck blocked the entrance, manned by a Marine armed with a .50-caliber machine gun aimed at the road ahead. New barricades went up along with extra sentries. "It was the kind of taut, concerted security precautions that almost surely would have prevented the truck-bomb explosion," Zucchino observed. "The new security measures were a grim concession by the Marines that their previous measures, though upgraded and comprehensive, had simply not been good enough. The failure of those procedures was all the more disturbing because it comes in the wake of a nearly identical truck-bombing that leveled a section of the U.S. Embassy here April 18."

Military officials, when questioned by the press, offered mixed views on the security in the lead-up to the Sunday bombing. "We thought we had good security," Commodore Rick France told reporters, "but obviously they got around it." Geraghty agreed with his boss. The Marines, whose mission was to serve as peacekeepers, did not want to project a bunker image. "We took every reasonable precaution to prevent terrorist attacks," the colonel said. "This particular operation was obviously well planned and timed and coordinated." But others disagreed, including Jordan. "We were too open around here," the public affairs officer said. "Any five-year-old could sit out there and figure out how to get in."

Tension between the press and the Marines persisted. The reporters did not always ingratiate themselves. That was the case for two ABC News journalists, whom public affairs officials evicted for failing to check in on arrival and for using combative language and a poor attitude with the Marines. "Mood of troops," one public affairs report noted that day, "ranges from shock and uncertainty to courageously confident." Many of the troops, like Glenn Dolphin, wanted the reporters gone. "I realized that they had a job to do, but I found their presence a huge invasion of privacy," he said. "You couldn't perform any task without hearing the shutter sounds as dozens of cameramen took photographs nonstop. I felt as if they had not earned the right to be there. To them it was a job. To us it was much more personal than that." In contrast, Dolphin marveled at Geraghty's strength. "For an officer who literally had the weight of the world on his shoulders," he said, "Geraghty was holding up remarkably well. I could not detect any change in his personality or leadership style, despite the unbelievable pressure he was under. His continued command presence and remarkable stamina fascinated me."

A similar recovery effort unfolded to the north, where French workers used dogs to sniff the rubble for survivors. President François Mitterrand, who flew out of Paris at 2 a.m. that morning, arrived in Beirut at dawn. He met with Gemayel, toured the French ruins, and then visited the Marines, all during his brief seven hours on the ground. At the airport, the French leader entered the morgue. Workers had placed nearly two hundred bodies in aluminum caskets, making the hangar resemble a warehouse for the dead. Those caskets sat atop pallets, stacked three across and four high, held down by nylon straps. A dozen pallets were lined up one after the other inside the darkened hangar. The colonel escorted the French president and his entourage inside, where Mitterrand froze, absorbing the sight. "His eyes opened wide, and his face became pallid," Geraghty recalled. "It was an expression that I will take to my grave."

The French president asked to pay his respects. Geraghty, of course, obliged. Mitterrand walked down the line, pausing before each pallet of caskets, where he made the sign of the cross. Other members of his presidential party did the same. He asked about the activity in the far corner of the hangar, an area shielded by curtains and illuminated by floodlights. Geraghty explained that Marines and sailors were sorting body parts. Mitterrand asked to see the area and again pay his respects. "When the presidential party departed," he said, "it was apparent to me that these men expressed the same heartfelt condolences for the American dead that they must have shown earlier to their fallen French peacekeepers not far away."

Geraghty returned to the hangar that afternoon as the first bodies were prepared to be loaded aboard a transport plane for the flight to Germany, the first stop on the long journey home. Ulick watched as the colonel paid his respects to his fallen Marines. "That has to be," he later wrote in a letter to his mother, "the loneliest man in the world." Pucciarelli joined Geraghty as a forklift rumbled over, lowered its mast, and scooped up the first pallet. The driver turned toward the plane when the colonel stopped him. The solemn occasion demanded an honor guard. Twenty-four Marines lined up in two rows of twelve facing one another. Geraghty gave the signal to continue. "As the pallet loads of caskets moved slowly between the columns of Marines, the colonel, myself, and the squad saluted," Pucciarelli said. "There were no television cameras, no important officials, no large formation. This was a personal, sincere gesture by our colonel who, in this private way, showed his respect for his fallen Marines."

Additional Marines touched down in Beirut that night, having left Cherry Point the day before. The callousness of many of the arrivals, who had served previously in Lebanon, angered the survivors, a tension no doubt exacerbated by grief, shock, and exhaustion. "This never would have happened," one new arrival remarked, "if we were still here."

That Monday night, thirty-six hours after the attack, Petit stretched out for some rest. Each time he closed his eyes, he saw the pile. He finally rose, pulled on his boots, and walked back over to the wreckage. Under the glare of floodlights, he watched men work. "The frantic pace had slowed," he said. "The workers moved a little more lethargically as they went about their grim task. Common sense dictated that there couldn't be any more survivors."

CHAPTER 48

I would simply ask that all Americans this evening, with a bended knee,
thank God that this country of ours can still produce young Americans
who are willing to lay down their life for free men everywhere.
—GENERAL PAUL KELLEY
October 24, 1983

Half a world away, General Kelley traveled that Monday morning to Andrews Air Force Base, where he would board a C-137 jet transport to Germany and then on to Beirut. The general told reporters that his trip had two objectives, the most important of which was to pay his respects to the dead and visit wounded Marines. His second goal was to serve as the president's emissary and share his condolences with the Marines who would stay in Beirut. "I'd just like to say that I've been a Marine for all of my adult life," he said, "and yesterday I have to say in sincerity and all honesty was the hardest day of my life."

Kelley touched down at 7:30 p.m. Monday night at Rhein-Main Air Base, outside Frankfurt, around the same time as a cargo plane carrying the remains of 144 slain Marines arrived. He asked to pay his respects. "I was not prepared for the flood of emotion which overcame me for I had never seen before, and Lord willing I will never see again, an aircraft as large as a C-141 filled to capacity with caskets, caskets of those Marines, sailors, and soldiers who had been so very much alive and full of youth and vitality during my visit to Beirut several weeks earlier," he said. "On this cold and windswept night in a distant land I watched as young airmen from our Air Force respectfully and tenderly removed each casket one by one."

"Lord," he asked himself, "where do we get such men?"

Of the sixty-eight evacuated sailors and Marines, thirty-six were sent to three different hospitals in Germany. Twelve others went to Italy, while another twenty landed in the British hospital in Cyprus. During his brief stopover in Germany, Kelley had time to visit only two of the three hospitals. At 7 a.m. on October 25, he flew by helicopter from Rhein-Main to the Air Force hospital in Wiesbaden, about twenty-eight miles away.

The message traffic revealed the horrific range of injuries the men suffered when the building came down on them, from burns and crush wounds to broken bones, impalements, and amputations. "Depressed left frontal skull fracture; comatose," one message read.

"Ruptured spleen," added another, "fractured right tibia and fibula."

"Respiratory failure; 1st and 2nd degree burns face/arm; 2nd degree burns legs."

The Air Force hospital in Wiesbaden had sixteen wounded. That compared to seventeen at Landstuhl Army Hospital and another three at the Army's 97th General Hospital in Frankfurt. At Wiesbaden that morning, five of the wounded dressed in bathrobes were placed in wheelchairs and rolled into the hall to meet the general, who presented each one with a Purple Heart. One of the men, Hospital Corpsman Third Class Pedro Alvarado, had recently spoken to his wife by telephone. He had good news to share with Kelley.

"We're gonna have a baby!" he told the general. "It's my first one, sir."

"God bless her," Kelley said.

The general visited nonambulatory troops in their rooms, where small American flags were displayed at the foot of each bed. Lance Corporal Burnham Matthews recounted being blown out of the third-floor window. The general asked if he was knocked unconscious.

"No, sir," he said. "I remember tumbling through the air and everything."

In another room, Kelley spoke with Corporal Joseph Schneider of Florida, who was shirtless, prompting the general to pin his Purple Heart to his pillow.

"I was just twenty feet from the building, sir," he said. "I was buried underneath the rubble."

"How long before they got you out?" Kelly asked.

"About thirty minutes," he said. "It went fast."

Army Sergeant Elvin Henry Jr. of South Carolina told him he didn't remember anything. "The next thing I know," he said, "I was on the *Iwo Jima*."

"Were you pretty shaken?" Kelley asked.

"I'm quite shook," he replied.

Kelley told each Marine he was proud of them.

The general paused over the bed of Lance Corporal Jeffrey Nashton of Rome, New York, who had suffered a broken leg, crushed arm, two collapsed lungs, and a fractured skull that would later require a steel plate in his head. Nashton couldn't see because of the concrete dust still trapped in his eyes. Kelley told Nashton that he was there. To verify, the blind Marine grabbed the general's camouflaged coat. He ran his hands up until he reached the collar, where he felt the four stars. "He held my hand with a firm grip. He was making signals and we realized he wanted to tell me something," Kelley said. "We put a pad of paper in his hand."

Everyone watched.

"Semper fi," Nashton scribbled. "Always faithful."

Kelley was so moved that when he left, he reached up and unfastened his stars. He later had them mounted on a framed velvet plaque adorned with the Marine Corps motto. The general presented it to Nashton the following month as he recovered at what was then Bethesda Naval Hospital. "When I left the hospital," Kelley said, "I realized I had met a great human being, and I took off those stars because at the time I felt they belonged more to him than to me."

CHAPTER 49

This is a disaster that has been waiting to happen.
—SENATOR SAM NUNN
October 24, 1983

Monday proved a busy day at the White House.

Larry Speakes met with reporters at 9:30 a.m. in his office, though a transcript of the session shows he had little new information since he briefed them the evening before. Speakes provided a quick rundown of the president's schedule for the day, including his luncheon with regional news editors and broadcasters. In addition, Reagan would meet with his advisors about Lebanon as well as talk with other leaders of the multinational force.

Reporters fired off a litany of questions. Would the Marines be put aboard ships or moved out of the airport? Did Reagan plan to speak to the families? Would the president visit the wounded in Germany? Did he plan to go on television and address the nation?

The transcript shows Speakes had few answers.

"There's no decision," he said at one point.

"I don't know," he added later.

"We haven't discussed that."

One of the few areas he was certain was Reagan's commitment to Lebanon, even as lawmakers had increased demands for the troops to come home. "The fact is," he said, "that there's no change in our mission and no change in our determination."

Another enlightening moment in the twenty-seven-minute briefing came when a reporter asked who precisely was the adversary. The question mirrored the one asked by the father of slain Marine Randy Clark, one that no doubt still stumped many Americans. Were the Soviets the threat? Or the Syrians who want to dominate Lebanon? Or the Iranians?

"Who," the frustrated reporter sputtered, "are we talking about?"

"All of the above," Speakes said.

Elsewhere in the White House, the president met his senior aides followed by the American ambassador to the Soviet Union. He then fielded phone calls with nearly a half dozen lawmakers, including Tip O'Neill and Howard Baker. Reagan had accomplished all this by the time he walked into a 12:09 p.m. luncheon with regional news editors and broadcasters. Gathered inside the State Dining Room were about eighty journalists, a mix of print, radio, and television media from the *Arizona Republic* to the *Cedar Rapids Gazette*. Gold silk drapes covered the windows, which offered views of the North Lawn. Above the fireplace hung an 1869 portrait of Abraham Lincoln painted by George P. A. Healy. On the mantel just below, Franklin Roosevelt had ordered workers to carve a quotation from a letter President John Adams wrote to his wife, Abigail, on the second night he stayed in the White House. "I pray Heaven to bestow the best of Blessings on this House and on all that shall hereafter inhabit it," it stated. "May none but honest and wise Men ever rule under this roof."

Reagan certainly needed those prayers.

The president addressed attendees from a lectern next to the fireplace at 1:05 p.m. "Good afternoon," he began. "Given what has happened in Lebanon, I've put aside the remarks that I was prepared to give here today. And I'd like to read you this statement."

"Yesterday's acts of terrorism in Beirut," he began, "which killed so many young American and French servicemen were a horrifying reminder of the type of enemy we face in many critical areas of the world today—vicious, cowardly, and ruthless. Words can never convey the depth of compassion that we feel for those brave men and for their loved ones."

Camera shutters rattled as the president spoke, periodically looking up from his printed remarks atop the lectern. "Many Americans are wondering why we must keep our forces in Lebanon," he continued. "The reason they must stay there until the situation is under control is quite clear. We have vital interests in Lebanon and our actions in Lebanon are in the cause of world peace." The president reiterated his goal of removing foreign forces from Lebanon so that the Gemayel government could restore sovereignty and security. "By promoting peace in Lebanon," he said, "we strengthen the forces for peace throughout the Middle East. This is not a Republican or a Democratic goal but one that all Americans share."

Peace in Lebanon, Reagan argued, was a cornerstone of regional stability—and that stability depended on America's presence. "We must not allow international criminals and thugs such as these to undermine the peace in Lebanon," the president continued. "The struggle for peace is indivisible. We cannot pick and choose where we will support freedom. We can only determine how. If it is lost in one place, all of us lose." If Lebanon were to fall, it would undermine America's strategic position not only in the eastern Mediterranean, but all of the Middle East, including the Arabian Peninsula. "The United States will not be intimidated by terrorists," he concluded. "We have strong circumstantial evidence linking the perpetrators of this latest atrocity to others that have occurred against us in the recent past, including the bombing of our Embassy in Beirut last April. Every effort will be made to find the criminals responsible for this act of terrorism so this despicable act will not go unpunished."

At the end of his six-minute statement, the president fielded questions.

"What are the options?" asked Linda Douglas of KNXT in Los Angeles. "Do we increase the number of troops in Lebanon? Do we withdraw the troops?"

"The option that we cannot consider is withdrawing," Reagan said, reiterating his earlier commitment. "The mission remains and it remains as yet unfulfilled."

Susan Hutchinson of KIRO-TV in Seattle noted that she was not only a journalist but also the spouse of a Marine Corps captain. "As such," she said, "I am personally grieved over the loss of lives." What would the president say, Hutchinson continued, to people upset over the American loss of life in a region that has long been a stranger to peace?

"I wish there were an instant answer here that would resolve all your concerns," Reagan said as he gripped the top of the lectern. "I understand your concern. I understand all Americans' concern, and I have to say that I don't know of anything that is worse than the job I have, than having to make the calls that I have made as a result of these snipings that have taken place in the past. I wish it could be without hazard." But the Middle East was too important, he continued, to let slide into chaos. He reminded attendees that Lebanon was once the prosperous and peaceful gateway to the east. "We believe," he said, "it can be again."

Why not, asked another reporter, let the Marines use real force?

That could lead, he argued, to a wider war against other Arab states. "That is not the road to peace," the president said. "Our mission, I think, makes sense."

What is America doing, pressed Lilly Flores of KIII-TV in Corpus Christi, Texas, to identify remains and notify families?

Because it was a headquarters building, Reagan said, many of the personnel records were destroyed. Few of the sleeping Marines wore dog tags.

All this combined to slow identification, which the president knew made a cruel delay for families. "You have touched upon," he concluded, "what is a heartbreaking part of this particular incident."

After lunch Reagan headed to the Oval Office, where he phoned French president Mitterrand, who had just returned from his day trip to Beirut. French rescuers were still busy, though an eventual tally would confirm fifty-eight dead paratroopers. Reagan had sent Mitterrand a telegram the day before about the bombings. "We deplore this cowardly and brutal attack which is aimed all too clearly at undermining our commitment to work for peace, stability and reconciliation in Lebanon," he wrote. "I want to assure you that the United States will not be deterred from pursing our common objectives in Lebanon by the actions of terrorists." The American Embassy in Paris doubted the attack would undermine French resolve for the mission in Lebanon. "Our assumption," the embassy cabled Washington, "is that the French will go along with the U.S. on whatever our initial response to the bombing is."

That was the news the president wanted to hear.

Mitterrand had returned at 7 p.m. to Paris, where he greeted reporters outside the Elysée Palace who noted the sixty-seven-year-old leader looked "pale and somber" after his seventeen-hour journey. "I say to everyone that a country is great by the force of its spirit, by its resolve and by the friendship and respect that it merits," Mitterrand said. "That's why in Lebanon, France remains and will remain faithful to its history and its engagements."

Talking points prepared for Reagan's call show that the president walked Mitterrand through America's actions to date, including the five hours he spent Sunday meeting with his advisors. He noted that General Kelley had been dispatched on a mission to assess security, while Secretary of State Shultz planned to reach out to his French counterpart on how the two nations might cooperate more closely to prevent any future attacks. Reagan then addressed his hope for a counterstrike. "For our part," he concluded, "we plan to retaliate—as you have done in the past—once we have determined who perpetuated this heinous crime."

October 1983–April 1984

All of a sudden, the building started falling apart.
Pieces of the concrete started going in different directions.
I remember falling through the air and feeling the different decks
or floors collapse underneath me. I felt the roof come down and hit
the third floor and the third floor hit the second floor and
the second floor hit the first floor, and each time it hit the
different floors, it was breaking off and falling.

—LANCE CORPORAL ROBERT CALHOUN, ABC NEWS INTERVIEW
October 23, 1987

Rescuers pull survivors out of the destroyed Battalion Landing Team headquarters
building on October 23, 1983. *AP Photo*

CHAPTER 50

Our Marines had become pawns in a larger game.
—GENERAL JOHN VESSEY
February 16, 2013

As the immediate shock of the attack subsided—and the scope of the casualties began to crystallize—many in Congress grew more hostile. A few argued that America needed to bring the Marines home, but most realized the nation had few immediate options. "There is no clear way out," said Democratic senator Alan Cranston of California. "We cannot retreat under fire, and if we were to declare war, we wouldn't know who to declare war against."

Many more demanded a reevaluation of the mission as well as improvements in security, both easier remedies in the short term. Democratic Speaker of the House Tip O'Neill drew fire from some members of his own party for his role in helping broker the previous month's compromise with the White House over the War Powers Resolution. A small group of Democrats, in fact, demanded Congress cut off cash for the Lebanon mission, a move that would force the Marines to come home. O'Neill fired back at his critics, reminding dissenters to put America ahead of the Democratic Party. "Our troops were there for the purpose of aiding and abetting diplomacy. Nobody anticipated anything of a terrorist action," O'Neill said. "If we run, it would happen again at all our embassies around the world."

Senate Majority Leader Howard Baker agreed. "This must not become a political football," he warned. "We must not be legislating at the point of a gun." Such admonishments, however, failed to stem the criticism. "I wouldn't want my son sitting at the end of that runway," declared Republican representative Toby Roth of Wisconsin. "Would you want your son there? And if not, how can you justify sending anyone else's son or daughter?"

"If you're smart, you know when to cut your losses," added Democratic representative Samuel Stratton of New York. "That's what we didn't understand in Vietnam."

To calm congressional concerns, Reagan dispatched his top lieutenants to Capitol Hill. Shultz met behind closed doors on Monday with members of both the Senate Foreign Relations Committee and the House Foreign Affairs Committee. His prepared remarks showed that he linked Lebanon to Reagan's larger ambition of creating regional peace. "We are in Lebanon because the outcome in Lebanon will affect our position in the whole Middle East," Shultz said. "To ask why Lebanon is important is to ask why the Middle East is important—because the answer is the same." The United States, he argued, had no choice but to remain and finish the job. "If we are driven out of Lebanon, radical and rejectionist elements will have scored a major victory," the secretary of state cautioned. "The message will be sent that relying on the Soviet Union pays off and that relying on the United States is a fatal mistake."

On Tuesday Weinberger followed Shultz to Capitol Hill, where he met in executive session with the Senate Armed Services Committee. Like Shultz, the transcript of the hearing shows he shared little new information. Circumstantial evidence still pointed to Iran—or at least Iranian individuals—as the likely culprit with help from Syria. Security was adequate, he said, for the risks at the time. The daily threat of mortar and sniper fire explained why so many Marines were inside the Battalion Landing Team headquarters at the time of the bombing. The Defense Department would have a better understanding of security and how to improve it for the Marines once General Kelley returned. That said, Weinberger warned that suicide attacks are hard to prevent. "Even the most stringent security precautions," the defense secretary said, "are not going to guarantee that an incident like this kind can't happen."

Neither cabinet member succeeded in quieting the concerns of lawmakers, many of whom had constituents still anxiously awaiting news of the fate of loved ones in Beirut. A few expressed regret for their support for the previous month's compromise that allowed the Marines to stay for another eighteen months. "I'm sure there are people who would like to have their votes back now," quipped Republican representative Jim Courter of New Jersey.

Republican representative Buddy Roemer of Louisiana agreed. "Shame on us," he said. "It's not just the president; it's us. We had our chance and did nothing."

Others demanded the White House clarify the mission. "The president needs to clearly define for the American people why their boys are being sent to die in Lebanon," argued Senator Robert Byrd of West Virginia. His fellow Democratic senator Edward Kennedy of Massachusetts agreed. "We must not accept," he barked, "an endless American involvement that maintains our Marines as nothing more than sitting ducks in the Lebanese civil war."

One area on which a majority of lawmakers agreed was the need to improve security, particularly given that this was the second such attack in less than six months. "The pattern is too close to the embassy bombing to understand why it was allowed to happen twice," said Senator Charles Mathias, a Maryland Republican. "It was not an isolated incident," added Representative John LaFalce, a New York Democrat, "but it is endemic to the warfare of the region."

The diversity of opinion on Capitol Hill mirrored the wide range of views that appeared on the editorial pages of newspapers nationwide. Some, including the *Philadelphia Inquirer*, advocated America leave. "Tragically," the paper opined, "it is time to recognize that there are honorable tasks on this earth that cannot be completed." The *Boston Globe* agreed. "Whatever comes of investigations," the paper declared, "grieving American families know only that their loved ones died in a helpless way in a seemingly hopeless cause."

Other papers echoed lawmakers in recognizing that America was all that stood between stability and chaos. "For a power with America's responsibilities," argued the *Washington Post*, "it is inconceivable to hand the bombers the victory they sought by pulling the Marines out. American influence through the region could collapse." *USA Today* lamented the nation's no-win predicament. "We are caught in a cruel vise," the paper wrote. "We cannot flee Lebanon and leave it to the vultures who now rejoice over the torn flesh of our fallen troops. Nor can we turn our Marines into warriors killing in the name of peace."

Lebanese officials likewise weighed in on the debate, no doubt hoping to shape American public opinion and prevent a sudden withdrawal of troops that might trigger the collapse of the Gemayel government. Lebanese ambassador Abdallah Bouhabib took a hard line in an interview with *U.S. News & World Report*, warning that American credibility was on the line. If the Marines were pulled out, he argued, it would be seen as "abandonment." Gemayel, in contrast, avoided the politics of pressure, focusing instead on the sorrow many felt over the loss of so many young lives. "These men are not just American and French, but are Lebanese martyrs as well," Gemayel wrote in a *Washington Post* essay. "The terrible tragedy of last Sunday burns at the heart and soul of us all. We mourn each and every life lost."

But the Lebanese were not the only foreign power to speak out.

Reagan's repeated threats of retaliation worried Syria, which sent diplomatic notes to Western European governments urging them to discourage the United States from action. Iran, in contrast, welcomed an American attack. "We are not afraid," the government declared. "This is our hope because we seek martyrdom. Let America do what it can."

Druze militia leader Walid Jumblatt, whose forces previously shelled American troops, denied any involvement in the bombing. So, too, did Amal militia leader Nabih Berri. "I do not want the Marines to leave," he assured staffers from the National Security Council who visited him in Beirut. "I will help you find the people who attacked the Marines."

Reporters even trekked up to the city of Baalbek in the Bekaa Valley to meet with Hussein al-Musawi, the bearded leader of Islamic Amal, the radical Shiite group that formed part of Hezbollah and who American intelligence suspected was responsible for the attack. At a stone headquarters off the town square, guards frisked reporters before ushering them inside, where al-Musawi perched in a green chair rolling a string of beads with his fingers. Through a translator, the militia leader denied any knowledge of the attack, even though he was the operation's architect. His Hezbollah colleague Imad Mugniyah, by some reports, in fact, watched the bombing through binoculars from a nearby rooftop. Al-Musawi applauded the suicide bombers. "I bow," he told reporters, "before the souls of the martyrs who carried out this operation."

Mail and telegrams meanwhile continued to flood the White House, where staff and volunteers dutifully opened and sorted them. Correspondence came from religious and business leaders as well as mayors, state representatives, and trade unions. Much like the editorial pages, opinions proved varied, reflecting a nation in mourning and in shock. "My prayers are with you," professed the Reverend James Hickey, archbishop of Washington.

"You are doing God's will," added Bishop John Chedid of Los Angeles.

More than a few were angry. Unlike the polished words of editorial writers, such letters were often blunt, even brutal. "I have been a strong supporter of you for years. Unfortunately, I have badly misjudged you. You are all talk and damn little action!" cabled Robert McNeil, town supervisor in Lisbon, New York. "You make Jimmy Carter look good."

Not all the ire was directed at Reagan. Others blamed the terrorists and the military for failing to safeguard against the attack. "There are no words strong enough to express my disgust at such brutality and lack of respect for human life," cabled Robert Wilbraham, the national commander of American Veterans of World War II, Korea, and Vietnam.

Some pleaded with Reagan to pull the Marines out of Lebanon, while others demanded he retaliate against the attackers. "Please," implored Robert Harris, a state representative from Vermont, "I beg you on bended knees, come to your senses, and bring the troops home before many more, perhaps hundreds, are senselessly killed or wounded."

The only unifying element to be found in the pages and pages of letters and telegrams that flooded the White House was the demand that Reagan, the seeker of compromise, at last take action. "Urge that you withdraw all America troops immediately," one demanded.

"Do something to protect our Marines," another wrote.

"Bring our men home now!"

The comments from lawmakers, editorial pages, and citizens all combined to increase the pressure on Reagan, who, as *New York Times* reporter Hedrick Smith observed, "looked exhausted, emotionally drained, even old for the first time in his presidency." The bombing of the Marine headquarters was a massive calamity. The families of the men killed, the Marines still in Beirut, and Americans everywhere all now looked to him, a sentiment best captured by Douglas Chamberlain, a state representative from Wyoming. "The grieving relatives and the nation," he wrote, "await your action to insure this will never happen again."

CHAPTER 51

I want someone to tell me why my son had to die.
—MARY LOU MEURER
October 24, 1983

As Monday rolled into Tuesday and then Wednesday, many families still anxiously awaited news from Beirut. The destruction of the Battalion Landing Team headquarters, which housed all the records, coupled with the fact few Marines wore dog tags as well as the physical destruction of the bodies, all combined to slow the identification process.

For families that translated into agony.

Throughout the week, casualty notification teams continued to fan out through communities nationwide, though the process proved glacial. As of 8 a.m. on Wednesday—more than seventy-two hours after the attack—only thirty-seven of the more than two hundred confirmed dead had been identified and their next of kin notified.

Many others learned only that their loved ones were missing. That was the case for Lisa Hudson, who anxiously awaited news about her husband while staying on her family's farm in Georgia. "The doorbell rang," she recalled. "I knew what that meant."

Her father summoned her to the door.

Two nervous young sailors in dress blues informed her that her husband was missing in action, news that was followed a day later by a Western Union telegram. "I deeply regret to confirm," the message began. "Your great anxiety in this situation is understood and when further information is available you will be promptly informed."

Under pressure from families, the Pentagon announced plans to release the names of the uninjured. Newspapers published partial lists of the dead and wounded. In Beirut, officers ordered surviving Marines to write letters home. A special flight would carry the letters back to the United States for distribution. The Marine Corps set up several hotlines where families could call for information, but many found the numbers busy. In a cruel hoax, someone claiming to be a Marine lieutenant phoned families, telling them their loved ones were either dead or wounded. This prompted the Pentagon to clarify the process. "A notification is always made in person," a spokesperson said, "both wounded or killed, never over the phone."

Mix-ups likewise occurred, as some Marines and sailors were initially reported wounded only for families to later learn those notifications were erroneous. That was the case for William Foster of Richmond, Virginia, who through a clerical error had received word his son and namesake was injured. "I am worse off now than I was before," said Foster. "We don't know anything now." His wife, Mary Miller, echoed him. "For two days and nights, we were so happy. We thought he was alive," she said. "Now, we're right back where we started."

Two Marine officers visited the New York home of Rose Lagoy, informing her that her son Lance Corporal Michael Balcom had been killed. Hours later, as the family wept and wrestled with their grief, her wounded son phoned from his hospital bed in Germany. "Most people don't believe in miracles," Lagoy said. "But I had one today."

Patricia Briscoe had the opposite experience. The Baltimore mother believed she had seen her son Lance Corporal Davin Green on the television Sunday, which had convinced her for days that he was safe. "Once I saw that picture of that Marine walking to the helicopter for the hospital in Naples," she recalled, "I was sure that was Davin. He was tall, brown-skinned and had the same hairline and the same skinny arms. I was sure he was alive."

She opened her door days later to find two Marines.

"Are you Patricia Briscoe?" one inquired.

"Yes," she confirmed, asking if the Marines had the number of her son's hospital.

"Ma'am," the Marine said. "We've come to tell you that Davin is dead."

The news floored her. "How do you know?" Briscoe stammered. "I saw him on TV Sunday and as he was walking to the helicopter. He looked fine."

Many others continued to wait in agony as the days ticked by. Friends, loved ones, and faith leaders visited with families to provide what comfort they could. In Massachusetts, the local grocery store kept John L'Heureux's parents supplied with food for six days until the family finally learned he was in Germany. Afraid to disturb them, neighbors left baskets of provisions on the front steps. Local schoolchildren offered prayers. "That whole week," recalled his stepfather, Richard Wells, "was just hell."

Few could work or even sleep. Most remained prisoners of television news, watching the broadcasts while waiting for either a call or a knock on the door. Charles Holland, who had lost another son two years earlier in a car wreck, knew his son Robert lived on the fourth floor of the Battalion Landing Team headquarters. "This will make an old man out of you fast," Holland said. "We are expecting the worst. It is terrible just sitting here waiting."

That nightmare played out in living rooms nationwide. "You just sit here waiting to see if a Marine Corps staff car drives up," added Charles Cavarello of Rhode Island, whose son Michael was a lance corporal in Beirut. "There isn't anything else you can do."

"We've got our fingers crossed and we're praying," said Eugene Dudley of Massachusetts, whose son Bruce was previously wounded in Beirut. "It's a sad thing to say. But I guess we're waiting for the score sheet to come out."

For others, word arrived with the slam of a car door. "As soon as I saw those two Marines coming up to the door, I knew," said Letha Kimm, whose son Edward was killed in the attack.

Carol Schak of New Jersey had a similar reaction when the Marines arrived on her porch with the news of her son James Langon's death. "I don't want to see you here," she confessed.

"We don't want to be here," the men replied.

Guillermo San Pedro opened the door of his Florida home to find a similar scene. "Are you here," he asked, "because my son is dead?"

In the weeks leading up to the bombing, families had learned through letters of the deteriorating situation in Beirut. "The cease-fire here is a crock," nineteen-year-old Alan Opra wrote his mother. "They're still shooting at us." Even as families waited for information, new letters sent on the eve of the bombing landed in mailboxes. That was the case for the mother of Army specialist Marcus Coleman of Dallas, who wrote of his fears as to whether he would survive. "I'm getting closer and closer," he wrote of coming home, "and I don't know whether I'm going to make it. I pray every night I do. I'm leaving it in God's hands."

Coleman did not survive.

Confirmation of the deaths brought out anger in some, including the family of Lance Corporal Ronald Meurer, who left behind a wife and three-month-old daughter. "As far as I'm concerned, my son died for nothing," said Mary Lou Meurer of Ohio. "Why isn't our president in Beirut now, like the president of France is?" Others agreed, questioning the purpose of the mission. That was true of John Price of Alabama, whose son James was killed. "I feel my son was sacrificed," he said. "I don't see any reason for those boys being there."

As the week wore on—and family stresses dominated news coverage—the American Telephone & Telegraph Company established two special circuits that connected the Beirut airport to the phone company's International Operating Center in Pittsburgh. Operators in Pennsylvania could then connect those calls to domestic numbers. Each Marine was allowed to make a two-minute call home. "This service is available to Marines 24 hours a day and it will be in operation until the need for it subsides," a company spokesperson said. "The free calls can only originate in Lebanon." In Beirut, Marines lined up to phone home. Enlisted men were given priority over officers. That's how the Norfleet family in Kentucky learned their son, Lance Corporal Charles "Tony" Norfleet, was safe. "We all screamed when we heard his voice," his mother said. "Then we hung up the phone and prayed."

CHAPTER 52

I have seen enough dead for 10 lifetimes.
—Private David Madaras, letter to his family
October 24, 1983

Work continued in Beirut as rescuers deconstructed the pile layer by layer, removing the remains of the fourth floor followed by the third, second, and finally the first. The dead continued to surface, each placed in body bags and shipped to Germany, where dentists and FBI agents used forensic science to identify the remains. On the third day, workers uncovered the remains of Bryan Earle, who had returned from his honeymoon the day before the bombing. His bride, Micheline, had rushed to the Marine compound, where she had kept a lonely and tearful vigil, interrupted only by visits to the local hospitals and morgues in search of news. "I had a bad feeling when I got there that he was dead," Micheline said. "I kept hoping somehow he was alive. You don't ever want to believe someone you love is dead."

Work on the pile proved emotional and exhausting. Sergeant Kim McKinney toiled all week, helping to remove fifty-seven bodies. "Why I kept count, I have no idea," McKinney later said. "Seven days of just slow torture, cutting out the concrete, cutting the steel, picking it up, removing the dead—seven days. It was just a never-ending nightmare."

Others packed up personal papers and belongings salvaged from the wreckage for shipment to families back in America. Unidentifiable papers and clothes, particularly those stained with blood, were collected and burned.

Dr. Jim Ware, who had played a tremendous role in the immediate aftermath of the terrorist bombing, still had one vital task to accomplish. "I want to see John Hudson," he repeatedly instructed the work crews. "I need to see him."

Hudson and Ware, who had attended the same medical school in Georgia, had first met back in May, rooming together for three weeks on board the *Austin* en route to Beirut. The fastidious Ware had spent six months preparing for deployment, packing everything he might need, right down to the foot powder. Hudson, in contrast, showed up with a single sack.

"What do you have there?" Ware asked in disbelief.

"Hell, I don't know," Hudson replied. "I packed last night."

The two had hit it off immediately, a bond that would only strengthen in the months ahead. "He had been my friend," the dentist recalled, "my sidekick and my jokester."

Crews fetched Ware several days after the bombing with the news that Hudson had been found. Unsure of what he would encounter, Ware made his way over to the pile, where Marines had freed Hudson from the rubble.

Would his friend be crushed?

Or his body torn in pieces?

"Where is he?" Ware asked as he approached.

"Right here," one of the workers replied.

Ware looked down on the lifeless body of his friend and was relieved to find him intact and free of any blood. Hudson, who had been asleep in his rack, wore a T-shirt but no shoes or dog tags. His right hand covered his face, the palm facing upward. The building where he had sought shelter from rockets and artillery had come down on top of him, killing him instantly. Ware paid his respects. "I wanted that moment with him," he said, "because he was a personal friend of mine."

"That's John," he confirmed for the rescuers.

Hudson had long feared his life would end in Beirut, a dread he touched on in so many of his letters. He prayed often that he would survive so that he could return home to his wife and infant son, to practice medicine in Georgia and play his beloved Dixieland jazz. In the top corner of each letter, he kept a running tally of his days in Beirut versus how many he had left. In his final letter, penned three days before the bombing, he noted he had spent 164 days on the beach and had only 24 days left. "Hopefully our long separation is quickly coming to an end. I sure hope so!" Hudson wrote. "I love you more than you'll ever know."

Naval criminal investigators—joined later by FBI agents—combed through the wreckage while reporters continued to prowl the bomb site's perimeter, interviewing those Marines willing to talk. Many focused on Lance Corporal Robert Calhoun, who had a dramatic story of being on the roof of the Battalion Landing Team headquarters when the attack occurred. Journalists encircled the twenty-one-year-old Texan, holding microphones up to his face as he recounted hearing the terrorist's truck crash through the guard shack and then explode. "Everything started falling," he remembered. "I was praying to God." Calhoun came to rest atop the rubble, where he froze for about twenty seconds. When he came to his senses, he unburied his friend Joe Martucci, who was next to him. That's when he heard the cacophony of voices.

"Help me!" people around him cried. "God, help me!"

The young Marine's voice broke. "His words began to run together," observed the *Philadelphia Inquirer*'s David Zucchino, "so somebody from the Public Affairs Office pulled him away to let him collect himself. Later, some other reporters asked to talk to him, but the public affairs people said, no, he had been under too much strain already."

Several wounded Marines in Germany likewise spoke with reporters, including Burnham Matthews. As he had done for General Kelley, he recounted his incredible story of being blown out of a third-floor window. "I remember objects flying past me," Matthews said. "I landed flat on my feet and I turned and watched as the roof of the building hit the ground."

Reporters asked if the Marines felt security had been adequate. Car bombs were a known threat, the men replied, but a suicide attack was beyond imagination. "It was a cheap shot," said Lance Corporal Lovelle Moore of Illinois. "You gotta be sneaky to fight best."

"You can't fight car bombs with a rifle," added Matthews.

A similar press event took place at the hospital in Naples, where other wounded Marines recuperated. Much like Calhoun, journalists zeroed in on twenty-year-old Lance Corporal Adam Webb of Ohio, who was atop the building and rode the rubble down. "I stayed on the roof until it hit the ground," he said. "Then I wound up sitting upright in a jeep."

Many of the young Marines still in Beirut struggled to process the tragedy. Few had time to reflect in the hours after the attack, but as the days passed and the size of the pile diminished, many had time to rest and contemplate. "Paranoia is high, so is stress and fear. Days have been long and tiresome, nights have been sleepless and terrible," Brad Ulick wrote in his diary. "As of yet, I have not mourned for my dear dead friends. I have not had time to fully think of it, nor have I accepted it. My mind cannot fully comprehend such mass death + destruction. Yet, I felt it, smelled it, and saw it." Some sought out Father Pucciarelli, asking for

Bibles and rosary beads. Others peppered him with questions. "What is death?" some asked. "What is my friend doing now? Where are my buddies? Are they part of the next dimension?"

The attack left many other Marines grateful. "I just thank God I'm alive," said Lance Corporal Mike Balcom of New York, who survived despite being buried under the rubble. "I am not ashamed to say that it scared the shit out of me," Private David Madaras wrote to his parents. "We were always saying how those guys in that building had it made—the easy life, living in a building with all the comfort. Well, I'm glad I live in a ditch."

"I cried a lot," recalled Michael Petit. "It didn't take much to cause my emotions to spill over: a photograph, a glimpse of a letter, part of a birthday card."

Most were exhausted by the sight of mangled bodies as well as the stench of rot that hung over the pile. "I have seen enough death and destruction to last for a thousand lifetimes," Grant McIntosh wrote. "It seems to me that the whole bloody world is going to Hell in a hand basket." The naval investigator worked for three days, packing bodies and photographing the crime scene, before he returned to the *Iwo Jima*. A letter from his wife with a photo of his daughter triggered a meltdown. "I broke, all I could see was the families and children of the dead Marines," McIntosh wrote. "Honey, I cried. I felt so much hate, anger, frustration and above all helplessness."

Henry Linkkila, who was on guard duty the morning of the attack, had been evacuated to the *Iwo Jima*. The explosion blew out both of his eardrums and left his ears with a constant ring, so much so that he struggled just to sleep. "I've vowed," the cook wrote his mother, "never to step foot in Beirut again." Many others felt the same. It was time to go home. "Boy," John Dalziel wrote his family, "the deck of that ship will feel like Heaven."

CHAPTER 53

*Just once in my lifetime, I would like to see the young men
go to Washington and send the old men out to die.*
—GEORGE PROKOP, LETTER TO THE EDITOR
October 28, 1983

General Kelley touched down Tuesday afternoon following his stop-over in Germany. The commandant was joined by presidential aide Edward Hickey and Representative John Murtha, a Pennsylvania Democrat who had come as an emissary to House Speaker Tip O'Neill. Kelley insisted on visiting the bomb site first, a gruesome scene that repulsed Murtha, even though he was a former Marine and Vietnam combat veteran. "The stench of bodies was just overwhelming," the lawmaker said. "It was the worst thing I have ever seen."

For forty minutes, the men surveyed the wreckage, watching as rescuers dug out the remains of two additional Marines. "You could see a foot sticking up. Then after a while, another foot," Murtha said. "And then, they lifted it out and you could see the whole body, bloated, disfigured, with one arm blown off. And I was thinking how just two days ago, this had been some young fella."

The scene proved equally as hard for Kelley. "There is nothing more devastating to a Marine," the general said, "than the loss of another Marine."

Hickey, in contrast, focused not on the dead, but on the heroic role of the rescuers, who toiled for days amid the rubble and rebar. In a report for the president, he singled out the extraordinary work of Rabbi Resnicoff and Father Pucciarelli, who helped rescue Chaplain Wheeler and comforted so many others. Hickey recounted the story of Resnicoff's makeshift yarmulke fashioned from the camouflage fabric of a helmet. "This morning I saw the rabbi in a hospital consoling the wounded. He still wore the yarmulke," Hickey cabled the White House. "He told me it was the greatest honor ever bestowed upon him."

During his two-day visit, Kelley reviewed the details of the bombing and examined the compound's security. Geraghty escorted him to meet with other multinational force leaders as well as General Tannous, where he discussed the latest intel surrounding the twin attacks against American and French forces. In a top-secret five-page report to the president—a draft of which he wrote by hand in the back of the plane on his return flight from Beirut—Kelley outlined his findings. This was not the work of a crazed fanatic, but a calculated attack by foreign actors designed to drive the United States out of Lebanon. The French reported that twelve individuals rapidly left the Iranian embassy less than fifteen minutes after the 6:22 a.m. attack. Ten of those were later identified as Syrian military officers. General Tannous stated that the first secretary to the Soviet Embassy in Beirut told one of his officers that "Reagan thought he won his re-election at Suk al-Gharb, but he will lose it in the streets of Beirut."

America needed to prepare, Kelley wrote, for a new form of warfare. "In my professional estimation our Marines have now been targeted for terrorism by highly professional non-Lebanese elements," he concluded. "In my view, these acts of violence will continue, and the perpetrators will carefully examine and analyze our vulnerabilities and make every effort to exploit them. In short, I firmly believe that the expertise for terrorism of the Soviet Union, Syria, Iran, and possibly Libya, will be focused upon our Marines in the months to come." Geraghty's security at the compound, Kelley added, was designed to defend against the daily attacks by artillery, mortars, and small-arms fire. "In this context, his security efforts had been successful. Not one Marine, sailor, or soldier protected by this building had been killed or wounded during a period of 13 months," the general wrote. "I have yet to find any intelligence which would have alerted the commander to this extraordinary 'truck-bomb' threat."

Kelley likewise argued that it was a mistake to compare the attack on the Marine headquarters with the April bombing of the embassy. "The dissimilarities," he noted, "far outweigh the similarities." In that case, a lone car drove up to the front and exploded. Security at the Marine compound would have prevented a similar strike, requiring a heavy and high-speed vehicle able to crash through concertina wire and sandbags. Kelley wrote that even General Tannous, who had vast experience with car bombs in Lebanon, concluded that this was different. "In his opinion," Kelley wrote, "this attack represents a new and unique terrorist threat, one which could not have been reasonably anticipated by the Commander on the scene."

The general addressed options to improve security. He ruled out moving the Marines to higher ground, since the Druze, Christians, and Lebanese military still battled in the mountains. Putting them aboard ship would increase their safety but would likely collapse the multinational force. That left staying at the airport and improving defenses. Primary security for the airport, he added, was the job of the Lebanese military. In addition, it was an active commercial airport, which the Marines had no authority to disrupt.

America needed a new approach.

Kelley recommended strengthening the coalition. "We must make every effort," the general wrote, "to have the multinational force both multinational and a force." It was clear that the Soviets, Syrians, and Iranians did not look at the four member nations as a cohesive unit, but as separate entities that could be individually targeted. "A truly combined command and operation, to include multinational patrols, presents the other side with a more difficult decision," Kelley wrote. "It may prove less attractive an option to kill a Marine, an Italian, a Frenchman and an Englishman than it would be to kill four Marines." The Lebanese likewise needed to improve intelligence sharing and security around the airport. Kelley warned that America should not be complacent or consider the attackers as intellectual inferiors. The terrorists, he noted, are suicidal, determined, and professional. "No amount of action on our part," he concluded, "will make us totally immune to suicidal terrorism."

At the end of his visit, Kelley sat down with Geraghty and other senior military and diplomatic leaders in the colonel's headquarters. If the Marines were going to stay put, then security needed to change and adapt to face the deadly new adversary. With input from the Marines, Kelley outlined a list of recommendations he planned to forward to the president. Those ranged from limiting vehicle and civilian access to blocking and reinforcing all entrances. The general urged additional guards throughout the compound as well as rifle companies to reinforce the perimeter aided by mobile patrols armed with antitank weapons.

In addition to Kelley's recommendations, the Marines had already adopted other measures, including shrinking the airport road from four lanes to two. Troops rolled out concrete and dirt-filled barricades and dug an anti-vehicle ditch around the compound. Geraghty added M60 machine guns with armor-piercing rounds to cover all roads and open areas around the airport. He likewise barred civilians, relocated the Lebanese military outside the perimeter, and increased the internal guard posts and added light antitank weapons.

Kelley's visit was followed on October 26 by one from Vice President George Bush, who, like Representative Murtha, described his brief time in Beirut "as one of my most difficult and emotional assignments." At 7:16 a.m. that Wednesday, Bush arrived on deck of the *Iwo Jima* via a helicopter from Cyprus. Geraghty met him on board and briefed him. The death toll as of that morning stood at 219. The vice president visited two wounded Marines in sick bay, presenting them Purple Hearts before jumping back into a helicopter at 8:33 a.m. for the flight to the beach. The bespectacled vice president shed his tie, but still wore gray slacks and a white button-down, which was accentuated by a camouflaged flak vest and helmet.

Bush refused to interrupt the work of the rescuers, speaking instead to reporters. "I hadn't expected this much destruction. You've heard it. You've read it. But until you feel it, see it . . . ," he said as his voice trailed off. "I guess it's the horror, just the cowardly horror. You know what happened, what somebody did." The vice president reiterated Reagan's commitment to Lebanon. "We're not going to let down friends," he said. "We're not going to let a bunch of insidious terrorist cowards shape the foreign policy of the United States."

Bush flew next to meet with Gemayel. In a report to the president, he wrote that Gemayel's "analysis of things in Lebanon was disturbing and disappointing" and that he "showed no enthusiasm and certainly no optimism" about the upcoming reconciliation talks in Geneva. With foreign armies in control of 80 percent of his country, Gemayel said the Americans were vital to his survival. "Without the Marines," Bush wrote, "he suggested the Soviet-backed Syrians would be sitting in his office." Not only did Gemayel argue that he could not let the Marines leave, but he also predicted more terrorist attacks in the future. "In short," Bush concluded, "he painted us into a quagmire with little hope for the future."

Bush's dour report dovetailed with the assessment of the American intelligence community. On the same day Bush met with Gemayel, CIA director William Casey sent White House Chief of Staff James Baker a special National Intelligence Estimate. "The prospects for a lasting political reconciliation among Lebanon's confessional factions are extremely bleak," the report warned. "Meaningful national reconciliation depends primarily on the Lebanese and for the present they seem unwilling to make the concessions and compromises necessary for a lasting accommodation. As a consequence, the prospects of achieving a sovereign and politically stable state free from foreign occupation are virtually nonexistent."

The parade of visitors in Beirut continued with the arrival on October 29 of an eleven-member delegation of lawmakers from the House Committee on Veterans' Affairs and the Committee on Armed Services. Geraghty greeted them upon arrival. In a sign of the hostility he would later face before Congress, Representative Larry Hopkins charged up to him.

"You are going to eat a shit sandwich!" the Kentucky Republican barked.

"I didn't blink, move a muscle, or say a word. But I did glare at him," the colonel recalled. "After a period, he apparently sensed my mood and finally backed off."

That same day, Geraghty filed his weekly situation report. Despite the tragedy, he applauded the tireless work of his troops. "Key leadership challenge is to put physical and emotional drain of the past week behind us and start looking ahead to sustain max readiness against the known and unknown enemy," he wrote. "The strength of our spirit has been severely tested this past week and not found wanting. Our faith and confidence in the men that form this magnificent Navy/Marine team has been again unquestionably confirmed."

As the days passed, the pile shrank.

Workers hauled the debris to an unused end of one runway, creating a six-foot-tall rubble field that stretched more than a half mile long and measured fifty yards wide. Two special agents from the Explosive Units of the FBI Laboratory Division arrived to comb through the tangle of rebar and concrete. The oblong-shaped bomb crater measured thirty-nine feet long by twenty-nine feet wide. Agents pinpointed the exact spot of detonation, which showed that the truck had penetrated thirteen feet inside the lobby. A clock recovered in the basement marked the time of the blast as 6:21:26. A rear axle was all that remained of the Mercedes. "A reinforced concrete slab," agents concluded, "which was approximately 4 feet x 8 feet x 7 inches thick with a 1-inch marble facing was driven eight feet into the crater by the explosive forces."

The FBI found traces of pentaerythritol tetranitrate, the same explosive used in the embassy bombing. Similar to the April attack, the terrorists had used gas containers such as oxygen or propane to magnify the blast. Agents conservatively estimated that the explosion equated to about

12,000 pounds of TNT, though experts conceded it could have ranged as high as 20,000 pounds, making the attack six to nine times larger than the one that rocked the embassy. The attack proved to be the largest non-nuclear blast the experts had ever examined.

The week wound down.

And the ruins gave up the last of the dead.

Petit was on hand to watch as the final victim emerged.

"Ho!" someone shouted.

A backhoe driver hit the brakes. Two Marines jumped down into the pit. The corporal peered in to see a hand rising up out of the dirt. The men worked carefully to unbury the body, which was curled up in the fetal position. "The smell of putrefied flesh was nauseating, and I wanted to leave," Petit said. "But I was unable to tear myself away."

The Marines pulled on one of the legs to try to free the body, but it would not budge. The men tossed aside shovels and used their hands to dig around the edges. "Eventually," Petit said, "they used a shovel as a lever and managed to pry him loose. I waited until they gently placed him into a body bag before I slowly walked to the command post."

CHAPTER 54

Whether Bill is alive or not, we know that he's with the Lord.
—BILL AND KAYE GAINES, LETTER TO RONALD REAGAN
October 26, 1983

Reagan felt the pressure.

From Congress.

From the families of the Marines.

From the nation.

In less than a week, the president had gone from enjoying golf amid the famed azaleas and dogwoods of Augusta National to enduring one of the worst terrorist attacks in modern history. In addition, he had surprised the public by ordering the October 25 invasion of Grenada—code-named Operation Urgent Fury—which involved more than 7,000 Marines and paratroopers. "It was," as Associated Press reporter Harry Rosenthal wryly noted, "the worst week of Ronald Reagan's presidency—save perhaps the time he was shot."

A White House tally revealed that from October 21 to 27, the administration had received 3,154 letters on the question of whether troops should remain in Beirut. Of those, 2,862 urged Reagan to bring the Marines home. Another 1,028 letters addressed retaliation, a majority of which demanded America strike back. Those letters and telegrams—some from the friends, siblings, and parents of men killed—offered a glimpse of the nation's diverse opinions. Some supported the president. Others did not. A few wrote more out of a sense of catharsis, including a private who had spent hours digging through the rubble for his friends. "As far as I know to date, everyone in my particular unit has been killed," he wrote. "Had I not switched assignments with my best friend, I would have been asleep in the Headquarters building I called home."

The emotion in others was raw, including for Kenneth Ellison. "They killed my son in Beirut," he wrote. "They killed him in his sleep."

Susan Ray, sister of slain Marine Joseph Moore, described the toll her brother's death had taken upon her family. "When Joseph was murdered, so was a part of my mother and father," she wrote. "These two people are not the same two people I once knew. What I see now are two angry, empty, and cold people." Her mother cried all day and refused to get out of bed, while her father tried to remain strong for the couple's five surviving children. "He's a poor actor," Kay wrote; "the lines in his face are proof of the sleepless nights, the nights he lays awake and swears he hears Joseph calling for him. My mother tells me that in the middle of the night this grown man weeps like a baby."

In the wake of the first Marine deaths in August and September, Navy corpsman Joseph Milano, who had fought to save them, had questioned what people would remember of the men. "I wonder," he wrote, "how long it will take before people forget about these Marines." Milano's own friends and family raised similar questions now that he, too, was gone. "Our grief is totally insurmountable," his friend Francine Minutoli wrote to Reagan. "We need something to help us reconcile his death. We need to hear, from you, his purpose in Lebanon."

Many others agreed.

As the flood of letters, congressional speeches, and editorials made clear, Reagan needed to rally the shell-shocked nation, still reeling from the images of destruction paraded across televisions screens, the stories of families desperate for news, and the interviews with survivors who recounted the horror of the attack. The president needed to define the mission and explain to the American public why so many young men had died. More importantly, he needed to buy time to nail down the identity of the attackers and chart a path forward. The charismatic former actor planned to do so in a nationally televised address on the night of October 27, a speech that would no doubt prove to be one of the most important of his entire career.

Suggestions from aides on what he should include poured into the Oval Office. Newt Gingrich sent eighteen pages of notes and proposed verbiage. "The American people and the American news media are, to some extent, in a stake of shock," the Georgia congressman wrote. "The combination of an unimagined scale of violence in Beirut and an unexpected invasion of Grenada have swamped the American system with information shock."

"Recent events," another aide wrote, "clearly have unleashed a major debate in the Congress and the country of the direction of broader Administration policy."

Rather than fall back on speechwriters, the president tackled it himself with a pen and notepad. He cleared much of his schedule the afternoon before and stayed up until 1 a.m. crafting his words. He continued to work on it throughout the day on Thursday.

At one point, Deputy Chief of Staff Michael Deaver gave him a copy of the story of Jeffrey Nashton's emotional bedside encounter with General Kelley in Germany. "If you can read it without choking up," Deaver told him, "I'll let you keep it."

But the softhearted president could not.

"All right," Deaver demanded, "give it back."

Reagan refused, choosing instead to insert the anecdote into his speech, which he repeatedly rehearsed until he could get through it. On October 27, Reagan ate a quick dinner with the First Lady at 7 p.m. before heading to the Oval Office forty minutes later.

Dressed in a navy-blue suit with white pocket square and dark tie, the president took a seat behind his oak desk, which was crafted from timbers salvaged from the ill-fated Arctic explorer HMS *Resolute*, an 1880 gift from Queen Victoria to then-president Rutherford Hayes. The American people tuned in at 8 p.m. to see the commander in chief, flanked by the American and presidential flags, address the nation.

Rather than gloss over the tragedy, the president walked Americans through the terrorist attack in detail. "This past Sunday," he began, "at twenty-two minutes after six Beirut time, with dawn just breaking, a truck, looking like a lot of other vehicles in the city, approached the airport on a busy, main road. There was nothing in its appearance to suggest it was any different than the trucks or cars that were normally seen on and around the airport. But this one was different. At the wheel was a young man on a suicide mission."

The president described the bombing, the collapse of the building, followed by the attack on the French. He reminded the nation that these were not the first American deaths in Lebanon. Others had been killed by mortars and snipers. After each death, he called the parents. "Sometimes there were questions," he said. "And now many of you are asking: Why should our young men be dying in Lebanon? Why is Lebanon important to us?"

Reagan explained that despite Lebanon's diminutive size—not to mention its location five and a half thousand miles away—it was a cornerstone for peace in a volatile region. Four times in the last three decades, Israel and its Arab neighbors had gone to war. "And each time," he said, "the world has teetered near the edge of catastrophe."

But America's interests went beyond Lebanon. It was vital to safeguard Israel and block Soviet influence in the region, an adversary that continued to aid Syria with weapons and advisors. He recalled his stalled plan for Middle East peace, which he hoped would build on the Camp David Accords. To make peace a reality, however, it was imperative to drive out foreign forces and end the fighting. "So why are we there?" the president asked. "Well, the answer is straightforward: to help bring peace to Lebanon and stability to the vital Middle East."

The multinational force, he said, was created as a tool for that purpose. Israel had agreed to leave, but Syria refused. In the meantime, Gemayel set up a new government while American troops had helped train the Lebanese army. "In the year that our Marines have been there, Lebanon has made important steps toward stability and order. The physical presence of the Marines lends support to both the Lebanese government and its army. It allows the hard work of diplomacy to go forward," Reagan said. "As to that narrower question—what exactly is the operational mission of the Marines—the answer is, to secure a piece of Beirut, to keep order in their sector, and to prevent the area from becoming a battlefield.

"If our Marines must be there, I'm asked, why can't we make them safer? Who committed this latest atrocity against them and why?"

Reagan said America was doing everything possible to keep the Marines safe, including sending the battleship *New Jersey* to the region. "We have strong circumstantial evidence that the attack on the Marines was directed by terrorists who used the same method to destroy our embassy in Beirut," the president said. "Those who directed this atrocity must be dealt justice, and they will be. The obvious purpose behind the sniping, and now this attack, was to weaken American will and force the withdrawal of U.S. and French forces from Lebanon."

The bombing, he argued, was actually a sign of the operation's success. "The multinational force was attacked precisely because it is doing the job it was sent to do in Beirut," Reagan said. "It is accomplishing its mission." Going forward, America planned to accelerate its push for peace and stability, including with the upcoming reconciliation talks in Geneva. The administration would work with allies to lend support to Lebanon. Lastly, America planned to improve security for the Marines. Leaving Lebanon would not only send the wrong message to the world, but would surrender the Middle East to the Soviets. "Brave young men have been taken from us. Many others have been grievously wounded. Are we to tell them their sacrifice was wasted?" Reagan said. "We're a nation with global responsibilities."

The president then walked viewers through the invasion of Grenada, explaining the need to rescue nearly a thousand Americans, including eight hundred medical students. The mission had proven a success as planeloads of students returned safely home. "The events in Lebanon and Grenada," Reagan said, "though oceans apart, are closely related." In both cases, Moscow assisted and encouraged violence. "The world has changed," he said. "Today, our national security can be threatened in faraway places." But the nation's resolve, through the attack in Beirut and the success in Grenada, had assured him that America would maintain peace and ensure freedom.

Reagan then shared the story of Kelley's encounter with Jeffery Nashton. He made it through without breaking down. "That Marine and all those others like him, living and dead, have been faithful to their ideas," the president said. "That young Marine and all of his comrades have given every one of us something to live up to.

"I will not ask you to pray for the dead," he concluded, "because they're safe in God's loving arms and beyond the need of our prayers. I would like to ask you all—wherever you may be in this blessed land—to pray for these wounded young men and to pray for the bereaved families of those who gave their lives for our freedom. God bless you, and God bless America."

The president's speech totaled a little more than four thousand words and ran twenty-five minutes. The response proved immediate. In the thirty-five minutes that followed, more than a thousand calls flooded the White House. By midnight, that number had jumped to 4,592 calls. Of those, 4,272 expressed support for the president, a margin of 13–1. The administration likewise received 1,167 telegrams, with 1,102 of those writing in praise of Reagan.

Congressional leaders likewise applauded the president.

"A powerful and moving speech," declared Senate Majority Leader Howard Baker. "Undoubtedly it will have a unifying effect on the American people."

"His finest hour," added Senator Paul Laxalt, a Nevada Republican.

"Masterful," announced Republican representative Jim Leach of Iowa.

His speech even drew praise from journalists, including CBS News commentators who weighed in on it that evening. "I have an idea," anchor

Dan Rather said, "that this may go down as one of the president's strongest, more effective speeches of his presidency."

"I think I'd put it right up there as one of his strongest speeches," agreed his colleague Bill Plante, the network's Washington correspondent.

An ABC News poll of 250 viewers that night showed support for the president's handling of Lebanon soared from 50 percent to 80 percent. As later polls indicated, that incredible jump likely reflected an emotional high experienced by viewers in the speech's immediate aftermath. A later joint *Washington Post/ABC News* poll of 1,246 people revealed a more modest rise in support, from 41 to 52 percent. That was more in line with other polls, including one by *USA Today* that revealed an increase in support from 39 to 53 percent.

Experts cautioned that the sudden bump in support for Reagan did not erase the deeper doubts expressed by a majority of respondents about America's long-term chance of success in Lebanon. "The public feels the Marine mission in Lebanon has been a failure so far—62 percent of those we interviewed felt that way," observed Jeffrey Alderman, the director of polling for ABC News. "Nearly half the public felt the United States has no clear policy for the Marines in Lebanon. Reagan's speech did little to turn around those basic attitudes."

A number of opinion writers zeroed in on that critical point. Reagan's speech certainly tapped an emotional vein for many Americans, but it offered no new ideas or plans for how to remedy what his own vice president that week had called a "quagmire."

He still had to deal with the notoriously weak Gemayel.

Plus an intractable and murderous Syria.

And now he faced the threat of Iranian-backed terrorism, which everyone from General Kelley to Gemayel predicted would continue to torment the Marines, a fact highlighted by journalists Robert Novak and Rowland Evans. "Prolonging of the Marines' Beirut encampment," the influential duo warned, "continues to be another disaster waiting to happen."

Reagan remained stuck in a no-win situation, one best described by the *Miami Herald*. "Get out or get in deeper," the paper declared. "Those seem to be the real choices that Washington is ducking." Others questioned the premise that peace in Lebanon was actually vital to American and regional interest, particularly since the country had been at war for nearly a decade. "We fear for the judgment of our policymakers," wrote the *Los An-*

geles Times, "if, in fact, they truly think that stability in the Middle East hangs on sorting out the implacable hostilities of Lebanon." The *Minneapolis Star Tribune* raised the specter of Reagan's hubris. "The president hears so clearly the call of destiny that he is untroubled by alarms ringing on all sides," the paper wrote. "In our view, there are good reasons for alarm."

But those voices of doubt and caution remained the minority, as evidenced by the continued flood of calls to the White House. The president, no doubt exhausted by the grueling week, ducked out Friday afternoon with the first lady for a weekend at Camp David, where the couple relaxed and caught the film *The Big Chill.* Over the next four days, White House staff and volunteers logged 16,009 calls. Of those, 13,401 were positive. "The Comments Office," one memo noted, "reports it was an enormously heavy response—unprecedented, in fact, and the single largest such telephone response in the course of this Administration."

CHAPTER 55

There is no way on God's Earth that rifle fire could have stopped that truck.
—General Paul Kelley, testimony before the
Senate Armed Services Committee
October 31, 1983

The first C-141 carrying the remains of American Marines and sailors killed in Beirut touched down at Dover Air Force Base at 3:52 a.m. on October 30. In the back of the transport plane were the caskets of fifteen men killed six days earlier in the terrorist attack. Officials at Dover had prepared all week for this solemn occasion, transforming a cavernous hangar normally used by the C-5 Galaxies—the Air Force's largest cargo plane—into a funeral chapel to receive the dead and their families. A massive American flag that measured thirty-eight feet long by twenty feet high hung from an overhead girder. Workers had arranged cinder blocks to hold the caskets. Others had set out three sets of portable aluminum bleachers and plastic chairs for families and dignitaries. A pair of flatbed trailers in the back would provide a platform for the media. A thirty-eight-piece Marine Corps band had rehearsed the Navy Hymn.

The arrival that predawn Saturday of the first remains represented the culmination of nonstop exhausting work that had taken place that week in Germany by teams of forensic dentists, fingerprint experts, pathologists, morticians, and volunteers. The initial casualty plan had called for all remains to be flown from Beirut to the U.S. Army Mortuary in Frankfurt for identification before returning them to the United States. The first thirty-seven bodies had arrived early Monday morning—less than twenty-four hours after the bombing—followed by a second flight later that day that delivered an additional 144 remains. The 181 bodies transported by those first two flights far exceeded the storage capacity of the Army's morgue, forcing the military to scramble for an alternative. Officials decided to use the Frankfurt morgue for the final preparation of remains, but settled on nearby Rhein-Main Air Base as the principal hub for storage and identification of the slain soldiers, sailors, and Marines.

To tackle the difficult task, the Air Force procured a large festival tent, which was erected in a base parking lot. Workers laid down plywood floors and used corrugated sheet metal to cordon off several workspaces, including an administrative area, holding zone, and examination suite for identifications. Electricians strung fluorescent lights overhead while folding tables were set up along with wooden sawhorses to support stretchers. The metal transfer cases were stacked in refrigeration trailers outside, covered by camouflage netting. In the era before DNA technology, identification was made primarily through fingerprint and dental analysis. That job fell to four FBI fingerprint experts, twenty dentists, twenty-three dental technicians, eight x-ray technicians, and one pathologist, plus another fifty air base staffers and an army of eight hundred volunteers, all of whom dressed in disposable surgical gowns, rubber gloves, and masks to filter out the odors. One of those was Dr. Robert Sundquist, a thirty-two-year-old dentist who had previously helped identify victims of the Jonestown mass suicide in Guyana. "Teeth are the most protected area of the body," he said. "Teeth will survive almost anything."

The process of identification began when workers carried the aluminum caskets from the refrigeration trucks to a staging area inside the tent. Teams then opened each and transferred the body bag to a stretcher. The condition of the remains varied widely. Some appeared to be sleeping, while many others were badly mangled by the building's collapse. Still others were swollen and black from decomposition. "Some of them," Sundquist recalled, "you couldn't even recognize as human." Incomplete bodies proved another challenge, forcing technicians to reassemble the remains, like a jigsaw puzzle. "At this time," one situation report noted, "we have four transfer cases containing unassociated body parts."

The remains would first be x-rayed and then fingerprinted. Those prints were then flown back to Washington each night for analysis by the FBI. X-rays were used to spot previously broken bones that might help with identification. After fingerprinting, dentists working in pairs charted each victim's teeth. One performed an inspection while the other took detailed notes. The duo then flipped roles and repeated the process to ensure their work was as precise as possible. This work was complemented by dental x-rays, which were taken with a portable machine. Dentists then compared those x-rays and charts to the records salvaged from the basement of the Battalion Landing Team headquarters, which at times proved a challenge since some of records were wet, torn, and mixed with concrete shards and dust.

Identified bodies were then sent to the mortuary in Frankfurt, which was staffed by a dozen Army and Air Force morticians, seven identification specialists, one Navy mortuary technician, and another two hundred volunteers. Workers cleaned the remains, inventoried any personal items included in the body bags, and drafted an anatomical chart. Once identification specialists reconfirmed the victim's identity, the remains were turned over to an embalmer. As a final step—and to guarantee absolute accuracy—a civilian specialist reviewed each file, anatomical chart, and embalming record. That final review could take anywhere from one and a half to as many as eight hours per body. "When the validator was certain of the correctness of the data," the mortuary report noted, "he would sign the death certification document."

The process that began that Monday night of October 24 would continue for seventeen days. Marines recovered the majority of the dead the day of the bombing, but rescuers would find dozens more during the deconstruction of the pile. Each body found was packed into a transfer case and flown to Germany. All told, forensic teams would process the remains of nearly all 241 soldiers, sailors, and Marines killed that Sunday morning. Of those, 68 were identified using both fingerprints and dental records. Another 131 were identified solely by dental analysis and 28 just with fingerprints. The remaining few were identified visually or by other medical records. "Ninety six percent of the remains were identified," the mortuary report stated, "by using a combination of dental and fingerprint information."

From Frankfurt, the bodies were flown to Dover, home to the military's largest mortuary and capable of accommodating up to a thousand dead. For the Jonestown mass suicide, which Sundquist had worked, the base had handled the remains of more than nine hundred men, women, and children. The plan called for planes to arrive between 2 and 4 a.m., a time picked to prevent the press from witnessing the removal of the caskets. Meanwhile, a working party would clean the hangar, arrange the seating, and position cinder blocks for the number of caskets expected. Once the caskets were in place, workers draped each one in an American flag. All this had to be accomplished by 7 a.m., when the arrival ceremony was scheduled to take place.

The C-141 that touched down in the predawn hours of October 30 would be the first of thirteen flights that would follow; one every day until the last victims came home on November 11—Veterans Day. Following the ceremony, workers would transport the remains via a closed truck to the Dover mortuary, where technicians would inspect each victim and perform cosmetic work on those few who would later have an open-casket funeral. Volunteers would dress the victims, which was a challenge since many had swollen by as much as five inches. For those remains that would not be viewed, volunteers wrapped them and laid uniforms atop each, pinned them in place, and removed any lint. Purple Hearts, many left over from Vietnam, had to be inspected. "Most were deteriorated and not suitable for presentation," one after-action report noted. "Rehabilitation was required which caused delay in mailing." Coffins were then sent to Philadelphia and Washington and shipped to the funeral homes that would handle each burial.

The first C-141 to come back carried the remains of fourteen Marines and one sailor. The plane taxied to the hangar, where Marines unloaded each of the caskets. At 7 a.m., the Marine Band from Quantico played "Eternal Father," the Navy's hymn. Chief of Chaplains Rear Admiral Neil Stevenson opened in prayer, choosing a familiar verse from the book of Matthew that the men in Beirut all knew. "Blessed are the peacemakers," he began.

Families listened and wept as the chaplain's words echoed inside the cavernous hangar. Stevenson then turned to face the twenty relatives in attendance that morning. "We stand in awe before your sons," the chaplain continued. "They have honored their families. They have witnessed their fidelity to our nation. They have evidenced their respect for humanity. They have presented themselves before Your Grace in pursuit of peace."

Chief of Naval Operations Admiral James Watkins spoke next. "We share the grief of the family and friends who lost loved ones in this terrible tragedy."

The admiral turned to the long row of caskets.

"I salute you, brave brothers," he continued, "and I ask God to give solace and comfort to your families in this hour of great need and personal loss."

General Kelley followed. The commandant of the Marine Corps had endured a difficult week. He had flown to Germany, where he witnessed the arrival Monday night of many of the dead. He had met with some of the wounded before flying to Beirut, where he watched rescuers pull even more bodies from the rubble. His words that morning mirrored the thoughts on the minds of many. "This cowardly and heinous act snuffed out the lives of over 220 brave Americans," Kelley said. "I pray to God that these brave men have not died in vain."

CHAPTER 56

*Personally, I'm doing good. Trying to get things
back to normal. If it will ever be.*
—CORPORAL JOHN DALZIEL, LETTER TO HIS FAMILY
October 28, 1983

At 8:11 a.m. on November 4, President Reagan and the first lady walked out onto the South Lawn of the White House and climbed aboard Marine One for a flight to Andrews Air Force Base. Eight minutes later, the couple touched down and transferred to Air Force One for the fifty-nine-minute trip south to Marine Corps Air Station Cherry Point, along the coast of North Carolina. The president was joined that Friday morning—twelve days after terrorists killed 241 soldiers, sailors, and Marines—by an entourage that included Shultz, Weinberger, McFarlane, and Treasury secretary Don Regan as well as the Tarheel State's two senators, Jesse Helms and John East, and representatives, John Martin and Charles Whitley. Ambassadors from England, France, Italy, and Lebanon rounded out the presidential party.

At Cherry Point, the president boarded a helicopter to nearby Camp Lejeune, home of the 24th Marine Amphibious Unit. Despite the White House's prediction of a mild fall day with partly sunny skies, Reagan disembarked to find cold and steady rain. Major General Alfred Gray greeted the president, who climbed into a motorcade that delivered him moments later to a nearby outdoor amphitheater where General Kelley awaited him.

The president had come this soggy morning to pay his respects and honor the men killed and wounded in Beirut. There was no more fitting place than Camp Lejeune, a sprawling 170-square-mile base in Jacksonville. Construction of the base in 1941 had caused this sleepy town of 800 residents to balloon into a city of 26,000. The base and the city enjoyed a symbiotic relationship. Jacksonville was where many young leathernecks bought their first cars, purchased homes, and started families of their own. "We love our Marines," said Madge Nelson, who sold stereo equipment at the Military Sales Company. "They're our bread and butter."

In the wake of the bombing, journalists representing more than fifty-five news organizations had descended upon this coastal community. Not since the invasion of Iwo Jima in 1945 had the United States lost so many Marines in a single day. Camp Lejeune stood at the epicenter of this loss. Symbols of support were everywhere, from the "Semper Fidelis" sign posted out in front of a local florist to the billboard that towered over Lejeune Boulevard that read: "All Our Thoughts and Support Are with Our Marine Families."

"This tragedy literally struck through the entire community," said Patrick Thomas, the Jacksonville city manager. "There is not a person in this town who doesn't know someone who lost somebody."

Dressed in a tan overcoat, Reagan arrived at around 10 a.m. at the amphitheater, where an estimated five thousand people gathered in the cold rain on the banks of the New River. About two dozen Marines wounded in the bombing sat in wheelchairs, covered by green ponchos. Before taking his seat, the president went down the line, speaking to each of them.

"Good morning," he said. "God bless you."

The service began with the presentation of colors followed by the national anthems of the United States, England, France, Italy, and Lebanon. Before the lectern, five M16 rifles leaned against one another, capped by a helmet and surrounded by scarlet and gold chrysanthemums. Navy chaplain Commodore John McNamara touched on the inclement weather. "The Lord," he began, "has given us a day to match our mood of anguish and grief."

The audience listened.

"I don't know why young men die," McNamara continued. "I don't know why we must endure this grief and pain. You would think it would break the heart of God."

General Gray followed, noting that hundreds of letters of support had poured in since the attack. "As I say a final farewell to our fine heroes," he told the audience, "I want to tell them we will always stand by your families and loved ones—that's the way we are."

The president did not speak during the service but stood along with others and sang as the band played the service hymns of the Army, Navy, and Marines.

"Where is my daddy?" a young boy cried out at one point.

His mother leaned down and embraced him. Another attendee lowered her umbrella and turned her face to the heavens, letting the rain wash away her tears.

"Taps" concluded the forty-five-minute service, during which Nancy wept.

"It was a dreary day with constant rain which somehow seemed appropriate," Reagan wrote that night in his diary. "It was a moving service & as hard as anything we've ever done." Others in his administration agreed, including Larry Speakes. "It was," the White House spokesman later wrote, "the most somber, heart-wrenching hour of his presidency."

After the service, the president met with about two hundred family members of those killed, spending forty-five minutes with them at the nearby Second Marine Division Headquarters.

"You have a most difficult job, Mr. President," one woman said.

"God bless you," he replied.

Reagan had no remarks prepared, but spoke spontaneously, which made him nervous. "No words can make things easier," he began. "All those we honor today, they chose to wear the uniform of their country. They believed in defending freedom, defending what this country stands for. They were willing to die for freedom for their country."

The families fell silent.

"Where do we find men like this?" the president continued. "We all know the answer. They come from families like yours, from farms and villages, towns and cities across this nation. What they did for us—for our country—is what America is all about."

The families embraced him. "They were so wonderful, sometimes widows or mothers would just put their arms around me, their head on my chest & quietly cry," Reagan wrote. "One little boy, 8 or 9, politely handed me a manila folder saying it was something he'd written about his father. Later when I could read it I found it was a poem entitled 'Loneliness.'"

The president then departed for Cherry Point.

"This has been," he confided in aides, "my most difficult moment."

At the Marine air station, Reagan gave a seven-minute talk. The president had learned that morning of yet another terrorist attack in Lebanon, this time aimed at the Israelis. At dawn, a suicide bomber driving a truck had blown up an Israeli intelligence headquarters building in the southern city of Tyre, killing sixty people. "Freedom is being tested throughout the world," he said. "Let no terrorist question our will, no tyrant doubt our resolve. Americans have courage and determination, and we must not and will not be intimidated by anyone anywhere."

CHAPTER 57

I pray to God through Jesus I never have to go through this again.
—BRAD ULICK, LETTER TO HIS MOTHER
October 26 (circa), 1983

Reagan's honoring of the Marines came as families nationwide prepared to bury the dead, who were delivered home each day from Germany. In big cities and small towns, from Texas and Tennessee to New York and Maine, families gathered to say farewell to the men killed in Beirut. In the tiny Ohio town of New Richmond—home to just 2,776 residents—people mourned two slain Marines, Gunnery Sergeant Lloyd West and Corporal Terry Abbot. "The community has been stunned by this," Mayor Betty Hinson said. "We've had nothing but bad news in the past two weeks. It's really hit the community hard."

Men who had gone off to a distant land on a mission of peace now returned to churches where some had been baptized and others married. Friends and loved ones recounted stories. So, too, did high school administrators and pastors. People read Bible verses and recited poems, including Lucian Ray, who wrote one in honor of his son, thirty-three-year-old Gunnery Sergeant Charles Ray. "He's passed the test, he's with the best, he finally made it home."

Such services were often followed by processions to the cemetery. Families gathered in folding chairs under tents alongside harvested fields and where the autumn leaves crackled underfoot or crunched on freshly fallen snow. Marine honor guards fired salutes while buglers blew "Taps," the mournful notes wafting over fields. Such solemn moments were at times interrupted by outbursts of grief. "Don't let them take him away from me," one mother cried out before her son's casket was lowered. "I didn't want him to die."

Unlike many of his fellow Marines, Bill Stelpflug was buried at sea, his ashes carried in an urn aboard the USS *Pensacola*. The Alabama Marine, whose letters showed he never lost his empathy for those suffering in Beirut, had planned to take the bus home for Christmas so he could savor the slow drive through the rural countryside he so loved. Three miles offshore, Chaplain Anthony Casimano performed the Catholic burial service. "With faith and hope in eternal life, let us commend him to the loving mercy of our Father," he said. "Father, unto your hands we commend our brother, William." The priest dropped the urn into the water. "Give him eternal rest, oh Lord, and may the Light shine on him forever."

Micheline Earle accompanied her husband's remains from Germany back to Ohio. The couple had been married only seven days before a terrorist made her a widow. His wedding ring, which medical examiners slipped off his finger and later sent to her, was bent. Earle had written to his family of his plans to marry, but news of his actual wedding surprised them. "I know," Earle had assured them in a letter, "you will like her." Because Earle had not yet submitted her residency paperwork, which was found uncompleted in his back pocket when he was pulled from the rubble, the United States government provided her with a temporary passport and visa. Her older brother Walid accompanied her on the journey from Germany to Ohio.

More than two hundred friends and family gathered for the graveside service. Amid a light drizzle, Micheline hugged his casket. "I will pray for him every day," she cried. "I will pray for everyone. He didn't deserve to die. They all deserved to stay forever in this world."

A similar story unfolded in Georgia, where Lisa Hudson prepared to bury her husband, whose casket arrived at Morris Funeral Home. She went to visit him, knowing his remains were inside. Lisa had just been in Greece with him barely two months earlier. Her final image of John was the morning he left Athens, walking down the long hotel corridor and out of her life forever. Lisa laid her arms across the casket and rested her head on its top.

"Oh, John," she cried. "I can't believe you're gone."

Lisa made the funeral arrangements with the help of her mother while her aunt cared for the couple's infant son, Will. Lisa chose to bury her husband on her family's dairy farm, which stretched across five hundred acres of rolling Georgia countryside. Her father had previously picked out a spot for his own eventual burial, which he relinquished to the son-in-law he so dearly loved. Lisa dug the first shovel of earth to mark the spot. Workers with the funeral home then used a backhoe, clawing out the red Georgia clay as she watched.

"Bless your heart," she said to John. "You never dreamed you would be in that red clay."

On November 6—two days after President Reagan visited Camp Lejeune—friends and family crowded into the wooden pews at First United Methodist Church in Milledgeville, the redbrick sanctuary with six white steeples where the couple was married three years earlier. Lisa reminded herself that Sunday of the need to stay strong. "You're going to hold yourself together. You're going to act like the person that you know yourself to be, and that John would want you to be," she told herself. "Don't act like you're feeling inside."

The Reverend William Childers led the funeral service. "We are hurting; we are angry; we are shocked; and we want to blame God or the government or somebody. The evil of this world has brought hurt to our loved one," he told those gathered. "But we know we can't go on blaming God or the government or somebody, for that solves nothing."

But the service in the end proved far more upbeat, marked by friends who remembered Hudson's large personality. "He was," recalled David Anders, "a musician, a mechanic, a physician, prankster, a scholar, a son, a father, a husband, a brother and a friend."

"There were several occasions when I sat next to John Hudson in the dean's office trying to explain some of the antics we pulled in class," remembered another friend, Matt Nathan. "He took his work seriously—he didn't take himself seriously."

After the church service, friends and family formed a funeral procession that stretched a mile long as it rolled through town and out into the country. Police officers in white gloves blocked intersections and saluted as the family's limousine passed.

Beneath a clear blue sky that fall afternoon as the sun cast long shadows across the fields, two sailors removed and folded the American flag. In honor of John, a trombonist—not a bugler—then played "Taps." With Will grasped in her right arm, Lisa placed a single rose atop the casket. As family and friends stood to leave, Raz'Mataz—the Dixieland jazz band Hudson played with at Six Flags Over Georgia—launched into "St. James Infirmary" before transitioning into the "Muskrat Ramble," one of Hudson's favorite tunes.

CHAPTER 58

Our country is dying.
—LEBANESE PRESIDENT AMIN GEMAYEL
November 1, 1983

In the wake of the bombing, Marines in Beirut hustled to tighten security. "We expect more attacks," Geraghty told reporters. "These are determined people." Amid this work, the colonel paused to give his troops a pep talk, letting them know how proud he was of their hard work in the wake of the attack. "The precise and proper response to this tragedy has been nothing more than what is expected of sailors and Marines of this team," he said. "I also think it a most fitting memorial to those who were killed that we continue to perform our mission as they did. They gave their lives in the cause for peace. We will continue the march."

Father Pucciarelli, who had spent countless hours performing last rites and comforting survivors, did the same. "My commendation goes to all who worked hard and steady day and night to extricate our fallen comrades' bodies and wounded from the building," he said. "There were some long and hard hours and some tedious moments for all, I know."

A flood of up to two thousand letters arrived each day in Beirut, as citizens wrote thank-you cards and sent packages of candy, brownies, and books, including one school that sent eighty-one boxes of cookies. "Your courage and bravery in the face of cowardly terrorists are inspiring to all Americans who love freedom," wrote the Hill family of Atlanta. "We pray for you and ask for your safe return home." American Legion Post 64, based in the tiny town of Cashmere, Washington, mailed fifteen boxes of paperbacks totaling some nine hundred books. "We are <u>proud</u> of you," wrote member Verne Vincent, "and wish you well."

First Lieutenant Ted Bowler received what was possibly the most surprising care package. A raging Celtics fan, Bowler used to drive through the Boston suburb of Brookline just so he could pass Larry Bird's house, keeping an eye out for the basketball star's black Chevrolet Trailblazer. A highlight was the day Bowler drove by and caught sight of Bird mowing his lawn. After the bombing, Bowler's mother knocked on Bird's door and told his fiancée about her son in Beirut. Soon after, the platoon commander received a care package. The return address stunned him. "I only know one person from Brookline," he said, "and that's Larry Bird." The Celtic's six-foot-nine power forward had sent Bowler a warm-up jacket along with a note letting him know he had free tickets waiting on him when he returned home. "He's a God in Boston," Bowler said. "He's possibly the most famous person in the Commonwealth. Everyone loves him."

November brought days of wind and heavy rains, which turned the Marines' Beirut compound into a sea of red mud. "I've started to look for wood," John Dalziel wrote home, "to start on an Ark." To combat the elements, troops drove in scores of stakes to hold tents down while others shoveled trenches to redirect the water. "Marines who had served in earlier deployments," Dolphin observed, "would have had difficulty recognizing the landscape."

Crews brought in shipping containers and covered them with dirt to serve as new hardened bunkers. Geraghty, meanwhile, ordered Alpha Company to abandon the university library, which was too isolated to protect. The spot had long offered the leathernecks high ground to watch over the surrounding slums and militias. But that tactical advantage had come at a price in the form of a bull's-eye on the peacekeepers' backs. It was there that Captain Michael Ohler was shot in the head by a sniper one week before the terrorist bombing. A reminder of Ohler's sacrifice remained taped to the wall as the convoy moved out before dawn on November 9, a crayon drawing from the captain's niece of Snoopy strolling through fall leaves beneath clouds colored red and yellow. "To Uncle Mike," she wrote. "I love you, Tiffany."

Colonel Geraghty ordered nonessential personnel back aboard ship. That included Alpha Company, which had endured some of the heaviest fighting in the months leading up to the bombing. Five of the six Marines killed before the attack had been from Alpha. "You can't dwell on it," Captain Paul Roy advised his men. "It'll tear you apart." Alpha Company would stand in reserve on the *Harlan County*. "The move left more work for fewer Marines to get done," Dolphin said, "but at least we knew that those Marines were now safe."

Troops, meanwhile, cleaned and packed equipment to send out to the ships in preparation for departure on November 19, the day Geraghty would hand over command to the 22nd Marine Amphibious Unit under the command of Brigadier General James Joy, whose forces were inbound from Grenada. The work at times was grueling, but the troops knew it was a necessary step. "We all got sailing home on our mind—so it eases the pain a little!" Dalziel wrote. "Once the gear is brought out to the ships, that only leaves one thing left—us." The days ticked past. "In many ways our last week in Lebanon was the hardest to endure," Dolphin said. "Aside from anticipation, I was fighting an ever-present feeling of dread."

Beyond the wire, a similar sense of doom hung over the Lebanese capital. Rifle fire rattled and mortars rained down, periodically closing the airport. Residents lined up for hours outside Western embassies, desperate for visas. Roadblocks designed to prevent car bombs strangled daytime traffic, while an 8 p.m. curfew turned people into prisoners each night. Gas shortages and electricity blackouts further disrupted daily life. "I'm choking," said George Zeiny, a local restaurant owner. "I'm just slowly choking." Even for a nation that had suffered eight years of war and violence, enough was enough. *New York Times* reporter Thomas Friedman observed that many Lebanese, who had initially welcomed America's intervention, had lost faith in its ability to bring about peace. Others feared that the gorgeous city once heralded as the Paris of the Middle East was gone. "As each day goes by," Friedman wrote, "it seems more and more people are beginning to admit to themselves that maybe there is no solution for Lebanon."

On November 16, a few days before the Marines would hand over duties and depart, Dolphin visited the ruins of the Battalion Landing Team headquarters. A few pieces of the foundation piers were all that remained. The lieutenant walked around the pit, recalling where the mess hall had once stood. On the building's south side, Marines had left mementos of lost friends. Dolphin let his eyes roam over packages of cigarettes, Copenhagen, and even a can of beer. Others had deposited letters with names scrawled on them, each held down by rocks.

"I'll never forget," one read.

"I'll be seeing you soon," stated another.

Dolphin paused to take in the scene. "I knew that once I left here," he said, "I would never return." Others did the same, offering a silent prayer or making the sign of the cross. "No one spoke. One by one they turned away and started walking back to their units."

CHAPTER 59

*The lives of American Marines are being wasted in
a foreign country that couldn't care less.*
—ROBERT GUILFORD, LETTER TO THE EDITOR
October 31, 1983

A merica zeroed in on the attackers.

Intelligence pointed to Hussein al-Musawi's terror group Islamic Amal, which was based in Baalbek and formed part of Hezbollah, and the Husayni Suicide Forces. More than a half dozen intercepts showed officials in Tehran and Damascus urging the Lebanese terrorists to attack American and French targets. The most damning of these was a September 22 message in which Iranian ambassador Mohtashemi in Damascus stated he had ordered Musawi to "undertake an extraordinary attack against the U.S. Marines."

Shultz, McFarlane, and the National Security Council staff urged the president to retaliate, only to run into interference from Weinberger and Vessey. While an air strike would no doubt assuage the anger felt by many, it risked pulling America deeper into a war in the Middle East at precisely the time the defense secretary was looking for an exit.

"Weinberger and Vessey opposed striking back at terrorists," recalled Howard Teicher. "Weinberger repeatedly argued with Shultz against retaliation unless the evidence was absolute. It seemed he would agree only if culpability could be proved in an American court of law."

But Reagan disagreed.

"Let's go after it," the president ordered. "Let's plan the mission, get ready and quick, and if possible do it with the French. But do it."

On October 28—the day after his Oval Office speech—Reagan signed National Security Decision Directive No. 111, which laid the groundwork for such an operation. "Subject to reasonable confirmation of locations of suitable targets," the president ordered, "attack those targets decisively, if possible in coordination with the French."

The National Security Council staff took it upon themselves to plan the mission. Philip Dur, who served as the director of political military affairs, flew to Paris to meet with General Jean Saulnier, the military advisor to French president Mitterrand. Dur confided in the general that the president had authorized the National Security Council to explore a retaliatory attack on the Sheikh Abdullah Barracks. "We believe that a joint strike with the French," Dur explained, "would be most desirable from both political and military points of view."

Did America's military leaders support this strike?

"*Bien sûr,*" Dur said. "Of course. The military would obey the president's orders."

Who on the American side would plan the mission?

The Pentagon, Dur confessed, had not been formally tasked to do so. The National Security Council was working with the Navy. Saulnier said he would run it up the French ladder. "I left that meeting," Dur recalled, "optimistic that the French would join us."

Dur returned to Washington and met with Vice Admiral James "Ace" Lyons, the deputy chief of naval operations for plans and policy. A colorful and outspoken admiral, whose tendency for blunt talk would later cost him his career, Lyons reviewed the Iranian intercepts. "If there ever was a 24-karat gold document, this was it," he later said. "This was not something from the third cousin of the fourth wife of Muhammad the taxicab driver."

In his office at the Pentagon, Lyons drafted a plan for an eight-plane air strike. He then sent it by courier to Rear Admiral Jerry Tuttle, the commander of the naval task force off Lebanon. A former carrier pilot, Tuttle proved an equally polarizing commander, who referred to himself as Sluf, which stood for "short little ugly fucker." Tuttle revised Lyon's plan, increasing it to a twelve-plane strike force. Reagan welcomed the news. "We believe we have a fix on a headquarters of the radical Iranian Shiites who blew up our Marines," he wrote in his diary on November 7. "We can take out the target with an airstrike & no risk to civilians. We'll meet at 7 a.m. tomorrow as to whether we order the strike now or while I'm away."

As the plan came together, so, too, did the opposition, which broke along the same fault lines that had handicapped the administration for months in

Lebanon. Weinberger led the charge against the strike. "I'm not an eye-for-an-eye man. You've got to have a purpose, and if your purpose is just to kill a lot of people, that's easy enough to do," he said. "But we didn't have the conclusive kind of target information that I think is essential."

Reagan met the following morning with his advisors in the Red Room, moments before he was scheduled to depart for a weeklong trip to Japan and South Korea. Weinberger and Vessey advocated the president hold off on a decision until his return, a move that would allow them more time to gather intelligence. Reagan recounted the session in his diary. "Began the day," he wrote, "with a short meeting re a possible air strike in Beirut against those who murdered our Marines. Decided we don't have enough intelligence info as yet."

For proponents of the strike, Reagan's departure that morning signaled defeat, robbing them of the momentum. Passions would die down and America would lose interest.

"I knew," recalled Undersecretary of State Eagleburger, "that was the end of it."

Reagan returned from Asia and regrouped with his advisors on November 14, but participants came away with contradictory interpretations of what transpired, which was not uncommon given the president's tendency to withdraw from fights. McFarlane was convinced Reagan had ordered the joint strike to take place in a few days. "It was," he recalled, "a direct, unambiguous decision." But others disagreed, including Weinberger, who fell back on the lack of decisive intel. Reagan's diary shows he was still unconvinced. "We have some additional intelligence," the president wrote, "but still not enough to order a strike."

On board the carrier *John F. Kennedy*, which steamed off the coast of Lebanon, tensions soared over the anticipated mission. "Several times crews were awakened from a sound sleep, ordered to dress in their flight and survival gear, briefed on the strike and ordered to the roof to man up the airplanes," observed *Washington Post* reporter George Wilson, who was embedded with the crew. "Higher Authority each time called off the raid at the last minute."

Admiral Tuttle was visited by his French counterpart, who brought a letter requesting America assist in an air strike on Baalbek on November 17. Tuttle agreed, but he needed permission from Washington, which once again never came.

Accounts differ on precisely what happened next. According to McFarlane, the national security advisor rolled into the White House when he received a call from Weinberger. He relayed to him that French defense minister Charles Hernu had reached out that morning to request America join the raid, but that Weinberger refused.

"I don't understand, Cap," McFarlane protested. "What went wrong?"

"I just don't think it was the right thing to do," he replied.

McFarlane was furious. "It was outrageous," he wrote. "Weinberger had directly violated a presidential order. Whatever his feelings about our role in Lebanon, whatever his disagreement with our policy, the fact was that a presidential decision had been made and an order given and that should have been that." McFarlane hustled to see Reagan. "There is no excuse for it, Mr. President," he stammered. "You approved this operation, and Cap decided not to carry it out. The credibility of the United States in Damascus just went to zero."

"Gosh, that's really disappointing," Reagan said, according to McFarlane. "We should have blown the daylights out of them. I just don't understand."

Weinberger relates a different story, characterizing McFarlane's accusation that he disobeyed a presidential order as "absurd." The defense secretary kept notes of his conversation with Hernu, who advised that the French could hold off for sixty-five minutes, if the Americans wanted to join. "The president has not made a decision; he is still considering it," Weinberger replied. "Unfortunately, it is a bit too late for us to join you in this one."

France went ahead with the strike, which followed one day after Israeli fighters targeted another Islamic Amal training camp in the Bekaa Valley in retaliation for the bombing in Tyre. Israel's strike, which killed or wounded as many as eighty Shia fighters, proved far more successful than the French operation. A handful of craters was all France had to show for a mission best described by historian David Crist as an "abject failure."

The media zeroed in on the missing player in the back-to-back attacks. "Today's air raids," as Thomas Friedman wrote in the *New York Times*, "left the Americans as the only force in Lebanon that has not retaliated in any way for the recent suicide truck-bomb attacks." The smoke had barely cleared when administration officials began to tamp down any speculation that America might also strike back. "There are still contingency plans all over town," one unnamed official told the *Washington Post*, "but I think the window has been closed."

That was confirmed in a top-secret memo from McFarlane to Shultz, Weinberger, Vessey, and CIA director William Casey. "In view of the

Israeli and French Actions of November 16 and 17, it is your recommendation to the President that a U.S. attack at this time is not appropriate. The President agrees with your judgment," the national security advisor wrote on November 22, 1983. "Accordingly, we should discontinue current plans and associated readiness to execute preemptive attacks in response to the October 23 tragedy."

The aborted mission infuriated members of the National Security Council staff. "I was despondent," Dur later wrote. So, too, was Teicher. Despite Reagan's apparent frustration with the missed opportunity, McFarlane realized it was largely an act for his sake. Reagan would never reprimand Weinberger. McFarlane had been outplayed. "Weinberger, for his part," he said, "had won a decisive battle in his now all-out effort to pull us out of Lebanon."

The aircrews on the *Kennedy* were equally as miffed to read about the lackluster French strike in photocopies of the *International Herald Tribune* passed around the air wing.

"They woke up the gardener," one officer huffed.

In the end, America would never retaliate. The deaths of 220 Marines, eighteen sailors, and three soldiers would go unavenged; America's only response would be to designate Iran as a state sponsor of terror in 1984.

In his memoir, Reagan took responsibility for the aborted air strike. "Our intelligence experts found it difficult to establish conclusively who was responsible for the attack on the barracks," the president wrote. "Although several air strikes were planned against possible culprits, I canceled them because our experts said they were not absolutely sure they were the right targets. I didn't want to kill innocent people."

CHAPTER 60

I firmly believe that highly sophisticated and well-trained terrorists
will target Marines in the months to come.
—GENERAL PAUL KELLEY, TESTIMONY BEFORE CONGRESS
November 1, 1983

The House Armed Services Committee—working in tandem with its Investigations Subcommittee—launched a probe into the Beirut bombing. The investigation had three stated goals: determine the policy objectives in Lebanon; analyze how the Marines' mission contributed to those objectives; and evaluate whether the risks to the Marines were adequately appreciated and if precautions were taken to counter them.

Between November 1 and December 15, the lawmakers held eight hearings in Washington and aboard the *Iwo Jima*, totaling a little more than forty-six hours. During that time, the committee members interviewed some three dozen witnesses, including a few, like Colonel Geraghty and Commodore Rick France, who testified more than once. The 654-page transcript, portions of which remain redacted, show that other witnesses ranged from General Kelley and Joint Chiefs Chairman General John Vessey down to individual Marines and eyewitnesses, including Burnham Matthews and Henry Linkkila.

Seven of the committee members had just returned from a two-day trip to Frankfurt and Beirut, where legislators had met with Geraghty, toured the blast site, and watched workers recover two bodies from the rubble. On that trip, lawmakers noted that security had improved. The Marines had moved some nonessential personnel aboard ships and dispersed others around the airport. Old cars and buses blocked unnecessary gates and weak spots in the fence line while civilian traffic was barred from the base. All agreed that the exposed location at the airport made the Marines an attractive target, but some questioned whether troops should have been better prepared in the wake of the embassy attack. "The delegation is divided," lawmakers noted, "on the question as to whether it was a lack of security at the Beirut International Airport or inadequate threat assessment that brought about such a successful bombing."

Committee members hoped the hearings would provide those answers. General Kelley testified first, taking a seat in room 2118 of the Rayburn House Office Building at 10:40 a.m. on November 1. The Marine commandant apologized that his opening remarks would be long. "We have an immense tragedy in this country," he began. "I owe it to the American public and I owe it to my Marines to explain the circumstances as best we know them."

The airport was a civilian environment, he said, one that was not tactically strong. But the Marines were not sent to Beirut as combatants. "Our basic mission is presence, and the logical question is how you define 'presence'?" he asked. "'Presence' is a mission that is not in any military dictionary. It is not a classic military mission, but the chain of command at the time correctly took 'presence' to mean: 'be visible.'" The Marines were a symbol of American strength and resolve. Since the troops were not engaged in combat, the use-of-force guidelines were designed for peacetime operations. "The rules of engagement were considered appropriate and adequate for the environment and for the threat which existed at the time."

Between the arrival of the Marines in September 1982 and the bombing in October 1983, conditions in Beirut had drastically deteriorated. The April bombing of the embassy triggered security upgrades at the airport, including stringing concertina wire across the parking lot and filling hundreds of thousands of sandbags. Rooftop surveillance increased. So, too, did foot patrols. The Marines considered and discounted other ideas, including digging tank ditches and planting a minefield in the parking lot where the terrorist began the attack. Such aggressive measures were ruled out because the airport was actively used by civilians and the threat assessment at the time did not warrant them. Furthermore, America did not want to project the image of an armed fortress, which would undermine the presence mission.

Verbal harassment of Marines on patrol picked up over the summer, followed by the first rocket and mortar attacks in July. To counter this, Marines dug in deeper. The primary threat, Kelley noted, remained shelling, which prompted troops to move into the concrete and steel–reinforced Battalion Landing Team headquarters. The building had survived both an Israeli artillery barrage and even a minor earthquake in

June. "It is very significant," he added, "that in a thirteen-month period, no Marine, no soldier, no sailor billeted in this building was killed or injured due to incoming artillery, mortar, rocket, or small-arms fire."

In September, tensions worsened when Israel moved south and the Lebanese military began to battle the Amal militia. The Marines hardened their positions, moved into reinforced buildings, and began to return fire when fired upon. "The shooting in and around Beirut was at ammunition levels rivaling any major battle that you can mention in World War II—over one million rounds of artillery ammunition was fired during that period."

The use of naval gunfire in support of the Lebanese military may have led some Muslims to perceive that the Marines were pro-Christian and no longer neutral, but Kelley said he was in no position to judge. The intelligence community, the general acknowledged, continued to warn of possible terrorist attacks against the Marines. "But the threat was nonspecific," he said. "It was general and overshadowed by the very real, very specific, and very active reality of conventional military action." Terrorism threats appeared more oriented around car bombs that targeted convoys. From June, a hundred such threats were received, some of which included the make, color, and license plate number. That intel was provided to sentries. Once the September cease-fire began to break down, however, artillery returned. "The terrorist threat remained vague while the active threat from artillery and small arms was increasing."

As for the terrorist attack, only a massive concrete wall could have stopped the bomber behind the wheel of a speeding five-ton truck. "The commander's security was oriented toward the threat of the past several months, that is to say, artillery, rockets, mortars, small-arms fire and car bombs. In this context, the security efforts had been successful," Kelley argued. "Obviously, the commander's security arrangements were inadequate to counter this form of kamikaze attack, but we have yet to find any shred, any single shred of intelligence which would have alerted a reasonable and prudent commander to this totally new and unique threat."

Attackers managed to surprise the French, Kelley added, who were experienced with terrorism. Even the Lebanese, who had long lived with car bombs, were stunned by this new form of attack. This was not the work of a random fanatic, but a well-planned and -executed strike designed to drive the United States out of Lebanon. "It is my professional estimate that our Marines have been targeted for terrorism by highly professional non-Lebanese elements," he concluded. "In my view these acts of violence will continue and the perpetrators will carefully examine and analyze our vulnerabilities and make every effort to exploit them."

Over the next two days, lawmakers peppered Kelley with questions, at times provoking heated responses. Representative Marjorie Holt asked why America did not reduce the size of the Marine force. "Isn't today the time to do something dramatically different in Lebanon?" the Maryland Republican asked. "We cannot let what happened happen again."

The force was the proper size for the mission, Kelley said. If it were down-sized, other nations would follow, which would unravel the multinational force. "If you are going to have a presence mission," he said, "then you have to have people who are present."

"We give the impression we are leaving them there as sitting ducks," Holt countered.

"We are doing everything right now humanly possible to protect them," the general said, "from a new form of terrorism which we had heretofore not experienced."

Others asked about closing the airport, moving the Marines back aboard ship, or replacing troops with more tanks. Kelley shot down each idea. America had no authority to shut down a civilian airport, while pulling troops back aboard ship would undermine the coalition force. "Tanks alone don't provide presence," he added. "People provide presence."

Why didn't America just leave?

Such a move would send a message to the world that terrorism works. "I promise you that the United States of America will be victimized by kook terrorists and nations supporting terrorists all over the world. There will be no end to the repercussions of a backdown from an act of terrorism," Kelley argued. "The answer is to go after the terrorist and the people who have supported that terrorist. Get to the disease. That is what we have to do."

Lawmakers zeroed in on the fact that the guards had unloaded rifles.

That was the decision of the on-scene commander, Kelley said, who over the months had wrestled with multiple accidental discharges. Given the speed and nature of the attack, the general stated that he doubted guards armed with M16 rifles would have had any real ability to stop a five-ton truck. He likewise surmised that the terrorists knew sentries were armed with rifles and had fortified the truck. "I would say in my pro-fessional opinion," Kelley added, "that the ability to stop that with M16 rifle fire would be almost impossible."

That assertion brought a rebuke from Representative Larry Hopkins. "One thing that we do know for sure," the Kentucky Republican countered, "an empty M16 with no magazine attached and nothing in the chamber can-not, and did not, and will not stop anything."

The focus by lawmakers on the attack's minutiae irked Kelley, who be-lieved it overlooked the larger lessons of the tragedy. That was clear from his exchange with Representative Bob Stump, an Arizona Republican. "We are wondering whether the guy had a magazine in his rifle or not, but nobody is addressing those guys that did it. And that is very frustrating," Kelley said. "I want to find the perpetrators and I want them brought to justice."

The general expanded on those points moments later, making a pre-diction that would prove haunting. "This is a new ball game, a totally new dimension," he said. "No one had forecast this kind of activity. It could have just as well been an airplane, and probably if it was, people would understand a little more clearly the insidious threat of massive kamikaze attack by suicidal individuals."

Over the course of multiple hearings, some of the more dramatic testi-mony came from the Marine eyewitnesses and survivors, including Henry Linkkila, who was one of the guards on duty that Sunday morning. The cook, who had both eardrums blown out in the bombing, was clearly nervous when he took a seat in the staff mess room on the *Iwo Jima*.

"I want you to relax, okay," one of the lawmakers assured him.

"Thank you," he replied.

Linkkila walked committee members through that morning, describing the Mercedes and how he first heard it when it tore through the concertina wire as he walked his post.

"Did you pick up your pace?" one lawmaker asked.

"No, ma'am," he said. "All I did was turn around."

"Just looked up?"

"Yes," he said.

The Mercedes blew past him. By the time he put a magazine into his rifle and chambered a round, the truck had reached the Battalion Landing Team headquarters.

"If you had gotten it in, what would you have done?"

"I would have emptied the magazine into the truck," he said, "but there wasn't any time."

"Would that have stopped the truck?"

"I don't know," Linkkila said, "but at least I could have tried."

Fellow guard Lance Corporal Eddie DiFranco testified that as soon as he saw the truck, he knew exactly what was about to happen. One of the committee members asked, if he had had his magazine in his rifle, could he have chambered a round and fired?

"Definitely," the Marine said.

"And the driver was less than about—"

"More or less within point-blank range," he said.

"So you could have killed the driver if you had had a round chambered?"

"Yes, sir," he declared.

Lance Corporal John Berthiaume described the impact of the attack, which knocked him to the ground as concrete chunks rained down on him. "I stood up and couldn't see like a foot in front of my face for the longest time."

Navy Petty Officer First Class Kenneth Densmore, who worked as an air traffic controller, had a unique perspective up in the tower 1,638 feet away. "You could see just black, like gunpowder going off, and then a brilliant yellow flash," he said. "I hollered for the guys to hit the floor and the windows in the tower were blown up at the time."

Burnham Matthews recounted his harrowing story of being hurled out of a third-floor window, while others talked about being on top of the building and riding it down.

Navy corpsman Donald Davidson described giving morphine to mortally wounded men trapped in the rubble to ease their suffering as they died. "You had to be there to see it, you know."

Hopkins, who had berated Geraghty on his recent trip to Beirut, likely got an answer he wasn't expecting when he asked Matthews who was responsible for the tragedy. "What is the general feeling about who is at fault there?" he asked. "Who do you blame?"

"I guess we blamed the Congress here, sir," the Marine replied. "Because we knew that's who was taking control of the situation."

The heart of the hearings, however, centered on the testimony of Commodore France and Colonel Geraghty. Both officers sat for hours, testifying in stark terms about the deadly environment the Marines faced in Beirut. "In this type of war," France told lawmakers, "you don't have any way to show that you are winning except that you are alive."

France made clear his loyalty to Geraghty, stating that he was the best officer in the United States for this mission. The Marines, who he testified took as many as three hundred rounds a day, used all the available sandbags in the Mediterranean to shore up defenses. One of the biggest challenges, however, was vague intelligence. "All you need is one slipup," France said. "That is really what we have. One we didn't think of. How many successes did we have? I think quite a bit when you look at the casualty figures versus the threat."

"Now we are starting to lose a lot of kids," one of the lawmakers countered.

"It seems to me," added Richard Ray, a Georgia Democrat, "that we ought to have anticipated that in that atmosphere and in that environment anything could happen."

France noted that over time security had increased as Marines added concertina wire, checkpoints, and guard posts. Sentries were on the lookout for car bombs.

"We put seven hundred people into one compound," Ray said, "and didn't expect the very worst."

"We didn't expect a truck, no, sir," France acknowledged.

Geraghty testified twice, once on board the *Iwo Jima* and a second time in Washington. The colonel knew he was in trouble. With 241 dead soldiers, sailors, and Marines, America was looking for someone to blame. "I was radioactive," he said.

"If at any time you feel you might need legal counsel, just stop me," advised Representative Nicholas Mavroules, a Massachusetts Democrat.

The colonel outlined his mission, balancing the need to show the flag while not appearing to be a fortress. "We walked a razor's edge," he said, "to maintain our neutrality and treated all the Lebanese factions alike, showing no favoritism toward one group or another."

Geraghty explained that the threat had increased dramatically, which coincided with the change in demographics among the populace and the rise in attacks against coalition forces. "Right now," he testified, "we are faced with a terrorist threat, a very sophisticated, well-coordinated, planned attack situation covering the spectrum of means and capability."

The airport location made security a challenge. Not only was the low ground tactically unsound, but the commercial activity gave him no control over passing vehicles, any one of which could park outside the wire, explode, and still do tremendous damage.

"You cannot guarantee security for your people there?" asked Mavroules.

"Not where I am," Geraghty said. "No, sir."

The colonel said he had dispersed his troops and hardened bunker sites. Over the months, the attacks had escalated from shelling to sniping. In each case, Geraghty said, the Marines had adapted to minimize the threat. Once troops figured out how to neutralize snipers, terrorists escalated the violence again with the truck bombing. The same types of attacks, he noted, had been executed against the French and the Israelis. Money was no issue, a fact highlighted by the time his troops stopped a car to find more than $3 million in cash. "We know they have the capability for this. We know they have resources and money unlimited, and the fanatics to drive them," he testified. "The environment that we are faced with today with this kind of threat, it is a loser's game. You are cutting losses for starters. They are going to get you."

Could the Marines lower the risk by moving elsewhere?

"It is the Americans and the uniform," Geraghty replied. "Not the location."

Why not go on the offensive?

"Who is the enemy?" he asked, drawing attention to one of the biggest challenges. "The enemy," he added, answering his own question, "is really small bands of terrorists."

Committee members asked Geraghty about the battle at Suk al-Gharb in which America had intervened to help the Lebanese military. "Were you apprehensive at that time that we were perhaps tipping the balance and ceasing to be neutral?" one lawmaker asked.

"That was a major change," he said. "That would be a milestone."

Why did the guards, committee members pressed, not have magazines in their rifles? "We had a number of accidental discharges which are not uncommon when you start carrying live rounds all the time," he said, adding that excessive airport traffic heightened the danger. "There was just too high a risk of having an accidental round killing a civilian."

Did he ever seek higher approval to improve his security?

"We were," the colonel said, "continually changing our defensive posture." Marines had requested and used the better portion of one million sandbags. "The main threat that I had to deal with in real life on a day-to-day basis," he continued, "was the increased shelling, which became very heavy, of multiple rocket launchers and heavy artillery, heavy mortars as well as small arms, antitank weapons, direct fire weapons, across the spectrum."

"In your opinion, are we going to lose more Marines even with the added security precautionary measures?" Mavroules asked.

"Yes, sir," Geraghty said. "Because in that environment, we are targets."

The colonel explained that the location of the Marines at a commercial airport handicapped his ability to secure it from future attacks. "I could take you by that airport," he said, "and stand there for an hour and we could count three hundred refuelers or airline catering trucks or dump trucks any of which could be loaded with the same or bigger bomb that would be moving ten feet from that fence and drive through it and blow it and kill eight hundred people."

Democratic representative Dan Daniel of Virginia asked if the attack was the result of political, military, planning, or judgmental failures.

"Well, sir, the mission was political. We were not tactically deployed in a military sense. By virtue of our location, there were considerable vulnerabilities," Geraghty said. "There may have been a fanatic driving that truck, but the fellow behind the execution and the planning had a pretty cold political mind. It is an act that I feel was committed with the motive of getting us out of Lebanon and if we leave the French and the others will follow."

"I understand what you are saying but that doesn't respond to the question."

"I don't think we can say one particular area was at fault," the colonel replied. "It was probably a part of a little bit of each."

Representative Sam Stratton of New York was one of the few who throughout the more than forty hours of testimony acknowledged the role of Congress in the tragedy. Stratton had visited the Marines in late September. He had returned home and warned Weinberger of his fears of a pending massacre. "We recognized that you were sitting ducks, that you were being targeted, and you had very little to respond," he said. "The Marines, in traditional combat, don't sit still and let the enemy fire at them. They believe that the best defense is a strong offense." Stratton said America's top leaders shared the blame, not just the immediate commander and troops on the ground. "When you give a force a mission that you don't really believe in," he concluded, "it seems to me that that responsibility has got to go to the top."

Even Hopkins, who had blamed Geraghty when he stepped off the plane in Beirut, agreed, thanking him for his service. "I think sending you into that position," Hopkins said, "would be very much like this committee looking at Niagara Falls and asking you to go there and stop its flow with a bucket and then criticizing you if you were not able to do so."

Such comments, however, stood in stark contrast to the final report.

The Investigations Subcommittee of the House Armed Services Committee, which had conducted six of the eight hearings, issued its findings in a December 19 report titled "Adequacy of U.S. Marine Corps Security in Beirut." The blistering three-page summary blamed all levels of command, from the on-scene commanders in Beirut to the Washington policymakers who sent them into harm's way. Much of the criticism, however, was aimed at Geraghty and France, who the report said sacrificed safety to appear visible. The lawmakers found no evidence that anyone in either diplomatic or political leadership denied requests that might have improved security. Furthermore, there was no excuse for security at the Marine compound to be less than at the temporary embassy. "While the subcommittee fully recognizes it is easy to be wise after the fact, it finds that the commander of the Marine Amphibious Unit made serious errors in judgment in failing to provide better protection for his troops within the command authority available to him," the report concluded. "As the commander, he bears the principal responsibility for the inadequacy of the security posture at the BLT headquarters."

The full seventy-eight-page report, which was released days later, attempted to soften the criticism of Geraghty, recognizing the impossible task he had faced. "Colonel Geraghty is a dedicated and talented officer who was given a difficult mission that, as he interpreted it, became increasingly more difficult to perform without exposing the Marines under his command to significant death or injury," it stated. "This is not a case of dereliction of duty, or of neglect. But it is a case of misjudgment with the most serious consequences."

In addition to the on-scene commanders, the subcommittee faulted senior military leaders in the chain of command, who failed to provide adequate intelligence support for the Marines as well as exercise sufficient oversight of the security in Beirut. "Visits by higher level commanders," the report stated, "were commonly familiarization briefings and appeared not to provide positive oversight, such as directives to improve security." The lawmakers likewise blamed the administration. "While of necessity calling attention to the failures of local commanders within their area of responsibility," it added, "the subcommittee must also call to account the higher policy-making authority that adopted and continued a policy that placed military units in a deployment where protection was inevitably inadequate."

The subcommittee urged the White House to review its Lebanon policy as well as apply pressure on Gemayel to find a political answer to his nation's ills. "The solution to Lebanon's problem will only be found at the bargaining table," the report said. "We must not in any way encourage the perception that a solution can be found on the battlefield with the participation of U.S. armed forces." On a larger level, the lawmakers questioned the administration's repeated assertion that America's Middle East policy was predicated upon victory in Lebanon. "Does the success of our policy really depend on a deadly deployment of Marines who weren't even there two years ago?" the report asked. "Sustained deployment of American personnel in a situation of certain further casualties is a grave, moral choice for policymakers: a choice in which the Congress must ultimately share. Such a choice should be made only if the policy objectives are visible, profoundly important and clearly obtainable."

The subcommittee voted 9–3 to accept the report. Republican representatives Bob Stump and David Martin, two of the three who voted against the report, submitted a dissenting view, arguing that it was too much to blame France and Geraghty for the attack. The lawmakers pointed to the successful bombing ten days later of the Israelis in Tyre. Guards there had loaded weapons and opened fire, yet the terrorist still was ultimately successful. "Only with hindsight do we feel the field commanders can be faulted for failing to perceive and protect against a threat of the nature and magnitude of the successful terrorist attack of October 23," the lawmakers concluded. "To assign culpability, for not defending against this specific type of attack, to those who did not have the benefit of 20-20 hindsight, while remembering that the mission had not changed although the conditions had changed drastically, is unfair."

CHAPTER 61

*The systematic, carefully orchestrated terrorism which we see in the
Middle East represents a new dimension of warfare.*
—REPORT OF THE LONG COMMISSION
December 20, 1983

Congress was not alone in its hunt for answers.

At the urging of General Kelley, Weinberger ordered a Pentagon probe of the bombing. To lead the investigation, the defense secretary turned to sixty-three-year-old Admiral Robert Long, a veteran submariner who began his career in the Pacific during World War II. Over the years, Long had ascended the ranks, serving as head of the Atlantic submarine force and later vice chief of naval operations. The four-star admiral had retired in July as the nation's Pacific Fleet commander when Weinberger called with an urgent request.

"You know," Long protested, "I just retired."

"I'm sorry, Bob," Weinberger said. "But I need you."

To aid with the investigation, the admiral tapped Marine Lieutenant General Lawrence Snowden, Air Force Lieutenant General Eugene Tighe Jr., and Army Lieutenant General Joseph Palastra Jr., a selection that guaranteed each service branch was represented. At Weinberger's request, he rounded out the commission with one civilian, Robert Murray, a Harvard faculty member and former undersecretary of the Navy and deputy assistant secretary for defense. These five commissioners, aided by nearly three dozen experts, convened on November 7, launching a six-week probe that would interview 125 witnesses spread across six countries. "Weinberger made it very clear to me that I had absolute carte blanche authority to look at anything, ask anyone, and in no way did he direct that my conclusions and recommendations should be limited in any way," Long recalled. "It was a very broad charter."

Unlike Congress, which held at least some public hearings and later produced a transcript of most of the testimony, witnesses before the Long

Commission appeared in closed session. Interviews were informal. No one testified under oath and no transcript was published. The entire board questioned primary witnesses, while secondary officials and experts were often interviewed by a single commission member and staff. All members visited Beirut and toured the blast site. Over the course of the investigation, the panel cast a wide net, examining the airport's security, the rules of engagement, failures in intelligence, and the role of the chain of command. "The Commission," as its report noted, "did not question the political decision to insert the Marines into Lebanon and did not address the political necessity of their continued participation in the Multinational Force following the 23 October 1983 terrorist attack."

The 166-page report—nineteen pages of which still remain classified even after more than four decades—reiterated many of the findings of the House Armed Services Committee's investigation. But unlike Congress, which focused largely on security breakdowns and individual culpability in the lead-up to the attack, the Long Commission sounded a much greater alarm, echoing the concerns raised by General Kelley and Colonel Geraghty. In short, terrorism was here to stay—and America needed to prepare. "The Commission believes that the most important message it can bring to the Secretary of Defense is that the 23 October 1983 attack on the Marine Battalion Landing Team headquarters in Beirut was tantamount to an act of war using the medium of terrorism," the report declared. "Much needs to be done, on an urgent basis, to prepare U.S. military forces to defend against and counter terrorist warfare."

The commissioners, as the report made clear, couldn't help but grudgingly admire the "true genius" of the terrorists, who managed to plan and execute an attack that exceeded the imagination of those responsible for the security of the Marines—a sucker punch that effectively floored everyone. "For the terrorists, the attack was an overwhelming success," the panel concluded. "It achieved complete tactical surprise and resulted in the total destruction of the headquarters, and the deaths of 241 U.S. military personnel." Proof of that success was evident in the continual stream of tragic images broadcast on American televisions, the debate that dominated editorial pages, and the fiery speeches of lawmakers who paced the floors of Capitol Hill. "The psychological fallout of the attack on the U.S. has been dramatic," the commissioners wrote. "The terrorists sent the U.S. a strong political message."

Such an act was possible in part because of a systemic breakdown in intelligence. The Marines not only lacked vital human intelligence, but also had no way to effectively process the flood of car bomb reports that arrived each week. "It is difficult to overstate," the report noted, "the magnitude of the intelligence problem in a milieu where high casualty terrorist acts are relatively easy to perpetrate yet hard to stop." The panel added that attacks like the one against the embassy or Marines require few resources or manpower, making them exceptionally hard to intercept in the planning stages. "The terrorists in Lebanon and the Middle East are formidable opponents. In general, they are intensely dedicated and professional," the report stated. "They are exceptionally well-trained, well-equipped and well-supported. With State sponsorship, these terrorists are less concerned about building a popular base and are less inhibited in committing acts which cause massive destruction or inflict heavy casualties."

The report charted how various factions in Lebanon, who had initially welcomed the Marines as heroes, increasingly came to view them as "pro-Israel, pro-Phalange, and anti-Muslim." The use of naval gunfire to support the Lebanese at Suk al-Gharb was the tipping point, cementing the reputation of the Marines as belligerents. "By the end of September 1983, the situation in Lebanon had changed to the extent that not one of the initial conditions upon which the mission statement was premised was still valid," the report noted. "The environment clearly was hostile." As the political situation deteriorated, America expanded the role of the Marines, including training local forces, supplying weapons and ammunition, and ultimately changing the rules of engagement to aid the Lebanese. America's intention was never to back one side in the conflict. "It is undeniable, however," the commission wrote, "that the facts of political life in Lebanon make any attempt on the part of an outsider to appear nonpartisan virtually impossible." Into this volatile mix landed Iran, which had no interest in Lebanese reconciliation. "Iranian operatives in Lebanon are in the business of killing Americans."

At this point, the commission argued, senior leaders in the chain of command should have intervened to help the Marines adapt to the evolving threats. Similar to Congress, the panel found no evidence that any visits by high-ranking officers to Beirut resulted in security improvements. In Long's interview with General Bernard Rodgers, commander of U.S. forces in Europe, the admiral zeroed in on that oversight. "Why did you not change the mission?" Long asked. "Why had you not given them adequate rules of engagement?"

"Bob," he replied, "I wouldn't think of telling Marines how to do their job."

That failure of oversight by upper echelons in the chain of command was a key factor in the attack's success. The rising threat demanded constant reassessment and "systematic and aggressive" attention to defend against possible terrorism. In addition, the commissioners noted that even the mission's basic concept of presence was interpreted differently throughout the chain of command. The panel therefore recommended the defense secretary take whatever administrative or disciplinary action he deemed appropriate. "The Commission holds the view that military commanders are responsible for the performance of their subordinates," the report stated. "The commander can delegate some or all of his authority to his subordinates, but he cannot delegate his responsibility for the performance of any of the forces he commands. In that sense, the responsibility of military command is absolute."

The commission likewise faulted Geraghty and Lieutenant Colonel Larry Gerlach, concluding that the security measures at the airport were not commensurate with the threat or sufficient to stop the attack. The panel acknowledged that Geraghty was deluged with intel, though none of it specifically related to such a strike. He likewise had never been briefed in detail about the embassy bombing and the destructive potential of gas-enhanced bombs. The commission added that while it may have appeared wise to house so many troops in the Battalion Landing Team building, that decision ultimately "contributed to the catastrophic loss of life." Despite circumstances beyond either Geraghty's or Gerlach's control, the panel recommended that the secretary of defense take either administrative or disciplinary action against them. Similar to Congress, the panel clearly was impressed by Geraghty, a fact made evident by comments Admiral Long later made about him in an oral history. "I don't think I have ever seen a finer young man than Colonel Geraghty," he said. "Extremely conscientious."

Even though the panel professed it would not examine politics, the report included what the *Washington Post* characterized as a "scarcely veiled indictment of the mission." America's response to the deteriorating environment on the ground had been to lean more heavily on the military, which was no longer feasible. It was time to find a diplomatic way out of the Lebanese fiasco. "The Commission recommends," the report concluded, "that the Secretary of Defense continue to urge that the National Security Council undertake a reexamination of alternative means of achieving U.S. objectives in Lebanon, to include a comprehensive assessment of the military security options being developed by the chain of command and a more vigorous and demanding approach to pursuing diplomatic alternatives."

On December 20, Admiral Long forwarded the report to Weinberger along with a letter signed by all the commissioners. "The completion of our work," Long wrote, "leaves us with a deep sense of loss because of the magnitude and viciousness of the tragedy, feelings of great pride in the patriotism and heroism of the people serving in the United States military and a firm conviction that our report brings you constructive findings and recommendations that can help you take steps to improve our defense capabilities in several critical areas."

The defense secretary pored through the commission's findings. Weinberger had been around Washington long enough to recognize that the report was, as he later described it, a "bombshell." Not only did it note systemic breakdowns, but more importantly it highlighted the larger battle that had raged for months over the use of force as a tool for diplomacy. It likewise singled out America's intervention at the Suk al-Gharb, which McFarlane had pushed, as the turning point. "The commission's findings," Weinberger said, "placed before the public many of the arguments I had been making privately for well over a year, such as the abysmal inadequacy of using a word such as 'presence' as a substitute for a valid and properly equipped military mission, and the nonsensical emphasis on quite inadequate military options as a tool of influence when, in fact, the Lebanese political landscape was cracking beneath our feet."

Weinberger forwarded the report to Reagan three days later with a five-page summary and a three-page breakdown of security upgrades instituted in the wake of the attack. Unless the president objected, Weinberger wrote that he planned to release the report that day at a press conference. "It will result in significant publicity," he predicted in his memo. "Terrorism and the situation in Lebanon both confront us with difficult days ahead."

But the White House balked.

Thirty minutes before Weinberger was scheduled to meet with the press, a Pentagon spokesman announced to reporters that the release would be delayed. A senior Defense Department official told the *New York Times* that Bud McFarlane had put the brakes on the report's release. "It's clear from the report," one official said, "that you can't pin blame on the Marine commanders in Beirut without holding their superiors equally responsible, and you can't blame the military without saying the policy was a major factor."

In a three-page top-secret memo to the president, McFarlane warned that punishing the Marines or senior commanders could open a Pandora's box, triggering a "long and corrosive process with a potentially serious and unpredictable outcome." The national security advisor had another idea—one based purely on politics, not altruism. As the commander in chief, Reagan should take responsibility for the tragedy. "In doing this, you would explain that there is blame enough to go around and that none of us fully anticipated or prepared for such a monstrous example of state-sponsored terrorism," McFarlane wrote. "You could further argue that hindsight leads to the conclusion that the <u>entire</u> chain of command should have been better prepared for this tragic eventuality. The sad but incontrovertible facts are that our troops in Lebanon, our military organization in general, and indeed our entire nation, were ill-quipped to deal with a trend which began with the Beirut Embassy bombing in April 1983."

McFarlane urged the president—despite 241 deaths coupled with the panel's recommendation that the White House find a new approach in Lebanon—to publicly declare his commitment to not back down. "Simply put, if we yield to pressure for withdrawal now, we will tacitly condone the use of terror as an instrument of policy," McFarlane wrote. "Pulling out the Marines will not solve the root cause of the tragedy in Beirut."

Reagan followed that advice.

At 9:16 a.m. on December 27—and one day prior to the report's public release—the president entered the White House Briefing Room armed with a three-page statement, which McFarlane and his staff had helped prepare. During his five-minute remarks, the president said that despite the difficult job, the United States had helped deliver positive changes in Lebanon. "We do not expect Utopia," Reagan said, "but I believe that we're on the verge of new progress toward national reconciliation and the withdrawal of foreign forces." The president likewise followed McFarlane's recommendation and shouldered the blame for the terrorist bombing. "I do not believe," Reagan continued, "that the local commanders on the ground, men who have already suffered quite enough, should be punished for not fully comprehending the nature of today's terrorist threat. If there is to be blame, it properly rests here in this office and with this president. And I accept responsibility for the bad as well as the good."

The president's acceptance of blame prior to the report's release was designed to detract from the commission's harsh criticism of his policies. To further minimize the political damage, the White House barred Weinberger from hosting his planned press conference, a move reporters complained was designed to rob television crews of footage. The administration likewise printed only minimal copies of the report for the media and Congress, forcing the public to wait a week. Despite such efforts, headlines showed the press zeroed in on the panel's criticism of the White House. "Pentagon Blasts Policy on Beirut," trumpeted the *Chicago Tribune*.

"Report Hits U.S. Reliance on Force in Lebanon," added the *Washington Post*.

"Pentagon Report Could Be Reagan Liability," declared the *Santa Cruz Sentinel*.

Many newspapers, ranging from the *Los Angeles Times* to the *Philadelphia Inquirer*, published the report's executive summary, which circumvented the administration's efforts to downplay the findings. The harsh back-to-back reports by Congress and the Pentagon reignited a furor among lawmakers, who would not reconvene until January 23. Democratic representative Barbara Mikulski of Maryland called for Weinberger's ouster, while House Speaker Tip O'Neill signaled it might be time to reconsider the eighteen-month deployment deal. "The president showed great courage in sending the Marines into what everyone knew would be a difficult assignment," said Republican senator William Roth Jr. of Delaware. "The president should now show that same courage by admitting that this course of action failed."

"The Marines are not heroes in Lebanon," added Representative Bill Alexander, an Arkansas Democrat, "but are victims of an unclear and vacillating policy."

Editorial pages around the country echoed those concerns. "The Beirut bombing is a lesson," argued the *Wichita Eagle*, "on the folly of militaristic diplomacy."

Many of the families of the Marines pored through the news accounts, which only salted wounds and sparked bitterness. Included among those was Bill Stelpflug's mother, who criticized Reagan's public posturing. "He should not make grandstand heroics like he's protecting the military," Peggy Stelpflug said. "It's his fault for putting them there."

How, she asked, after all that had happened, could the Marines remain?

"It's too late for Billy," she concluded. "It's not too late for the others."

CHAPTER 62

Day by day the United States moves deeper into the Lebanese quagmire.
—ANTHONY LEWIS, *NEW YORK TIMES*
December 15, 1983

Amid the continued violence in Lebanon—and the political furor of the investigations in Washington—Colonel Geraghty and his Marines returned home on the morning of December 7. The *Austin* was the first of the five ships in the flotilla to ease into port at Morehead City, ending a nearly three-week journey across the Mediterranean and the Atlantic. The return that cold morning to the same port where the Marines had embarked back in May brought an end to the 210-day deployment, a mission of peace that had proven anything but peaceful.

The troops who lined the rails, anxious to catch a glimpse of loved ones on the pier below, were the survivors, men who had endured the escalating violence in Beirut followed by the catastrophic terrorist attack. The Marines had learned en route home that eight more of their comrades had been killed in Beirut, victims of a Druze rocket attack. "Sometimes it seems like we left here just yesterday. But if you look back at everything that happened," recalled Lance Corporal Chris Vlask, "it feels like we were there several years."

On the pier below stood four hundred fathers and mothers, wives and children, many waving yellow flags and cheering. Joining them were three bands—one from the Marine Corps and two from East and West Carteret high schools—as well as an army of kindergartners from Beaufort Elementary School. The children, dressed in jackets, hats, and gloves to fend off the cold, held up single letters that together spelled "Merry Christmas." "We just wanted to show them that we love them," said teacher Pat Muller. "We are just proud to be Americans."

Families scanned the faces at the rails. "It's him!" Jerri Aycock shouted when she spotted her son, Lance Corporal Kenneth Newton. "It's really him. He's alive."

Major General Alfred Gray came aboard to give the troops a pep talk, ending with the three words the men so longed to hear: "Let's go ashore!" the general hollered.

The troops erupted in cheers.

At 10:41 a.m., the Marines, dressed in fatigues and carrying rifles and packs, saluted the flag and filed one after the other down the thirty-seven steps of the ship's gangway. The troops boarded Trailways buses for the forty-mile ride to Jacksonville, where the Chamber of Commerce had hung red, white, and blue bunting and tied yellow ribbons around every utility pole leading into town. Signs in front of businesses heralded the arrival of the hometown heroes while residents emerged from houses to applaud. The outpouring of support overwhelmed some of the troops. "I've never been any more proud of being a Marine than I was that day," recalled Mark Singleton. "It made you cry." Others agreed. "To be back home still feels like a dream," said Lance Corporal Michael Cerniglia. "It's just so good to be back alive."

The Marines came from all over the country, which meant not everyone had loved ones on hand to welcome them. As the dismissed troops rushed into the arms of wives and children, others drifted to a nearby row of phone booths. A news reporter watched one Marine step inside, prop his rifle up against the glass, and pick up the receiver.

"Hello, Mom," he announced, wiping tears from his eyes. "I'm home."

Despite Reagan's acceptance of blame for the attack, Weinberger insisted on punishing the commanders. He checked with the White House, discovering that the president's absolution applied only to courts-martial, not administrative reprimands. Based on that information, Secretary of the Navy John Lehman issued Geraghty and Lieutenant Colonel Gerlach "nonpunitive letters of instruction." For Geraghty, it was one more blow. Two days after the colonel arrived home to the joyous celebrations at Camp Lejeune, he was relieved of command. His Marine Corps career was effectively over. "Although this letter will not be placed in your official record," Lehman wrote, "it is intended as a nonpunitive reminder that your actions, as commander, were not sufficient to prevent this tragedy."

Gerlach, who most had believed would succumb to his injuries, had miraculously survived. He had spent days in a coma in a Shiite hospital before being transferred to the *Iwo Jima*, Cyprus, and Germany before returning home to a Veterans Administration hospital in Boston. Gerlach was in a hospital bed, recovering from wounds that would leave him dependent on a wheelchair for the rest of his life, when his letter of reprimand reached him.

No one else would ever be punished.

CHAPTER 63

*Perhaps the greatest American miscalculation was believing that
Lebanon, after nine years of civil war, could be put back together again.*
—THOMAS FRIEDMAN, *NEW YORK TIMES*
February 19, 1984

The fallout from the back-to-back investigations into Beirut was only one challenge the president faced. As 1983 wound down, the situation in Lebanon escalated. On December 3, Syrian antiaircraft guns and surface-to-air missiles in the Bekaa Valley targeted American reconnaissance planes. This prompted the Navy—with White House approval—to plan a retaliatory strike the following morning. Gunfire from the *New Jersey* was ruled out since there was no forward spotter to help guarantee accuracy. Furthermore, as Chief of Naval Operations Admiral James Watkins explained, a carrier strike was considered a more proportional response. "If you are shot at," the admiral declared, "you shoot back."

It was ironic that Syria's targeting of American reconnaissance planes warranted retaliation, but the murder of 241 soldiers, sailors, and Marines did not. The December strike, which would be the first air combat mission over Lebanon, involved twenty-eight planes from the carriers *Independence* and *John F. Kennedy*. Planners scheduled the mission for 11 a.m. but pressure from Washington forced the strike to move up to 6:30 a.m. This made it impossible to arm and launch all the planes on time, which created stragglers, as well as put the rising sun directly in the eyes of the pilots. A morning haze that obscured the targets added to the challenge, forcing the aircrews to fly low and into enemy fire.

"SAMs! SAMs! SAMs," airmen radioed.

"I'm hit!" one pilot announced moments later. "I'm hit!"

The morning mission quickly devolved into chaos.

"Mayday! Mayday! This is three zero five. I'm proceeding over the water now."

Commander Edward Andrews managed to guide his burning A-7 Corsair over the Mediterranean, where he ejected and was later plucked from the sea by a Christian fisherman and his son. Syrian missiles also brought down a two-seat A-6 Intruder. The airmen ejected, but pilot Lieutenant Mark Lange landed hard, during which time his left leg was severed. He ultimately bled to death. Bombardier and navigator Lieutenant Robert Goodman, who suffered some broken ribs and a separated left shoulder, was captured by the Syrians.

The botched strike demoralized the Navy's airmen. George Wilson, the *Washington Post* reporter embedded on the *Kennedy*, made the rounds that afternoon to interview the mission's planners and aircrews. "I found rage, bitterness, sadness, rationalization, and protest," he said. "I heard no more talk about bombing Lebanon back to the Stone Age."

On December 14, after pilots reported more Syrian antiaircraft fire, the *New Jersey* joined the fight, firing her massive sixteen-inch guns for the first time since the Vietnam War. The gunfire from the 59,000-ton battleship, which steamed just two miles offshore, rattled the capital as 1,900-pound rounds thundered overhead. "Everything was shaking along the coast," one Marine on the beach recalled. "People were rushing to the beach to watch."

When Congress reconvened in January, the battle moved from the Middle East to Washington. Speaker of the House Tip O'Neill, who had helped Reagan pass his compromise to keep Marines in Beirut for another eighteen months, announced it was time to bring the troops home. House Democrats readied a resolution demanding a withdrawal. "We are trying to keep this as nonpolitical as we possibly can," the Massachusetts Democrat said. "We want to bring those boys home as quickly and as safely as we can."

O'Neill's about-face infuriated the president. "He may be ready to surrender," Reagan retorted, "but I'm not. As long as there is a chance for peace, the mission remains the same."

But O'Neill pushed back. "Lebanon is not a test of how tough we are," he countered, "but of how smart we are."

The president's masterful speech on October 27 had bought him some much-needed time to find a solution in Lebanon, which the administration had since squandered. Gemayel's heralded reconciliation talks in Geneva had failed to deliver any real results. Neither had Shultz nor McFarlane, whose habitual answer was to expand the military's role. Other ideas ranged from inviting new countries to join the multinational force to encouraging Iraq and Turkey to stir up tensions along their borders with Syria to distract Assad. Despite efforts to forge ahead, analysts prepared a fallback plan, one with scaled-back objectives that would allow America to hurry up and leave Lebanon but not look defeated. "We must avoid the appearance of being forced out or of forsaking our commitments," one discussion paper stated. "But we must plan for and create the conditions that permit us to leave in a credible way."

Weinberger had his own idea on how to accomplish that goal. The defense secretary advocated America pull the Marines back aboard ship. "This is consistent," he urged the president, "with the view that I have expressed in the past. Placing our forces offshore would allow us to fulfill our commitment and support our basic objectives, and at the same time maintain public and Congressional support for the job we are doing in Lebanon."

Lebanon remained a fiasco—and the public knew it. "Virtually all of the serious press," one memo noted, "has turned against us." Polls showed six out of ten Americans disapproved of the president's handling of the situation in Lebanon. An equal number believed it was time to bring the troops home. Scorching editorials and commentary reflected the public's views. "How long," asked Tom Brokaw of NBC's *Nightly News,* "can this go on?"

"The solution, for a change, is simple," added the *Los Angeles Times.* "Get the Marines out, do it now."

The *Miami Herald* agreed. "It is time," the paper declared, "to cut America's losses in a place where nothing is to be gained."

Three former CIA directors—William Colby, Admiral Stansfield Turner, and James Schlesinger—went on the Sunday morning talk shows to urge Reagan to withdraw the Marines. "The worst of all policies," Schlesinger said, "is simply to hang in there."

The eight Democratic presidential candidates—all united in demanding America's withdrawal—used it as a sledgehammer to pound the president, who faced reelection that fall. This came as two more Marines died in January, one in a rocket-propelled grenade attack and the other in a battle with Shiite militiamen. In what no doubt humiliated Reagan, the Reverend Jesse Jackson, who was running for the Democratic presidential nomination, flew to Damascus and secured the release of downed Navy pilot Lieutenant Goodman.

Lebanon was a political bleeder that needed a tourniquet.

Faced with this reality, Reagan's diary shows that on January 26, 1984, the president and his national security advisors settled on a plan to redeploy the Marines back aboard ship, a move he first wanted to run past Gemayel. "We were," one Pentagon official admitted, "desperate to get out."

Even McFarlane realized it was over, a fact that crystallized in a conversation with Chief of Staff James Baker. "Bud," he asked, "what is the light at the end of the tunnel?"

"There really isn't any," McFarlane finally acknowledged.

For days after that secret decision, Reagan continued to trumpet America's support for Lebanon, even as he continued to publicly feud with Tip O'Neill. "The situation in Lebanon is difficult, frustrating, and dangerous," the president said in his weekly radio address on February 4. "But that is no reason to turn our backs on friends and to cut and run."

Forty-eight hours later, Beirut exploded in violence.

Thousands of Druze and Amal militiamen, who for days had battled the Lebanese military in the southern slums, overran the capital on February 6. Terrified residents fled, creating gridlock amid a cacophony of car horns. Many chose to abandon their vehicles in the streets as artillery rained down and fires erupted. Throughout Beirut, machine guns rattled. The army declared a 1:30 p.m. shoot-to-kill curfew. "Panic gripped the city today," the *Washington Post* reported, "in the face of a breakdown of what was left of law and order."

"It's a living hell," declared resident Lilly Klink. "We have rockets coming down on us one a minute. There are no lights and smoke is everywhere."

In a blow to Gemayel, the nation's Sunni prime minister, Shafik Wazzan, resigned along with the entire cabinet. But that paled compared to the next punch. Lebanon's army of 37,000 soldiers, many of whom were trained by the Marines and who had represented America's hope for a stable future, suddenly disintegrated. As many as 40 percent of the officers and enlisted men defected to join the militias, bringing their American-made weapons with them. Militiamen rumbled through Beirut in tanks and armored personnel carriers. "In the streets and the rubble and at former army checkpoints," observed the *Philadelphia Inquirer*'s David Zucchino, "soldiers kissed their new militia brothers in ritualistic rapprochement." Such scenes demoralized the Marines. "It was," recalled Major Ernest Van Huss, "just a helpless feeling."

American leaders watched in horror as much of Gemayel's government and military collapsed. "It was an intolerable situation," recalled Army attaché Major Joseph Englehardt. "There was no more good to be done." On February 7, one day after violence engulfed Beirut, President Reagan announced plans to pull the Marines back aboard ships. He did so, not in a televised speech, but in a written statement handed out to reporters in Las Vegas as he traveled to his California ranch. The White House planned to keep the Marines off the coast for now, a move that allowed the administration to downplay any suggestion that America was abandoning Lebanon. "We don't consider this a withdrawal," Larry Speakes assured reporters, "but more of a redeployment."

But many in the press saw through the administration's effort to put a positive spin on the pullout. *Chicago Tribune* editorial cartoonist Jeff MacNelly lampooned the White House's characterization in a cartoon that compared Beirut to "Napoleon's Redeployment from Moscow" and "Custer's Last Redeployment." The president attempted to balance the news of the pullout by expanding the use of naval gunfire and airpower against any units firing into Beirut, including from areas controlled by Syria. "Those who conduct these attacks," Reagan declared, "will no longer have sanctuary from which to bombard Beirut at will."

Reagan's announcement drew praise on Capitol Hill even as many lawmakers argued that the decision was long overdue. "The president has recognized the irreversible drift of events," observed Senator Charles Mathias Jr., a Maryland Republican.

But not all were pleased, including Senator Barry Goldwater. The Arizona Republican was the lone lawmaker who had advocated bringing the Marines home after the embassy bombing the previous April, a position that at the time drew scorn from fellow lawmakers and opinion writers. "Moving them out to the ships is not enough," Goldwater argued. "I'd move them all the way home."

The Marines in Lebanon, who had hunkered down amid the fighting, welcomed the news. Since arriving in November, when the smell of rot still hung in the air, troops had turned the airport into a fortress. "The work," as Major Van Huss recalled, "was continuous day and night." Aided by seventy-four Navy Seabees and another ninety-nine Marine combat engineers, troops had sunk more than 400 shipping containers into the ground and built another 348 bunkers and two-man fighting holes. A tank ditch and a nine-foot-tall earthen berm that encircled the Marine compound added to the security upgrades, all of which America planned to abandon.

"I'm ready to go," exclaimed Lance Corporal Samuel Lee. "I've got women to meet and beers to drink." Others were more reflective. "There's no hope for this country," explained Lance Corporal Adam Morales. "They've been fighting for centuries. You can't change that."

America's decision to withdraw triggered an exodus among the other multinational forces. The British left on February 8, followed twelve days later by the Italians. The French, who had once controlled Lebanon, were the only force that planned to remain.

In the days ahead, Marines packed supplies and hauled them out to the ships. Others built bonfires to torch records. On February 26, the last of the Marines prepared to depart, bringing an end to America's year-and-a-half involvement in Lebanon.

Throughout that morning, helicopters ferried troops out to ships while tanks and amphibious vehicles plunged into the surf. Navy gunboats patrolled the shoreline. Artillery thundered in the mountains while black smoke drifted over the beach. News reporters traipsed through the sand for final interviews. "No more wounded, no more killed," said Gunnery Sergeant Michael McGilberay. "Let these people kill themselves."

"This place is crazy," added Lance Corporal Michael Bullard.

Unfortunately, policy dictated that the Marines had to leave behind several mongrel dogs, who sported names like Bunker and Ceasefire, strays who watched from the shore as the troops departed. "They were the only real friends we had in Lebanon," lamented Staff Sergeant Jeffery Roberts.

The last personnel carrier hit the beach around 12:30 p.m. The officer hollered at his troops to load up. "Get in there! I don't care how, just get in!" he shouted. "You all fit when we came and you better do it now. Let's go! Let's get out of here!"

At 12:37 p.m. the personnel carrier rumbled across the sand and into the surf, headed toward the landing ship USS *Manitowoc*.

The reporters all watched.

"Goodbye, folks," Staff Sergeant Gerry Elokonich shouted.

Three minutes later, a jeep flying the green flag of the Amal militia rolled up onto the beach, followed by a pickup truck with a .50-caliber machine gun. At 12:43—six minutes after the Marines left—militiamen ran the Amal flag up over the watchtower.

One unnamed Marine left behind a poem penned in blue ink on the doorframe of an underground bunker, twenty-seven words that would serve as the mission's epitaph:

THEY SENT US TO BEIRUT,
TO BE TARGETS WHO COULD NOT SHOOT.
FRIENDS WILL DIE INTO AN EARLY GRAVE,
WAS THERE ANY REASON FOR WHAT THEY GAVE?

Within the hour, as Marines settled aboard the ships, the *New Jersey* once again opened fire, hurling sixteen one-ton shells at Syrian gun positions in the mountains. The destroyer *Caron* joined the fight, firing another fifty rounds from its five-inch guns.

The Marines remained offshore as the days turned to weeks, time to allow the political turmoil in Washington to die down. By then, too, it had become clear that the political situation in Lebanon was truly hopeless, a fact that coincided with the continued unraveling of security in the capital.

In January, terrorists assassinated Dr. Malcolm Kerr, the president of the American University in Beirut, in his campus office building.

Kerr's assassination was followed in March by the kidnapping of CNN bureau chief Jeremy Levin, who managed to escape after almost a year in captivity.

Levin proved far more fortunate, however, than CIA station chief William Buckley. The former Army Special Forces officer and Vietnam veteran was grabbed that same month by Shiite terrorists and would later die a prisoner of Hezbollah.

The deteriorating situation no doubt prompted France to reverse course and announce plans to pull out on March 24. "The mission," President François Mitterrand declared, "has been fulfilled and we cannot be one of the factors intervening in what is a civil war."

In the war for Lebanon, Syria was the clear victor. Gemayel, in an effort to save himself, caved to Assad's demands and repudiated the May 17 agreement that Shultz had taken such pride in and that had once served as the blueprint for America's diplomatic efforts. "As the U.S. tide goes out," one reporter observed, "the Syrian tide comes in."

On March 30, 1984, Reagan sent his final report to Congress, alerting lawmakers that he planned to officially terminate America's involvement with the multinational force, ending the nation's eighteen-month misadventure in Lebanon. America's intervention, he wrote, had come at the steep price of 264 killed and another 137 wounded. The unsuccessful operation, the president added, had cost taxpayers $60 million, a figure that in today's dollars would run nearly $200 million. "These were," Reagan wrote, "heavy burdens and grievous losses for our country." In an effort to save face, the president noted that the embassy remained open while a limited number of American troops would help train and advise what was left of the Lebanese military. "The United States," Reagan wrote, "has not abandoned Lebanon."

The backroom brawl that pitted Shultz, McFarlane, and the National Security Council staff against Weinberger, Vessey, and the Joint Chiefs spilled out into the open in the form of dueling public speeches, best characterized by a *Washington Post* reporter as a "cockfight." America's failure in Lebanon had bruised Shultz, who blamed both Congress for meddling via the War Powers Resolution and Weinberger for his reluctance to use military force. "The hard reality is that diplomacy not backed by military strength is ineffectual," the secretary of state argued. "Leverage, as well as good will, is required. Power and diplomacy are not alternatives. They must go together, or we will accomplish very little in this world."

Never one to back down from a fight, the defense secretary countered. The nebulous mission in Lebanon had clarified his views on the use of force, which he distilled into six criteria leaders should consider before sending troops into combat. In what became known as the Weinberger Doctrine, the defense secretary argued that leaders first should make sure any commitment of troops is vital to American national interest and that the nation has a clear intent to win. Political and military objectives must clearly be defined, and reassessments made continually as the situation evolves. There should be a reasonable expectation that Congress and the public would support the conflict, and finally force must be used only as the last resort. "Employing our forces almost indiscriminately and as a regular and customary part of our diplomatic efforts," Weinberger argued, "would surely plunge us headlong into the sort of domestic turmoil we experienced during the Vietnam war, without accomplishing the goal for which we committed our forces. Such policies might very well tear at the fabric of our society."

The tragedy of Lebanon would forever haunt Reagan. "Every day since the death of those boys," he wrote years later in his memoir, "I have prayed for them and their loved ones." After he decided in March to bring the troops home, Reagan sat down with a pen and paper and recorded his thoughts on the tragedy. His personal secretary later typed his notes and delivered them to White House speechwriters for possible inclusion in a future address, but the president's private words would never be uttered in public. His five pages read like an anguished apology to the men he had sent into harm's way, men who had lived up to the finest traditions of the United States Marine Corps. "The goal we sought in that troubled place was worthy of their best and they gave their best. They were no part of our failure to achieve that goal. In the end, hatreds centuries old were too much for all of us," Reagan concluded. "Yes, our Marines are coming home—but only because they did all that could be done. Semper Fi and God bless them."

CHAPTER 64

The road that led 1,800 U.S. Marines to the hell of
Beirut was paved with noble intentions.
—MIAMI HERALD EDITORIAL
January 26, 1984

O ver the years, the violence continued.

More kidnappings. More hijackings. More bombings.

But Hussein al-Musawi, the architect of the bombing of the Battalion Landing Team headquarters, saw his terrorism stardom fade, compared to his Hezbollah colleague Imad Mugniyah. By the mid-1990s, news coverage of the bearded terror leader, who had once prompted Western journalists to trek up to his Bekaa Valley headquarters, dwindled to a trickle, with at least one report claiming that an Israeli air strike snuffed him out.

Mugniyah, in contrast, who reportedly watched the bombing of the Marine headquarters, would experience a meteoric rise up the list of the world's most notorious terrorists, building a résumé in cordite and blood. In addition to the attack on the Marines, Mugniyah was accused of bombing the American Embassy six months earlier, as well as the subsequent kidnapping, torture, and murder of CIA station chief William Buckley. Authorities fingered him for the hijacking of TWA Flight 847 from Athens to Rome, which led to the murder of Navy diver Robert Stethem, as well as the 1996 bombing of the Khobar Towers in Saudi Arabia, an attack that killed 19 American airmen and wounded more than 400 others.

The Israelis wanted Mugniyah for the 1992 bombing of their embassy in Argentina, followed two years later by an attack on a Jewish community center in Buenos Aires. The two bombings killed a combined total of 114 people and wounded hundreds more.

The $5 million bounty the United States initially offered for Mugniyah soon jumped to a staggering $25 million. "There was an open license," one American official recalled, "to find, fix, and finish Mugniyah and anybody affiliated with him."

But Mugniyah proved hard to catch.

The elusive terrorist, nicknamed the "father of smoke," reportedly turned to plastic surgery to disguise his appearance. But in 2007 intelligence authorities learned that he was living in Damascus. Operatives shadowed the terrorist, monitoring his routine and associates. The CIA and the Mossad, which were working at the time to arrest the nuclear ambitions of Syria and Iran, began to plan a joint operation to assassinate him, one sanctioned by then-president George W. Bush. Authorities settled on a bomb, but rather than use a typical explosive that might result in civilian casualties, technicians developed what amounted to a claymore mine, one that was tested approximately two dozen times at a secret facility in North Carolina. "It was designed," one source recalled, "to throw out everything in a specific direction."

Once perfected, the bomb was flown to Jordan and then smuggled into Syria. Operatives obtained a local sport utility vehicle. Technicians loaded the bomb, which had a two-second delay, into the rear-mounted spare tire. The operation was set.

On February 12, 2008, Mugniyah met with Hezbollah commanders in a neighborhood in the Syrian capital. The terror leader left around 10:30 p.m. and strolled back to his 2006 Mitsubishi Pajero. CIA operatives pressed the detonator.

One second passed.

Then two.

The bomb exploded in a violent cloud of shrapnel. "It separated Mr. Mugniyah's arms, legs, and head from the remainder of his torso, which was catapulted about 50 feet through a window," one participant recalled. "It worked exactly like it was supposed to."

The United States and Israel publicly denied any involvement, though officials welcomed the news of his death. "The world is a better place without this man in it," State Department spokesman Sean McCormack told reporters at the time. "He was a cold-blooded killer, a mass murderer and terrorist responsible for countless innocent lives lost."

Iran's ambassador to Syria, who had encouraged "an extraordinary attack" on the Marines, barely avoided a similar fate. In 1984, Israeli operatives sent Hojjat ol-Eslam Ali Akbar Mohtashemi a bomb hidden inside a book about Shiite holy places. When he opened the Valentine's Day gift, the bomb blew off his right hand and robbed him of two fingers on his left. In the end, however, it was not a bomb or an assassin's bullet that took him down. That honor fell to the coronavirus, which finished him off in a Tehran hospital in June 2021.

Seven years after Mugniyah's death, dogged American journalists tracked down and published details of the clandestine operation to take out the former terror leader. When interviewed, an unnamed former CIA operative in the Middle East offered an important message on Mugniyah's death, one that no doubt resonated with the victims of his terrorism. "We will track you down," the operative said, "no matter how much time it takes."

Epilogue

Lebanon has long been a land of deadly myths and delusions.
—Fouad Ajami, Middle East expert
February 12, 1984

Beirut was only the beginning.

The attacks suffered at the hands of Islamic terrorists kicked off four decades of war that led American troops to battle in the mountains of Afghanistan and the streets of Iraq. Along the way, the United States suffered similar attacks again and again, from the bombing of our embassies in Kenya and Tanzania to the attack on the USS *Cole* in Yemen.

General Kelley's greatest fear—the one he highlighted during his 1983 testimony before Congress—came true eighteen years later on a cool September morning when hijackers flew planes into the World Trade Center and the Pentagon while another crashed into a field in Pennsylvania. The horror that Marines had suffered in the battered capital of Lebanon had come home.

America would never be the same.

The passage of time has offered a clearer view of the origins of what became America's global war on terrorism, allowing historians and participants to weigh in on the mission's value.

Was the attempt to bring stability to Lebanon worth the cost in blood and treasure?

Secretary of State George Shultz believed so. As the administration's leading advocate for intervention, he never wavered in his view that Lebanon was a vital building block of a stable Middle East. In his 1993 memoir, Shultz lamented the missed opportunity to enact change in 1982 when Israel and Syria were weakened by war. He placed blame, not so much on himself as America's top diplomat, but on special envoys Philip Habib

and Morris Draper. He likewise continued to point at the Pentagon's reluctance to use force to aid diplomatic negotiations. "Success would have
been of immense strategic value to us," Shultz wrote. "Peace in Lebanon
could contribute to peace elsewhere."

Others in the administration disagreed, including Draper. "Contrary
to some of the rhetoric at the time it was not of vital interest to us," he
said. "We could have just abandoned Lebanon quite easily." Joint Chiefs
of Staff Chairman General John Vessey agreed. The general, who never
supported the mission, called the deaths of 241 service members a "senseless tragedy." "What were we trying to accomplish? What did we expect
to accomplish with a battalion of Marines?" he asked. "If we were going to
change Lebanon, it would take probably four or five divisions and then we
probably would not have succeeded."

The deaths in Beirut scarred many in the Reagan administration. "For
me personally," Vessey added, "it was the saddest day of my military career." The attack so upset Marine Commandant General Paul Kelley, who
described it as "the worst emotional trauma of my life," that the first line
of his 2020 obituary in the *New York Times* mentioned his grief. The terrorist bombing likewise affected senior civilian leaders, including Michael
Deaver, Reagan's deputy chief of staff. "What a hellish waste it had all
been," he lamented. Former press officer Larry Speakes echoed him. "Lebanon," he wrote, "was a place none of us in the Reagan administration ever
wanted to hear about again after October 23, 1983."

Few wrestled with the grief as much as the president, who called the parents and spouses of each Marine killed in the lead-up to the bombing. After
the terrorist attack, he met with dozens of family members on a somber visit
to Camp Lejeune. "The loss of Marines hit Reagan hard," Vessey recalled.
"You could see it in his face. Whenever he mentioned it, it was clearly difficult for him." His own son, Michael Reagan, confirmed, noting that the loss
of so many men would haunt the president until his death in 2004 at the age
of ninety-three. "My father never really forgave himself for Beirut," he said,
"and took those Marine lives to his grave."

Fears of political damage from Lebanon proved elusive. Though Reagan
would go on to win reelection with ease in 1984—he captured a staggering
525 electoral votes to Walter Mondale's 13—the tragedy prompted much
soul-searching for White House officials. "The question that has nagged at
me ever since the bombing of the Marines is how much did our opposition

to being there affect our performance in ways that may have permitted the bombing," Vessey wondered. "How much did our hopes to get out of there affect our ability to protect ourselves?"

Both Vessey and Defense Secretary Caspar Weinberger, who led the opposition to America's involvement, regretted not pushing harder to pull the Marines out before the terrorist attack. "It was a disaster waiting to happen," Weinberger said. "It was terrible to be proven right under such horrible circumstances. They should have been pulled out earlier."

Unlike others in the administration, Bud McFarlane never publicly apologized or even acknowledged his own role in the catastrophe. If anything, he emerged more brazen, which led to his downfall during the Iran-Contra Affair in 1986, a scandal in which the White House secretly sold arms to Khomeini in exchange for prisoners. The proceeds were then funneled to the Contra rebels in Nicaragua, who were battling the communist Sandinistas. In a stunning and humiliating fall from grace, McFarlane was hauled before Congress to testify.

On February 8, 1987, he popped thirty Valium pills, chasing them with wine in an attempt to end his life. He then climbed into bed next to his wife, hoping he would never wake up. He instead opened his eyes in the intensive care unit at Bethesda Naval Hospital. "My life," he wrote, "apparently, was meant to go on."

The following year, the former national security advisor pleaded guilty to charges of withholding information to Congress and was sentenced to two hundred hours of community service.

President George H. W. Bush pardoned McFarlane on Christmas Eve of 1992.

"I so let the country down," McFarlane later admitted.

He died in 2022 at the age of eighty-four.

Historians have proven equally as harsh in assessing the mission. "The story of the Reagan administration's involvement in Lebanon is a case study of foreign policy calamity," argued biographer Lou Cannon. "More than any other undertaking, the U.S. involvement in Lebanon demonstrates the naivete, ignorance and undisciplined internal conflict characteristic of the Reagan presidency." William Quandt, a former National Security Council staffer, professor, and Middle East expert, was more diplomatic in his assessment. "The best laid of plans," he observed, "have a way of coming unraveled in Lebanon."

That remains true today.

Lebanon's civil war dragged on until 1990. The terror group Hezbollah, born in the Bekaa Valley in the early 1980s, is now a dominant political party. Similar to the Palestine Liberation Organization, Hezbollah operates like a state within a state, complete with its own military. In 2006, the militant group fought a thirty-four-day war against Israel. More recently, Lebanon's economy has flatlined to the point it teeters on becoming a failed state.

For the survivors and their families, and the families of those killed in the attack, Beirut would forever alter their lives, from coping with life-changing injuries and post-traumatic stress to dealing with the death of a husband, son, or father. "This was a tragedy of people, where each was unique, and each had a story," Rabbi Arnold Resnicoff so eloquently wrote afterward. "Each had a past, and each had been cheated of a future."

Micheline Earle, who had married Bryan Earle one week before the bombing, faced deportation from the United States since her husband had been killed before he completed her residency application. As such, the teenager, who was on a temporary visa, could not leave the United States after his funeral, or else she risked not being able to return. She felt that Earle's family, who were always hospitable, blamed her for his death, since he had volunteered to return so he could marry her. Micheline also blamed herself. "Even to this day," she said recently, "I still question it."

But Earle's goal, as he told his friends in Beirut, was to give her a new life outside war-torn Lebanon. Furthermore, to return home to an increasingly dangerous and radicalized country as the widow of an American sailor could spell her doom.

So she stayed and fought for her citizenship.

She lived in an apartment while lawmakers slowly worked on special legislation that would grant her permanent residency. "If Micheline Earle's husband had not been killed in the tragic bombing," said Democratic senator Howard Metzenbaum of Ohio, who sponsored the bill to help her, "she would now be a permanent resident of the United States. It is only fitting that the Congress correct this injustice in honor of her husband's sacrifice."

One year turned to two.

And then three.

For a young girl in a foreign land the experience was lonely. Her only connection to home came via long-distance phone calls on which she could hear gunfire and explosions in the background. "I miss my mom," she told a reporter, "more than anybody else, more than anything else."

In May 1986, Congress passed legislation granting her permanent residency, which Reagan signed into law. Four years later, on April 27, 1990, she became a United States citizen. Micheline later remarried and had two daughters. Many of her family members have since moved from Lebanon and settled in America. Her first love, however, remains in her heart. "I have a lot more to celebrate in life and a lot more to be grateful for," she said recently. "But there will never, ever be another Bryan. No one will ever take his memory away."

Lisa Hudson struggled.

Dr. Jim Ware, who had been close with John Hudson, visited her in Georgia after he returned from Beirut. Lisa's parents, like so many others wrestling with grief, questioned whether Hudson might have somehow survived, even though they had held a funeral and buried the young father on the family's farm in Georgia.

"No," Ware assured her. "He's not alive."

Ware related his insistence upon seeing Hudson when he was found in the rubble. He described his friend in a T-shirt with no shoes or dog tags. His right hand, Ware noted, covered his face with the palm facing upward. At the mention of that detail, Lisa jumped up and darted out of the room, only to return a moment later with a photograph.

"Is this what he looked like?" she asked.

The photo showed Hudson asleep with his hand over his face, his palm turned outward.

Yes, the dentist confirmed.

"That's the way he slept," Lisa announced.

The photograph proved that Hudson had never heard the bomb's blast or felt the rush of terror, but had instead died, like so many others, in his sleep. "For me that was a wonderful moment, because I had calmed her fears," Ware said. "Only I could do that."

Lisa Hudson never remarried.

She never met a man she loved as much as John Hudson, the irreverent trombonist who had once entertained thousands at Six Flags Over Georgia. Lisa went back to work and raised the couple's son with help from her parents. At the thirtieth reunion of the Beirut veterans, Will Hudson delivered a powerful and emotional speech about what it was like to grow up without a father, a story that echoes through the lives of so many other children of the men killed in Lebanon. As a four-year-old, Will Hudson asked his father's best friend if he would be his dad. On a father-son Cub Scout campout three years later, he cried himself to sleep. "I have lived every day of my life with a hole in my heart that will never be filled," he said. "I have never heard my father's voice and I have never seen his face. I will never know what it feels like to have someone call you their 'son' and I will never know what it feels like to call someone 'dad.' Every joyful milestone in my life has also been a painful reminder of what I was also missing."

Many of the men who survived the bombing carry the physical and emotional scars of that day. Lieutenant Colonel Larry Gerlach remains dependent on a wheelchair. Navy hospital corpsman Don Howell is blind in his right eye. Brad Ulick not only suffers breathing problems from the dust he inhaled, but his hands are tattooed with scars from where he rubbed them raw digging through the rubble.

Scores more suffer with the guilt of surviving, including Stephen Russell and Henry Linkkila, both of whom were on duty that day. "I was Sergeant of the Guard that morning and to this day hold myself personally responsible for what happened. At that exact moment in time I was responsible for the security of each and every Marine, sailor, and soldier," Russell said. "Survivors guilt is real and I am reminded every single day that I should not be there." That guilt is one of the reasons Linkkila doesn't feel comfortable going to Beirut reunions. "I was the guy at the gate when it happened. I was the man standing there," he said. "I find it hard to look at people."

Ulick's emotional anguish is so severe that he has contemplated suicide.

Why, he asks, did he survive and so many others did not? "Every day I wake up, I have to tell myself that today is not the day I give up," he said. "I feel so guilty for living."

America's refusal to strike back in the wake of the attacks on the embassy and the Marines still troubles many, including Geraghty. "The failure of the United States to retaliate against this act of war sent the wrong message to the terrorist state powerbrokers in Tehran and Damascus," he said. "Our timidity whetted the jihadists' appetite."

Survivors and the families of those killed instead have increasingly turned to the courts for help. In 2001, eighty-three victims and families sued Iran for its role in the embassy bombing. Four years later, a federal court judge ordered Iran to pay $126 million. "The lawsuit is our way of fighting back," survivor Anne Dammarell said at the time. "It is the only way we have to make Iran accountable for the incredible pain it inflicted."

Others have followed suit, including twenty-six survivors and nearly a thousand family members of the troops killed in the bombing of the Battalion Landing Team headquarters in Beirut. In 2007, a federal court ordered Iran to pay another $2.65 billion to those victims. "This court is sadly aware that there is little it can do to heal the physical wounds and emotional scars," Judge Royce Lamberth said at the time. "These individuals, whose hearts and souls were forever broken, waited patiently for nearly a quarter-century for justice to be done."

Collecting that money has proven a challenge.

The United States passed legislation in 2012 to make it easier for victims to seize assets from frozen accounts held by Bank Markazi, Iran's central bank. Lawyers for the bank sued, arguing that the legislation clearly targeted one entity and therefore violated the Constitution. The case went all the way to the U.S. Supreme Court, which in 2016 ruled 6–2 that Iran must pay up. Deborah Peterson, whose brother Corporal James Knipple died in the Marine bombing, was one of the plaintiffs. "I don't think you ever really have closure," she said after the ruling. "I'll always be sad that Jim didn't have a whole life, a full life."

Despite the legal and financial setbacks, Iran has continued to publicly deny any involvement. In October 2023, however, a senior government official slipped up and publicly admitted his nation's role during an interview with the state-controlled Islamic Republic News Agency. Sayyed Issa Tabatabai, who serves as Iran's representative in Lebanon, acknowledged that he traveled to Lebanon to help with the "martyrdom operations." He likewise talked about Iran's efforts to nurture Hezbollah in the Baalbek area. The news agency quickly scrubbed those portions of the interview from its website, but not before international media outlets copied it. "God made it possible," Tabatabai said, "for me to continue the military activity."

Colonel Geraghty, a conscientious officer who many believed would one day serve as commandant of the Marine Corps, saw his career ruined by Beirut. He retired from the service in 1986. Geraghty went on to work for the CIA in its Counterterrorist Center and later the private sector, applying the information he learned in Lebanon to his service in the intelligence field. He lives today in Arizona. Though Congress and the Pentagon blamed him for the attack, his own men do not. That was evident when he approached the lectern at the fortieth Beirut veterans reunion in 2023.

"I will follow you anywhere, sir!" one man yelled from the back.

Geraghty wrote a book in 2009 titled *Peacekeepers at War*, in which he laid out the tremendous challenges he faced in Beirut and examined the pressure from Washington. America's mission, he concluded, was a noble undertaking that saved many lives before it was sadly undermined by terrorists intent to drive the multinational force from Lebanon. "Civilized rules of behavior and moral codes," he wrote, "are anathema to Islamic extremists."

Over four decades later, Beirut remains a part of all the men who served there. Ware stayed in the Navy, where he later commanded the 1,200-bed hospital aboard the USNS *Comfort*, which helped with the rescue of earthquake victims in Haiti in 2010. After his retirement as a captain, he returned to his native Savannah, where he still practices dentistry. His good friend and fellow dentist Dr. Gil Bigelow retired from the Navy as a captain after a career that spanned the globe. A master parachutist and scuba diver, he now lives in Virginia.

Chaplain Danny Wheeler, the last survivor pulled from the wreckage, remained on active duty for another two and a half years before he transferred to the Naval Reserves. He returned home to Wisconsin, where he continued to serve as a Lutheran pastor. Now retired, Wheeler divides his time between Wisconsin and Hilton Island, South Carolina. His good friend Rabbi Resnicoff retired from the Navy as a captain in 2001 after almost three decades of service. Resnicoff, who lives in Washington, donated his camouflage kippa to the Navy Chaplain Corps Museum along with the broken and charred welcome plaque from the Peacekeeping Chapel that was salvaged from the rubble.

Don Howell, who was buried in the basement of the headquarters building, went back to school and became a trauma nurse. He lives today near where he grew up along the warm South Carolina coast in Charleston. Emanuel Simmons settled in Jacksonville, North Carolina, near Camp Lejeune. He owns a gym, 10 Rounds of Fitness, where he trains boxers and helps people with Parkinson's disease. Burnham Matthews, who was hurled from a three-story window, stayed in the service for twenty-four years. Upon retirement, he worked for the Marine Corps Warfighting Laboratory in Quantico, Virginia, and later the FBI before he retired to the mountains of western North Carolina.

Pablo Arroyo, who was also thrown out of the third-floor window and buried in the rubble, remained in uniform for four more years. Arroyo went on to serve for another two decades with the Connecticut State Police and later the U.S. Department of Homeland Security. Kenny Farnan left the Marines soon after the bombing. Like Arroyo, he, too, went into law enforcement, serving as a police officer with the city of Pittsburgh until his retirement in 2013.

Mark Singleton retired from the Marines as a lieutenant colonel in 2004. He returned home to South Carolina, where he teaches history at Coastal Carolina University and is president of Rogue Kinetics, a self-defense, risk, and security consultancy. Bob Jordan and Randy Gaddo, who handled public affairs in Lebanon, helped found the Beirut Veterans of America. Gaddo even reprised his role in authoring and editing a new version of the *Root Scoop*.

In 1986, the city of Jacksonville erected a monument on Lejeune Boulevard to honor the men killed in Beirut and Grenada. The memorial features a wall engraved with the 273 names of those who died. A bronze statue of a solitary soldier presides over the memorial, on which is etched a single sentence: "They Came in Peace."

Every year at 6 a.m. on the anniversary of the bombing, survivors and families gather at the memorial for a candlelight vigil. Each victim's name is read aloud. At 6:22 a.m.—the moment the bomb detonated—the reading pauses and a moment of silence follows. Gaddo led the early morning service on October 23, 2023, to mark the fortieth anniversary. "They are not just names," he reminded attendees, "they are real people, with personalities and passions, virtues and vices, good days and bad days, and with people who love them."

Hundreds listened in silence on that cool fall morning.

"When we read each name," Gaddo continued, "that person comes alive again in our mind and in this place, where they join with us and their fellow heroes to continue celebrating their lives. We who read the names and listen to the names are only visitors—the men behind these names will live here for another year, waiting to remind us again next year that they died as heroes, American Marines, sailors, and soldiers—as peacekeepers."

Those in attendance nodded as he spoke.

"So," Gaddo said in conclusion, "our first duty is to remember."

And remember we will.

Acknowledgments

Producing a work of narrative nonfiction is a team effort. As such, we are indebted to a wealth of historians, archivists, and researchers, as well as Beirut veterans, rescuers, and the wives, siblings, and children of the men killed in that awful terrorist attack. Dr. Charlie Neimeyer, the former director of Marine Corps history, encouraged this project from the beginning, sharing his terrific insight as well as making introductions at the Marine Corps History Division at Quantico, Virginia. At the Marine archives, we want to thank Stephen Coode, John Lyles, Tyler Reed, and Nancy Whitfield for the great help during our on-site research as well as in the months that followed. Archivist Aimee Muller at the Ronald Reagan Presidential Library in California was an enormous help both in person and from afar, graciously hunting down information and answering numerous questions.

Historian André Sobocinski with the Navy's Bureau of Medicine and Surgery was another invaluable resource, sharing oral histories, records, and contacts with survivors. At the National Archives, we want to thank Nate Patch and Todd Crumley. Jared Galloway assisted us at the National Naval Aviation Museum in Pensacola, Florida. So, too, did our diligent research assistant David Meron, who helped scan hundreds of pages of letters. Historian and good friend Jon Jordan reached out to former senator Sam Nunn on our behalf. Thank you as well to Becky Sherman at Emory University for her help with the senator's papers. At the U.S. Naval Institute, we want to thank Janis Jorgensen. We also want to thank the excellent military historians and our friends at the Citadel, Doctors Brian Jones, Kyle Sinisi, and David Preston.

We owe a special thanks to Major General James Lariviere, who served as a young Marine lieutenant in Beirut in the months leading up to the bombing. General Lariviere has since become one of the nation's leading scholars on the bombing, and we benefited immensely from his expertise as well as his prepublication review of the manuscript. At the law firm Crowell & Moring in Washington, D.C., we want to thank Stuart Newberger, who generously provided copies of the court records from the litigation surrounding the April 1983 bombing of the American Embassy. Similarly, Caragh Fay and Amanda Fox Perry with the Fay Law Group were a huge help in sharing transcripts from the litigation involving the attack on the Battalion Landing Team headquarters six months later. Katie Rasdorf, who has proven to be an indispensable resource over many years and books, doggedly helped hunt down many of the photos used in this book.

This book never would have been possible, however, without the tremendous help of dozens of Beirut veterans and their families, whose stories form the heart of this narrative. Thank you to Dr. James Ware, who not only spent the better part of a day recounting his experiences in Beirut, but also kindly reviewed the manuscript in advance of publication. We owe a special thanks as well to his colleague and dear friend, Dr. Gilbert Bigelow, who was equally as kind and gracious. Thank you to Rabbi Arnold Resnicoff and Chaplain Danny Wheeler, both of whom spent many hours sharing their experiences. Over the last four decades, Randy Gaddo has done a herculean job keeping the story of the bombing alive through articles and speeches, as well as the hard work he and others invest to plan reunions. From the beginning, Randy was an enormous help and great friend to this project, answering myriad questions, sharing photos, and providing a keen review of an early draft of this book. We likewise want to thank John Dalziel, who gave us each a piece of the rubble from the Battalion Landing Team headquarters. That haunting piece of broken concrete helped bring alive this awful tragedy.

We owe a special thanks to Lisa Hudson, who spent hours relaying stories about her late husband, John. Lisa likewise shared more than six hundred pages of John's letters and nine hours of recordings he made on cassette tapes while in Beirut, allowing us to hear his voice four decades after his death. Those personal records afforded us a real connection to John that punctuates the tragedy of his death. On a similar note, we want to thank Gail Ohler Osborne, whose husband, Michael, was killed by a sniper days before the bombing. Gail shared wonderful information about Michael and helped us secure copies of his letters, which are on file at the National Naval

Aviation Museum. Thank you as well to her daughter Sarah, her soon-to-be son-in-law Ryan Prong, and her husband, Chris Osborne. We likewise want to thank Micheline Thompson, who recounted for us the story of her love and brief marriage to Bryan Earle.

Colonel Timothy Geraghty was a wonderful resource and true gentleman. It was an honor to enjoy dinner with the colonel, his wife, Karen, and son Sean at the fortieth reunion in Jacksonville, North Carolina. We owe a special thanks to Kathryn Dempsey, who provided us with letters, newspaper accounts, and other personal writings from her brother George Losey. We likewise want to thank Kathryn's husband, Michael, and her siblings and their spouses, Susan and Geoff Losey and Beth and Holt Stevens, all of whom provided us with warm and colorful accounts of George. Thank you as well to Mark Singleton and Don Howell, tremendous individuals and friends who not only shared their harrowing stories but graciously reviewed an early draft of the manuscript to help with accuracy. We likewise want to thank Stephen Russell and Henry Linkkila, who were on duty that morning. Both related their accounts in person and via email of that tragic day and the guilt they still wrestle with today. Henry likewise provided us with scores of his personal letters, which helped enrich this book.

Along similar lines, we want to thank Brad Ulick, who shared his diary and letters with us as well as sat for a lengthy interview. David Madaras likewise generously shared with us his personal letters, while Michael Toma provided us with his diary. Others we are indebted to include Burnham Matthews, Pablo Arroyo, Ken Farnan, and Emanuel Simmons, all of whom recounted in detail what it was like in the Battalion Landing Teams headquarters building the morning of the attack. We want to thank Mark Hacala for his great help and for providing us his own research materials, not to mention a copy of the latest *Bluejacket's Manual*, which he coedited. Mark and fellow veteran Darius Eichler likewise were a huge help in researching the story of their good friend Bryan Earle. Anthony Pais was an enthusiastic helper. Anthony not only related his personal story but loaned us his archive of records. Others we want to thank include Neal Morris, Blaine Cosgrove, Rodney Burnette, Steve Combes, Tim McCoskey, Philip Amrhein, Peter Ferraro, Paul Dziadon, John Snyder, John L'Heureux and his stepfather, Richard Wells, Jack Cress, Ed Tuthill, Myron Kyle, and Myron Harrington.

An important part of the story is the medical rescue. We want to thank Dr. Fraser Henderson, Dr. Pat Hutton, and Mauricio Aparicio, all of whom shared with us what it was like on board the *Iwo Jima*. On a similar note, thank you to Dr. Robert Sundquist, who recounted his story of handling the identification of the deceased in Germany.

To all the Beirut veterans and families, we want to say a special thank-you for all the help and encouragement. It has been a privilege and an honor to tell your story.

In Honor of the Fallen

Terry W. Abbott Marine Corps
Clemon Alexander Marine Corps
John R. Allman Marine Corps
Moses Arnold, Jr. Marine Corps
Charles K Bailey Marine Corps
Nicholas Baker Marine Corps
Johansen Banks Marine Corps
Richard E. Barrett Marine Corps
Ronny K. Bates Navy
David L. Battle Marine Corps
James R. Baynard Marine Corps
Jesse W. Beamon Navy
Alvin Belmer Marine Corps
Shannon D. Biddle Marine Corps
Stephen B. Bland Marine Corps
Richard L. Blankenship Marine Corps
John W. Blocker Marine Corps
Joseph J. Boccia, Jr. Marine Corps
Leon W. Bohannon, Jr. Marine Corps
John R. Bohnet, Jr. Marine Corps
John J. Bonk, Jr. Marine Corps
Jeffrey J. Boulos Marine Corps
David R. Bousum Marine Corps
John N. Boyett Marine Corps
Anthony K. Brown Marine Corps
David W. Brown Marine Corps
Bobby B. Buchanan, Jr. Marine Corps

John B. Buckmaster Marine Corps
William F. Burley Marine Corps
Alfred L. Butler, III Marine Corps
Jimmy R. Cain Marine Corps
Paul L. Callahan Marine Corps
Mecot E. Camara Marine Corps
Bradley J. Campus Marine Corps
Randall A. Carlson Army
Johnie D. Ceasar Marine Corps
Sam Cherman Marine Corps
Randy W. Clark Marine Corps
Marc L. Cole Marine Corps
Marcus E. Coleman Army
Juan M. Comas Marine Corps
Robert A. Conley Marine Corps
Charles D. Cook Marine Corps
Curtis J. Cooper Marine Corps
Johnny L. Copeland Marine Corps
Bert D. Corcoran Marine Corps
David L. Cosner Marine Corps
Kevin P. Coulman Marine Corps
Manuel A. Cox Marine Corps
Brett A. Croft Marine Corps
Rick R. Crudale Marine Corps
Kevin P. Custard Marine Corps
Russell E. Cyzick Marine Corps
David L. Daugherty Marine Corps
Andrew L. Davis Marine Corps
Sidney J. Decker Marine Corps
Michael J. Devlin Marine Corps
Thomas A. Dibenedetto Navy
Nathaniel G. Dorsey Marine Corps
Frederick B. Douglass Marine Corps
George L. Dramis Marine Corps
Timothy J. Dunnigan Marine Corps
Bryan L. Earle Navy
Roy L. Edwards Marine Corps

William D. Elliot, Jr. Navy
Jesse J. Ellison Marine Corps
Danny R. Estes Marine Corps
Sean F. Estler Marine Corps
Thomas A. Evans Marine Corps
James E. Faulk Navy
Richard A. Fluegel Marine Corps
Steven M. Forrester Marine Corps
William B. Foster, Jr. Navy
Michael D. Fulcher Marine Corps
Benjamin E. Fuller Marine Corps
Michael S. Fulton Marine Corps
William R. Gaines, Jr. Marine Corps
Sean R. Gallagher Marine Corps
David B. Gander Marine Corps
George M. Gangur Marine Corps
Leland E. Gann Marine Corps
Randall J. Garcia Marine Corps
Ronald J. Garcia Marine Corps
Edward J. Gargano Marine Corps
David D. Gay Marine Corps
Harold D. Ghumm Marine Corps
Warner Gibbs, Jr Marine Corps
Timothy R. Giblin Marine Corps
Michael W. Gorchinski Navy
Richard J. Gordon Marine Corps
Harold F. Gratton Marine Corps
Robert B. Greaser Marine Corps
Davin M. Green Marine Corps
Tomas A. Hairston Marine Corps
Freddie L. Haltiwanger, Jr. Marine Corps
Virgel D. Hamilton Marine Corps
Gilbert Hanton Marine Corps
William Hart Marine Corps
Michael S. Haskell Marine Corps
Michael A. Hastings Marine Corps
Jefferey T. Hattaway Marine Corps

Paul A. Hein Marine Corps
Douglas E. Held Marine Corps
Mark A. Helms Marine Corps
Ferrandy D. Henderson Marine Corps
Matilde Hernandez, Jr. Marine Corps
Rodolfo Hernandez Marine Corps
Stanley G. Hester Marine Corps
John W. Henderickson Marine Corps
Donald W. Hildreth Marine Corps
Richard H. Holberton Marine Corps
Robert S. Holland Marine Corps
Bruce A. Hollingshead Marine Corps
Melvin D. Holmes Marine Corps
Bruce L. Howard Marine Corps
John R. Hudson Navy Reserve
Terry L. Hudson Marine Corps
Lyndon J. Hue Marine Corps
Maurice E. Hukill Marine Corps
Edward S. Iacovino, Jr. Marine Corps
John J. Ingalls Marine Corps
Paul G. Innocenzi, III Marine Corps
James J. Jackowski Marine Corps
Jeffrey W. James Marine Corps
Nathaniel W. Jenkins Marine Corps
Michael H. Johnson Navy
Edward A. Johnston Marine Corps
Steven Jones Marine Corps
Thomas A. Julian Marine Corps
Marion E. Kees Navy
Thomas C. Keown Marine Corps
Edward E. Kimm Marine Corps
Walter V. Kingsley Marine Corps
Daniel S. Kluck Army
James C. Knipple Marine Corps
Todd A. Kraft Marine Corps
Freas H. Kreischer, III Marine Corps
Keith J. Laise Marine Corps

Thomas G. Lamb Marine Corps
Mark A. Lange Navy
James J. Langon, IV Marine Corps
Michael S. Lariviere Marine Corps
Stephen B. Lariviere Marine Corps
Richard L. Lemnah Marine Corps
David A. Lewis Marine Corps
Val S. Lewis Marine Corps
Joseph R. Livingston Marine Corps
Donald G. Losey, Jr. Marine Corps
Paul D. Lyon, Jr Marine Corps
John W. Macroglou Marine Corps
Samuel Maitland Marine Corps
Charlie R. Martin Marine Corps
Jack I. Martin Marine Corps
David S. Massa Marine Corps
Michael R. Massman Marine Corps
Joseph J. Mattacchione Marine Corps
Ben Henry Maxwell Army
John McCall Marine Corps
James E. McDonough Marine Corps
Timothy R. McMahon Marine Corps
Robert V. McMaugh Marine Corps
Timothy D. McNeely Marine Corps
George N. McVicker, II Navy
Louis Melendez Marine Corps
Richard H. Menkins, II Marine Corps
Michael D. Mercer Marine Corps
Ronald W. Meurer Marine Corps
Joseph P. Milano Navy
Joseph P. Moore Marine Corps
Richard A. Morrow Marine Corps
John F. Muffler Marine Corps
Alex Munoz Marine Corps
Harry D. Myers Marine Corps
David J. Nairn Marine Corps
Luis Nava Marine Corps

Michael J. Ohler Marine Corps
John A. Olson Marine Corps
Robert P. Olson Marine Corps
Alexander M. Ortega Marine Corps
Richard C. Ortiz Marine Corps
Jeffrey B. Owen Marine Corps
Joseph A. Owens Marine Corps
Ray Page Marine Corps
Ulysses G. Parker Marine Corps
Mark W. Payne Marine Corps
John L. Pearson Marine Corps
Marvin H. Perkins Marine Corps
Thomas S. Perron Marine Corps
John A. Phillips, Jr. Marine Corps
George W. Piercy Navy
C. Wayne Plymel Marine Corps
William H. Pollard Marine Corps
Rafael Pomalestorres Marine Corps
Victor M. Prevatt Marine Corps
James C. Price Marine Corps
Patrick K. Prindeville Marine Corps
Eric A. Pulliam Marine Corps
Diomedes J. Quirante Navy
David M. Randolph Marine Corps
Charles R. Ray Marine Corps
David L. Reagan Marine Corps
Rui A. Relvas Marine Corps
Terrence L. Rich Marine Corps
Warren Richardson Marine Corps
Jaun C. Rodriquez Marine Corps
Louis J. Rotondo Marine Corps
Mark E. Salazar Army
Guillermo San Pedro, Jr. Marine Corps
Michael C. Sauls Marine Corps
Charles J. Schnorf Marine Corps
Scott L. Schultz Marine Corps
Peter J. Scialabba Marine Corps

Gary R. Scott Marine Corps
Ronald L. Shallo Marine Corps
Thomas A. Shipp Marine Corps
Jerryl D. Shropshire Marine Corps
James F. Silvia Marine Corps
Larry H. Simpson Marine Corps
Stanley J. Sliwinski Marine Corps
Kirk H. Smith Marine Corps
Thomas G. Smith Marine Corps
Vincent L. Smith Marine Corps
Edward Soares Marine Corps
Allen H. Soifert Marine Corps
William S. Sommerhof Marine Corps
Michael C. Spaulding Marine Corps
John W. Spearing Marine Corps
Stephen E. Spencer Marine Corps
Bill J. Stelpflug Marine Corps
Horace R. Stephens Marine Corps
Craig S. Stockton Marine Corps
Jeffrey G. Stokes Marine Corps
Thomas D. Stowe Marine Corps
Eric D. Sturghill Marine Corps
Devon L. Sundar Marine Corps
James F. Surch Navy
Dennis A. Thompson Marine Corps
Thomas P. Thorstad Marine Corps
Stephen D. Tingley Marine Corps
John J. Tishmack Marine Corps
Henry Townsend, Jr. Marine Corps
Lex D. Trahon Marine Corps
Richard Twine Army
Pedro J. Valle Marine Corps
Donald H. Vallone, Jr. Marine Corps
Michael R. Wagner Navy
Eric R. Walker Marine Corps
Leonard W. Walker Marine Corps
Eric G. Washington Marine Corps

Obrian Weekes Marine Corps
Tandy W. Wells Marine Corps
Steven B. Wentworth Marine Corps
Allen D. Wesley Marine Corps
Lloyd D. West Marine Corps
John R. Weyl Marine Corps
Burton D. Wherland, Jr. Marine Corps
Dwayne W. Wigglesworth Marine Corps
Rodney J. Williams Marine Corps
Scipio Williams, Jr Marine Corps
Johnny A. Williamson Marine Corps
Walter E. Wint, Jr Marine Corps
William E. Winter Marine Corps
John e. Wolfe Marine Corps
Donald E. Woollett Marine Corps
David E. Worley Navy
Craig L. Wyche Marine Corps
James G. Yarber Army
Jeffrey D. Young Marine Corps
William A. Zimmerman Marine Corps
John P. Giguere Marine Corps
Jeffrey R. Scharver Marine Corps
Jeb F. Seagle Marine Corps
Kenneth V. Welch Army

A Note on Sources

To tell the story of the tragedy that befell American diplomats and Marines in Beirut in 1983 required extensive archival work as well as more than a hundred hours of interviews with survivors and family members. The Marine Corps History Division in Virginia should be the first stop for anyone interested in learning more about America's involvement in Lebanon. The archive houses thousands of pages of primary source materials. Those include the monthly Command Chronologies, weekly situation reports, and daily message traffic, not to mention dozens of oral histories, many conducted right before and after the October 1983 bombing. The archive also features the rich personal collections of many of the Marines who served. These records include powerful personal letters, a complete set of the weekly *Root Scoop*, and even the after-action report of the mortuary teams trusted to identify the remains.

Another vital stop for any researcher is the Ronald Reagan Presidential Library in California. This archive, perched atop a mountain with incredible views, boasts the official White House records related to Lebanon and Grenada. This includes Reagan's daily schedules, meeting agendas, discussion papers, media releases, memos, press conference transcripts, and correspondence from the public as well as the families of the men who served. To supplement the official records, we consulted the published memoirs and diaries of President Reagan as well as many of his top advisors, including Secretary of State George Shultz, Defense Secretary Caspar Weinberger, and National Security Advisor Bud McFarlane.

Other important secondary sources include Thomas Friedman's *From Beirut to Jerusalem* and Robert Fisk's *Pity the Nation*. These two books from Beirut-based journalists are an invaluable window into the political turmoil of Lebanon in the early 1980s. Marine Corps historian Benis Frank wrote an excellent book titled *U.S. Marines in Lebanon, 1982–1984*, which avoids the political component of the mission, but does provide a detailed service history. Several Marines have written powerful first-person accounts of their experiences. Those works include Michael Petit's *Peacekeepers at War* and Glenn Dolphin's *24 MAU*. Colonel Geraghty published his own book, which like Petit's book is titled *Peacekeepers at War*, that lays out in great detail the tremendous struggle he faced as Lebanon spiraled into chaos. While there have been several books done on the rise of the terror group Hezbollah, one that proved invaluable to us was David Crist's *The Twilight War*, an excellent work of scholarship.

In addition to primary and secondary sources, we benefited enormously from the help of dozens of Beirut veterans and families. We interviewed more than forty survivors as well as spouses, parents, and children of the men who served and died in Lebanon. Those veterans and families provided us with a treasure trove of never-before-published papers, including more than a thousand pages of letters and diaries as well as scores of photographs. John Dalziel, in fact, graciously gave us each a piece of the Battalion Landing Team headquarters that he salvaged. These contemporaneous records, which are quoted liberally throughout the book, help form the emotional heart of this tragic story. It is important to note that all quotations and dialogue come from letters, diaries, military and political reports, oral histories, interviews, speeches, transcripts, and radio messages, all of which are documented in the detailed notes that follow.

Abbreviations

BUMED U.S. Navy Bureau of Medicine and Surgery, Falls Church, Virginia
LOC Library of Congress, Washington, D.C.
MCHD Marine Corps History Division, Archives Branch, Quantico, Virginia
NNAM National Naval Aviation Museum, Pensacola, Florida
RRPL Ronald Reagan Presidential Library and Museum,
    Simi Valley, California

Notes

PART I

1   "You are about": "Message from the President to the U.S. Marine Forces
     Participating in the Multi-National Force in Beirut, Lebanon," Aug. 25, 1982,
     Box 15, Office of Media Relations, Ronald Reagan Presidential Library
     (RRPL), Simi Valley, Calif.

CHAPTER 1

3   "Beirut has become": "Horror in Beirut," editorial, *Pittsburgh Post-Gazette*,
     April 20, 1983, p. 6.

3   The black GMC: Robert Baer, *See No Evil: The True Story of a Ground Soldier in
     the CIA's War on Terrorism* (New York: Crown, 2002), pp. 65–66.

3   A mile away: "Middle East: The Horror, the Horror!" *Time*, May 2, 1983, p. 28.

3   Shoppers browsed: William E. Farrell, "In Beirut, 'Bells Not Bullets' After
     Year of Carnage," *New York Times*, Dec. 26, 1982, p. 1.

4   Others queued: "Beirut Cinemas Turn Corner as Biz Normalizes," *Variety*, vol.
     309, no. 1, Nov. 3, 1982, p. 1.

4   "People were just": Thomas L. Friedman, "Counting the Casualties in Beirut
     and Beyond," *New York Times*, April 24, 1983, p. E3.

4   In the previous: Jonathan C. Randal, "Attacks on Patrols in Beirut Wound
     5 U.S. Marines, 8 Italians," *Washington Post*, March 17, 1983, p. A1; "5 U.S.
     Marines and 9 Italians Wounded," *New York Times*, March 17, 1983, p. A1.

4   Only four days: Kai Bird, *The Good Spy: The Life and Death of Robert Ames* (New
     York: Crown, 2014), p. 296.

4   A dusting of snow: David Ignatius, "A Blast Still Reverberating; 25 Years Ago,
     a New Kind of War Began in Beirut," *Washington Post*, April 17, 2008, p. A23.

4   Locals in search: "Blood and Terror in Beirut," *Newsweek*, May 2, 1983, p. 22.

4   Up on the embassy's: Don Chubb testimony, in Proposed Findings of Fact and
     Conclusions of Law, Anne Dammarell, et al., vs. Islamic Republic
     of Iran, et al., p. 253.

4   The day before: Robert Essington testimony, April 9, 2003, in vol. 3 of the trial
     transcript of Anne Dammarell, et al., vs. Islamic Republic of Iran, et al.

4   The twenty-one: Testimony of Earl McMaugh, Annie Mullins, Teresa
     McMaugh Younts, Michael McMaugh, and Cherie Lynn Jones, April 10, 2008,

in vol. 4 of the trial transcript of Anne Dammarell, et al., vs. Islamic Republic of Iran, et al.; Sager, Mike, "Private Farewells: Friends Remember Marine Killed in Beirut," *Washington Post*, April 27, 1983, p. A1.

5   "I'll give you": Ronnie Tumolo testimony, in Proposed Findings of Fact and Conclusions of Law, Anne Dammarell, et al., vs. Islamic Republic of Iran, et al., p. 95.

5   "How are you doing": Dorothy Pech testimony, April 9, 2003, in vol. 3 of the trial transcript of Anne Dammarell, et al., vs. Islamic Republic of Iran, et al.

5   The bespectacled: Bird, *The Good Spy*, pp. 10–17, 70, 117–18.

5   "He was": Yvonne Blakely Ames testimony, April 15, 2003, in vol. 5 of the trial transcript of Anne Dammarell, et al., vs. Islamic Republic of Iran, et al.

6   "I've got": Allison Haas testimony, in Proposed Findings of Fact and Conclusions of Law, Anne Dammarell, et al., vs. Islamic Republic of Iran, et al., p. 111.

6   Up on the eighth: Robert Dillon oral history with Charles Stuart Kennedy, May 17, 1990, Foreign Affairs Oral History Collection of the Association for Diplomatic Studies and Training, Library of Congress (LOC), Washington, D.C.

6   During the Lebanese: Douglas Watson, "Attaché, Driver Also Murdered," *Washington Post*, June 17, 1976, p. A1; Nora Boustany, "U.S. Ambassador Dean Ambushed in Lebanon, Escapes Attack Unhurt," *Washington Post*, Aug. 28, 1980, p. A40.

6   In the meantime: Thomas Tracy testimony, June 28, 1983, in U.S. Congress, House, *The U.S. Embassy Bombing in Beirut, Hearing Before the Committee on Foreign Relations and its Subcommittee on International Operations and on Europe and the Middle East*, 98th Cong., 1st Sess., June 28, 1983 (Washington, DC: U.S. Government Printing Office, 1983), pp. 4–7.

7   "Let's go down": Anne Dammarell oral history with Charles Stuart Kennedy, June 10, 2013, Foreign Affairs Oral History Collection of the Association for Diplomatic Studies and Training, LOC.

7   "This is either": Anne Dammarell, "Hidden Fears, Helpful Memories: Aftermath of the 1983 Bombing of the United States Embassy in Beirut" (master's thesis, Georgetown University, 1994), p. 14.

7   A brief break: Baer, *See No Evil*, pp. 66–67.

7   The explosion: David Zucchino, "Bomb Kills 39 at U.S. Embassy," *Philadelphia Inquirer*, April 19, 1983, p. A1; Herbert H. Denton, "Bomb Wrecks U.S. Embassy," *Washington Post*, April 19, 1983, p. 1; Thomas L. Friedman, "Building in Ruins," *New York Times*, April 19, 1983, p. 1.

8   "Everything went black": Anne Dammarell oral history with Charles Stuart Kennedy, June 10, 2013.

CHAPTER 2

9   "I don't know": Scott MacLeod, "Beirut Bombing," *Pacific Daily News*, April 26, 1983, p. 11.

9   The explosion: Philio Dibble, "The Beirut Bombing: Report from Embassy Says 7 Floors 'Collapsed, One After the Other,'" *State*, June 1983, p. 2.

9   "I thought": Terry A. Anderson, "A Quiet Day . . . and Then Terror," *Kansas City Star*, April 24, 1983, p. 6A.

9   Byers miraculously: Rayford Byers testimony, April 9, 2003, in vol. 3 of the trial transcript of Anne Dammarell, et al., vs. Islamic Republic of Iran, et al.

10   "Mr. Essington": Robert Essington testimony, April 9, 2003, in ibid.

10   "When I came": Faith Lee testimony, in Proposed Findings of Fact and Conclusions of Law, Anne Dammarell, et al., vs. Islamic Republic of Iran, et al., p. 55.

10   *"My god"*: Ibid.

10   "Holy shit": Ronnie Tumolo testimony, in Proposed Findings of Fact and Conclusions of Law, Anne Dammarell, et al., vs. Islamic Republic of Iran, et al., p. 97.

10   "My bedroom door": Ibid., pp. 97–98.

10   "Even though": Charles Light testimony, April 10, 2003, in vol. 4 of the trial transcript of Anne Dammarell, et al., vs. Islamic Republic of Iran, et al.

10   "My hearing": Ibid.

11   "Just as I looked": Ibid.

11   "Mohammed took": Ibid.

11   "Mostashfa": Ibid.

11   "Everything seemed": Robert Dillon oral history with Charles Stuart Kennedy, May 17, 1990.

11   "We all started": Ibid.

11   "We were astounded": Ibid.

12   "Relax": Anne Dammarell oral history with Charles Stuart Kennedy, June 10, 2013.

12   "She looked": Robert Dillon testimony, April 7, 2003, in vol. 1 of the trial transcript of Anne Dammarell, et al., vs. Islamic Republic of Iran, et al.

12   *"She's not"*: Ibid.

12   "May we enter": Dibble, "The Beirut Bombing."

12   "People were walking": Faith Lee testimony, in Proposed Findings of Fact and Conclusions of Law, Anne Dammarell, et al., vs. Islamic Republic of Iran, et al., p. 55.

12   "It was chaos": John Reid oral history with Charles Beecham, Sept. 4, 2002, Foreign Affairs Oral History Collection of the Association for Diplomatic Studies and Training, LOC.

12   "From the top": Herbert H. Denton, "Bomb Wrecks U.S. Embassy," *Washington Post*, April 19, 1983, p. 1.

13   "It's gonna blow": Robert Fisk, *Pity the Nation: The Abduction of Lebanon* (New York: Atheneum, 1990), p. 479.

13   "Rescue workers": Zucchino, "Bomb Kills 39 at U.S. Embassy."

13   "We tripped": Fisk, *Pity the Nation*, p. 479.

13   "It was a catastrophic": James Mead oral history with Benis Frank, May 23, 1983, Box 3, Operations Other than War: Beirut Oral History Transcripts, Marine Corps History Division (MCHD), Archives Branch, Quantico, Va.

13   "One platoon": Ibid.

13 "Damn, damn": Zucchino, "Bomb Kills 39 at U.S. Embassy."

13 "My buddy": Ibid.

13 The terror organization: Ihsan A. Hijazi, "Islamic Attackers Seen as Pro-Iran," *New York Times*, April 19, 1983, p. A12; "Pro-Iranian Force Claims Role in Many Attacks in Lebanon," *Washington Post*, April 20, 1983, p. A25.

13 "This is part": Denton, "Bomb Wrecks U.S. Embassy."

13 Over them all: Terry A. Anderson, "Lunchtime Crowds Pack Streets When Firestorm Hits," *Orlando Sentinel*, April 19, 1983, p. A7.

14 "He was": "Bloody Monday: An Inside Look," *San Francisco Examiner*, April 24, 1983, p. 1.

14 "The more hysterical": Thomas L. Friedman, "Building in Ruins," *New York Times*, April 19, 1983, p. 1.

14 "With the giant": "Middle East: The Horror, the Horror!" *Time*, May 2, 1983, p. 28.

14 "vicious": "Remarks of the President on the Bombing of the U.S. Embassy in Beirut," April 18, 1983, Box 15, Office of Media Relations, RRPL.

14 "cowardly": Ibid.

14 "This criminal attack": Ibid.

14 "The ones": "Bloody Monday: An Inside Look," *San Francisco Examiner*, April 24, 1983, p. 1.

14 "I tried to get": Diane Dillard oral history with Charles Stuart Kennedy, March 7, 1990, Foreign Affairs Oral History Collection of the Association for Diplomatic Studies and Training, LOC.

15 "Now, I think": Ibid.

15 "I realized": Ibid.

15 "The attendant": "Bloody Monday: An Inside Look," *San Francisco Examiner*, April 24, 1983, p. 1.

15 "A body": Susan M. Morgan, "Beirut Diary," *Studies in Intelligence*, Summer 1983, p. 3.

15 "I look briefly": Ibid.

15 "The only thing": Ibid.

16 "I retrieve": Ibid., p. 4.

CHAPTER 3

17 "Lebanon, if it": Loren Jenkins, "There Is No Lebanon Anymore," *Washington Post*, Oct. 10, 1982, p. C1.

17 The seed of strife: Thomas L. Friedman, *From Beirut to Jerusalem* (New York: Farrar, Straus & Giroux, 1989), pp. 11–13.

17 "social time bomb": Jenkins, "There Is No Lebanon Anymore."

17 The intervening decades: Friedman, *From Beirut to Jerusalem*, pp. 16–17, 119–25, 135–36; Fisk, *Pity the Nation*, pp. 73–75.

18 Those tensions climaxed: Friedman, *From Beirut to Jerusalem*, pp. 17–18.

18 The nineteen-month: James M. Markham, "Lebanon, 19 Months After Civil War, Remains Divided," *New York Times*, Aug. 21, 1977, p. 3; James M. Markham, "The War That Won't Go Away," *New York Times*, Oct. 9, 1977, p. SM9.

18 "The sheer scope": Ray Vicker, "In the Wake of Lebanon's Civil War," *Wall Street Journal*, Nov. 10, 1976, p. 24.

18 "Lebanon had become": Caspar W. Weinberger, *Fighting for Peace: Seven Critical Years in the Pentagon* (New York: Warner Books, 1990), p. 136.

19 "They were Christians": Friedman, *From Beirut to Jerusalem*, p. 137.

19 "Gemayel was something": Ibid., p. 138.

19 "The Israelis": Ibid.

19 Syria's role in Lebanon: Ze'ev Schiff and Ehud Ya'ari, *Israel's Lebanon War*, ed. and trans. Ina Friedman (New York: Simon & Schuster, 1984), pp. 32–37.

19 "We won't let them": Ibid., p. 34.

19 "Lebanon was a powder": Weinberger, *Fighting for Peace*, p. 138.

20 Onto this stage: Friedman, *From Beirut to Jerusalem*, pp. 126–28, 142–43.

20 That came: Fisk, *Pity the Nation*, p. 197.

20 "Beirut is outside": Schiff and Ya'ari, *Israel's Lebanon War*, p. 105.

20 Prime Minister Begin: Ibid., p. 106.

20 He instead: Ibid., p. 217.

20 "Bekaa Valley": Edward C. Keefer, *Secretaries of Defense Historical Series*, vol. X, *Caspar Weinberger and the U.S. Military Buildup, 1981–1985* (Washington, DC: U.S. Government Printing Office, 2023), p. 275.

20 "Even in Lebanon": Jack Anderson, "In West Beirut, Rays of Peace in War Clouds," *Washington Post*, Aug. 20, 1982, p. B7.

20 American military observers: Robert Dillon oral history with Charles Stuart Kennedy, May 17, 1990.

20 "The siege": Ibid.

20 "Bekaa Valley": Edward C. Keefer, *Secretaries of Defense Historical Series*, vol. X, *Caspar Weinberger and the U.S. Military Buildup, 1981-1985* (Washington, DC: U.S. Government Printing Office, 2023), p. 275.

20 "Walking the streets": Colin Smith, "Killing Time Runs Out in Beirut," *Guardian*, July 11, 1982, p. 10.

20 "The entire fabric": "West Beirut Shellshocked," *New York Times*, Aug. 6, 1982, p. A1.

21 As July rolled: Hedrick Smith, "In Congress, the Invasion Has Eroded Israel's Almost Automatic Support," *New York Times*, July 21, 1982, p. A8.

21 Republican senator Jesse Helms: "Helms Talks of Breaking with Israel," *Washington Post*, Aug. 8, 1982, p. A18.

21 Reagan's aides: Steven R. Weisman, "Aides Fear Mideast Is Hurting Reagan," *New York Times*, Aug. 16, 1982, p. B6; "President Stops Sending Israel Artillery Shells," *Wall Street Journal*, July 28, 1982, p. 4.

21 "The United States": George Shultz, *Turmoil and Triumph: My Years as Secretary of State* (New York: Charles Scribner's Sons, 1993), p. 43.

21 "The slaughter": Ronald Reagan diary, July 31–Aug. 1, 1982, in Ronald Reagan, *The Reagan Diaries*, ed. Douglas Brinkley (New York: HarperCollins, 2007), p. 95.

21 "Mr. President": Michael K. Deaver with Mickey Herskowitz, *Behind the Scenes: In Which the Author Talks About Ronald and Nancy Reagan . . . and Himself* (New York: William Morrow, 1987), pp. 165–66.

21 "Menachem": H. W. Brands, *Reagan: The Life* (New York: Anchor Books, 2015), p. 386.

21 "It has gone": Deaver, *Behind the Scenes*, p. 166.

21 "Twenty mins.": Ronald Reagan diary, Aug. 12, 1982, in Reagan, *The Reagan Diaries*, p. 98.

21 "I didn't know": Deaver, *Behind the Scenes*, p. 166.

22 "Sticking Americans": John Vessey oral history with Thomas Saylor, Feb. 16, 2013, Concordia University, St. Paul, Minn.

22 "The American debacle": David C. Martin and John Walcott, *Best Laid Plans: The Inside Story of America's War Against Terrorism* (New York: Harper & Row, 1988), p. 93.

22 "Part of my heart": Jay Ross, "Arafat Sails from Lebanon," *Washington Post*, Aug. 31, 1982, p. A1.

22 "The time has come": "Address to the Nation on United States Policy for Peace in the Middle East," Sept. 1, 1982, https://www.reaganlibrary.gov/archives/speech/address-nation-united-states-policy-peace-middle-east.

23 "Begin": Deborah Hart Strober and Gerald S. Strober, *The Reagan Presidency: An Oral History of the Era* (Washington, DC: Brassey's, 2003), p. 217.

23 The outraged: Weinberger, *Fighting for Peace*, p. 147.

23 "A friend does not": "Text of Begin's Letter to Reagan Dealing with Lebanon and the West Bank," *New York Times*, Sept. 6, 1982, p. 4.

23 "I saw in Bashir": Robert Dillon oral history with Charles Stuart Kennedy, May 17, 1990.

23 "All of us": Ibid.

23 "You could crush": Shultz, *Turmoil and Triumph*, p. 79.

23 Gemayel, who had: Edward A. Gargan, "Bashir Gemayel Lived by the Sword," *New York Times*, Sept. 15, 1982, p. A8; Nora Boustany, "Remote-Control Bomb Kills 8 in Beirut," *Washington Post*, Feb. 24, 1980, p. A2.

23 "Let me tell": Schiff and Ya'ari, *Israel's Lebanon War*, p. 247.

24 "The final proof": Ibid., p. 248.

24 "There were almost": Robert Dillon oral history with Charles Stuart Kennedy, May 17, 1990.

24 "I don't want": Schiff and Ya'ari, *Israel's Lebanon War*, p. 255.

24 "Fisky": Fisk, *Pity the Nation*, p. 357.

25 "When we had seen": Ibid., p. 360.

25 "The bullet": Ibid., p. 362.

25 "Jesus Christ": Ibid., p. 360.

25 "Sabra and Shatila": Friedman, *From Beirut to Jerusalem*, p. 164.

25 "I could see": Fisk, *Pity the Nation*, p. 364.

25 "All of us": Ibid., p. 360.

25 "I have a representative": Schiff and Ya'ari, *Israel's Lebanon War*, p. 276.

25 "I was shaken": Shultz, *Turmoil and Triumph*, p. 105.

26 "All people": "Statement on the Murder of Palestinian Refugees in Lebanon," Sept. 18, 1982, https://www.reaganlibrary.gov/archives/speech/statement-murder-palestinian-refugees-lebanon.

26 "We had promised": Martin and Walcott, *Best Laid Plans*, p. 95.

26 "We shouldn't be": Shultz, *Turmoil and Triumph*, p. 108.

26 "I recognize" John Vessey oral history with Thomas Saylor, Feb. 16, 2013.

26 "The participation": "Address to the Nation Announcing the Formation of a New Multinational Force in Lebanon," Sept. 20, 1982, https://www. reaganlibrary.gov/archives/speech/address-nation-announcing-formation-new-multinational-force-lebanon.

26 "We didn't have": John Benson Matthews, "United States Peacekeeping in Lebanon, 1982–1984: Why It Failed" (PhD diss., Washington State University, 1994), p. 53.

CHAPTER 4

27 "The American public": "Beirut 'Much More Dangerous' Now for Marines," *Arizona Republic*, Sept. 22, 1982, p. A12.

27 "American military": Strober and Strober, *The Reagan Presidency*, p. 213.

27 "The multinational force": Ibid., p. 215.

27 "We figured": Martin and Walcott, *Best Laid Plans*, p. 98.

27 "What is presence?": James Mead speech, Sept. 14, 1983, Box 3, Operations Other than War: Beirut Oral History Transcripts, MCHD.

27 "Jim, the reason": Ibid.

28 "A lot of us": Margot Hornblower, "Hill Gives Troop Plan Mixed Review," *Washington Post*, Sept. 21, 1982, p. A10.

28 "We're going right": Ibid.

28 "interposition force": Ronald Reagan to Thomas O'Neill, Jr., Sept. 29, 1982, Box 16, Office of the Counsel to the President, RRPL.

28 "In carrying out": Ibid.

28 "I recognize": National Security Decision Directive Number 64, "Next Steps in Lebanon," Oct. 28, 1982, Box 4, Executive Secretariat, NSC: NSDDs, RRPL.

28 "It was a wonder": Morris Draper statement, in "Marines in Lebanon, A Ten-Year Retrospective: Lessons Learned," May 3, 1993, symposium transcript, Box 1, Operations Other Than War, Beirut Lessons Learned and After-Action Reports, MCHD, p. 18.

29 "corrupt": Robert Dillon oral history with Charles Stuart Kennedy, May 17, 1990.

29 "notorious womanizer": Ibid.

29 "He had all": Friedman, *From Beirut to Jerusalem*, p. 177.

29 "We saw": Robert Dillon oral history with Charles Stuart Kennedy, May 17, 1990.

29 "It is a tribal": Thomas Friedman statement, in "Marines in Lebanon, A Ten-Year Retrospective: Lessons Learned," May 3, 1993, p. 33.

29 "Lebanon was a": Morris Draper statement, in ibid., p. 42.

29 "There are no": Thomas Friedman statement, in ibid., p. 31.

29 "If President": Loren Jenkins, "There Is No Lebanon Anymore," *Washington Post*, Oct. 10, 1982, p. C1.

30 "There is a feeling": David B. Ottaway, "Marines Keep Hopes High, Profile Low in Beirut," *Washington Post*, Oct. 8, 1982, p. A1.

CHAPTER 5

31 "We were fully": Robert Dillon, "Remarks at Commemorative Ceremony on the 25th Anniversary of the Bombing of the U.S. Embassy in Beirut, Lebanon," April 18, 2008, https:/2001-2009.state.gov/p/nea/rls/rm/103864.htm.

31 "Lord forgive me": Ronald Reagan diary, April 19, 1983, in Reagan, *The Reagan Diaries*, p. 146.

31 "Is anyone": Thomas L. Friedman, "Toll at Least 40 in Beirut Bombing as Dead Are Taken from Rubble," *New York Times*, April 20, 1983, p. A1.

31 "Excavation teams": Ibid.

31 Two days after: Herbert H. Denton, "Manassas Marine's Body Is Found in Grisly Search of Beirut Rubble," *Washington Post*, April 21, 1983, p. A22; Andrew Mull, "The Embassy," undated manuscript, Andrew K. Mull Collection, MCHD.

32 Troops loaded: James Mead oral history with Benis Frank, May 23, 1983.

32 "The ceremony": David Zenian, "Bodies of 16 Americans Killed in Lebanon Returned to U.S.," *Daily Sentinel-Tribune*, April 23, 1983, p. 2.

32 The blast: Thomas L. Friedman, "Debris at Embassy Suggests Car Bomb," *New York Times*, April 23, 1983, p. 4.

32 But those minuscule: Bird, *The Good Spy*, p. 335.

32 "At this time": SECSTATE WASH DC to ALL DIPLOMATIC AND CONSULAR POSTS, 050424Z May 83, "AMEMBASSY Beirut Bombing," Box 2, Executive Secretariat, NSC: Cable File, RRPL.

32 Diane Dillard turned: Diane Dillard oral history with Charles Stuart Kennedy, March 7, 1990; John Reid, "The Deadliest Attack Ever," *American Diplomacy*, October 2013, https://americandiplomacy.web.unc.edu/2013/10/the -deadliest-attack-ever/.

33 The embassy's main: Herbert H. Denton, "Staff of Embassy in Beirut Functions in Private Abodes," *Washington Post*, May 5, 1983, p. A17.

33 "His master bedroom": "Search Is On for New Base of Operations," *State*, June 1983, p. 5.

33 "Jordanians share": AMEMBASSY AMMAN to RUEHC/SECSTATE WASH DC, 0181823Z April 83, "Letter of Condolence from King Hussein," Box 51, Executive Secretariat, NSC: Cable File, RRPL.

33 "I and my ministers": Sultan Qaboos of Oman to Ronald Reagan, April 20, 1983, #145470, Box 146, WHORM Subject File: CO 118, RRPL.

33 "We mourn": SECSTATE WASHDC to RUEHTV/AMEMBASSY TEL AVIV, 201946Z April 83, "Condolence Letters from Begin and Shamir," Box 2, Executive Secretariat, NSC: Cable File, RRPL.

33 "the terror capital": David Zucchino, "Openness of U.S. Embassy Was Unusual for Violent Beirut," *Philadelphia Inquirer*, April 24, 1983, p. 1F.

33 "Beirut is a war": "Security Inadequate at U.S. Posts Abroad," editorial, *Today*, April, 20, 1983, p. 10A.

33 "The embassy": "The Beirut Bombing," editorial, *Winston-Salem Journal*, April 20, 1983, p. 4.

33 "Believe me": Zucchino, "Openness of U.S. Embassy Was Unusual for Violent Beirut."

33 "An American embassy": Herbert H. Denton, "U.S. Delegation in Beirut to Escort Dead Home," *Washington Post*, April 23, 1983, p. A13.

34 "In the end": Zucchino, "Openness of U.S. Embassy Was Unusual for Violent Beirut."

34 "I think it's high": "Attack Fails to Deter U.S., Reagan Says," *Philadelphia Inquirer*, April 19, 1983, p. 1.

34 "If the Marines": "Cut and Run?" editorial, *Arizona Republic*, April 21, 1983, p. A6.

34 "as low-class": Robert Dillon oral history with Charles Stuart Kennedy, May 17, 1990.

34 Berri was not: Elaine Sciolino, "Pivotal Figure in the Beirut Crisis," *New York Times*, June 18, 1985, p. A1.

34 The balding: David Ignatius, "The Warlord," *Wall Street Journal*, Sept. 8, 1983, p. 1.

35 "If there were": Friedman, *From Beirut to Jerusalem*, p. 197.

35 He sent an army: David Crist, *The Twilight War: The Secret History of America's Thirty-Year Conflict with Iran* (New York: Penguin Books, 2012), pp. 122–31.

35 "You could": Morris Draper statement, in *Marines in Lebanon, A Ten-Year Retrospective: Lessons Learned*, May 3, 1993, p. 17.

35 "The American Embassy": Herbert H. Denton, "Toll in Beirut Bombing Rises to 46," *Washington Post*, April 20, 1983, p. A1.

35 "It is unfortunate": Herbert H. Denton, "Manassas Marine's Body Is Found in Grisly Search of Beirut Rubble," *Washington Post*, April 21, 1983, p. A22.

35 "Sometimes": Thomas L. Friedman, "Counting the Casualties in Beirut and Beyond," *New York Times*, April 24, 1983, p. E3.

36 More than three: Ken Ringle, "Thousands Honor Beirut Dead at Memorial Services," *Washington Post*, April 27, 1983, p. A20.

36 Three days later: "Remarks of the Director of Central Intelligence at the Memorial Ceremony Held at Headquarters on 29 April 1983," https://www.cia.gov/readingroom/docs/CIA-RDP85B01152R000100020047 -6.pdf.

36 The State Department: Charles Tyson to John Poindexter, "Memorial Service for Foreign Service Personnel," April 26, 1983, #143207, WHORM Subject File: IV 083, RRPL.

36 The president: "Schedule of the President for Saturday, April 23, 1983," Arrival Ceremony for the Casualties of the Lebanon Embassy Bombing, Box 6, Office of Presidential Advance, RRPL.

36 More than 150: "Reagan: 'They Truly Were Peacemakers,'" *San Francisco Examiner*, April 24, 1983, p. 1; "President Honors Americans Killed by Explosion in Beirut," *New York Times*, April 24, 1983, p. 14.

36 "There can be": "Remarks of the President at Ceremony Honoring the Victims of the Beirut Bombing," April 23, 1983, Box 6, Office of Presidential Advance, RRPL.

37 "It was a": Ronald Reagan diary, April 23, 1983, in Reagan, *The Reagan Diaries*, p. 147.

37 "Nancy and I": Jacqueline Trescott, "Laughter Left Aside," *Washington Post*, April 25, 1983, p. D1.

CHAPTER 6

38   "All our eggs": "Separate Observations of Congressman William L. Dickinson," in U.S. Congress, House, *Lebanon: Limited Interest, Limited Involvement, Frequent Accounting, Report of the Delegation to Lebanon—1983*, 98th Cong., 1st Sess., Oct. 18, 1983 (Washington, DC: U.S. Government Printing Office, 1983), p. 9.

38   The process: William Clark to Ronald Reagan, "The Middle East," Feb. 4, 1983, Box 4, William P. Clark Files, RRPL.

38   "fruitless mediation": Harry Cochrane to Richard Beal, March 31, 1983, Box 1, Richard S. Beal Files, RRPL.

38   "A policy": Ibid.

38   Against such odds: Shultz, *Turmoil and Triumph*, p. 198.

38   After three years: Michael Getler, "The Knives Have Come Out for Shultz, Clark on Policy," *Washington Post*, April 24, 1983, p. A1.

39   In many ways: Bernard Gwertzman, "The Shultz Method," *New York Times Magazine*, Jan. 2, 1983, p. SM12.

39   The only colorful: "Personalities," *Washington Post*, Feb. 27, 1987, p. C3.

39   "Reagan Plan's": Karen Elliott House, "Reagan Plan's Failure Began at Home," *Wall Street Journal*, April 20, 1983, p. 30.

39   "The Bungled": Anthony Lewis, "The Bungled Initiative," *New York Times*, April 24, 1983, p. E21.

39   "The Knives": Getler, "The Knives Have Come Out for Shultz, Clark on Policy."

39   "Because the president": House, "Reagan Plan's Failure Began at Home."

39   "I shared": Shultz, *Turmoil and Triumph*, p. 196.

39   "History as much": James MacManus, "Assad's Grand Design for a Greater Syria," *Guardian*, May 2, 1981, p. 17.

40   Assad's previous: Neil MacFarquhar, "Hafez al-Assad, Who Turned Syria into a Power in the Middle East, Dies," *New York Times*, June 11, 2000, p. 51.

40   "He wanted Lebanon": Shultz, *Turmoil and Triumph*, p. 197.

40   The Jewish state: Ibid.; "Prospects for Lebanon in the Next 6–12 Months," March 27, 1983, Box 1, Richard S. Beal Files, RRPL.

40   "One is to restore": National Security Decision Directive Number 92, "Accelerating the Withdrawal of Foreign Forces from Lebanon," April 27, 1983, Box, 5, Executive Secretariat, NSC: NSDDs, RRPL.

41   "The mood": Shultz, *Turmoil and Triumph*, p. 200.

41   "It's simply incredible": Karen Elliott House, "Shultz, After a Sobering Tour of Beirut, Tackles Issues Splitting Israel, Lebanon," *Wall Street Journal*, April 29, 1983, p. 4.

41   Gemayel had few: David Mack oral history with Charles Stuart Kennedy, Oct. 24, 1995, Foreign Affairs Oral History Collection of the Association for Diplomatic Studies and Training, LOC.

41   "We're not talking": Shultz, *Turmoil and Triumph*, p. 213.

41   "The Lebanese": Ibid.

41   "I feel like": Ibid.

41   "There are a lot": Ibid.

41 "The negotiations": David Mack oral history with Charles Stuart Kennedy, Oct. 24, 1995.

41 The proposed plan: Shultz, *Turmoil and Triumph*, p. 220.

42 On May 6: Ibid., p. 215.

42 "ultimate betrayal": Bureau of Intelligence and Research, Analysis, Feb. 8, 1984, Box 4, Donald R. Fortier Files, RRPL.

42 "The real Syrian": James MacManus, "Syria Tries to Kill Shultz Deal," *Guardian*, May 11, 1983, p. 1.

42 "Lebanon will become": Larry Pintak, *Beirut Outtakes: A TV Correspondent's Portrait of America's Encounter with Terror* (Lexington, MA: Lexington Books, 1988), p. 106.

42 Shultz detected: Shultz, *Turmoil and Triumph*, p. 217.

42 Only a year earlier: David Ignatius, "Bulldozers Ply Ruins of a City That Held Foes of Syria's Chief," *Wall Street Journal*, May 6, 1982, p. 1; Thomas L. Friedman, "A Syrian City Amid Rubble of Rebellion," *New York Times*, May 29, 1982, p. 1; Nicholas D. Kristof, "Pulling Back the Curtain on Syria," *New York Times*, Sept. 8, 2013, p. SR1.

42 "Assad": Evan Galbraith to Robert McFarlane, Oct. 24, 1983, Box 15, Robert McFarlane Files, RRPL.

42 The violence showed: MacFarquhar, "Hafez al-Assad, Who Turned Syria into a Power in the Middle East, Dies."

42 "His manner": Shultz, *Turmoil and Triumph*, p. 217.

43 "This agreement": Weinberger, *Fighting for Peace*, p. 156.

CHAPTER 7

44 "One of the things": George Converse to Mary Ann Converse, June 10, 1983, Box 2, George Converse Collection, MCHD.

44 A native of Saint Louis: Timothy J. Geraghty, *Peacekeepers at War: Beirut 1983—The Marine Commander Tells His Story* (Washington, DC: Potomac Books, 2009), pp. 13–17.

44 "We are": Timothy Geraghty interview, March 6, 2023.

44 "He had a way": Glenn E. Dolphin, *24 Mau: 1983: A Marine Looks Back at the Peacekeeping Mission to Beirut, Lebanon* (Baltimore: Publish America, 2005), pp. 18, 20.

45 Such units: Geraghty, *Peacekeepers at War*, pp. ix, 17–19.

45 "But everyone": Michael Petit, *Peacekeepers at War: A Marine's Account of the Beirut Catastrophe* (Boston: Faber & Faber, 1986), p. 23.

46 "They will get hit": James Mead oral history with Benis Frank, May 23, 1983, Box 3, Operations Other than War: Beirut Oral History Transcripts, MCHD.

46 "Terrorism": Timothy Geraghty oral history with Benis Frank, May 28, 1983, Box 2, Operations Other than War: Beirut Oral History Transcripts, MCHD.

46 "While we are here": Maurice Hukill to family, May 23, 1983, in Mary Ellen Jackowski and Peggy A. Stelpflug, eds., *Voices from Beirut: The Peacekeepers Speak* (Albany, NY: Fuller's, 2013), p. 57.

46 "I gave up smoking": Bill Stelpflug to Kathy Stelpflug, May 21, 1983 (postmark date), Bill Stelpflug Collection, MCHD.

46 "I had never": John Hudson to Lisa Hudson, May 15, 1983.

46 "I never knew": Bill Stelpflug to Kathy Stelpflug, May 21, 1983 (postmark date).

46 "The water is so blue": Bill Stelpflug to Peggy and William Stelpflug, May 21, 1983, Bill Stelpflug Collection, MCHD.

46 "Let me tell you": Henry Linkkila to Patricia Roy, June 5, 1983 (postmark date).

47 "We are all nervous": Bruce Hollingshead to family, May 23, 1983, in Jackowski and Stelpflug, *Voices from Beirut*, p. 55.

47 "Can you believe": John Hudson to Lisa Hudson, May 28, 1983.

47 "I felt": Henry Linkkila to Patricia Roy, June 5, 1983 (postmark date).

47 Explosives teams: Benis M. Frank, *U.S. Marines in Lebanon, 1982–1984* (Washington, DC: History and Museums Division, Headquarters, U.S. Marine Corps, U.S. Government Printing Office, 1987), p. 24.

47 "We were": Carl Stiner statement, in *Marines in Lebanon, A Ten-Year Retrospective: Lessons Learned*, May 3, 1993, p. 45.

47 A couple old: George Converse to Mary Ann Converse, June 1, 1983, Box 2, George Converse Collection, MCHD.

47 "Blessed are the": George Converse to Mary Ann Converse, June 3, 1983, Box 2, George Converse Collection, MCHD.

48 "I half expected": Dolphin, *24 Mau*, p. 70.

48 "Welcome to the": Ibid., p. 69.

48 "It is infested": William Pollard to Stacy and Maggie Pollard, June 1, 1983, in Jackowski and Stelpflug, eds., *Voices from Beirut*, p. 93.

48 "You ought to see": Henry Linkkila to Patricia Roy, June 5, 1983 (postmark date).

48 "Everything here": Mecot Camara to Theresa Camara Riggs, June 5, 1983, in Jackowski and Stelpflug, eds., *Voices from Beirut*, p. 18.

48 "Most of the Marines": John Hudson to Lisa Hudson, May 31, 1983.

49 "All in all": George Converse to Mary Ann Converse, June 1, 1983, Box 2, George Converse Collection, MCHD.

49 The cooks: Henry Linkkila interview, May 30, 2023.

49 A gifted: Interviews with Lisa Hudson (Feb. 9–10, 2023) and James Ware (Jan. 6, 2023).

49 "The whole ship": John Hudson to Lisa Hudson, May 22, 1983.

50 "We really don't have": John Hudson audio recording, October (no day listed), 1983.

50 Bigelow had worked: Gilbert Bigelow interview, Jan. 25, 2023.

50 Ware had attended: James Ware interview, Jan. 6, 2023.

50 A Massachusetts: Steve Marantz, "Priest Haunted by Beirut Deaths," *Boston Globe*, Dec. 30, 1983, p. 13.

50 Wheeler had spent": Danny Wheeler interview, Jan. 19, 2023.

51 "Whenever you have": "From the Chaplains," *Root Scoop*, June 10, 1983, p. 4.

51 "It's the pits": William Pollard to Stacy and Maggie Pollard, June 1, 1983.

51 "Poor people": David Madaras to Ann and Charles Madaras, June 7, 1983 (postmark date).

51 "Some parts": George Converse to Mary Ann Converse, June 1, 1983, Box 2, George Converse Collection, MCHD.

51 On the morning: "Earthquake Rattles Lebanon," *Tampa Tribune*, June 4, 1983, p. 23.

51 "It was pretty": Bill Stelpflug to Peggy and William Stelpflug, June (no day listed) 1983, Bill Stelpflug Collection, MCHD.

51 "Hell, some people": Bill Stelpflug to Kathy Stelpflug, June 29, 1983 (postmark date), Bill Stelpflug Collection, MCHD.

51 "We may or may not": "Services Scheduled for State Marine," *Daily Oklahoman*, Nov. 9, 1983, p. 16.

51 "I'm excited": "Scoop on Root Vets," *Root Scoop*, June 17, 1983, p. 4.

51 "To me": Ibid.

51 "When on post": Recommended ROE Card for Issue to Individual Marine, For Official Use Only, Guidelines for ROW, undated.

52 The leathernecks jumped: 24th MAU, Command Chronology, 11 May–30 June 1983, MCHD.

52 "We try to let": Tim Bennett, "Mobile Patrols: A Highly Visible Job of Showing the Flag and Gathering Information," *Root Scoop*, Aug. 5, 1983, p. 1.

52 "That patch": Ibid.

52 The daily patrols: CTF SIX ONE to COMSIXTHFLT, 200300Z June 83, "CTF 61/62 Joint Daily Intelligence Summary (DISUM) 020 for the Period 181800-191759Z Jun 83," in 24th MAU, Command Chronology, 11 May – 30 June 1983, MCHD.

52 These actions: TWO FOUR MAU to CG FMFLANT, 191540Z June 83, "TWO FOUR MAU SITREP No. 13," Beirut, Lebanon CD Collection, 24th MAU SITREPS, Mar-Nov 1983, MCHD.

52 "The anti-American": CTF SIX ONE to RUFRQJQ/COMSIXTHFLT, 172359Z June 83, "CTF 61/62 Joint Daily Intelligence Summary (DISUM) 018 for the Period 161800-171759Z Jun 83," in 24th MAU, Command Chronology, 11 May–30 June 1983, MCHD.

52 "Barriers are being": CTF SIX TWO to COMSIXTHFLT, 010735Z May 83, "Rules of Engagement," in 24th MAU, Command Chronology, 11 May–30 June 1983, MCHD.

52 "It had a sobering": "Embassy Platoon," *Root Scoop*, June 10, 1983, p. 2.

52 Beyond patrols: 24th MAU, Command Chronology, 11 May–30 June 1983, MCHD.

53 Dr. Hudson delivered: John Hudson to Lisa Hudson, June 11, 1983.

53 A group of 102: 24th MAU, Command Chronology, 11 May–30 June 1983, MCHD.

53 The colonel wrestled: Matthews, "United States Peacekeeping in Lebanon," pp. 207–8.

53 The worst: CTF SIX TWO to CTF SIX ONE, illegible (circa June 16, 1983), "Shooting Incident of 15 JUN 83," in Beirut, Lebanon CD Collection, Messages and General Correspondence for June 1983, MCHD.

53 "The Lebanese": John Hudson to Lisa Hudson, June 16, 1983.

53 "What surprised me": Geraghty, *Peacekeepers at War*, p. 40.

53 "The clang": Petit, *Peacekeepers at War*, p. 83.

53 "If you had": Dolphin, *24 Mau*, pp. 70–71.

54 "Within a short": Ibid., p. 68.

54 "Yes, we're a long": "From the Chaplain," *Root Scoop*, July 15, 1983, p. 4.

54 For a taste: The weekly schedule for AFRTS Beirut Channel 8 can be found in the *Root Scoop*.

54 "It stopped traffic": Don Howell interview, Jan. 25, 2023.

CHAPTER 8

55 "There are no": Roger Simon, "One Things About Beirut Remains the Same—Terror," *Herald*, April 28, 1983, p. 4.

55 Against this backdrop: David B. Ottaway, "Beirut Picks Itself Up, Dusts Itself Off and Starts to Rebuild," *Washington Post*, Oct. 11, 1982, p. A1.

55 "This country": Thomas L. Friedman, "Lebanese Patch Up the Scars of War," *New York Times*, Feb. 13, 1983, p. 18.

55 "Life in this city": Thomas L. Friedman, "Living with the Violence in Beirut," *New York Times*, July 17, 1983, p. SM12.

56 "The pharmacist's wife": Friedman, *From Beirut to Jerusalem*, p. 26.

56 "It is a reflection": Judith Miller, "A Reporter's Notebook: Beirut's Artillery Parrot," *New York Times*, Nov. 7, 1983, p. A10.

56 "The newcomer": Ibid.

56 "People ate valium": Pintak, *Beirut Outtakes*, p. 37.

56 "Kids five or six": Ibid., p. 42.

56 "Any time, anyplace": Friedman, "Living with the Violence in Beirut."

56 "Beirutis talk": Friedman, *From Beirut to Jerusalem*, p. 39.

56 "Beirut Hotel": "Beirut Hotel Torn by Blast," *Los Angeles Times*, July 21, 1983, p. 2.

56 "Man Driving": "Man Driving Bomb-Laden Car Kills 2 at Beirut Resort Complex," *Washington Post*, July 21, 1983, p. A19.

57 "Sense of Doom": Jack Redden, "Sense of Doom Pervades Beirut," *Philadelphia Daily News*, July 25, 1983, p. 16.

57 "Snipers and shelling": Friedman, "Living with the Violence in Beirut."

57 "She was just": Samuel Koo, "Car Bomb Kills Woman in Mid-Interview After Attack," *Washington Post*, Aug. 7, 1982, p. A2.

57 "All car bomb": Friedman, "Living with the Violence in Beirut."

57 "After a while": Ibid.

57 "On any given": William Claiborne, "Beirut's Bomb Expert Finds 'Plenty of Work,'" *Washington Post*, Dec. 8, 1983, p. A1.

57 "A bomb was thrown": "Situation Report for 3 June 1983," in Beirut, Lebanon CD Collection, Messages and General Correspondence for June 1983, MCHD.

57 "The Libyan": "Situation Report for 5 June 1983," in ibid.

57 "A Datsun": "Situation Report for 13 June 1983," in ibid.

58 "It blew up": Bill Stelpflug to Peggy and William Stelpflug, June (no day listed) 1983, Bill Stelpflug Collection, MCHD.

58   "Boy I jumped": David Madaras to Ann and Charles Madaras, June 15, 1983.
58   "The White House": Harold Jackson, "Shultz Ponders His Next Mideast
      Move," *Guardian*, June 4, 1983, p. 8.

CHAPTER 9
59   "There is little": Robert Long et al., "Report of the DOD Commission on
      Beirut International Airport Terrorist Act, October 23, 1983" (hereafter
      Report of the Long Commission), Dec. 20, 1983, p. 127.
59   The four-story: Nan Robertson, "House to Open $122 Million Office
      Building," *New York Times*, Jan. 2, 1965, p. 1; Comptroller General of the
      United States Report to the Congress of the United States, "Examination of
      Construction and Related Costs, Rayburn House Office Building, April 1967.
59   "It is quite": Ada Louise Huxtable, "Complaints Grow on New House Office
      Building," *New York Times*, March 30, 1965, p. 32.
60   The Capitol Hill: "U.S. Tells of Embassy Attack," *New York Times*,
      June 29, 1983, p. A9.
60   That was more: "What's News," *Wall Street Journal*, June 29, 1983, p. 1.
60   "The United States": All subsequent quotations in this chapter come from
      U.S. Congress, House, *The U.S. Embassy Bombing in Beirut, Hearing Before the
      Committee on Foreign Relations and Its Subcommittee on International Operations
      and on Europe and the Middle East*, 98th Cong., 1st Sess., June 28, 1983
      (Washington, DC: U.S. Government Printing Office, 1983), pp. 1–25.

CHAPTER 10
63   "You can't keep": Larry Gerlach statement, May 3, 1993, in Matthews, "United
      States Peacekeeping in Lebanon," p. 253.
63   To improve security: TWO FOUR MAU to CG FMFLANT, 022014Z July
      83, "TWO FOUR MAU SITREP No. 15," in Beirut, Lebanon CD Collection,
      24th MAU SITREPS, Mar–Nov 1983, MCHD.
63   "I hate Marines": CTF SIX TWO to COMSIXTHFLT, 022033Z July 83, in
      Beirut, Lebanon CD Collection, Messages and General Correspondence for
      July 1983, MCHD.
63   "Americans no good": CTF SIX TWO to CTF SIX ONE, 041505Z July
      83, "OPREP 1/5 Feeder 37/4 July 1983," in Beirut, Lebanon CD Collection,
      Messages and General Correspondence for July 1983, MCHD.
63   "Incidents of children": TWO FOUR MAU to CG FMFLANT, 100955Z
      July 83, "TWO FOUR MAU SITREP No. 16," in Beirut, Lebanon CD
      Collection, 24th MAU SITREPS, Mar-Nov 1983, MCHD.
63   Doctors Bigelow: Ibid.; Geraghty, *Peacekeepers at War*, p. 46.
63   In early July: "Marines Serving Lebanese Children," *Root Scoop*,
      June 10, 1983, p. 3.
64   "I loved": Bill Wright, "Playground a Reality for Beirut Children," *Root Scoop*,
      July 8, 1983, p. 3.
64   "I just wish": Ibid.
64   "I felt sorry": Petit, *Peacekeepers at War*, p. 63.

64   "Look at the faces": Miles A. Burdine, "Life on the Front Lines Isn't Easy,"
      Root Scoop, Aug. 19, 1983, p. 3.

64   "Many people": William Gaines Jr. to Kaye and Bill Gaines, Sept. 21, 1983,
      Box 75, Anne Higgins Files, RRPL.

64   Geraghty continued: 24th MAU, Command Chronology, 1 July–31
      July 1983, MCHD.

64   "The men dismounted": Ibid.

64   Troops continued: Ibid.

64   "If things got": Petit, *Peacekeepers at War*, p. 85.

65   "Like the blind": John Dalziel to Rosie and Rod Dalziel, Sept. 6, 1983.

65   "Rifle bolts": TWO FOUR MAU to CG FMFLANT, 161607Z July 83,
      "TWO FOUR MAU SITREP No. 17," in Beirut, Lebanon CD Collection,
      24th MAU SITREPS, Mar–Nov 1983, MCHD.

65   "He feels": Ibid.

65   Beyond meetings: 24th MAU, Command Chronology, 1 July–31 July 1983,
      MCHD.

65   "Too many VIPs!": George Converse to Mary Ann Converse, July 4, 1983, Box
      2, George Converse Collection, MCHD.

65   "The congressmen": Petit, *Peacekeepers at War*, p. 96.

65   "I wonder": Dolphin, *24 Mau*, p. 97.

65   "It is hot": Bill Stelpflug to Kathy Stelpflug, June 29,1983 (postmark date), Bill
      Stelpflug Collection, MCHD.

66   "You can lose": "A Hot Spot, a Hot Box for U.S. Marines," *U.S. News & World
      Report*, Sept. 12, 1983, p. 28.

66   Despite the heat: "Charlie Co. Captures First in Boxing," *Root Scoop*,
      July 15, 1983, p. 4.

66   "Contestants": Tom Nowaczyk, "Marines Capture 5K, 10K Road Races,"
      Root Scoop, July 1, 1983, p. 2.

66   "I felt real": Tim Bennett, "10K Winner Exceeds His Expectations," *Root Scoop*,
      July 1, 1983, p. 2.

66   "In the end": Tim Bennett, "Marines Celebrate July 4 with Festivities," *Root
      Scoop*, July 8, 1983, p. 1.

66   "We have a great": Ibid.

66   "Barbecues replaced": "The Fourth: Everyone's Celebration," *Tribune*,
      July 4, 1983, p. 1.

67   "On June 29th": Michael Ohler to Gail Ohler, July 1, 1983, Michael Ohler
      Collection, National Naval Aviation Museum (NNAM), Pensacola, Fla.

67   "I was dumbfounded": Ibid.

67   "God has blessed": Ibid.

67   "How do you want": John Hudson to Lisa Hudson, July 6, 1983.

67   "I couldn't believe": Ibid.

67   "The majestic scenery": Geraghty, *Peacekeepers at War*, p. 48.

68   "I felt": Ibid.

68   "On the return": Ibid.

68   "It is unbelievable": John Hudson to Lisa Hudson, June 17, 1983.

68 Those brave enough: Interviews with Neal Morris (July 11, 2023); Mark Singleton (Dec. 21, 2022); Tim McCoskey (March 2, 2023); and Emanuel Simmons (Dec. 31, 2022).

68 "It smelled": Emanuel Simmons interview, Dec. 31, 2022.

68 "It was like": Mark Singleton interview, Dec. 21, 2022.

68 "The other night": Bill Stelpflug to Kathy Stelpflug, June 9, 1983 (postmark date), Bill Stelpflug Collection, MCHD.

68 Jim Ware actually: Interviews with James Ware (Jan. 6, 2023) and Blaine Cosgrove (June 1, 2023).

69 "We watch nightly": Grant McIntosh Jr. to Grant McIntosh Sr., Aug. 7, 1983, Box, 1, Grant McIntosh Collection, MCHD.

69 "My parish": "Wheeler Recalls Danger-Filled Wait for Rescue," *Dunn County News*, Dec. 21, 1983, p. 3.

69 "How are you doing?": Ibid.

69 "This place": John Hudson to Lisa Hudson, June 28, 1983.

69 More than anything: John Hudson to Lisa Hudson, June 14, 1983.

69 "I cannot believe": John Hudson to Lisa Hudson, June 16, 1983.

69 Hearing their voices: John Hudson to Lisa Hudson, May 24, 1983.

69 "I pray": John Hudson to Lisa Hudson, May 19, 1983

69 "I'm sorry": John Hudson to Lisa Hudson, May 28, 1983.

69 "I love you": John Hudson to Lisa Hudson, June 28, 1983.

70 "Some people at night": John Allman to Anne Allman, June 29, 1983, in Jackowski and Stelpflug, *Voices from Beirut*, p. 9.

70 "The Sea is pretty": Davin Green to Sheria Scott, undated, in ibid., p. 49.

70 "I may be": Henry Linkkila to Patricia Roy, June 5, 1983 (postmark date).

70 "As you can probably": Henry Linkkila to Patricia Roy, July 17, 1983.

70 "I hate this place": Henry Linkkila to Patricia Roy, June 25, 1983 (postmark date).

70 "This place": Henry Linkkila to Patricia Roy, July 14, 1983.

70 "I wanna": Henry Linkkila to Patricia Roy, Aug. 15, 1983 (postmark date).

70 To help: "From the Chaplain," *Root Scoop*, July 1, 1983, p. 4.

70 "Thank God": Bill Stelpflug to Peggy and William Stelpflug, August (no day listed) 1983, Bill Stelpflug Collection, MCHD.

70 "Keep looking": "From the Chaplain," *Root Scoop*, July 22, 1983, p. 4.

71 "When the second": John Hudson to Lisa Hudson, July 22, 1983.

71 "It sported": Petit, *Peacekeepers at War*, p. 83.

71 "The ground shook": Dolphin, *24 Mau*, p. 101.

71 "We're being shelled": Petit, *Peacekeepers at War*, p. 99.

71 "I pulled the shrapnel": John Hudson to Lisa Hudson, July 22, 1983.

71 "He wanted me": Ibid.

71 Eleven 122mm: 24th MAU, Command Chronology, 1 July–31 July 1983, MCHD.

72 "Both of these": John Hudson to Lisa Hudson, July 22, 1983.

72 "I definitely": Ibid.

72 "Despite the close": Dolphin, *24 Mau*, p. 102.

72   "Caught between": TWO FOUR MAU to CG FMFLANT, 241234Z July 83,
     "TWO FOUR MAU SITREP No. 18," in Beirut, Lebanon CD Collection,
     24th MAU SITREPS, Mar-Nov 1983, MCHD.

CHAPTER 11

73   "The Lebanese": "Withdrawing from Lebanon," editorial, *Washington Post*,
     July 31, 1983, p. D6.

73   "Like a fisherman": James MacManus, "Assad's Demolition Job Leaves Peace
     in His Palm," *Guardian*, July 8, 1983, p. 13.

73   "I wish I could": Don Oberdorfer, "Shultz Ends Trip to Mideast with No
     Pullout Accord," *Washington Post*, July 8, 1983, p. A1.

73   "I'm not sure": Bernard Gwertzman, "Square One: Miscalculation on Mideast
     Add Up to Near Zero for U.S.," *New York Times*, July 10, 1983, p. E1.

73   "Shultz ends": James MacManus and David Landau, "Shultz Ends Tour with a
     Message of Failure," *Guardian*, July 8, 1983, p. 6.

73   "Miscalculations": Gwertzman, "Square One."

73   "Back to": Colin Smith, "Back to Square One in the Lebanon Quagmire,"
     Observer, July 10, 1983, p. 11.

73   "It really is": Ronald Reagan diary, July 20, 1983, in Reagan, *The Reagan
     Diaries*, p. 168.

73   Not only: Herbert H. Denton, "Beirut Bomb Misses Prime Minister,"
     Washington Post, July 8, 1983, p. A14.

74   "The American": Thomas L. Friedman, "Is Lebanon Sliding Toward
     Partition?" *New York Times*, July 31, 1983, p. E2; Thomas L. Friedman,
     "Beirut's Latest Trauma Is Economic Crisis," *New York Times*, July 24,
     1983, p. E3.

74   "sometime playboy": Friedman, *From Beirut to Jerusalem*, p. 177.

74   The weekly return: Richard Bernstein, "Begin's Melancholy Mood Is Causing
     Concern in Israel," *New York Times*, July 23, 1983, p. 3.

74   "Was this disaster": David Ignatius, "Brooding Begin Is Shrouded in Gloom,"
     Wall Street Journal, Aug. 8, 1983, p. 20.

74   Along a seventy: David Zucchino, "Israel Defends New Pullback as
     Temporary," *Philadelphia Inquirer*, Aug. 21, 1983, p. 1G; James M. Markham,
     "Israelis Build New Defenses as Lebanon Pullback Nears," *New York Times*,
     Aug. 21, 1983, p. 14.

74   "one of the world's": Thomas L. Friedman, "Vicious Little Feud in Lebanon
     Makes Israelis Want to Wash Their Hands," *New York Times*, July 14,
     1983, p. A10.

75   "Syria and its Lebanese": David Hirst, "Airport Hit as Beirut Is Bombarded,"
     Guardian, July 23, 1983, p. 4.

75   "Our support": George Shultz to Ronald Reagan, "Your Meeting with
     Lebanon's President, Amin Gemayel, Friday, July 22, 1983," July 19, 1983, Box
     4, Robert McFarlane Files, RRPL.

75   "possessed none": Robert C. McFarlane with Zofia Smardz, *Special Trust*
     (New York: Cadell & Davies, 1994), p. 210.

75 "For better or worse": William Clark to Ronald Reagan, "Meeting with Amin Gemayel, President of Lebanon," undated, Box 4, Robert McFarlane Files, RRPL.

75 With that: Daily Diary of President Ronald Reagan, July 22, 1983.

75 "I'm impressed": "Remarks of the President and of President Amin Gemayel of Lebanon Upon Departure," July 22, 1983, Box 15, Office of Media Relations, RRPL.

CHAPTER 12

76 "The world": Ronald Reagan diary, August 10, 1983, in Reagan, *The Reagan Diaries*, p. 174.

76 McFarlane came: McFarlane, *Special Trust*, pp. 112–45.

76 "What was clear": Ibid., p. 141.

76 "Working for such": Ibid., p. 154.

77 "Ultimately, what he": Ibid., p. 155.

77 "Following in Kissinger's": Martin and Walcott, *Best Laid Plans*, p. 112.

77 Even McFarlane's hobbies: Jane Leavy, "McFarlane and the Taunting Glare of Truth," *Washington Post*, May 7, 1987, p. C1.

77 "He spoke": Martin and Walcott, *Best Laid Plans*, p. 112.

77 "Never kick": McFarlane, *Special Trust*, p. 212.

78 "My arguments": Ibid., pp. 212–13.

78 "Reagan": Ibid., p. 211.

78 "criminally irresponsible": Ibid.

78 "When it came": Ibid., p. 241.

79 "Tell me": Ibid., p. 238.

79 "My mind raced": Ibid.

79 "But they are not": Ibid.

79 "Six and a half": Ibid., p. 239.

80 "We can take": Ibid., p. 245.

80 "Amin is a fop": Ibid., p. 246.

80 "Each head": Ibid.

81 "Assad respects": Ibid., p. 247.

81 "Assad was determined": Ibid., p. 248.

CHAPTER 13

82 "The status quo": George W. Pucciarelli, "After the Beirut Bombing," *Proceedings*, January 1987, p. 64.

82 A group of Marines: CTF SIX TWO to CTF SIX ONE, 311437Z July 83, in 24th MAU, Command Chronology, 1 July–31 July 1983, MCHD.

82 "Attack was definitely": Ibid.

82 "The number": CTF SIX TWO to CFT SIX ONE, 012200Z Aug. 83, in Beirut, Lebanon CD Collection, Messages and General Correspondence for August 1983, MCHD.

82 "The danger": TWO FOUR MAU to CG FMFLANT, 071148Z Aug. 83, "TWO FOUR MAU SITREP No. 20," in Beirut, Lebanon CD Collection, 24th MAU SITREPS, Mar–Nov 1983, MCHD.

82   At the start: Geraghty, *Peacekeepers at War*, pp. 48–49.

83   "Our tactical": William Tuohy, "U.S. Warship Experiences First Combat," *Los Angeles Times*, Sept. 22, 1983, p. 12.

83   "Tactically": Timothy Geraghty testimony, Nov. 12, 1983, in U.S. Congress, House, *Review of Adequacy of Security Arrangements for Marines in Lebanon and Plans for Improving That Security, Hearings before the Committee on Armed Service and the Investigations Subcommittee of the Committee on Armed Services*, 98th Cong., 1st sess., Nov. 1, 2, 12, 13 and Dec. 8, 9, 14, 15, 1983 (Washington, DC: U.S. Government Printing Office, 1985), pp. 262–63.

83   The Italians observed: CTF SIX TWO to CTF SIX ONE, 082100Z Aug. 83, "CTF 62 Daily Intel Summary for 8 Aug. 83," in Beirut, Lebanon CD Collection, Messages and General Correspondence for August 1983, MCHD.

83   "There is every": Ibid.

83   "A new crowd": Timothy Geraghty testimony, Nov. 12, 1983, in *Review of Adequacy of Security Arrangements*, p. 260.

83   "When I first arrived": Dan Williams, "Marines' Role Draped in Verbal Camouflage," *Miami Herald*, Sept. 11, 1983, p. 1.

83   "It's a weird": Henry Linkkila to Patricia Roy, Aug. 17, 1983.

84   "This place": John Hudson to Lisa Hudson, Aug. 8, 1983.

84   "These rounds indicate": Geraghty, *Peacekeepers at War*, p. 49.

84   At 5:23 a.m.: Point Paper, "Attack on Marine Positions; 10 Aug. 1983," Aug. 10, 1983, in Beirut, Lebanon CD Collection, Messages and General Correspondence for August 1983, MCHD.

84   "I heard it": Michael Toma text message, June 18, 2023.

84   "Shit hit": Michael Toma diary, Aug. 10, 1983.

84   "It did a better": John Dalziel to Rosie and Rod Dalziel, Aug. 11, 1983.

84   "I heard it": Neal Morris interview, July 11, 2023.

84   "Hey, Marine": Ibid.

84   "Holy shit": Ibid.

85   "He is so lucky": John Hudson to Lisa Hudson, Aug. 10, 1983.

85   "The incident": Geraghty, *Peacekeepers at War*, p. 49.

85   "Incoming rockets": CTF SIX TWO to RUEKJCS/NMCC WASHINGTON DC, 100549Z Aug. 83, in Beirut, Lebanon CD Collection, Messages and General Correspondence for August 1983, MCHD.

85   "The rockets": Dolphin, *24 Mau*, p. 109.

85   The Army's new: Geraghty, *Peacekeepers at War*, pp. 49–50.

85   "This let the Druze": Dolphin, *24 Mau*, p. 110.

85   "I feel": TWO FOUR MAU to CG FMFLANT, 141218Z Aug. 83, "TWO FOUR MAU SITREP No. 21," in Beirut, Lebanon CD Collection, 24th MAU SITREPS, Mar–Nov 1983, MCHD.

85   The closure: David Zucchino, "Druze Attacks Erode Confidence in Lebanon's Shaky Government," *Philadelphia Inquirer*, Aug. 14, 1983, p. C1.

86   To add insult: Thomas L. Friedman, "Lebanese Druse Assault Army, Seize Ministers," *New York Times*, Aug. 11, 1983, p. A1; Herbert H. Denton,

"Druze Militiamen Kidnap 3 Beirut Cabinet Ministers," *Washington Post*, Aug. 11, 1983, p. A1.

86 "We've got": Herbert H. Denton, "Druze Gunners Keep Airport Shut," *Washington Post*, Aug. 14, 1983, p. A24.

86 "The withdrawal": CTF SIX TWO to CTF SIX ONE, 042130Z Aug. 83, "CTF 62 Daily Intel Summary for 3–4 Aug. 83," in Beirut, Lebanon CD Collection, Messages and General Correspondence for August 1983, MCHD.

86 "When the Israelis": John Hudson to Lisa Hudson, Aug. 12, 1983.

86 "We may not": Anne Keegan, "In Beirut, Marines Duck, Hold Their Fire," *Pittsburgh Press*, Aug. 14, 1983, p. A24.

86 "The Can't": Anne Keegan, "One Beer a Day," *Detroit Free Press*, Aug. 18, 1983, p. 1.

86 "It's the story": Ibid.

86 "What I don't": John Hudson to Lisa Hudson, Aug. 12, 1983.

86 Bigelow and Ware: Interviews with James Ware (Jan. 6, 2023) and Gilbert Bigelow (Jan. 25, 2023).

87 "He wasn't": James Ware oral history with Jan Herman, André Sobocinski, and Karen Stokes, June 21, 2011, Bureau of Medicine and Surgery (BUMED), Falls Church, Va.

87 "It's guard duty": Keegan, "In Beirut, Marines Duck, Hold Their Fire."

87 "The best part": Henry Linkkila to Patricia Roy, Aug. 17, 1983.

87 "The sight": Dolphin, *24 Mau*, p. 116.

87 "Marines have been": Samira Kawar, "Marines in Lebanon 'Won't Be Intimidated,'" *Fresno Bee*, Aug. 17, 1983, p. C6.

87 "A logical question": David Zucchino, "Israel: Lebanon Must Police Its Peace," *Philadelphia Inquirer*, Aug. 17, 1983, p. 12A.

87 August saw: Tim Bennett, "Library Opens at BLT Headquarters," *Root Scoop*, Aug. 12, 1983, p. 7.

87 "There you will": George Pucciarelli, "From the Chaplain," *Root Scoop*, Aug. 12, 1983, p. 6.

88 "The only requirement": "Alcoholics Anonymous Group Forming Here, *Root Scoop*, Aug. 5, 1983, p. 4.

88 The lull: "Alpha Company Captures Ironman Competition," *Root Scoop*, Aug. 26, 1983, p. 6.

88 On August 18: TWO FOUR MAU to CG FMFLANT, 211400Z Aug. 83, "TWO FOUR MAU SITREP No. 22," in Beirut, Lebanon CD Collection, 24th MAU SITREPS, Mar–Nov 1983, MCHD.

88 "I haven't had": Lisa Hudson interview, Feb. 10, 2023.

88 "It's so great": Lisa Hudson to Louise and James Helton, Aug. 23, 1983.

88 "His personality": Lisa Hudson interview, Feb. 10, 2023.

88 "Don't go": Ibid.

88 "We hugged": Ibid.

88 "I'll be back": Ibid.

88 "I have to hug": Ibid.

88 "We held": Ibid.

CHAPTER 14

89   "The mission": Geraghty, May 3, 1983, in Matthews, "United States Peacekeeping in Lebanon," p. 155.

89   "The fighting": Geraghty, *Peacekeepers at War*, p. 54.

89   "The outpost": C. W. Rowe, "Marines Killed in Battle with Lebanese Militia," *Hawaii Marine*, Sept. 7, 1983, p. 1.

89   "Fighting continued": CTF SIX TWO to CTF SIX ONE, 281829Z Aug. 83, in Beirut, Lebanon CD Collection, Messages and General Correspondence for August 1983, MCHD.

90   "Fighting continues": CTF SIX TWO to CTF SIX ONE, 290511Z Aug. 83, in Beirut, Lebanon CD Collection, Messages and General Correspondence for August 1983, MCHD.

90   "Groups of armed": CTF SIX TWO to CTF SIX ONE, 290720Z Aug. 83 in Beirut, Lebanon CD Collection, Messages and General Correspondence for August 1983, MCHD.

90   At 9:40 a.m.: Frank, *U.S. Marines in Lebanon*, p. 78.

90   "It just hit": David Zucchino, "A Chance to Return the Fire Is Welcomed by Marines," *Philadelphia Inquirer*, Aug. 31, 1983, p. 11A.

90   "Staff Sergeant Ortega": Mark Singleton interview, Dec. 21, 2022.

90   Marine amtracks: CTF SIX TWO to CTF SIX ONE, 290910Z Aug. 83, "Marine Casualties 29 Aug. 83," in Beirut, Lebanon CD Collection, Messages and General Correspondence for August 1983, MCHD.

90   "Casualty section": List of Deceased, undated (circa Aug. 29, 1983), in Beirut, Lebanon CD Collection, Messages and General Correspondence for August 1983, MCHD.

90   The Marines meanwhile: Geraghty, *Peacekeepers at War*, p. 55; Frank, *U.S. Marines in Lebanon*, p. 78.

91   "The Druze battery": CTF SIX TWO to CTF SIX ONE, 030010Z Aug 23, in Beirut, Lebanon CD Collection, Messages and General Correspondence for August 1983, MCHD.

91   America had suffered: C. W. Rowe, "Marines Strike Back at Their Attackers," *Root Scoop*, Sept. 2, 1983, p. 1.

91   Over the span: CTF SIX TWO to CTF SIX ONE, 310010Z Aug. 83, "OPS Summary 28-29 August 83," in Beirut, Lebanon CD Collection, Messages and General Correspondence for August 1983, MCHD.

91   "The small arms": Ibid.

91   In at least: Ibid.

91   "It was a very": David Zucchino, "A Chance to Return the Fire Is Welcomed by Marines," *Philadelphia Inquirer*, Aug. 31, 1983, p. 11A.

92   "Our hands": Ibid.

92   "The Can Shoot": Frank, *U.S. Marines in Lebanon*, p. 79.

92   "I know it is tough": CMC WASHINGTON DC to TWO FOUR MAU, 290924Z Aug, 83, in Beirut, Lebanon CD Collection, Messages and General Correspondence for August 1983, MCHD.

92   "The firing is": Robert H. Reid, "Lebanese Oust Militia Units," *Hartford Courant*, Sept. 1, 1983, p. 1.

92 "Beirut Battle": Julie Flint, "Beirut Battle Plunges Country Back into Chaos," *Guardian*, Aug. 31, 1983, p. 1.

92 "Heavy Fighting": David Lamb, "2 Marines Die as Heavy Fighting Edges Lebanon Toward Civil War," *Fresno Bee*, Aug. 30, 1983, p. 1.

92 "Marines Now": "Marines Now Caught in Beirut's Quagmire," *Tampa Tribune*, Aug. 30, 1983, p. 4A.

92 On the last: Herbert H. Denton, "Troops Capture Militia Positions," *Washington Post*, Sept. 1, 1983, p. A1; Richard Bernstein, "Key Beirut Areas Retaken by Army from Militia Units," *New York Times*, Sept. 1, 1983, p. A1.

93 "Keeping the peace": TWO FOUR MAU to CG FMFLANT, 042130Z Sept. 84, "TWO FOUR MAU SITREP No. 24," Beirut, Lebanon CD Collection, 24th MAU SITREPS, Mar-Nov 1983, MCHD.

CHAPTER 15

94 "We have given": Otis Pike, "Lebanon: Marines in Harm's Way," *San Francisco Examiner*, Sept. 2, 1983, p. B3.

94 Nestled on 688 acres: Ann Devroy, "Reagan's Ranch Is 'Magic,'" *Green Bay Press-Gazette*, Sept. 4, 1983, p. A8; Lou Cannon, "Reagan's Ranch a Retreat, Tax Shelter—and Security Risk," *Washington Post*, July 5, 1980, p. A2.

94 National Security Advisor: Terence Hunt, "White House Portrays President Actively Involved in Beirut Crisis," *Greenwood Commonwealth*, Sept. 1, 1983, p. 11.

94 Based on those: John M. Goshko and Helen Dewar, "U.S. Rules Out Any Expansion of Marine Force," *Washington Post*, Sept. 1, 1983, p. A1; Saul Friedman, "Regan Orders No Change in Marines' Role in Beirut," *Philadelphia Inquirer*, Aug. 30, 1983, p. 8A.

94 "We condemn": David Hoffman, "Attack Is Blamed on Syrians' Role," *Washington Post*, Aug. 30, 1983, p. A1.

95 "Only 5 more months": "A Last Letter," *Democrat and Chronicle*, Aug. 30, 1983, p. 3A.

95 "We got bombed": Ibid.

95 "I started having": Steve Crosby and Jim Myers, "Death in Beirut Touches Home," *Democrat and Chronicle*, Aug. 30, 1983, p. 1.

95 "Members of the family": Ibid.

95 "Mr. President": Ibid.

95 "You don't": Ibid.

96 "Mr. Reagan": Ibid.

96 "I want nothing": Ibid.

96 "I loved him": Ibid.

96 The six-foot-three: Kathryn Dempsey, Geoffrey Losey, and Elizabeth Stevens interviews, Oct. 23, 2023.

96 "He thought": Kathy Doherty and Bruce Henderson, "N.C. Marine, in Lebanon to Help Dies There," *Charlotte Observer*, Aug. 30. 1983, p. 1.

96 "He developed": Ramiro Lagos, "Requiem for a Patriot and a Friend," undated (circa September 1983).

96 "George was a strong": Kathryn Dempsey email, Aug. 14, 2023.

96 "I went there": Doherty and Henderson, "N.C. Marine, in Lebanon to Help Dies There."

96 "Neighbors and relatives": Ray Rollins, "Marine Had Sought Assignment," *Winston-Salem Journal*, Aug. 30, 1983, p. 1.

97 "He was very": Tom Sieg, "'He Wanted to Serve . . . His Country,'" *Sentinel*, Aug. 30. 1983, p. 1.

97 "If there's anything": Ibid.

CHAPTER 16

98 "Politics is the art": Steven V. Roberts, "Congress Agrees to Allow Marines to Stay in Beirut," *New York Times*, Sept. 30, 1983, p. A1.

98 "The United States": Harold Jackson, "Congress Row on Death of Marines," *Guardian*, Aug. 30, 1983, p. 6.

98 "Our troops": Saul Friedman, "Reagan Orders No Change in Marines' Role in Beirut," *Philadelphia Inquirer*, Aug. 30, 1983, p. 8A.

98 "I want to": Ronald Reagan to Thomas O'Neill Jr., Sept. 29, 1982, Box 16, Office of the Counsel to the President, RRPL.

99 "I believe": Ronald Reagan to Thomas O'Neill Jr., Aug. 30, 1983, ibid.

99 "I believe": Bernard Gwertzman, "Marines Are Neither Combatants Nor Targets in Beirut, U.S. Insists," *New York Times*, Sept. 1, 1983, p. A1.

99 "Reagan Insists": Saul Friedman, "Reagan Insists Marines Not Involved in 'Combat,'" *Miami Herald*, Aug. 31, 1983, p. 12A.

99 "Marines Aren't": "Marines Aren't Facing Imminent Hostilities in Beirut, Shultz Says," *Ventura County Star*, Sept. 1, 1983, p. B8.

99 "This is a difficult": Bernard Gwertzman, "Officials Call Attacks a Surprise; U.S. Role in Lebanon Questioned," *New York Times*, Aug. 31, 1983, p. A1.

99 Refusing to label: George Skelton and David Wood, "Administration Won't Call Lebanon Strife 'Combat,'" *Los Angeles Times*, Aug. 31, 1983, p. 26.

99 "We have people": John M. Goshko and Helen Dewar, "U.S. Rules Out Any Expansion of Marine Force," *Washington Post*, Sept. 1, 1983, p. A1.

99 "American forces": Robert Byrd to Ronald Reagan, Aug. 31, 1983, #161289, Box 119, WHORM Subject File: CO 086, RRPL.

99 "In these conditions": Henry Gonzalez to Ronald Reagan, Sept. 2, 1983, #161467, ibid.

100 A Gallup poll: "More Than Half Polled Want Marine Pullout," *News and Observer*, Sept. 4, 1983, p. 3A.

100 "It should be": "Invitation to Disaster," editorial, *Asbury Park Press*, Sept. 4, 1983, p. C2.

100 "Is America": "Is America Caught in a Trap?" *U.S. News & World Report*, Sept. 12, 1983, p. 26.

100 "In bewilderment": Flora Lewis, "Time to Cut Losses," *New York Times*, Sept. 2, 1983, p. A19.

100 "Keeping the peace": "Casualties Must Not Lessen U.S. Resolve," editorial, *Durham Sun*, Aug. 31, 1983, p. 4A.

100 "leaving the Marines": Friedman, *From Beirut to Jerusalem*, p. 199.

100 "The only thing": Henry Linkkila to Patricia Roy, Sept. 2, 1983.

100 "No one wants": Dan Williams, "Marines' Role Draped in Verbal Camouflage," *Miami Herald*, Sept. 11, 1983, p. 1.

100 "When the shelling": "A Hot Spot, a Hot Box for U.S. Marines," *U.S. News & World Report*, Sept. 12, 1983, p. 28.

101 "I don't think": George Converse to Mary Ann Converse, Aug. 22, 1983, Box 2, George Converse Collection, MCHD.

101 "Lebanon is lost": Anne Keegan, "Marines in Beirut Duck and Shrug It Off," *Chicago Tribune*, Aug. 14, 1983, p. 1.

101 "Our troops": Grant McIntosh Jr. to Grant McIntosh Sr., Aug. 7, 1983, Box, 1, Grant McIntosh Collection, MCHD.

101 "I don't like": Robert Conley to Jim Conley, June 11, 1983, in Jackowski and Stelpflug, eds., *Voices from Beirut*, pp. 21–22.

CHAPTER 17

102 "These past": Dan Williams, "Marines' Role Draped in Verbal Camouflage," *Miami Herald*, Sept. 11, 1983, p. 1.

102 The special envoy: McFarlane, *Special Trust*, p. 248.

102 "Gemayel is just": Robert McFarlane statement, in *Marines in Lebanon, A Ten-Year Retrospective: Lessons Learned*, May 3, 1993, p. 29.

102 "sons-of-bitches": Robert Dillon oral history with Charles Stuart Kennedy, May 17, 1990.

102 "That situation": Ibid.

102 "To these ends": Charles Hill to William Clark, "Lebanon: Discussion Paper for September 3 NSC Meeting," Sept. 3, 1983, https://www.cia.gov /readingroom/docs/CIA-RDP85M00363R000300630019-4.pdf.

103 "Assad": Howard Teicher and Gayle Radley Teicher, *Twin Pillars to Desert Storm: America's Flawed Vision in the Middle East from Nixon to Bush* (New York: William Morrow, 1993), p. 228.

103 "use a massive": Robert McFarlane statement, in *Marines in Lebanon, A Ten-Year Retrospective: Lessons Learned*, May 3, 1993, p. 27.

103 "This was": McFarlane, *Special Trust*, p. 248.

103 "strange": Weinberger, *Fighting for Peace*, p. 360.

103 "indrawn": Ibid.

103 "McFarlane is a man": Ibid.

103 Weinberger was not: Ibid., pp. 1–22; Theodore H. White, "Weinberger on the Ramparts," *New York Times*, Feb. 6, 1983, p. SM14.

104 "I did not arm": Caspar Weinberger with Gretchen Roberts, *In the Arena: A Memoir of the 20th Century* (Washington, DC: Regnery, 2001), p. 313.

104 "For any Lebanese": McFarlane, *Special Trust*, p. 249.

104 "War": Carl von Clausewitz, *On War*, ed. and trans. by Michael Howard and Peter Paret (Princeton, NJ: Princeton University Press, 1984), p. 87.

104 "The president": Shultz, *Turmoil and Triumph*, p. 109.

104 "One has to think": *Meet the Press*, Nov. 6, 1983, transcript, in *Selected Works of*

General John W. Vessey, Jr., Tenth Chairman of the Joint Chiefs of Staff, 22 June 1982–30 September 1985 (Washington, DC: Joint History Office, Office of the Chairman of the Joint Chiefs of Staff, 2008), p. 90.

105 "My own feeling": Weinberger, *Fighting for Peace*, pp. 159–60.

105 "That's nonsense": George J. Church, "Force and Personality," *Time*, Dec. 24, 1984, p. 13.

105 "I think that is": Caspar Weinberger oral history with Stephen Knott and Russell Riley, Nov. 19, 2002, Miller Center of Public Affairs, University of Virginia, Charlottesville.

105 "as one of the greatest": James McCartney, "Curtain Falls on Bureaucratic Feud," *Miami Herald*, Nov. 5, 1987, p. 7A.

105 "Both were capable": Lou Cannon, *President Reagan: The Role of a Lifetime* (New York: Simon & Schuster, 1991), p. 403.

106 "This trait": Ibid., p. 402.

106 The president's calendar: Daily Diary of President Ronald Reagan, Sept. 3, 1983.

106 "The purpose": William P. Clark, "National Security Planning Group Meeting," Sept. 3, 1983, https://www.thereaganfiles.com/19830903-nspg-68-briefing.pdf.

107 There are no minutes: Aimee Muller (RRPL archivist) email, July 14, 2023.

107 The agenda: Agenda, National Security Planning Group Meeting, Sept. 3, 1983, https://www.cia.gov/readingroom/docs/CIA-RDP85M00363R000300630019-4.pdf.

107 "We are at a": Charles Hill to William Clark, "Lebanon: Discussion Paper for Sept. 3 1983 NSC Meeting," Sept. 3, 1983, including "NSPG Discussion Paper on Lebanon," undated, ibid.

107 "In the worse case": William P. Clark, "National Security Planning Group Meeting," Sept. 3, 1983.

107 "If this demarche": Ibid.

107 "Such actions": Ibid.

108 "The line": "NSPG Discussion Paper on Lebanon," undated.

108 "The meeting": Teicher, *Twin Pillars to Desert Storm*, p. 250.

108 "No new decisions": Ibid., p. 251.

CHAPTER 18

109 "The war": John Hudson to Lisa Hudson, Sept. 4, 1983.

109 The *Eisenhower*: 24th MAU, Command Chronology, 1 September–30 September 1983, MCHD.

109 "An eerie": Geraghty, *Peacekeepers at War*, p. 58.

109 News correspondents: 24th MAU, Command Chronology, 1 September–30 September 1983, MCHD.

109 "The Beirut press": Bob Jordan, "The Presence: Part II (The Conclusion)," *Leatherneck*, February 1989, p. 24.

110 "The peacekeeping": Geraghty, *Peacekeepers at War*, p. 58.

110 On September 2: Herbert H. Denton, "Tanks Guard Beirut Rites for

Marines," *Washington Post*, Sept. 3, 1983, p. A1; "Memorial Service Honors Marines, *Root Scoop*, Sept. 15, 1983, p. 2.

110 "We come together": "Marines in Lebanon Honor Dead Comrades," *Akron Beacon Journal*, Sept. 3, 1983, p. C7.

110 "Our country": Denton, "Tanks Guard Beirut Rites for Marines."

110 First Lieutenant Mark Singleton: Mark Singleton interview, Dec. 21, 2022.

111 "We were both": Jim Schlosser, "Lt. Losey's Body Is Returned Home," *Greensboro Record*, Sept. 2, 1983, p. 1.

111 "Tell us what": Mark Singleton interview, Dec. 21, 2022.

111 On September 4: Kathryn Dempsey interview, Aug. 11, 2023.

111 "Lord": Ramiro Lagos, "Requiem for a Patriot and a Friend," undated (circa September 1983).

111 "He made the greatest": Gary Terpening, "City Marine Is Honored at Funeral," *Winston-Salem Journal*, Sept. 5, 1983, p. 1.

111 "The precision": Ibid.

112 "Fire the volley": Leslie M. Allen, "Hundreds Come to honor Marine," *Greensboro Record*, Sept. 5, 1983, p. 1.

112 "There is": Ibid.

112 Ortega's funeral: Ervin L. Hawk, "He Died for Beliefs," *Morning Call*, Sept. 7, 1983, p. 1; Marguerite Del Giudice, "Hometown, Pa., Salutes a Hero," *Philadelphia Inquirer*, Sept. 7, 1983, p. 1B.

112 "The Bible reminds": Barbara Vancheri, "They Buried 'The Best of the Best,'" *Democrat and Chronicle*, Sept. 7, 1983, p. 1.

112 "Alex loved": Terry Rang, "A Hero Is Laid to Rest," *Pottsville Republican*, Sept. 7, 1983, p. 1.

113 "Staff Sergeant Ortega": "Marine Slain in Beirut Is Buried," *Pittsburgh Press*, Sept. 7, 1983, p. A19.

113 "Years ago": John Hudson to Lisa Hudson, Aug. 29, 1983.

113 "It was getting": Dolphin, *24 Mau*, pp. 133–34.

113 "The President": John Hudson to Lisa Hudson, Aug. 31, 1983.

113 Dolphin feared: Dolphin, *24 Mau*, pp. 134–35.

114 "At this stage": Herbert H. Denton, "Israeli Troops Start Pullback to South Lebanon Positions," *Washington Post*, Sept. 4, 1983, p. A1.

114 "No soap": Ronald Reagan diary, Sept. 3, 1983, in Reagan, *The Reagan Diaries*, p. 176.

114 "In the Commodore": Fisk, *Pity the Nation*, p. 490.

114 "That night": Geraghty, *Peacekeepers at War*, p. 59.

114 "For the entire": Richard Bernstein, "Militias in Beirut Battle for Land Vacated by Israel," *New York Times*, Sept. 5, 1983, p. 1.

114 "Being here": John Hudson to Lisa Hudson, Sept. 4, 1983.

115 "What irony": Ibid.

115 "The time of flight": 24th MAU, Command Chronology, 1 September–30 September 1983, MCHD.

115 "Babe it was real": Bradley McLaughlin to Karen McLaughlin, Sept. 9, 1983, in "'It's Like I'm Just Existing Here,'" *Democrat and Chronicle*, Oct. 24, 1983, p. 4A.

115 "The massive": 24th MAU, Command Chronology, 1 September–30
     September 1983, MCHD.

115 "Stakes are being": TWO FOUR MAU to CG FMFLANT, 111800Z Sept. 83,
     "TWO FOUR MAU SITREP No. 25," in Beirut, Lebanon CD Collection,
     24th MAU SITREPS, Mar–Nov 1983, MCHD.

CHAPTER 19

116 "The only thing": Bill Stelpflug to Peggy and William Stelpflug, September 18,
     1983, Bill Stelpflug Collection, MCHD.

116 "When the Marines": Robert Friedman, "Marine Paid 'Blood Tax' in
     Lebanon," *Daily News*, Sept. 11, 1983, p. 24.

116 "Ever since": Nancy J. Schwerzler and Karen Love, "Dead Marines' Towns
     Two Different Worlds," *Sun*, Sept. 7, 1983, p. A5.

116 At 5:49: Daily Diary of President Ronald Reagan, Sept. 6, 1983.

116 "Be calm": "Reagan Phones Marine's Dad," *Daily News*, Sept. 7, 1983, p. 14.

117 "Pedro sacrificed": Ibid.

117 "Don't worry": "A Thousand Mourn Marine's Death at Memorial Service,"
     Daily Spectrum, Sept. 15, 1983, p. 2.

117 Reagan reached: Daily Diary of President Ronald Reagan, Sept. 6, 1983.

117 "Why do we have": Randy Furst, "Dead Marine's Dad: Why Our Boys?" *Star
     and Tribune*, Sept. 7, 1983, p. 1.

117 "I'm sure as hell": Ibid.

117 "I called": Ronald Reagan diary, Sept. 6, 1983, in Reagan, *The Reagan Diaries*,
     p. 177.

117 "The reality has hit": "Bombings Sour Marines' Views of Beirut Duty,"
     Indianapolis Star, Sept. 11, 1983, p. 15A.

117 "We didn't expect": Scott MacLeod, "'We Do a Lot of Praying,'"
     Pennsylvanian, Sept. 11, 1983, p. 1.

118 Two hundred tired: "Beirut Comrades Honor Slain Marines," *News-Press*,
     Sept. 14, 1983, p. 10A.

118 "Both were highly": "Marines Pay Last Respects to Comrades," *Herald*,
     Sept. 14, 1983, p. 2.

118 "The Marines": Clayton LaVerdiere, "Winslow Native: "Marines Will Stay,"
     Morning Sentinel, Sept. 22, 1983, p. 7.

118 "The strain": Dolphin, *24 Mau*, p. 144.

118 "It was evident": "Memorial Service Honors Marines," *Root Scoop*,
     Sept. 15, 1983, p. 2.

118 "By their ultimate": Ibid.

118 In the gymnasium: Ron Seely, "The Way It Was for Randy Clark," *Wisconsin
     State Journal*, Sept. 14, 1983, p. 1.

119 The high school: "Slain Marine Wrote Letter That Said He Feared for Life,"
     Leader-Telegram, Sept. 4, 1983, p. 1.

119 "We are confused": Gene Prigge, "Mourners Ask for Explanation of Clark's
     Death," *Leader-Telegram*, Sept. 15, 1983, p. 1.

119 "Who are we": Ibid.

CHAPTER 20

120 "It is really": Bradley McLaughlin to Karen McLaughlin, Sept. 9, 1983, in "'It's Like I'm Just Existing Here,'" *Democrat and Chronicle*, Oct. 24, 1983, p. 4A.

120 "The most popular": Bob Jordan, "The Presence," *Leatherneck*, January 1989, p. 31.

120 Troops filled: 24th MAU, Command Chronology, 1 September–30 September 1983, MCHD.

120 This brought: Report of the Long Commission, p. 73.

120 "If the filling of sandbags": Dolphin, *24 Mau*, p. 154.

120 "Bunkers were dug": Randy Gaddo, "Better Homes and Bunkers???" *Root Scoop*, Sept. 22, 1983, p. 2.

120 "Sometimes we go": John Dalziel to Rod Dalziel, Sept. 20, 1983 (postmark date).

121 "I can honestly": Michael Massman to Patricia Lou Smith, Sept. 24, 1983, in John F. Brown, "'At Least I Know He's Alive,'" *Times Herald*, Oct. 26, 1983, p. 1.

121 "I have no emotional": Bradley McLaughlin to Karen McLaughlin, Sept. 9, 1983.

121 "I can't help": Joseph Milano to Angela and Peter Milano, undated, in Jackowski and Stelpflug, eds., *Voices from Beirut*, p. 78.

121 "It is so sad": John Hudson to Lisa Hudson, Sept. 13, 1983.

121 "This whole thing": Henry Linkkila to Patricia Roy, Sept. 6, 1983.

121 "I won't be happy": Henry Linkkila to Patricia Roy, Sept. 10, 1983.

121 "Can't wait": Bill Stelpflug to Kathy Stelpflug, September 10, 1983 (postmark date), Bill Stelpflug Collection, MCHD.

121 "I saw the most": Ibid.

121 "Beirut is not": John Hudson letter to Lisa Hudson, Sept. 15, 1983.

122 "No matter how": Michael Ohler to Gail Ohler, Sept. 10, 1983, Michael Ohler Collection, NNAM.

122 "She looks": Ibid.

122 "Is it okay": "Wheeler Recalls Danger-Filled Wait for Rescue," *Dunn County News*, Dec. 21, 1983, p. 3.

122 "Don't dwell": Michael Ohler to Gail Ohler, Sept. 5, 1983, Michael Ohler Collection, NNAM.

122 "God is in control!": Michael Ohler to Gail Ohler, Sept. 1, 1983, ibid.

122 "Ollie the Mad": 24th MAU, Command Chronology, 1 September–30 September 1983, MCHD.

122 "Everyone reacted": Petit, *Peacekeepers at War*, p. 133.

122 "My hearing": Dolphin, *24 Mau*, p. 153.

122 "You feel hopeless": E. J. Dionne Jr., "Some Marines 'Feel Helpless,'" *New York Times*, Sept. 7, 1983, p. A1.

122 "We are sitting": Scott MacLeod, "'We Are Sitting Ducks,'" *Arizona Republic*, Sept. 18, 1983, p. A4.

123 "Sixty-five dollars": Petit, *Peacekeepers at War*, p. 129.

123 "Essentially, we're": Dionne Jr., "Some Marines 'Feel Helpless,'" p. A1.

123 "The old warhorse": Dolphin, *24 Mau*, p. 147.

123 *"This son of a bitch"*: Ibid.

123 "That one small": Ibid.

123 "Who is it?" Geraghty, *Peacekeepers at War*, pp. 62–63.

CHAPTER 21

125 "The fact": "Test of Fire," editorial, *Miami Herald*, Sept. 8, 1983, p. 26A.

125 With McFarlane: Teicher, *Twin Pillars to Desert Storm*, p. 251; Philip A. Dur, *Between Land and Sea: A Cold Warrior's Log* (Austin, TX: Lioncrest, 2022), p. 202.

125 Dur was: John Gans, *White House Warriors: How the National Security Council Transformed the American War of War* (New York: Liveright, 2019), pp. 63–74.

125 "accelerated and expanded": National Security Decision Directive Number 103, "Strategy for Lebanon," Sept. 10, 1983, Box, 10, Executive Secretariat, NSC: NSDDs, RRPL.

125 A tally showed: Caspar Weinberger to William Clark, "Response to 10 September 1983 NSDD, Strategy for Lebanon," Sept. 12, 1983, https://www .esd.whs.mil/Portals/54/Documents/FOID/Reading%20Room/MDR _Releases/FY19/FY19_Q1/Response_10Sep1983_Strategy_12Sep1983.pdf.

125 "tactical intelligence": National Security Decision Directive Number 103, "Strategy for Lebanon," Sept. 10, 1983.

125 "aggressive self-defense": Ibid.

125 Weinberger and Vessey: Teicher, *Twin Pillars to Desert Storm*, p. 252.

126 "The situation": Ronald Reagan diary, Sept. 10, 1983, in Reagan, *The Reagan Diaries*, p. 178.

126 "tough little": Robert Dillon oral history with Charles Stuart Kennedy, May 17, 1990.

126 "It was the moment": McFarlane, *Special Trust*, p. 250.

126 "sky-is falling": Cannon, *President Reagan*, p. 421.

126 "This is": AMEMBASSY BEIRUT to RUEHC/SECSTATE WASHDC, 111038Z Sept. 83, "McFarlane/Fairbanks Mission: Strategic Escalation of the Battle," Box 54, Executive Secretariat, NSC: Subject File, RRPL.

127 "It was time": McFarlane, *Special Trust*, p. 251.

127 "I wanted some": Robert Dillon oral history with Charles Stuart Kennedy, May 17, 1990.

127 Back in Washington: Teicher, *Twin Pillars to Desert Storm*, p. 253.

127 "Assistance for this": "Addendum to NSDD 103 on Lebanon of September 10, 1983," Sept. 11, 1983, Box, 10, Executive Secretariat, NSC: NSDDs, RRPL.

127 "I understood": Geraghty, *Peacekeepers at War*, p. 65.

128 His own intel: Ibid.

128 "What followed": Ibid.

128 "General": Ibid.

128 "Sir, I can't": Ibid.

128 "President Reagan's": Ibid., p. 67.

128 "I wondered": Ibid., p. 66.

128 "Our increasing": Ibid., pp. 68-69.

129 No sooner: Ibid., p. 69.

129 "Anyone on the street": CTF SIX ONE to COMSIXTHFLT, 200300Z Sept. 83, "CTF 61/62 Joint Daily Intelligence Summary (DISUM) 110 for the Period 181800Z-191759Z Sept. 83," in 24th MAU, Command Chronology, 1 September–30 September 1983, MCHD.

129 In addition: Geraghty, *Peacekeepers at War*, p. 71.

129 "Military observers": Ibid., p. 70.

130 "I gave the orders": Ibid., p. 72.

130 At 10:04: Ibid.

130 "It was a dilemma": Ibid.

130 "My gut instinct": Ibid.

CHAPTER 22

131 "This country": Michael Ohler to Gail Ohler, Sept. 28, 1983, Michael Ohler Collection, NNAM.

131 "chewing gum": Crist, *The Twilight War*, p. 106.

131 What began: Ibid., pp. 122–23.

132 "Baalbek": Robin Wright, *Sacred Rage: The Wrath of Militant Islam* (New York: Touchstone Books, 1986), p. 81.

132 Iranian forces: Crist, *The Twilight War*, p. 125.

132 "We are": Ibid., p. 127.

132 "Imad Mugniyah": Ibid., p. 130.

132 "poor man's": Ibid., p. 129.

132 "If Hezbollah": Ibid.

132 The organization's first: Ibid., pp. 128–29.

133 "special targets": Ibid., p. 133.

133 "yes, you should": Ibid., p. 134.

133 "You should": Ibid.

CHAPTER 23

134 "How many Marines": "Goldwater Says U.S. Should Leave Lebanon," *News*, Sept. 12, 1983, p. 22.

134 "What that means": Hedrick Smith, "War Powers Dispute," *New York Times*, Sep 17, 1983, p. 4.

135 "What is at stake": Ibid.

135 "There are few": Ibid.

135 Despite the bluster: Gerald F. Seib, "Reagan Wants Congress to Back Marines in Beirut," *Wall Street Journal*, Sept. 14, 1983, p. 37; Steven V. Roberts, "U.S. Blames Soviet for Syrians' Role in Lebanese Strife," *New York Times*, Sept. 22, 1983, p. A1; Helen Dewar, "Senate Democrats Dig in Their Heels," *Washington Post*, Sept. 18, 1983, p. A1.

135 The proposed deal: Steven V. Roberts, "1½ -Year Extension," *New York Times*, Sept. 21, 1983, p. A1; Lou Cannon and T. R. Reid, "Marines Could Stay in Area 18 Months," *Washington Post*, Sept. 21, 1983, p. A1.

135 "I am especially": Roberts, "1½ -Year Extension."

136 "These objectives": All committee quotations come from U.S. Congress, House,

Statutory Authorization Under the War Powers Resolution—Lebanon, Hearing and Markup Before the Committee on Foreign Affairs, 98th Cong., 1st Sess., Sept. 21-22, 1983 (Washington, DC: U.S. Government Printing Office, 1983), pp. 1–51.

141 Shultz headed: Daily Diary of President Ronald Reagan, Sept. 21, 1983.

141 "Are we going": Shultz, *Turmoil and Triumph*, p. 227.

141 "I was, if anything": Ibid.

141 The questions raised: U.S. Congress, House, *Lebanon: Limited Interest, Limited Involvement, Frequent Accounting, Report of the Delegation to Lebanon—1983 of the Committee on Armed Services*, 98th Cong., 1st Sess., Oct. 18, 1983 (Washington, DC: U.S. Government Printing Office, 1983), pp. 1–10.

141 "I don't want": "Hopkins Wants Troops Out of Lebanon," *Messenger*, Sept. 27, 1983, p. 3.

141 "You're going": Patrick J. Sloyan, "U.S. in Lebanon: Anatomy of a Foreign Policy Failure," *Newsday*, April 8, 1984, p. 1.

141 "My God": Bill Arthur, "S.C. Congressman Questions Marine Role," *Charlotte Observer*, Sept. 28, 1983, p. 6A.

142 "Marines are trained": John O'Brien, "Rep. Ray Says He's Uneasy About Marines in Lebanon," *Columbus Ledger*, Sept. 28, 1983, p. 1.

142 "It was perfectly": Bob Redding, "Spratt Sees Peril in U.S. Policy," *Item*, Sept. 28, 1983, p. 1.

142 "Standing in the ship's": "Separate Observations of Congressman William L. Dickinson," in *Lebanon: Limited Interest, Limited Involvement, Frequent Accounting*, p. 9.

142 A *Washington Post*: Barry Sussman, "U.S. Majority Favors Limiting Deployment to 6 Months or Less," *Washington Post*, Sept. 29, 1983, p. A1.

142 The United States: "The Toll in Lebanon," *News Tribune*, Sept. 27, 1983, p. A3.

142 "The Thatcher": William Clark to Ronald Reagan, "Visit of British Prime Minister Thatcher," undated, Box 11, Executive & Soviet Affairs Directorate, NSC: Records, RRPL.

142 "The arms": Sloyan, "U.S. in Lebanon: Anatomy of a Foreign Policy Failure."

143 On September 28, 1983: T. R. Reid, "House Votes 18-Month Limit on Marines' Use in Lebanon," *Washington Post*, Sept. 29, 1983, p. A1.

143 The Republican-controlled: T. R. Reid, "Congress Clears 18-Month Marine Stay in Lebanon," *Washington Post*, Sept. 30, 1983, p. A1.

143 The House then: Ibid.

143 "The vote": Shultz, *Turmoil and Triumph*, p. 227.

143 "Today's vote": Steven V. Roberts, "Congress Agrees to Allow Marines to Stay in Beirut," *New York Times*, Sept. 30, 1983, p. A1.

143 "We're all troubled": "Briefly Said," *Pittsburgh Press*, Sept. 25, 1983, p. B2.

143 "Staying is bad": Roberts, "1½-Year Extension."

143 "We all agree": Steven V. Roberts, "Senate Unit Backs Lebanon Measure," *New York Times*, Sept. 24, 1983, p. 6.

143 "What is our": Reid, "House Votes 18-Month Limit on Marines' Use in Lebanon."

143 "If we are there": Ibid.

CHAPTER 24

144 "Basically everything": John Dalziel to Rosie and Rod Dalziel, Oct. 3, 1983.

144 "By the way": McFarlane, *Special Trust*, p. 253.

144 "It was a final": Ibid.

144 "I really need": Ibid., pp. 253–54.

144 "Let's go": Ibid., p. 254.

145 "The cease-fire": Ibid.

145 "'Cease-fire'": Geraghty, *Peacekeepers at War*, p. 80.

145 "We have just": "Colonel Geraghty: Don't Lose Sight of Our Peacekeeping Mission Here," *Root Scoop*, Oct. 6, 1983, p. 1.

145 "It was another": Geraghty, *Peacekeepers at War*, p. 72.

145 "I was also convinced": Ibid., p. 73.

145 "The pilot circled": Thomas L. Friedman, "Lebanese Reopen Beirut's Airport," *New York Times*, Sept. 30, 1983, p. A8.

146 That afternoon arrival: Report of the Long Commission, p. 67.

146 "All things": TWO FOUR MAU to CG FMFLANT, 091908Z Oct. 83, "TWO FOUR MAU SITREP No. 29," in Beirut, Lebanon CD Collection, 24th MAU SITREPS, Mar–Nov 1983, MCHD.

146 "All was quiet": George Converse to Mary Ann Converse, Oct. 1, 1983, Box 2, George Converse Collection, MCHD.

146 "Beirut appeared": Sender illegible to COMSIXTHFLT, date illegible, subject line illegible, in 24th MAU, Command Chronology, 1 September–30 September 1983, MCHD.

146 "Things are so": John Hudson to Lisa Hudson, Oct. 1, 1983.

146 "I can't believe": Bill Stelpflug to Peggy and William Stelpflug, October (no day listed) 1983, Bill Stelpflug Collection, MCHD.

146 "All of your letters": Henry Linkkia to Patricia Roy, Oct. 3, 1983.

146 The situation remained: TWO FOUR MAU to CG FMFLANT, 091908Z Oct. 83, "TWO FOUR MAU SITREP No. 29," Beirut, Lebanon CD Collection, 24th MAU SITREPS, Mar–Nov 1983, MCHD; Geraghty, *Peacekeepers at War*, p. 88.

146 "When the shelling": John Dalziel to Rosie and Rod Dalziel, Sept. 30, 1983.

146 "Our major": "Beirut Football League Holds First Games," *Root Scoop*, Oct. 13, 1983, p. 5.

147 "I wanted": "Mrs. Ortega Sends Gifts, Best Regards," *Root Scoop*, Sept. 29, 1983, p. 2.

147 Captain Michael Ohler: Michael Ohler to Gail Ohler, Sept. 21, 1983, and Oct. 5, 1983, Michael Ohler Collection, NNAM.

147 "To be together": Michael Ohler to Gail Ohler, Oct. 1, 1983, ibid.

147 "People are starting": John Hudson to Lisa Hudson, Oct. 12, 1983.

PART II

149 "Terrorists can attack": Brian Michael Jenkins, "The Lessons of Beirut: Testimony Before the Long Commission," February 1984, Alfred M. Gray Marine Corps Research Center, Quantico, Va.

CHAPTER 25

151 "The Lebanese people": Morris Draper oral history with Charles Stuart Kennedy, Feb. 27, 1991, Foreign Affairs Oral History Collection of the Association for Diplomatic Studies and Training, LOC.

151 "Sniper fired": "Situation Report for 5 Oct. until 0700 6 Oct. 1983," in Beirut, Lebanon CD Collection, Messages and General Correspondence for October 1983, MCHD.

151 "A white Peugeot": "Situation Report for 01 0700 Oct. until 02 0700 Oct. 1983," in ibid.

151 "Armed men": "Situation Report for 300700 Sep.–010700 Oct. 83," in ibid.

151 "During the shelling": CTF SIX TWO to CTF SIX ONE, 011036Z Oct. 83, "Threat Awareness During Cease Fire," in ibid.

151 "The cease-fire": Petit, *Peacekeepers at War*, p. 138.

152 "Positions and buildings": 24th MAU, Command Chronology, 1 October–31 October 1983, MCHD.

152 "The driver": 24th MAU, Command Chronology, 1 September–30 September 1983, MCHD.

152 "I figured": Petit, *Peacekeepers at War*, p. 136.

152 A livid: Geraghty, *Peacekeepers at War*, p. 76.

152 "His face": Petit, *Peacekeepers at War*, p. 136.

152 "A single round": 24th MAU, Command Chronology, 1 October–31 October 1983, MCHD.

152 "The vulnerability": Ibid

152 On October 9: Ibid.

152 Four days later: Ibid.

153 In his room: John Hudson to Lisa Hudson, Oct. 15, 1983.

153 "I don't know": David Madaras to Ann and Charles Madaras, Oct. 5, 1983.

153 "The direct threat": TWO FOUR MAU to CG FMFLANT, 161444Z Oct. 83, "TWO FOUR MAU SITREP No. 30," Beirut, Lebanon CD Collection, 24th MAU SITREPS, Mar–Nov 1983, MCHD.

153 At 10:03 a.m.: 24th MAU, Command Chronology, 1 October–31 October 1983, MCHD.

153 "He was still": John Hudson to Lisa Hudson, Oct. 15, 1983.

153 "Our Father": Danny Wheeler interview, Jan. 19, 2023.

153 "He looked": John Hudson to Lisa Hudson, Oct. 15, 1983.

153 "I can't do": Danny Wheeler interview, Jan. 19, 2023.

153 "You could hear": Ibid.

153 "I pronounced": John Hudson to Lisa Hudson, Oct. 15, 1983.

153 "I can't tell": Craig Stockton to Dona Stockton, Oct. 15, 1983, in Jackowski and Stelpflug, eds., *Voices from Beirut*, p. 114.

154 At 10:03 p.m.: 24th MAU, Command Chronology, 1 October–31 October 1983, MCHD.

154 "Being shot": Jack Kelly, "Dream Haunted Dead Marine's Dad," *Poughkeepsie Journal*, Oct. 18, 1983, p. 1.

154 "We've taken": Michael Ohler to Gail Ohler, Oct. 13, 1983, Michael Ohler Collection, NNAM.

154 His plan: Gail Ohler Osborne interview, Oct. 15, 2023.

154 "Always remember": Michael Ohler to Gail Ohler, Oct. 13, 1983.

154 "It is so sad": John Hudson to Lisa Hudson, Oct. 17, 1983.

154 "It's a different": John Hudson to Lisa Hudson, Oct. 14, 1983.

154 "One hell": Henry Linkkila to Patricia Roy, Oct. 17, 1983.

155 "You never know": John Dalziel to Rosie and Rod Dalziel, Oct. 22, 1983.

155 "If fired upon": William Claiborne, "U.S. Troops Kill Snipers in Lebanon," *Washington Post*, Oct. 16, 1983, p. A1.

155 Marine Snipers: William Claiborne, "Marine Draws a Bead on a Beirut 'Castro,'" *Washington Post*, Oct. 20, 1983, p. A1.

155 "It is strange": Thomas Friedman, "Beirut Sniper Attacks Reveal Vulnerability of Marine Posts," *New York Times*, Oct. 19, 1983, p. A1.

155 At 4:22 p.m.: 24th MAU, Command Chronology, 1 October–31 October 1983, MCHD.

155 "Shit man": Michael Toma diary, Oct. 15, 1983.

155 A six-by-six: CTF SIX ONE to NMCC WASHINGTON DC, 191814Z Oct. 83, in 24th MAU, Command Chronology, 1 October–31 October 1983, MCHD.

155 "I hope": Michael Toma diary, Oct. 15, 1983.

155 First Lieutenant Mark Singleton: Mark Singleton interview, Dec. 21, 2022.

155 "It is amazing": John Hudson to Lisa Hudson, Oct. 20, 1983.

CHAPTER 26

156 "War is hell": John Hudson to Louise and James Helton, Sept. 1, 1983.

156 The only bright: Micheline Thompson interview, Nov. 6, 2023.

156 "It was": Karen E. Henderson, "Soldier's Widow Faces Life Bravely," *Plain Dealer*, Oct. 18, 1987, p. 1B.

156 "I never really": Karen E. Henderson, "Widow of Slain Sailor Fights to Remain in U.S.," *Plain Dealer*, Oct. 23, 1984, p. 8A.

156 "They fell in love": Ibid.

156 "The days together": Mairy Jayn Woge, "Death Brings War Bridge to U.S.," *Plain Dealer*, Nov. 9, 1983, p. 13A.

157 "I found somebody": Darius Eichler interview, Nov. 1, 2023.

157 "He was infatuated": Ibid.

157 Arranging a marriage: Micheline Thompson interview, Nov. 6, 2023; John Hudson to Lisa Hudson, Oct. 16, 1983.

157 "Our hearts": Micheline Thompson text message, Nov. 18, 2023.

157 "You'll be visiting": Ibid.

157 "I love you": Ibid.

CHAPTER 27

158 "Things will have": Jimmy Ray Cain to Doris Collins, Oct. 7, 1983, #268556, WHORM Subject File: ND 007, RRPL.

158 Back in Washington": Daily Diary of President Ronald Reagan, Oct. 14, 1983.

158 "In the days": Ronald Reagan to Gail Ohler, Oct. 21, 1983, Michael Ohler Collection, NNAM.

158 "It was a moment": McFarlane, *Special Trust*, p. 257.

158 "You are the last": Patricia Nakhel to Ronald Reagan, Oct. 6, 1983, Box 75, Anne Higgins Files, RRPL.

159 "I promise you": Ronald Reagan to Patricia Nakhel, Nov. 28, 1983, ibid.

159 "The ceasefire": George Shultz to Ronald Reagan, "Our Strategy in Lebanon and the Middle East," Oct. 13, 1983, Box, 10, Executive Secretariat, NSC: NSDDs, RRPL.

159 "The static position": Caspar Weinberger to Robert McFarlane, "US Policy in Lebanon and the Middle East," Oct. 21, 1983, Box 4, Donald R. Fortier Papers, RRPL.

160 What to do: National Security Planning Group, Agenda, Oct. 18, 1983, Box 125, Executive Secretariat, NSC: Country File, RRPL; Daily Diary of President Ronald Reagan, Oct. 18, 1983.

160 No minutes exist: Aimee Muller (RRPL archivist) email, Aug. 7, 2023.

160 "All the options": Ronald Reagan diary, October 18, 1983, https://www.reaganfoundation.org/ronald-reagan/white-house-diaries/diary-entry-10181983/.

160 "We too are": Tom Keyser, "Nashua Marine Eulogized as Hero, Martyr," *Valley News*, Oct. 19, 1983, p. 1.

CHAPTER 28

161 "In Beirut": Charles Rowe, "Col. Geraghty Calls His Job as 24th MAU Boss the Best Job in the Corps for a Colonel," *Root Scoop*, Aug. 12, 1983, p. 1.

161 For the operation: Crist, *The Twilight War*, p. 134.

161 "The detonators": Ibid., p. 135.

161 Accounts vary: Ibid., pp. 135, 592.

CHAPTER 29

162 "Please don't worry": Edward Johnston to Mary Ann Johnston, Oct. 13, 1983, in Jackowski and Stelpflug, eds., *Voices from Beirut*, p. 68.

162 "We will be leaving": Henry Linkkila to Patricia Roy, Oct. 17, 1983.

162 "We have something": Danny Wheeler, "Chaplain's Corner: Getting Ready to Return Home," *Root Scoop*, Oct. 13, 1983, p. 2.

162 "Real good, huh": Henry Linkkila to Patricia Roy, Oct. 17, 1983.

163 "I so want": John Hudson to Lisa Hudson, Aug. 29, 1983.

163 "I say a prayer": John Hudson to Lisa Hudson, June 6, 1983.

163 "Enclosed with": John Hudson to Lisa Hudson, May 28, 1983.

163 "I have never": Hampson, Rick, "25 Years Later, Bombing in Beirut Still Resonates," *USA Today*, Oct. 18, 2008, p. 1.

163 "I know everyone": Bernadette Hearne, "Old Glory, Tears Honor Dead Marine," *Greensboro News & Record*, Nov. 6, 1983, p. 1B.

163 "I'm writing": Richard Blankenship to family, undated, Richard Blankenship Collection, MCHD.

164 "I just can't wait": "Family Loses Son in Beirut Tragedy," *Indiana Gazette*, Oct. 25, 1983, p. 6.

164 "I think I've lost": Bill Stelpflug to Peggy and William Stelpflug, Sept. 18, 1983, Bill Stelpflug Collection, MCHD.

164 "I think I'll take": Bill Stelpflug to Peggy and William Stelpflug, Oct. 19, 1983, ibid.

164 "I think I'll take": Bill Stelpflug to Kathy Stelpflug, October (no day listed) 1983, ibid.

164 "I'll know": Danny Wheeler interview, Jan. 19, 2023.

164 "Chaplain": Ibid.

165 "Marines greatly": CTF SIX TWO to CTF SIX ONE, 221700Z Oct. 83, in 24th MAU, Command Chronology, 1 October–31 October 1983, MCHD.

165 Lance Corporal: Interviews with Burnham Matthews (Dec. 29, 2022) and James Ware (Jan. 6, 2023).

165 "It occurred": Dolphin, *24 Mau*, p. 168.

165 Earle needed: Micheline Thompson interview, Nov. 6, 2023.

165 "Good night, Johnny": Danny Wheeler interview, Jan. 19, 2023.

165 "What up": Don Howell interview, Jan. 25, 2023.

CHAPTER 30

166 "Is the glorious": Lars-Erik Nelson, "Is It Worth American Blood?" *Daily News*, Oct. 19, 1983, p. 34.

166 "I was looking": Ronald Reagan, *An American Life* (New York: Simon & Schuster, 1990), p. 449.

166 Tensions had: Weinberger, *Fighting for Peace*, p. 101–13.

167 Amid this tension: Daily Diary of President Ronald Reagan, Oct. 21, 1983; Ronald Reagan diary, Oct. 21, 1983, in Reagan, *The Reagan Diaries*, p. 189.

167 "The operative": McFarlane, *Special Trust*, p. 261.

167 "The United States": Ibid., pp. 261–62.

167 "You're dead": Ibid., p. 262.

167 "Do it": Reagan, *An American Life*, p. 450.

167 At 9:31 a.m.: Daily Diary of President Ronald Reagan, Oct. 22, 1983.

167 "I know": Ed Magnuson, "D-Day in Grenada," *Time*, Nov. 7, 1983, pp. 22–28.

167 Reagan then hit: Reagan, *An American Life*, p. 452; Cannon, *President Reagan*, p. 442.

168 Charles Harris: William E. Schmidt, "Reagan Incident Figure Is Said to Be "Troubled," *New York Times*, Oct. 24, 1983, p. A14.

168 "Normally, I wouldn't": Reagan, *An American Life*, p. 452.

168 "This is Ronald": Francis X. Clines, "Reagan Unhurt as Armed Man Takes Hostages," *New York Times*, Oct. 23, 1983, p. A1.

168 "The man hung up: Reagan, *An American Life*, p. 452.

168 "One by one": Ronald Reagan diary, Oct. 21, 1983, in Reagan, *The Reagan Diaries*, p. 189.

CHAPTER 31

169 "It felt": "'Don't Leave Us,' Trapped Men Cry," *New York Times*, Oct. 24, 1983, p. A1.

169 The first light: Warren L. Nelson to File No. 83, "Visibility on Day of BLT Attack," Nov. 18, 1983, in *Review of Adequacy of Security Arrangements*, pp. 177–78.

169 "Saturday night": Geraghty, *Peacekeepers at War*, p. 91.

169 "Sunday is my": John Hudson to Lisa Hudson, July 23, 1983.

169 The Navy Broadcasting Service: Navy Broadcasting Service, Mobile Detachment One, Television Schedule, *Root Scoop*, Oct. 20, 1983, p. 7.

169 "Sunday was normally": Randy Gaddo, "Beirut Bombing," *Leatherneck*, February 1984, p. 16.

169 Gaddo was one: Randy Gaddo interview, Jan. 4, 2023.

170 "Life is dear": George Pucciarelli, "Chaplain's Corner," *Root Scoop*, Oct. 20, 1983, p. 3.

170 "The birds": Randy Gaddo remarks, "Memorial Day in Peachtree City," May 26, 2008.

170 "Your rifle": Burnham Matthews interview, Dec. 29, 2022.

170 "You don't know": Pablo Arroyo interview, Jan. 29, 2023.

171 Chaplain Wheeler: Interviews with Danny Wheeler (Jan. 19, 2023); Emanuel Simmons (Dec. 31, 2022); James Ware (Jan. 6, 2023); and Don Howell (Jan. 25, 2023).

171 Security that morning: Report of the Long Commission, pp. 94–99.

172 "That's the first": Kenny Farnan interview, Jan. 31, 2023.

172 Unlike earlier: Eddie DiFranco testimony, Nov. 13, 1983, in *Review of Adequacy of Security Arrangements*, pp. 307–26.

172 "I caught only": Eddie DiFranco handwritten report, undated (circa Oct. 23, 1983), Box 2, George Converse Collection, MCHD.

172 "I would have": Henry Linkkila testimony, Nov. 12, 1983, in *Review of Adequacy of Security Arrangements*, p. 168.

172 Sergeant of the Guard: Stephen Russell emails, Jan. 26–27, 2023, and Feb. 5, 2023.

173 *"What is that truck"*: Report of the Long Commission, p. 95.

173 "Get the fuck": Geraghty, *Peacekeepers at War*, p. 96.

173 "Hit the deck!": Report of the Long Commission, p. 95.

173 "I just watched": Kenny Farnan interview, Jan. 31, 2023.

173 "Son of a bitch": "Beirut Bombing 25 Years Later," *USA Today*, https://www.youtube.com/watch?v=XBSE0JndWeo.

173 The clock: Prepared Statement of John W. Hicks, Dec. 8, 1983, in *Review of Adequacy of Security Arrangements*, p. 399.

173 The blast: Ibid., pp. 398–99.

173 "The FBI": Report of the Long Commission, p. 99.

173 "It was like": Brad Ulick interview, Oct. 26, 2023.

174 "The building": Report of the Long Commission, p. 99.

174 "We saw the center": Joseph Martucci testimony, Dec. 8, 1983, in *Review of Adequacy of Security Arrangements*, p. 374.

174 "It's Beirut": Pablo Arroyo interview, Jan. 29, 2023.

174 "There is something": Burnham Matthews interview, Dec. 29, 2022.

174 "I turned around": Ibid.

174 "I was in the eye": Kenny Farnan interview, Jan. 31, 2023.

175 "It felt like": Don Howell interview, Jan. 25, 2023.

175 "I never heard": Emanuel Simmons interview, Dec. 31, 2022.

175 "I didn't hear anything": Danny Wheeler interview, Jan. 19, 2023.

CHAPTER 32

176 "Bodies—and pieces": Rabbi Arnold Resnicoff, undated report, Box 14, Peter M. Robinson Files, RRPL.

176 "Shards of glass": Geraghty, *Peacekeepers at War*, p. 91.

176 "What the hell": Ibid., p. 92.

176 "There were long": Dolphin, *24 Mau*, p. 171.

176 "Is everybody": Harry Slacum oral history with Benis Frank, Nov. 21, 1983, Box 3, Operations Other Than War: Beirut Oral History Transcripts, MCHD.

176 "God, you have": Ibid.

177 "I knew": Geraghty, *Peacekeepers at War*, p. 92.

177 "My God": Ibid.

177 "I can't explain": Timothy Geraghty oral history with Benis Frank, Nov. 21, 1983, Box 2, Operations Other Than War: Beirut Oral History Transcripts, MCHD.

177 "The BLT": Harry Slacum oral history with Benis Frank, Nov. 21, 1983.

177 "You won't believe": Ibid.

177 "It was deathly": Ibid.

177 "I heard no": Ibid.

177 The executive officer: ibid.

178 "My mind": Geraghty, *Peacekeepers at War*, p. 94.

178 "To buttress": Ibid.

178 "There must be": Dolphin, *24 Mau*, p. 172.

178 "Everything and everyone": Ibid.

178 "The BLT": Ibid.

CHAPTER 33

179 "I couldn't get": Danny Wheeler interview, Jan. 19, 2023.

179 "You have a choice": Pablo Arroyo interview, Jan. 29, 2023.

179 "When I looked": Nora Boustany, "Seven Years Later: Marine Nightmare from Beirut," *Washington Post*, Nov. 4, 1990, p. C4.

179 "I was so frustrated": Pablo Arroyo interview, Jan. 29, 2023.

180 "Dude": Ibid.

180 "It sucked": Kenny Farnan interview, Jan. 31, 2023.

CHAPTER 34

181 "This isn't combat": "Iran Group Takes Credit for Truck-Bombs Driven by 2 Suicide Terrorists," *Democrat and Chronicle*, Oct. 24, 1983, p. 1.

181 "It was just": Gilbert Bigelow interview, Jan. 25, 2023.

181 "God, what was": James Ware oral history with Jan Herman, André Sobocinski, and Karen Stokes, June 21, 2011.

181 "Is anybody hurt": Ibid.

181 "What's the walkie": Ibid.

181 "We think the BLT": Ibid.

182 "Jim, prepare": Ibid.

182 "I knew": Gilbert Bigelow interview, Jan. 25, 1983.

182 "Some of these": Ibid.

182 "All patients": James J. Ware to Commanding Officer 2D Dental Battalion 2D Force Service Support Group (REIN), "After Action—Report in Preparation of Triage for Mass Casualties, Medical Support and Personnel/Record Accountability for Victims of the Bombing at BLT Headquarters October 23, 1983," Dec. 3, 1983.

183 "Are you okay": James Ware oral history with Jan Herman, André Sobocinski, and Karen Stokes, June 21, 2011.

183 "At this point": Ware, "After Action," Dec. 3, 1983.

183 "*I wonder what*": James Ware oral history with Jan Herman, André Sobocinski, and Karen Stokes, June 21, 2011.

183 "*Holy shit*": James Ware interview, Jan. 6, 2023.

183 "My main concern": Ware, "After Action," Dec. 3, 1983.

183 "I had sectioned": James Ware oral history with Jan Herman, André Sobocinski, and Karen Stokes, June 21, 2011.

184 "I jumped around": Ibid.

184 "All morphine": Ware, "After Action," Dec. 3, 1983.

184 "His left arm": Dolphin, *24 Mau*, p. 175.

184 "I don't want": Ibid.

184 "I was convinced": Ibid.

184 "If you want": Ibid.

184 "His vacant": Ibid.

184 "They're dead": Brad Ulick interview, Oct. 26, 2023.

184 "My eye": Ibid.

184 "Some of these guys": Gilbert Bigelow interview, Jan. 25, 2023.

185 "His whole body": James Ware interview, Jan. 6, 2023.

185 "I could see": Ibid.

185 "It was a multi-ring": Ibid.

CHAPTER 35

186 "We just got": Mark Singleton interview, Dec. 21, 2022.

186 Commodore France: CTF SIX ONE to NMCC WASHINGTON DC, 230543Z Oct. 83, in 24th MAU, Command Chronology, 1 October–31 October 1983, MCHD.

186 "Extent of casualties": Ibid.

186 "Get up!": Richard Camp and Suzanne Pool-Camp, "'They Came in Peace,'" *VFW Magazine*, October 2019, p. 38.

186 "So what's new?": Anthony Pais interview, Dec. 29, 2022.

187 "There was nobody": Camp and Pool-Camp, "'They Came in Peace,'" p. 38.

187 "All I saw": Anthony Pais interview, Dec. 29, 2022.

187 On the ground: Geraghty, *Peacekeepers at War*, p. 97.

187 "You could smell": David Madaras interview, Feb. 4, 2023.

187 "Bodies were lying": "'Don't Leave Us,' Trapped Men Cry," *New York Times*, Oct. 24, 1983, p. A1.

187 "Get us out": Ibid.

187 "I glanced down": Petit, *Peacekeepers at War*, p. 157.

187 "There was a leg": Dolphin, *24 Mau*, p. 174.

188 "What the hell": Don Howell interview, Jan. 25, 2023

188 "All I felt": Emanuel Simmons interview, Dec. 31, 2022.

189 "I was angry": Danny Wheeler interview, Jan. 19, 2023.

190 "Follow me": Arnold Resnicoff interview, Jan. 2, 2023.

190 "I started giving": George Pucciarelli oral history with Benis Frank, Nov. 21, 1983, Box 3, Operations Other Than War: Beirut Oral History Transcripts, MCHD.

190 "There were bodies": Arnold Resnicoff interview, Jan. 2, 2023.

190 "Over here": George Pucciarelli oral history with Benis Frank, Nov. 21, 1983.

191 "Have we not": Rabbi Arnold Resnicoff, undated report, Box 14, Peter M. Robinson Files, RRPL.

191 "Well, we have": George Pucciarelli, "After the Beirut Bombing," *Proceedings*, January 1987, p. 64.

191 "In the midst": Ibid.

191 "Whatever you need": Geraghty, *Peacekeepers at War*, p. 99.

191 "I felt strongly": Ibid., pp. 99–100.

192 "There's someone alive": Petit, *Peacekeepers at War*, pp. 155–56.

192 "I hear you": Randy Gaddo interview, Jan. 4, 2023.

192 "It was literally": Geraghty, *Peacekeepers at War*, p. 113.

192 "There was a dying": Dolphin, *24 Mau*, p. 182.

193 "By the time": Brad Ulick interview, Oct. 26, 2023.

193 "All of a sudden": Randy Gaddo interview, Jan. 4, 2023.

193 "We tried to pull": Ibid.

193 "Many bodies": Geraghty, *Peacekeepers at War*, p. 100.

193 "To put it bluntly": Ibid.

193 "My first": Ibid.

193 *"Here lie"*: Ibid.

193 "I was trying": Danny Wheeler interview, Jan. 19, 2023.

194 Given the language: Harry Slacum oral history with Benis Frank, Nov. 21, 1983.

194 "The groans": Mark Singleton interview, Dec. 21, 2022.

194 "Once a blood": Dolphin, *24 Mau*, p. 180.

194 "I grasped": Ibid., p. 184.

195 "As the dead": Pucciarelli, "After the Beirut Bombing."

195 "We ran out": Geraghty, *Peacekeepers at War*, p. 101.

195 "I saw one man": "'Don't Leave Us,' Trapped Men Cry," *New York Times*, Oct. 24, 1983, p. A1.

195 "He was just": Dolphin, *24 Mau*, p. 177.

195 "There were a lot": David Zucchino, "In Shock: Marines Wake to Grisly Horror," *Philadelphia Inquirer*, Oct. 24, 1983, p. 1.

195 "Pooch and I": Rabbi Arnold Resnicoff, undated report, Box 14, Peter M. Robinson Files, RRPL.

195 "What is that purple": Danny Wheeler interview, Jan. 19, 2023.

196 "I didn't realize": Rabbi Arnold Resnicoff, undated report, Box 14, Peter M. Robinson Files, RRPL.

197 "Racked with pain": Ibid.

197 "My Marines": Danny Wheeler interview, Jan. 19, 2023.

197 "How many patients": James Ware oral history with Jan Herman, André Sobocinski, and Karen Stokes, June 21, 2011.

CHAPTER 36

198 "If you saw": "Reception Pleases Beirut Wounded," *Green Bay Press-Gazette*, Oct. 30, 1983, p. 1.

198 At 12:30 a.m.: Carla Hall and Lois Romano, "After the Alarm from Beirut, Scrambling to Pass the Word," *Washington Post*, Oct. 25, 1983, p. C1.

198 The two-story: John W. Finney, "Pentagon Permits a Glimpse of Ultra-Secret 'War Room,'" *New York Times*, July 10, 1976, p. 20.

198 "Dr. Strangelove": Ibid.

198 "Explosion at BLT": Frank, *U.S. Marines in Lebanon*, p. 94.

198 At the same time: Hall and Romano, "After the Alarm from Beirut, Scrambling to Pass the Word."

198 "As it became": Ibid.

199 "The news came": Colin L. Powell with Joseph E. Persico, *My American Journey* (New York: Ballantine Books, 1995), p. 290.

199 "I felt": McFarlane, *Special Trust*, p. 262.

199 "How could this": Ibid., p. 263.

199 "The role there": Martin Tolchin, "Key Questions in Tug-of-War on War Powers," *New York Times*, Sept. 3, 1983, p. 7.

199 "McFarlane argued": Juan Williams, "Reagan's Days Off Erupt in Crisis," *Washington Post*, Oct. 24, 1983, p. A14.

199 Reagan authorized: Ibid.

199 "Those sons": Robert Timberg, *The Nightingale's Song* (New York: Simon & Schuster, 1995), p. 337.

200 "Let's go back": McFarlane, *Special Trust*, p. 263.

200 "There was to be": Reagan, *An American Life*, p. 453.

200 At 6:34: Daily Diary of Ronald Reagan, Oct. 23, 1983.

200 "A somber": Speakes, *Speaking Out*, p. 165.

200 "I know": "Statement by the President on Bombings of Multi-National Forces in Lebanon," 8:38 a.m., Oct. 23, 1983, Box 15, Office of Media Relations, RRPL.

201 "Remind me": Weinberger, *Fighting for Peace*, p. 113.

201 The seven items: Meeting on Lebanon, Agenda, Oct. 23, 1983, Box 125, Executive Secretariat, NSC: Country File, RRPL; Daily Diary of President Ronald Reagan, Oct. 18, 1983.

201 "He was in a white": Oliver L. North with William Novak, *Under Fire: An American Story* (New York: HarperCollins, 1991), p. 198.

201 "Well make them": Ibid.

CHAPTER 37

202 "Pro-Iranian Lebanese": SSO DIA to INFO SSO DIA, 231935Z Oct. 83, "Lebanon Situation/DIA INTSUM 7 (as of 231600Z Oct. 83)," Box 126, Executive Secretariat, NSC: Country, RRPL.

202 In the offices: "A Letter from the Publisher," *Time*, Oct. 31, 1983, p. 2.

202 CBS claimed: Tom Shales, "On TV, Diffusing the Anger, Sharing the Grief," *Washington Post*, Oct. 25, 1983, C1.

202 "Such late breaking": "A Letter from the Publisher," *Time*, Oct. 31, 1983, p. 2.

202 "By 5:30 a.m.": Hall and Romano, "After the Alarm from Beirut, Scrambling to Pass the Word."

202 "In almost four": "A Letter from the Publisher," *Time*, Oct. 31, 1983, p. 2.

203 "This is the latest": "Magazines Delay Press Run," *New York Times*, Oct. 25, 1983, p. A10.

203 "This is big": Shales, "On TV, Diffusing the Anger, Sharing the Grief."

203 Word likewise: Hall and Romano, "After the Alarm from Beirut, Scrambling to Pass the Word."

203 "We should not leave": T. R. Reid and Helen Dewar, "Hill Urges New Look at Mission," *Washington Post*, Oct. 25, 1983, p. A1.

CHAPTER 38

204 "We are no longer": Bob Dart, "Nunn Wants a U.N. Force to Replace Marines," *Atlanta Constitution*, Oct. 24, 1983, p. 8A.

204 Deputy Press Secretary: Speakes, *Speaking Out*, pp. 3–117; Michael Shear, "Larry Speakes, Public Face of Reagan Era, Dies at 74," *New York Times*, Jan. 10, 2014, p. A12.

204 Since the days: Don Oberdorfer, "Plushier Place for White House Press," *Washington Post*, April 3, 1970, p. B1.

204 "This is better": Don Oberdorfer, "Nixon Shows LBK New Press Room," *Washington Post*, April 7, 1970, p. A4.

205 "The information": All subsequent quotations in this chapter come from "Press Briefing by Larry Speakes," transcript, 9:15 a.m., Oct. 23, 1983, Box 15, Office of Media Relations, RRPL.

CHAPTER 39

207 "We have put": U.S. Congress, House, *Hearing Before a Subcommittee of the Committee on Appropriations, Situation in Lebanon and Grenada*, 98th Cong., 1st Sess. (Washington, DC: U.S. Government Printing Office, 1983), p. 8.

207 At the same time: Lesley Stahl, *Reporting Live* (New York: Touchstone, 1999), pp. 178–80; Lou Cannon and Juan Williams, "U.S. May Station Many Offshore," *Washington Post*, Oct. 24, 1983, p. A1.

207 "We're awfully": Stahl, *Reporting Live*, pp. 178–80.

208 "Can't we do": Crist, *The Twilight War*, p. 140.

208 "I almost wept": Stahl, *Reporting Live*, p. 179.

208 "I was very well": Weinberger, *Fighting for Peace*, pp. 116–17.

208 "Mr. Secretary": All subsequent quotations in this chapter come from "SECDEF Appearance on 'Face the Nation,'" transcript, Oct. 23, 1983, Box 126, Executive Secretariat, NSC: Country File, RRPL.

CHAPTER 40

210 "The volume": Patrick Hutton interview, Jan. 27, 2023.

210 With a deck: "Welcome Aboard, USS Iwo Jima (LPH 2)," undated pamphlet (circa September 1982–February 1984) distributed to embarked Marines, Jeremiah Walsh Collection, MCHD.

210 "It is": "Welcome Aboard, USS Iwo Jima (LPH 2)," undated pamphlet (circa January 1981–September 1982) distributed to embarked Marines, Box 1, Grant McIntosh Collection, MCHD.

210 Like any city: Eric R. Frykberg, Patrick M. J. Hutton, and Richard H. Balzar Jr., "Disaster in Beirut: An Application of Mass Casualty Principles," *Military Medicine* 152 (November 1987): 563–66; CTF SIX ONE to COMSIXTHFLT, 071100Z Nov. 83, Box 22, George Converse Papers, MCA.

210 "The wisdom": Ibid., p. 564.

211 "You always": Frazier Henderson interview, Jan. 23, 2023.

211 "My mission": Ibid.

211 That plan: Report of the Long Commission, p. 108.

211 "Everyone knew": Frazier Henderson interview, Jan. 29, 2023.

211 "Each of the wounded": Zachary S. Hubbard, Fraser Henderson Jr., Rocco A. Armonda, Alejandro M. Spiotta, Robert Rosenbaum, and Fraser Henderson Sr., "The Shipboard Beirut Terrorist Bombing Experience: A Historical Account and Recommendations for Preparedness in Events of Mass Neurological Injuries," *Neurosurgical Focus* 45 (December 2018): 1–7.

211 "Identification was": Frazier Henderson interview, Jan. 29, 1983.

212 "There were": Hubbard et al., "The Shipboard Beirut Terrorist Bombing Experience."

212 "All of them": Frazier Henderson interview, Jan. 29, 1983.

212 The sixty-five: Frykberg et al., "Disaster in Beirut"; Report of the Long Commission, p. 109.

212 Of that total: Brett A. Scott, J. Raymond Fletcher, Morris W. Pulliam, and Robert D. Harris, "The Beirut Terrorist Bombing," *Neurosurgery* 18, no. 1 (January 1986): 107–10.

212 "Am I going": Patrick Hutton interview, Jan. 27, 2023.

213 "The idea": Ibid.

213 "I talked": Ibid.

213 "Keep your head": Frazier Henderson interview, Jan. 29, 2023.

213 "Everyone was just": Ibid.

213 "Nobody was yelling": Mauricio Aparicio interview, Jan. 26, 2023.

213 "I woke up": John L'Heureux interview, Jan. 26, 2023.

213 "While I was": Michael Toma, "Reflections on My Service," June 28, 2016, https://marines.togetherweserved.com/usmc/servlet/tws.webapp. WebApp?cmd=ShadowBoxReflectionProfile&type=Person&ID=5445.

213 "Tell the guys": Emanuel Simmons interview, Dec. 31, 2022.

213 Starting at 12:30 p.m.: Report of the Long Commission, p. 108.

214 "Patient was judged": CTF SIX ONE to COMSIXTHFLT, 071100Z Nov. 83, Box 22, George Converse Papers, MCA.

214 At 2:21 p.m.: Report of the Long Commission, p. 108.

214 "Pablo, I thought": Nora Boustany, "Seven Years Later: Marine Nightmare from Beirut," *Washington Post*, Nov. 4, 1990, p. C4.

214 "Did he make it": Don Howell interview, Jan. 25, 2023.

CHAPTER 41

215 "Beirut was just": Gilbert Bigelow interview, Jan. 25, 2023.

215 "All of the rescuers": Geraghty, *Peacekeepers at War*, p. 104.

215 "During the day": Dolphin, *24 Mau*, p. 188.

215 "The energy": Gilbert Bigelow interview, Jan. 25, 2023.

215 The thirty reported: The escalating numbers can be found in the message traffic included with the 24th MAU, Command Chronology, 1 October–31 October 1983, MCHD.

215 "I've got to": James Ware interview, Jan. 6, 2023.

216 Workers placed: Interviews with Brad Ulick (Oct. 26, 2023) and John Snyder (Jan. 18, 2023).

216 Over it all: Petit, *Peacekeepers at War*, p. 160.

216 "Mom, I put": Brad Ulick to Marilyn Peterson, Oct. 26 (circa), 1983.

216 "Elusive": Thomas L. Friedman, "Elusive Targets: Peacekeepers Become Another Warring Faction," *New York Times*, Oct. 23, 1983, p. E1.

216 "This is incredible": Fisk, *Pity the Nation*, p. 513.

216 "This was": Ibid.

216 From that day: 24th MAU, Command Chronology, 1 October–31 October 1983, MCHD.

216 "We let them": Randy Gaddo interview, Jan. 4, 2023.

217 "The men are": "'Get Us Out . . . Don't Leave Us,'" *Arizona Republic*, Oct. 24, 1983, p. 1.

217 "How does this": Randy Gaddo interview, Jan. 4, 2023.

217 "I only wish": David Zucchino, "In Shock: Marines Wake to Grisly Horror," *Philadelphia Inquirer*, Oct. 24, 1983, p. 1.

217 "We're speaking": Ibid.

217 "Some of the .45s": Dolphin, *24 Mau*, p. 197.

217 "loose ends": Zucchino, "In Shock: Marines Wake to Grisly Horror."

217 "When you picked": Mark Singleton interview, Dec. 21, 2022.

217 "Bastards": "Marine Death Toll at 183," *Philadelphia Daily News*,
    Oct. 24, 1983, p. 3.
217 A similar story: Zucchino, "In Shock: Marines Wake to Grisly Horror."
218 "What beasts": Ibid.
218 "You motherfuckers": Dolphin, *24 Mau*, p. 183.
218 Father Pucciarelli: George Pucciarelli oral history with Benis Frank,
    Nov. 21, 1983.
218 "It's like salt": John Dalziel interview, April 19, 2023.
218 Naval dental technician: Paul Dziadon interview, Jan. 20, 2023.
218 "Lieutenant": James Ware oral history with Jan Herman, André Sobocinski,
    and Karen Stokes, June 21, 2011.
218 "He was a hero": Ibid.
218 "The smell": Petit, *Peacekeepers at War*, pp. 163–64.
219 "I am all right": Arnold Resnicoff to Barbara Resnicoff, Oct. 23, 1983.
219 "Every time": Brad Ulick interview, Oct. 26, 2023.
219 "I saw enough": Paul Dziadon interview, Jan. 20, 2023.
219 "Are you okay": Petit, *Peacekeepers at War*, p. 165.

CHAPTER 42
220 "Jesus, why": Brad Ulick diary, Oct. 24, 1983.
220 "The assessment": All quotations in this chapter come from "Press Briefing by
    Larry Speakes," transcript, 11:13 a.m., Oct. 23, 1983, Box 15, Office of Media
    Relations, RRPL.

CHAPTER 43
222 "No reason": Molly Markert to Ronald Reagan, Oct. 25, 1983, #175803,
    WHORM Subject File: ND 016, RRPL.
222 "If there was": Helen Dewar, "Congress Expects a Bitter Tangle Over U.S.
    Troops in Lebanon," *Washington Post*, Oct. 24, 1983, p. A1.
222 "The role": Ibid.
222 "What are": Steven V. Roberts, "Legislators Say Reagan Must Reassess U.S.
    Role," *New York Times*, Oct. 24, 1983, p. A8.
222 "People say": W. Dale Nelson, "Congress Moves to Reopen Peacekeeping
    Force Debate," *Tampa Tribune*, Oct. 24, 1983, p. 4A.
222 After finishing: Daily Diary of President Ronald Reagan, Oct. 23, 1983.
223 "issues bearing": National Security Planning Group, Agenda, Oct. 23, 1983,
    Box 2, Executive Secretariat, NSC: NSPGs, RRPL.
223 Even after more: Withdrawal Sheet, File Folder NSDD 109/111, Lebanon and
    Middle East, Box 1, Philip Dur Files, RRPL.
223 "Our best judgement": "Talking Points for the DDCI," Oct. 23, 1983, https://
    www.cia.gov/readingroom/docs/CIA-RDP85T00287R000801160001-7.pdf.
223 "principally responsible": Ibid.
223 "There is also": Ibid.
223 "The French": SSO DIA to [Redacted], 230802Z Oct. 83, "DIA Spot Report,"
    Box 125, Executive Secretariat, NSC, Country File, RRPL.

223 "We all believe": Ronald Reagan diary, Oct. 22–23, 1983, in Reagan, *The Reagan Diaries*, p. 190.

224 "We need": Crist, *The Twilight War*, p. 141.

224 "It must be": Ibid.

224 "We must show": Ibid.

224 "The Director": National Security Decision Directive Number 109, "Responding to the Lebanon Crisis," Oct. 23, 1983, Box, 10, Executive Secretariat, NSC: NSDDs, RRPL.

224 "Vaya con Dios": Frank, *U.S. Marines in Lebanon*, p. 101.

CHAPTER 44

225 "What is Mr. Reagan": "Voice of the People: Differing Views on U.S. Actions," *Akron Beacon Journal*, Oct. 28, 1983, p. A4.

225 Just like in the wake: Multiple such examples can be found in various files at the Reagan Library.

225 The African nation: AMEMBASSY LOME to SECSTATE WASHDC, 241329Z Oct. 83, "Togolese Government Declares Period of Mourning," Box 126, Executive Secretariat, NSC: Country File, RRPL.

225 "A feeling of great": "Pope Expresses 'Horror' at Beirut Bomb Attacks," *Daily News*, Oct. 24, 1983, p. 4.

225 A few leaders: David C. Wills, *The First War on Terrorism: Counter-Terrorism Policy During the Reagan Administration* (New York: Rowman & Littlefield, 2003), p. 65.

225 "We should not": AMEMBASSY CAIRO to SECSTATE WASDC, 261143Z Oct. 83, "Lebanon-Message from President Mubarak to President Reagan," Box 60, Executive Secretariat, NSC: Cable File, RRPL.

225 "Only a political": Helmet Kohl to Ronald Reagan, Oct. 24, 1983, #175758, WHORM Subject File: ND 016, RRPL.

226 As of 4 p.m.: Anne Higgins to Ronald Reagan via Dick Darman, "Incoming Telephone Calls and Telegrams," Oct. 23, 1983, Box 75, Anne Higgins Files, RRPL.

226 "My son": Ibid.

226 "The tragedy": Mr. and Mrs. Thomas O'Hara to Ronald Reagan, Oct. 23, 1983, ibid.

226 "Don't you think": James Cobb to Ronald Reagan, Oct. 23, 1983, ibid.

226 "Stop the politics": Ron Rackley to Ronald Reagan, Oct. 23, 1983, ibid.

226 "Please bring": Mrs. Love to Ronald Reagan, Oct. 23, 1983, ibid.

CHAPTER 45

227 "It is plain": "Beirut Outrage Requires New Look at U.S. Role," editorial, *Buffalo News*, Oct. 24, 1983, p. B2.

227 "If you're just": Mark Wolf, "Time of Bombing Gave TV Coverage a Slow Start," *Charlotte Observer*, Oct. 24, 1983, p. 9A.

227 "Don't turn": Lisa Hudson interview, Feb. 10, 2023.

228 "I couldn't watch": Jim Gallagher, "Fearful Families of Marines Wait, Pray," *Pittsburgh Post-Gazette*, Oct. 24, 1983, p. 1.

228 "I'm nuts": John Froonjian, "S.J. Families Wait, Hope," *Press*, Oct. 24, 1983, p. 1.

228 "Every time": Janet Kelley, "Mother Waits in Fear for Stranger Who May Bring News of Her Son," *Lancaster New Era*, Oct. 24, 1983, p. 1.

228 "You're afraid": Thomas Tolliver, "Waiting Is Hard," *Lexington Herald-Leader*, Oct. 24, 1983, p. A7.

228 "I know I won't": "Families Wait by the Phone for Sons' Calls from Beirut," *St. Petersburg Times*, Oct. 24, 1983, p. 11A.

228 NBC interrupted: Tom Shales, "On TV, Diffusing the Anger, Sharing the Grief," *Washington Post*, Oct. 25, 1983, p. C1.

228 "It's those kinds": Valeria M. Russ, "A Mother Prays 'for All the Boys,'" *Philadelphia Daily News*, Oct. 24, 1983, p. 4.

229 "Just send some": "Families Across U.S. Await Word of Relatives in Blast," *Spokane Chronicle*, Oct. 24, 1983, p. 1.

229 "That's my son!": Thomas Moran, "Family Says Photo Is of Local Marine," *Poughkeepsie Journal*, Oct. 24, 1983, p. 1.

229 "Every hour": Debbie M. Price and Valerie M. Russ, "Back Home, No News Is Good News," *Philadelphia Daily News*, Oct. 24, 1983, p. 4.

229 "No news": David Maraniss, "Marines Bring Painful News to Relatives of Beirut Victims," *Austin American-Statesman*, Oct. 24, 1983, p. A5.

229 Once collected: David Goeller, "Officers Beginning Grim Duty," *Paducah Sun*, Oct. 24, 1983, p. A2.

229 "Not since": "Messengers of Death Notify the Survivors," *Daily Herald*, Oct. 24, 1983, p. 2.

229 "The initial": Goeller, "Officers Beginning Grim Duty."

229 At the same: Bill Krueger and Joan Oleck, "Camp Lejeune Mourns Slain Marines," *News and Observer*, Oct. 24, 1983, p. 1; Michael Hirsley, "'300 to 400' Marines on Way to Lebanon," *Chicago Tribune*, Oct. 24, 1983, p. 6; "Grim but Ready, Marine Replacements Leave U.S.," *San Francisco Examiner*, Oct. 24, 1983, p. 5.

230 "We have a mission": "Marine Replacements Move Out as Families Wait for Word," *Birmingham Post-Herald*, Oct. 24, 1983, p. A7.

230 "If we were barbaric": Dennis Patterson, "'If We Were Barbaric, We Could Defend Against This Sort of Thing,'" *Fort Myers News-Press*, Oct. 24, 1983, p. 8A.

CHAPTER 46

231 "We are dealing": Jo Mannies, "Area Congressmen Say U.S. Role in Lebanon Should Be Restudied," *St. Louis Post-Dispatch*, Oct. 24, 1983, p. 12A.

231 "One thing is clear": All quotations in this chapter come from "Press Briefing by Larry Speakes," transcript, 7:06 p.m., Oct. 23, 1983, Box 15, Office of Media Relations, RRPL.

CHAPTER 47

233 "It was total": Kathy Kiely, "Grisly Beirut Scene Haunts Murtha," *Pittsburgh Press*, Oct. 30, 1983, p. A20.

233 "It is a long": "Bomb Toll in Lebanon Almost 200," *Cincinnati Inquirer*, Oct. 25, 1983, p. 1.

233 "Marines are performing": CTF SIX TWO to CTF SIX ONE, 24031Z Oct. 83, in 24th MAU, Command Chronology, 1 October–31 October 1983, MCHD.

233 "Many of the bodies": Dan Williams, "191 Americans Dead; Iranian Link Pursued," *Miami Herald*, Oct. 25, 1983, p. 1.

233 "One of them": David Zucchino, "The Face of Death Was Smiling," *Philadelphia Inquirer*, Oct. 25, 1983, p. 11A.

234 "At 12:03 p.m.": Ibid.

234 "Give that": Ibid.

234 "It was hopeless": George Pucciarelli, "After the Beirut Bombing," *Proceedings*, January 1987, p. 64.

234 "You knew": Anthony Pais interview, Dec. 29, 1983.

234 "I came across": Ibid.

234 "Put it in the bag": Ibid.

235 "Marines on their": Williams, "191 Americans Dead; Iranian Link Pursued."

235 *"How ironic"*: Petit, *Peacekeepers at War*, p. 166.

235 "Today, it's slowed": Zucchino, "The Face of Death Was Smiling."

235 "The task": Petit, *Peacekeepers at War*, p. 170.

235 "I don't know how": Ibid.

235 "It was that kind": David Zucchino, "Base Security Tightens in Grim U.S. Concession," *Philadelphia Inquirer*, Oct. 25, 1983, p. 1.

235 "We thought": Ibid.

235 "We took every": Williams, "191 Americans Dead; Iranian Link Pursued."

236 "We were too": Ibid.

236 That was the case: CTF SIX TWO to COMSIXTHFLT, 241855Z Oct. 83, in Beirut, Lebanon CD Collection, Messages and General Correspondence for October 1983, MCHD.

236 "Mood of the troops": Ibid.

236 "I realized": Dolphin, *24 Mau*, p. 198.

236 "For an officer": Ibid., 195.

236 A similar recovery: James MacManus, "Lebanon Factions Deplore Bombing," *Guardian*, Oct. 25, 1983, p. 1.

236 President François Mitterrand: John Vinocur, "Mitterrand Visits Beirut Barracks," *New York Times*, Oct. 25, 1983, p. A14; William Claiborne, "Beirut Rubble Yields Victims," *Washington Post*, Oct. 25, 1983, p. A1.

236 "His eyes": Geraghty, *Peacekeepers at War*, pp. 107–8.

237 "When the presidential": Ibid., p. 108.

237 "That has to be": Brad Ulick to Marilyn Peterson, Oct. 26 (circa), 1983.

237 "As the pallet": Pucciarelli, "After the Beirut Bombing."

237 "This never": Petit, *Peacekeepers at War*, p. 169.

237 "The frantic": Ibid., p. 171.

CHAPTER 48

238 "I would simply": General P. X. Kelley, "Departure from Andrews AFB," Oct. 24, 1983, #181975, WHORM Subject File: ND 016, RRPL.

238 "I'd just like": Ibid.

238 "I was not": Geraghty, *Peacekeepers at War*, pp. 109–10.

238 "Lord": Ibid., p. 110.

238 Of the sixty-eight: Tyler Marshall, "Many of Wounded Not Told of Deaths of Their Buddies," *Los Angeles Times*, Oct. 25, 1983, p. 14.

239 At 7 a.m.: "Marine Pins Purple Heart Medals on Wounded Troops," *Journal Tribune*, Oct. 25, 1983, p. 3.

239 "Depressed left": CDR LARMC LANDSTHUL GERMANY to RHDLCNE / CINCUSNAVEUR LONDON UK, 241646Z Oct. 83, "Report of Injury/Admittance Landstuhl Army Hosp Germany," in Beirut, Lebanon CD Collection, Messages and General Correspondence for October 1983, MCHD.

239 "Ruptured spleen": CBF CYPRUS to US CINCEUR VAIHINGEN GE, 231600Z Oct. 1983, in ibid.

239 "Respiratory failure": CDR LARMC LANDSTHUL GERMANY to RHDLCNE / CINCUSNAVEUR, 241646Z Oct. 83.

239 The Air Force: "Injured Marine Clings to Motto," *Miami Herald*, Oct. 26, 1983, p. 1.

239 "We're gonna": Ibid.

239 "No, sir": Ibid.

239 "I was just": Ibid.

239 "The next thing": "For Semper Fi, the Purple Heart," *Omaha World-Herald*, Oct. 25, 1983, p. 25.

239 The general paused: Nora Boustany, "Seven Years Later: Marine Nightmare from Beirut," *Washington Post*, Nov. 4, 1990, p. C4.

240 "He held": "Injured Marine Clings to Motto," *Miami Herald*, Oct. 26, 1983, p. 1.

240 The general presented: Eve Zibart, "'Semper Fi' Marine Gets a General's Stars," *Washington Post*, Nov. 16, 1983, p. A1.

240 "When I left": Ibid.

CHAPTER 49

241 "This is a": Harold Jackson, "Pentagon Faces Renewed Congressional Opposition," *Guardian*, Oct. 24, 1983, p. 1.

241 "There's no decision": "Press Briefing by Larry Speakes," transcript, 9:30 a.m., Oct. 24, 1983, Box 119, White House Office of Speech Writing, RRPL.

242 Elsewhere in the White House: Daily Diary of President Ronald Regan, Oct. 23, 1983.

242 "Good afternoon": All subsequent quotations in this chapter, unless otherwise noted, come from "Remarks of the President at Luncheon with Regional Editors and Broadcasters," Oct. 24, 1983, Box 15, Records of the Office of Media Relations, RRPL.

244 "We deplore": SECSTATE WASHDC to RUFHFR/AMEBAMSSY PARIS, 240509Z Oct. 83, "President's Letter on Beirut Bombings," Box 126, Executive Secretariat, NSC: Country File, RRPL.

244 "Our assumption": AMEBAMSSY PARIS to SECSTATE WASHDC, 241517Z Oct. 83, "Attack on US and French MNF Contingents: Initial French Reaction," Box 125, Executive Secretariat, NSC: Country File, RRPL.

244 "pale and somber": Vinocur, "Mitterrand Visits Beirut Barracks."

244 "I say to everyone": Ibid.

244 "For our part": "Talking Points for Call to President Mitterrand," undated, Box 125, Executive Secretariat, NSC: Country File, RRPL

PART III

245 "All of a sudden": ABC News transcript, Oct. 23, 1987, Box 2, Grant McIntosh Collection, MCHD.

CHAPTER 50

247 "Our Marines": John Vessey interview with Thomas Saylor, Feb. 16, 2013, Concordia University, St. Paul, Minn.

247 "There is no clear": Steven V. Roberts, "Legislators Say Reagan Must Reassess U.S. Role," *New York Times*, Oct. 24, 1983, p. A8.

247 A small group: Steven V. Roberts, "Some Democrats Want Marines Out," *New York Times*, Oct. 25, 1983, p. A16.

247 "Our troops": Judith Bender and Myron S. Waldman, "Capitol Full of Doubts," *Newsday*, Oct. 25, 1983, p. 5.

247 "If we run": T. R. Reid and Helen Dewar, "Hill Urges New Look at Mission," *Washington Post*, Oct. 25, 1983, p. A1.

247 "This must not": Bender and Waldman, "Capitol Full of Doubts."

247 "I wouldn't want": Reid and Dewar, "Hill Urges New Look at Mission."

247 "If you're smart": Roberts, "Some Democrats Want Marines Out."

248 "We are in Lebanon": Secretary Shultz, "The Situation in Lebanon," Oct. 24, 1983, Current Policy No. 520, Box 8, Department of State Publications, RRPL.

248 "Even the most": U.S. Congress, Senate, *The Situation in Lebanon, Hearings Before the Committee on Armed Services*, 98th Cong., 1st Sess., Oct. 25 and 31, 1983 (Washington, DC: U.S. Government Printing Office, 1983), p. 14.

248 "I'm sure": "2 N.J. Congressmen Question if Marines Belong in Lebanon," *Asbury Park Press*, Oct. 25, 1983, p. A7.

248 "Shame on us": Mike Feinsilber, "Reagan Vows Marines Will Stay in Beirut," *Tampa Tribune*, Oct. 25, 1983, p. 1.

248 "The president needs": "Security of Marines Challenged," *Asbury Park Press*, Oct. 25, 1983, p. A7.

249 "We must not": Edward Kennedy, "The Wanton Terrorist Attack," *Congressional Record*, 98th Cong., 1st sess., Oct. 24, 1983, p. 29015.

249 "The pattern": "U.S. Considers Transferring Troops to Offshore Positions," *Miami Herald*, Oct. 25, 1983, p. 9A.

249 "It was not": Douglas Turner, "Area Democrats Rap Marines' Security," *Buffalo News*, Oct. 25, 1983, p. A10.

249 "Tragically": "Excerpts from Editorials on the Bombing of Marine Headquarters in Beirut," *New York Times*, Oct. 25, 1983, p. A15.

249 "Whatever comes": Ibid.

249 "For a power": Ibid.

249 "We are caught": Ibid.

249 "abandonment": "What Lebanon Wants of U.S.," *U.S. News & World Report*, Nov. 7, 1983, p. 28.

249 "These men": Amin Gemayel, "Lebanon: After the Bombing," *Washington Post*, Oct. 30, 1983, p. C8.

250 Reagan's repeated: Director of Central Intelligence, National Intelligence Daily, Oct. 28, 1983, https://www.cia.gov/readingroom/docs/CIA-RDP85T01094R000500020035-2.pdf.

250 "We are not afraid": AMEMBASSY BEIRUT to RUEHC/SECSTATE WASHDC, "Marine Bombing: Reactions from Iranians and Hussein Musawi," Oct. 28, 1983, Box 60, Executive Secretariat, NSC: Cable File, RRPL.

250 Druze militia leader: William Claiborne, "French Suffer at Least 26 Dead," *Washington Post*, Oct. 24, 1983, p. A1.

250 "I do not want": AMEMBASSY TEL AVIV to RUEHBL/AMEMBASSY BEIRUT, "McFarlane/Fairbanks Mission: Meeting with Nabih Berri," Oct. 24, 1983, Box 60, Executive Secretariat, NSC: Cable File, RRPL.

250 Reporters even: Tom Infield, "Beirut Bombing Was a 'Good Deed,'" *Philadelphia Inquirer*, Oct. 28, 1983, p. 8A.

250 His Hezbollah colleague: Matthew Levitt, *Hezbollah: The Global Footprint of Lebanon's Party of God* (Washington, DC: Georgetown University Press, 2013), p. 28.

250 "I bow": "Muslim Radical Blesses Attack," *Philadelphia Daily News*, Oct. 28, 1983, p. 36.

250 "My prayers": James Hickey to Ronald Reagan, Oct. 23, 1983, #175773, WHORM Subject File: ND 016, RRPL.

250 "You are doing": John Chedid to Ronald Reagan, Oct. 24, 1983, #175777, WHORM Subject File: ND 016, RRPL.

250 "I have been": Robert McNeil to Ronald Reagan, Oct. 24, 1983, #182339, WHORM Subject File: ND 016, RRPL.

250 "There are no words": Robert Wilbraham to Ronald Reagan, Oct. 26, 1983, #176017, WHORM Subject File: ND 016, RRPL.

251 "Please, I beg": Robert Harris to Ronald Reagan, Oct. 24, 1983, #176047, WHORM Subject File: ND 016, RRPL.

251 "Urge that you": Thomas Rotondo, Jr., to Ronald Reagan, Oct. 23, 1983, #175767, WHORM Subject File: ND 016, RRPL.

251 "Do something": John Zampieri to Ronald Reagan, Oct. 24, 1983, #8334351, WHORM Subject File: ND 016, RRPL.

251 "Bring our men": Terry Fewell to Ronald Reagan, Oct. 25, 1983, #175804, WHORM Subject File: ND 016, RRPL.

251 "looked exhausted": Hedrick Smith, "A President Under Siege," *New York Times*, Oct. 25, 1983, p. A1.

251 "The grieving": Douglas W. Chamberlain to Ronald Reagan, Oct. 28, 1983, #176305, WHORM Subject File: ND 016, RRPL.

CHAPTER 51

252 "I want someone": "Families Await News of Death or Survival," *Tyler Morning Telegraph*, Oct. 26, 1983, p. 7.

252 As of 8 a.m.: "Pentagon Releases Partial List of Servicemen Who Survived," *Tampa Tribune*, Oct. 27, 1983, p. 13A.

252 "The doorbell": Lisa Hudson interview, Feb. 10, 2023.

252 "I deeply regret": David Harlow to Lisa Hudson, Oct. 26, 1983.

252 Under pressure: "Pentagon Plans List of Marines Who Escaped in Beirut Blast," *Omaha World-Herald*, Oct. 27, 1983, p. 4.

252 In Beirut: "Bombing Survivors Ordered to Write to Their Loved Ones," *Boston Globe*, Oct. 27, 1983, p. 2.

253 The Marine Corps: "Calls Pour Into Marine Hotline," *Omaha World-Herald*, Oct. 27, 1983, p. 4.

253 "A notification": "Families' Agonizing Wait Goes On," *Palm Beach Post*, Oct. 27, 1983, p. 8A; "Crackpot Calls Add to Marine Families' Woes," *Tampa Tribune*, Oct. 27, 1983, p. 13A.

253 "I am worse": Ibid.

253 "For two days": Ibid.

253 "Most people": Patricia O'Brien and Joyce Gemperlein, "An Old Agony of War with Some Brutal New Twists," *Philadelphia Inquirer*, Oct. 26, 1983, p. 20A.

253 "Once I saw": Arax, Mark, and Robert Hilson Jr., "A Marine's Mother Learns That Bad News Comes in Person," *Tampa Tribune*, Oct. 27, 1983, p. 13A.

254 "That whole week": Richard Wells interview, Jan. 30, 2023.

254 "This will make": Hunt Helm and Bill Powell, "Dreaded News Comes to Louisville Mother; Others Wait and Hope," *Courier-Journal*, Oct. 25, 1983, p. 1.

254 "You just sit here": Thomas Harper, "Some Families Wait, For Others the Waiting Is Over," *Missoulian*, Oct. 25, 1983, p. 2.

254 "We got our": Ibid.

254 "As soon as I": Ibid.

254 "I don't want": "Sorrow for Some, Relief for Others," *Courier-Post*, Oct. 25, 1983, p. 3A.

254 "Are you here": "Kin Fear Messages of Death," *Cincinnati Inquirer*, Oct. 26, 1983, p. A2.

254 "The cease-fire": "Marines' Families Can Only Wait for Word," *Detroit Free Press*, Oct. 25, 1983, p. A.

254 "I'm getting closer": "Crackpot Calls Add to Marine Families' Woes," *Tampa Tribune*, Oct. 27, 1983, p. 13A.

255 "As far as": Helm and Powell, "Dreaded News Comes to Louisville Mother."

255 "I feel my son": "The Longest Wait," *Journal Tribune*, Oct. 25, 1983, P. 3.

255 "This service": "AT&T Opens Phone Lines for Marines," *Omaha World-Herald*, Oct. 27, 1983, p. 4.

255 "We all screamed": Jack Warner, "Families Grieve for Beirut Dead," *Press-Tribune*, Oct. 27, 1983, p. 1.

CHAPTER 52

256 "I have seen": David Madaras to Ann and Charles Madaras, Oct. 24, 1983.

256 "I had a bad": Karen E. Henderson, "Widow of Slain Sailor Fights to Remain in U.S.," *Plain Dealer*, Oct. 23, 1984, p. 8A.

256 "Why I kept": ABC News transcript, Oct. 23, 1987, Box 2, Grant McIntosh Collection, MCHD.

256 Unidentifiable papers: TWO FOUR MAU to CG FMFLANT, 260927Z Oct. 83, "Return of Destroyed/Damaged Equip and Personal Effects," in Beirut, Lebanon CD Collection, Messages and General Correspondence for October 1983, MCHD.

256 "I want to see": James Ware interview, Jan. 6, 2023.

257 "What do you": James Ware oral history with Jan Herman, André Sobocinski, and Karen Stokes, June 21, 2011.

257 "He had been": James Ware interview, Jan. 6, 2023.

257 "Where is he?": James Ware oral history with Jan Herman, André Sobocinski, and Karen Stokes, June 21, 2011.

257 "I wanted": Ibid.

257 "Hopefully our long": John Hudson to Lisa Hudson, Oct. 20, 1983.

257 Many focused: Timothy J. McNulty, "Marine Retells 4-Floor Ride Over Death, Fire," *Sun-Sentinel*, Oct. 25, 1983, p. 10A.

258 "Everything started": "Thousands Cried, 'God Help Us . . . ,'" *Charlotte News*, Oct. 25, 1983, p. 7.

258 "Help me!": Ibid.

258 "His words": David Zucchino, "The Face of Death Was Smiling," *Philadelphia Inquirer*, Oct. 25, 1983, p. 11A.

258 "I remember objects": "Wounded Give Account of Beirut Attack," *Fort Myers News-Press*, Oct. 27, 1983, p. 10A.

258 "It was a cheap": John Tagliabue, "Wounded Marines Tell of Ordeal That Was Beirut," *New York Times*, Oct. 27, 1983, p. A9.

258 "You gotta": "3 Survivors Feared Car Bombs, but Felt Security at Headquarters Was Adequate," *Tampa Tribune*, Oct. 27, 1983, p. 13A.

258 "You can't fight": "Marines Say Attack Threat Was Constant," *Kansas City Times*, Oct. 27, 1983, p. 1.

258 "I stayed": "'I Heard the Sentry; Then It All Blew Up,'" *Pittsburgh Press*, Oct. 27, 1983, p. 1.

258 "Paranoia is high": Brad Ulick diary, Oct. 29, 1983.

259 "What is death?": "Marines in Beirut Think of Revenge," *Scrantonian*, Oct. 30, 1987, p. A2.

259 "I just thank": Jane P. Shoemaker, "From the Confusion, Vivid Memories," *Philadelphia Inquirer*, Oct. 27, 1983, p. 19A.

259 "I am not ashamed": David Madaras to Ann and Charles Madaras, Oct. 24, 1983.

259 "I cried": Petit, *Peacekeepers at War*, p. 174.

259 "I have seen": Grant McIntosh to Janice McIntosh, Oct. 26, 1983, Box, 1, Grant McIntosh Collection, MCHD.

259 "I broke": Ibid.

259 "I've vowed": Henry Linkkila to Patricia Roy, Nov. 8, 1983 (postmark date).

259 "Boy": John Dalziel to Rosie and Rod Dalziel, Oct. 30, 1983.

CHAPTER 53

260 "Just once": "Readers Angered by Terrorists' Bombing of Marines in Lebanon," *Sacramento Bee*, Oct. 28, 1983, p. B11.

260 "The stench": Kathy Kiely, "Grisly Beirut Scene Haunts Murtha," *Pittsburgh Press*, Oct. 30, 1983, p. A20.

260 "You could see": Ibid.

260 "There is nothing": Dan Williams, "Marines on Alert Amid Worries of Repeat Bombing," *Miami Herald*, Oct. 26, 1983, p. 15A.

260 "This morning": Edward Hickey to James Baker, Michael Deaver, and Robert McFarlane, Oct. 27, 1983, Box 125, Executive Secretariat, NSC: Country File, RRPL.

261 In a top-secret: Frank Libutti oral history with Benis Frank, Feb. 7, 1984, Box 3, Operations Other Than War: Beirut Oral History Transcripts, MCHD.

261 "Reagan thought": P. X. Kelley to Ronald Reagan, "Visit to Beirut, 25–26, 1983," Nov. 2, 1983, Box 10, Executive Secretariat, NSC: NSDDs, RRPL.

261 "In my professional": Ibid.

262 In addition to Kelly's: COMSIXTHFLT to CINCUSNAVEUR LONDON UK, 260800Z Oct. 83, in Beirut, Lebanon CD Collection, Messages and General Correspondence for October 1983, MCHD; Geraghty, *Peacekeepers at War*, pp. 115–16.

263 "as one of my": George H. W. Bush, *All the Best, George Bush: My Life in Letters and Other Writings* (New York: Scribner, 2013), p. 330.

263 At 7:16 a.m.: CTF SIX ONE to NMCC WASHINGTON DC, 261427Z Oct. 83, and CTF SIX ONE to COMSIXTHFLT, 272330Z Oct. 83," both in Beirut, Lebanon CD Collection, Messages and General Correspondence for October 1983, MCHD.

263 "I hadn't expected": "Bush: Terrorist Won't Shift U.S. Mideast Policy," *Tampa Tribune*, Oct. 27, 1983, p. 1.

263 "analysis of things": George Bush to Ronald Reagan, "Visit to Gemayel in Lebanon," Oct. 26, 1983, in Bush, *All the Best*, pp. 330–31.

263 "The prospects": William Casey to James Baker, Oct. 26, 1983, with excerpt from the Special National Intelligence Estimate, "Prospects for Lebanon," Box 125, Executive Secretariat, NSC: Country File, RRPL.

264 "You are going": Geraghty, *Peacekeepers at War*, p. 117.

264 "I didn't blink": Ibid.

264 "Key leadership": CTF SIX ONE to COMSIXTHFLT, 292215Z Oct. 83,

"Commander's Weekly SITREP," in Beirut, Lebanon CD Collection, Messages and General Correspondence for October 1983, MCHD.

264 Workers hauled: Prepared Statement of John W. Hicks, Dec. 8, 1983, in *Review of Adequacy of Security Arrangements*, p. 398.

264 The oblong-shaped: Ibid., p. 399.

264 "A reinforced": Ibid.

265 "Ho!": Petit, *Peacekeepers at War*, p. 180.

CHAPTER 54

266 "Whether Bill": Bill and Kaye Gaines to Ronald Reagan, Oct. 26, 1983, Box 75, Anne Higgins Files, RRPL.

266 "It was": Harry Rosenthal, "Reagan's Week: Series of Crises," *News/Sun-Sentinel*, Oct. 30, 1983, p. 1.

266 A White House tally: Tally Sheet, Major Issues (Mail), October 21 thru October 27, 1983, Box 75, Anne Higgins Files, RRPL.

266 "As far as I": A. E. Jones III to Ronald Reagan, Nov. 2, 1983, #202605, WHORM Subject File: ND 016, RRPL.

266 "They killed": Kenneth Ellison to Ronald Reagan, undated, Box 75, Anne Higgins Files, RRPL.

267 "When Joseph": Susan A. Ray to Ronald Reagan, Jan. 31, 1984, #209193, WHORM Subject File: ND 016, RRPL.

267 "I wonder": Joseph Milano to Angela and Peter Milano, undated, in Jackowski and Stelpflug, eds., *Voices from Beirut*, p. 78.

267 "Our grief": Francine Minutoli to Ronald Reagan, Oct. 31, 1983, Box 75, Anne Higgins Files, RRPL.

267 "The American people": Newt Gingrich to Ken Duberstein, "Explaining a Violent World to the American People," Oct. 25, 1983, #183642, WHORM Subject File: ND 016, RRPL.

267 "Recent events": Charles Hill to Robert McFarlane, "Presidential Speech on Lebanon and Grenada," Oct. 26, 1983, Box 101, Executive Secretariat, NSC: Subject File, RRPL.

268 Rather than fall: Ronald Reagan diary, Oct. 27, 1983, in Reagan, *The Reagan Diaries*, p. 191.

268 "If you can": Peter Goldman and Tony Fuller, *The Quest for the Presidency* (New York: Bantam Books, 1985), pp. 29–30.

268 On October 27: Daily Diary of President Ronald Reagan, Oct. 27, 1983.

268 "This past Sunday": "Text of an Address by the President to the Nation," Oct. 27, 1983, Box 15, Office of Media Relations, RRPL.

270 In the thirty-five: Larry Speakes to Ronald Reagan, Oct. 27, 1983, Box 45, Michael Deaver Files, RRPL.

270 By midnight: "President's Speech Receives Strong Support," undated, Box 10, Michael Baroody Files, RRPL.

270 "A powerful": Ibid.

270 "His finest": Ibid.

270 "Masterful": Ibid.

270 "I have an idea": White House News Summary, "CBS Commentary After President Reagan's Televised Address," Oct. 28, 1983, Box 10, Michael Baroody Files, RRPL.

271 "I think I'd put": Ibid.

271 An ABC News poll: "President's Speech Receives Strong Support," undated, Box 10, Michael Baroody Files, RRPL.

271 A later joint: Barry Sussman, "Reagan's Talk Gains Support for Policies," *Washington Post*, Oct. 10, 1983, p. A1.

271 That was more: Mark Mayfield, "'Great Communicator' Rallies USA," *USA Today*, Oct. 31, 1983, in Box 10, Michael Baroody Files, RRPL.

271 "The public feels": Jeffrey D. Alderman, "After Reagan Speech Public Supports Grenada Invasion; Lebanon Also Viewed More Positively," ABC News/Washington Post Poll, Oct. 15-28, 1983, Box 10, Michael Baroody Files, RRPL.

271 "Prolonging": "The Reagan Administration," *Evans-Novak Political Report*, Nov. 1, 1983, p. 2.

271 "Get out": "Why Lebanon," editorial, *Miami Herald*, Oct. 31, 1983, p. 12A.

271 "We fear": "The President's Message," editorial, *Los Angeles Times*, Oct. 28, 1983, p. 6.

272 "The president hears": "A Traumatic Week for the United States," editorial, *Minneapolis Tribune*, Oct. 30, 1983, p. 22A.

272 The president: Daily Diary of President Ronald Reagan, Oct. 28–29, 1983.

272 "The Comments Office": Peter Roussel to Larry Speakes, "Summary Regarding Speech Reaction," Oct. 31, 1983, Box 10, Michael Baroody Files, RRPL.

CHAPTER 55

273 "There is no": Paul Kelley testimony, Oct. 31, 1983, in U.S. Congress, Senate, *The Situation in Lebanon, Hearings Before the Committee on Armed Services*, 98th Cong., 1st Sess., Oct. 25 and 31, 1983 (Washington, DC: U.S. Government Printing Office, 1983), p. 91.

273 The first C-141: Don Singleton, "16 Marines Decorated with Tears," *Daily News*, Oct. 30, 1983, p. 5.

273 Officials at Dover: Fraser C. Smith, "At Dover Air Force Base, the Fallen Will Return with Honor," *Baltimore Sun*, Oct. 27, 1983, p. 2A; Joe Starita, "U.S. Soldiers Killed in Blast Return to U.S.," *Miami Herald*, Oct. 30, 1983, p. 23A; Jeffrey W. Peters, "Dover AFB Prepares for Grim Task," *Evening Star*, Oct. 26, 1983, p. 1.

273 The initial casualty: After Action Report, "Lebanon Bombing Casualty Handling Procedures," undated, Jeremiah Walsh Collection, MCHD.

273 The first thirty seven: "Air Force Transport Flies Bodies to West Germany for Identification," *Macon Telegraph and News*, Oct. 25, 1983, p. 9A.

273 Officials decided: After Action Report, "Lebanon Bombing Casualty Handling Procedures," undated.

274 "Teeth are the most": Robert Sundquist interview, Aug. 28, 2023.

274 "Some of them": Ibid.

274 "At this time": HQ USAFE RAMSTEIN AB GE to SECDEF WASH DC, 271345Z Oct. 83, "Beirut Killed in Action (KIA) SITREP 002," in Beirut, Lebanon CD Collection, Messages and General Correspondence for October 1983, MCHD.

275 "When the validator": After Action Report, "Lebanon Bombing Casualty Handling Procedures," undated.

275 "Ninety six percent": Ibid.

275 For the Jonestown: Starita, "U.S. Soldiers Killed in Blast Return to U.S."

275 The plan called: After Action Report, "Lebanon Bombing Casualty Handling Procedures," undated.

276 "Most were deteriorated": Ibid.

276 "Blessed are": Singleton, "16 Marines Decorated with Tears."

276 "We stand in awe": Ibid.

276 "We share": Starita, "U.S. Soldiers Killed in Blast Return to U.S."

276 "I salute": Singleton, "16 Marines Decorated with Tears."

276 "This cowardly": Starita, "U.S. Soldiers Killed in Blast Return to U.S."

CHAPTER 56

277 "Personally": John Dalziel to Rosie and Rod Dalziel, Oct. 28, 1983.

277 At 8:11 a.m.: Daily Diary of President Ronald Reagan, Nov. 4, 1983.

278 "We love": Larry King, "Town That Loves Marines Shares in Their Courage," *Greensboro News & Record*, Oct. 30, 1983, p. 1.

278 In the wake: John Monk, "Lejeune Community Waits, Worries" *Charlotte Observer*, Oct. 26, 1983, p. 1.

278 Symbols of support: King, "Town That Loves Marines Shares in Their Courage."

278 "This tragedy": "Tragedy Unites Marine Community," *Durham Sun*, Oct. 31, 1983, p. 3C.

278 "Good morning": David Hoffman, "Day of Grief," *Washington Post*, Nov. 5, 1983, p. A1.

278 "The Lord": Ibid.

278 "As I say": Jerry Allegood and Joan Oleck, "Reagan Consoles Marine Families," *News and Observer*, Nov. 5, 1983, p. 1.

278 "Where is my": Hoffman, "Day of Grief"; Francis X. Clines, "Reagan at Camp Lejeune," *New York Times*, Nov. 5, 1983, p. 1.

279 "It was a dreary": Ronald Reagan diary, Nov. 4, 1983, in Reagan, *The Reagan Diaries*, p. 194.

279 "It was": Speakes, *Speaking Out*, p. 166.

279 "You have a most": Allegood and Oleck, "Reagan Consoles Marine Families."

279 "No words": "Excerpts of the President's Remarks to the Families of the Victims of Lebanon and Grenada," Nov. 4, 1983, Box 15, Office of Media Relations, RRPL.

279 "They were so": Ronald Reagan diary, Nov. 4, 1983, in Reagan, *The Reagan Diaries*, p. 194.

279 "This has been": Hoffman, "Day of Grief."

279 "Freedom is being": "Remarks of the President to Cherry Point Marine Corps Air Station Personnel and Families," Nov. 4, 1983, Box 15, Office of Media Relations, RRPL.

CHAPTER 57

280 "I pray to God": Brad Ulick to Marilyn Peterson, Oct. 26 (circa), 1983.

280 "The community": "Death of 2 Marines Hit Small Town Hard," *Bucyrus Telegraph-Forum*, Nov. 8, 1983, p. 2.

280 "He's passed": "Services Console Service Families," *Bremerton Sun*, Nov. 3, 1983, p. 40.

280 "Don't let": "Marine Victim Buried at Indiantown Gap Cemetery," *Indiana Gazette*, Nov. 3, 1983, p. 29.

281 "With faith": Dave Goodwin, "Marines Bury Fallen Comrade," *Pensacola Journal*, Dec. 3, 1983, p. 1C.

281 His wedding ring": Micheline Thompson interview, Nov. 6, 2023.

281 "I know": Karen E. Henderson, "Medics Marriage a Mystery, *Plain Dealer*, Oct. 27, 1983, p. 1.

281 "I will pray": Karen E. Henderson, "Bride, Mother Weep at Rites for Navy Medic," *Plain Dealer*, Nov. 11, 1983, p. 5B.

281 "Oh, John": Lisa Hudson interview, Feb. 10, 2023.

282 "Bless your": Don Schanche Jr., "Bomb Victim, Widow Questioned U.S. Role," *Macon Telegraph and News*, Nov. 7, 1983, p. 1.

282 On November 6: John Lancaster, "Navy Doctor Buried Near Home," *Atlanta Journal*, Nov. 7, 1983, p. 1E.

282 "You're going": Lisa Hudson interview, Feb. 10, 2023.

282 "We are hurting": Don Schanche Jr., "Mourners Fill Church," *Macon Telegraph and News*, Nov. 7, 1983, p. 1.

282 "He was a musician": Lancaster, "Navy Doctor Buried Near Home."

282 "There were several": Ibid.

282 Beneath a clear: Ibid.

CHAPTER 58

283 "Our country": Thomas L. Friedman, "Lebanese Warned 'Country Is Dying,'" *New York Times*, Nov. 1, 1983, p. 1A."

283 "We expect": "Marines in Beirut Tighten Security," *Cincinnati Enquirer*, Nov. 4, 1983, p. A14.

283 "The precise": Cal Openshaw, "24th MAU Commander Reflects on Wake of BLT Bombing, Charges Members to Carry On," *Root Scoop*, Nov. 3, 1983, p. 1.

283 "My commendation": George Pucciarelli, "Chaplain's Corner," *Root Scoop*, Nov. 3, 1983, p. 2.

283 A flood: Harry Slacum oral history with Benis Frank, Nov. 21, 1983.

283 "Your courage": "Letters from Concerned People Continue to Flow into Beirut," *Root Scoop*, Nov. 3, 1983, p. 2.

283 "We are proud": Ibid.

284 "I only know": Hugh Hawthorne, "Larry Byrd Warms Up to Marine Fans," *Root Scoop*, Nov. 17, 1983, p. 7.

284 "I've started": John Dalziel to Rosie and Rod Dalziel, Nov. 13, 1983.

284 "Marines who had served": Dolphin, *24 Mau*, p. 212.

284 "To Uncle Mike": Glenn Frankel, "'Fishbowl' Outpost," *Washington Post*, Nov. 10, 1983, p. A1.

284 "You can't dwell": Ibid.

284 "The move left": Dolphin, *24 Mau*, p. 213.

285 "We all got": John Dalziel to Rosie and Rod Dalziel, Nov. 8, 1983.

285 "Once the gear": John Dalziel to Rosie and Rod Dalziel, Nov. 3, 1983.

285 "In many ways": Dolphin, *24 Mau*, p. 218.

285 "I'm choking": Thomas L. Friedman, "Beirut, the City of Despair," *New York Times*, Nov. 28, 1983, p. A1.

285 "As each day": Ibid.

285 "I'll never": Dolphin, *24 Mau*, p. 222.

285 "I knew that once": Ibid.

CHAPTER 59

286 "The lives": Robert Guilford, "The Marines' Deaths: Grief, Outrage, and Doubt," letter to the editor, *Miami Herald*, Oct. 31, 1983, p. 12A.

286 More than a half: McFarlane, *Special Trust*, p. 270.

286 "undertake extraordinary": Ibid.

286 "Weinberger and Vessey": Teicher, *Twin Pillars to Desert Storm*, p. 264.

286 "Let's go after": Robert L. Pfaltzgraff Jr. and Jacquelyn K. Davis, eds., *National Security Decisions: The Participants Speak* (Lexington, MA: Lexington Books, 1990), p. 309.

286 "Subject to reasonable": National Security Decision Directive Number 111, "Next Steps Toward Progress in Lebanon and the Middle East," Oct. 28, 1983, Box, 10, Executive Secretariat, NSC: NSDDs, RRPL.

287 "We believe": Dur, *Between Land and Sea*, p. 210.

287 "Bien sur": Ibid.

287 "I left that meeting": Ibid., p. 211.

287 "If there ever": James Lyons Jr., testimony, March 17, 2003, trial transcript, in Deborah D. Peterson, et al., vs. the Islamic Republic of Iran, et al., p. 55.

287 In his office: Martin and Walcott, *Best Laid Plans*, p. 136; Crist, *The Twilight War*, p. 143.

287 "We believe": Ronald Reagan diary, Nov. 7, 1983, in Reagan, *The Reagan Diaries*, p. 194.

288 "I'm not": Martin and Walcott, *Best Laid Plans*, pp. 137–38.

288 Reagan met: Crist, *The Twilight War*, p. 144.

288 "Began the day": Ronald Reagan diary, Nov. 8–9, 1983, in Reagan, *The Reagan Diaries*, p. 197.

288 "I knew": Martin and Walcott, *Best Laid Plans*, p. 137.

288 "It was": McFarlane, *Special Trust*, p. 270.

288 "We have some": Ronald Reagan diary, Nov. 14, 1983, in Reagan, *The Reagan Diaries*, p. 197.

288 "Several times": George C. Wilson, *Supercarrier: An Inside Account of Life Aboard the World's Most Powerful Ship, the USS John F. Kenney* (New York: Macmillan, 1986), pp. 122–23.

288 Admiral Tuttle: Martin and Walcott, *Best Laid Plans*, p. 138.

289 "I don't understand": McFarlane, *Special Trust*, pp. 270–71.

289 "absurd": Weinberger, *Fighting for Peace*, p. 161.

289 "The president": Crist, *The Twilight War*, p. 147.

289 France went ahead: Thomas L. Friedman, "French Jets Raid Bases of Militia Linked to Attacks," *New York Times*, Nov. 18, 1983, p. A1; Crist, *The Twilight War*, p. 145.

289 "abject failure": Crist, *The Twilight War*, p. 148.

289 "Today's air raids": Friedman, "French Jets Raid Bases of Militia Linked to Attacks."

289 "There are still": John M. Goshko and Fed Hiatt, "A Similar Reprisal by U.S. Is Unlikely," *Washington Post*, Nov. 17, 1983, p. A1.

289 "In view": Robert McFarlane to George Shultz, Caspar Weinberger, William Casey, and John Vessey Jr., "Countering Terrorist Attacks Against U.S. Forces and Facilities in Lebanon," Nov. 22, 1983, Box 10, Executive Secretariat, NSC: NSDDs, RRPL.

290 "I was despondent": Dur, *Between Land and Sea*, p. 212.

290 So, too, was Teicher: Teicher, *Twin Pillars to Desert Storm*, pp. 266–68.

290 "Weinberger, for his": McFarlane, *Special Trust*, p. 271.

290 "They woke up": Wilson, *Supercarrier*, p. 123.

290 "Our intelligence": Reagan, *An American Life*, pp. 463–64.

CHAPTER 60

291 "I firmly believe": Paul Kelley testimony, Nov. 1, 1983, in *Review of Adequacy of Security Arrangements*, p. 24.

291 The House: Unless otherwise noted, all quotations in this chapter come from the above-cited congressional transcript.

291 "The delegation": U.S. Congress, House, *Beirut Tragedy: "A New Crowd in Town" and Beirut Casualties: Care and Identification, Report Together with Supplemental Views of the Delegation to Beirut of the Committee on Armed Services and Committee on Veterans' Affairs*, 98th Cong., 1st sess. (Washington, DC: U.S. Government Printing Office, 1983), p. 4.

300 "While the subcommittee": U.S. Congress, House, *Adequacy of U.S. Marine Corps Security in Beirut: Summary of Findings and Conclusions* (hereafter *Summary of Findings and Conclusions*), *Report of the Investigations Subcommittee of the Committee on Armed Services*, 98th Cong., 1st sess., Dec. 19, 1983 (Washington, DC: U.S. Government Printing Office, 1983), p. 1.

300 "Colonel Geraghty": U.S. Congress, House, *Adequacy of U.S. Marine Corps Security in Beirut* (hereafter *Adequacy of U.S. Marine Corps Security in Beirut*), *Report Together with Additional and Dissenting Views of the Investigations Subcommittee of the Committee on Armed Services*, 98th Cong., 1st sess., Dec. 19, 1983 (Washington, DC: U.S. Government Printing Office, 1983), p. 47.

300 "Visits by higher": *Summary of Findings and Conclusions*, p. 1.

300 "While of necessity": Ibid.

301 "The solution": Ibid., p. 3.

301 "Does the success": *Adequacy of U.S. Marine Corps Security in Beirut*, p. 69.

301 The subcommittee voted: Margaret Shapiro, "House Unit Faults U.S. Security in Oct. 23 Bombing," *Washington Post*, Dec. 20, 1983, p. A1.

301 "Only with hindsight": *Adequacy of U.S. Marine Corps Security in Beirut*, p. 77.

CHAPTER 61

302 "The systematic": Report of the Long Commission, p. 127.

302 "You know": Robert Long oral history with Paul Stillwell, March 5, 1993, U.S. Naval Institute, Annapolis, Md.

302 "Weinberger made it": Ibid.

303 "The Commission": Unless otherwise noted, all quotations in this chapter come from the Report of the Long Commission.

304 "Why did you": Robert Long oral history with Paul Stillwell, March 5, 1993.

305 "I don't think": Ibid.

305 "scarcely veiled": "Mr. Reagan's Responsibility," editorial, *Washington Post*, Dec. 29, 1983, p. A16.

306 "The completion": Robert Long to Caspar Weinberger, "Letter of Transmittal," Dec. 20, 1983, Box 4, National Security Affairs, Assistant to the President for: Chron Files, RRPL.

306 "bombshell": Weinberger, *Fighting for Peace*, p. 163.

306 "The commission's findings": Ibid., pp. 163–64.

306 "It will result": Caspar Weinberger to Ronald Reagan, "Long Commission Report on October 23 Bombing," Dec. 23, 1983, Box 4, Donald R. Fortier Files, RRPL.

306 Thirty minutes: Philip Taubman, "Pentagon Delays Publishing Report on Beirut Attack," *New York Times*, Dec. 24, 1983, p. 1.

306 "It's clear": Ibid.

307 "long and corrosive": Robert McFarlane to Ronald Reagan, "Long Commission Report," undated, Box 4, National Security Affairs, Assistant to the President for: Chron Files, RRPL.

307 "We do not expect": "Statement by the President on the Long Commission Report on Lebanon," Dec. 27, 1983, Box 15, Office of Media Relations, RRPL.

308 To further minimize: Philip Taubman, "Intelligence Cited," *New York Times*, Dec. 29, 1983, p. A1; "No Copies Issued to Public," *New York Times*, Dec. 29, 1983, A. 14.

308 "Pentagon Blasts": "Pentagon Blasts Policy on Beirut," *Chicago Tribune*, Dec. 29, 1983, p. A.

308 "Report Hits": Fred Hiatt, "Report Hits U.S. Reliance on Force in Lebanon," *Washington Post*, Dec. 29, 1983, p. A1.

308 "Pentagon Report": Fred Hoffman, "Pentagon Report Could Be Reagan Liability," *Santa Cruz Sentinel*, Dec. 29, 1983, p. A8.

308 Many newspapers: "Excerpts from Pentagon Report on Beirut Bombing," *Los Angeles Times*, Dec. 29, 1983, p. 11; "The Findings of the Inquiry into the Beirut Bombing," *Philadelphia Inquirer*, Jan. 1, 1984, p. 4F.

308 Democratic representative: "Congresswoman Calls for Weinberger's Ouster," *Enterprise*, Dec. 28, 1983, p. 1; "O'Neill Reassessing 18-Month Pullout for Beirut Marines," *Atlanta Constitution*, Dec. 30, 1983, p. 2A.

308 "The president": "Roth Has Restated Lebanon Position," *News Journal*, Jan. 2, 1983, p. A6.

308 "The Marines": "O'Neill Calls for Meeting to Review Lebanon Role," *Newsday*, Dec. 30, 1983, p. 3.

308 "The Beirut bombing": "The Lesson of the Beirut Bombing," editorial, *Wichita Eagle-Beacon*, Dec. 30, 1983, p. 2B.

308 "He should not": Sara Fritz and Karen Tumulty, "Some of Marine Victims' Kin Grow Bitter," *Los Angeles Times*, Dec. 30, 1985, p. 1.

CHAPTER 62

309 "Day by day": Anthony Lewis, "Deeper and Deeper," *New York Times*, Dec. 15, 1983, p. A31.

309 The *Austin*: Jerry Allegood, "Marines' Return from Beirut Duty Is 'Like Christmas,'" *News and Observer*, Dec. 8, 1983, p. 1.

309 "Sometimes it seems": Dale Russakoff, "Marines Come Home in Joy and Sorrow," *Washington Post*, Dec. 8, 1983, p. A1.

309 On the pier below: Allegood, "Marines' Return from Beirut Duty Is 'Like Christmas,'" p. 1.

309 "We just wanted": "1,700 Marines Return from Lebanon to Rousing Welcome," *Winston-Salem Journal*, Dec. 8, 1983, p. 1.

309 "It's him!": Russakoff, "Marines Come Home in Joy and Sorrow."

310 "Let's go ashore!": John Monk, "This Time, Tears at Camp Lejeune Flow from Joy," *Charlotte Observer*, Dec. 8, 1983, p. 1.

310 At 10:41 a.m.: Ibid.

310 "I've never been": Mark Singleton interview, Dec. 21, 2022.

310 "To be back home": William E. Schmidt, "A Hero's Welcome for Beirut Troops," *New York Times*, Dec. 8, 1983, p. A1.

310 "Hello, mom": "Beirut Peacekeepers Welcomed Home," *Post*, Dec. 8, 1983, p. A18.

310 Despite Reagan's acceptance: Fred S. Hoffman, "Weinberger May Order Review of Beirut Officers," *Newsday*, Jan. 1, 1984, p. 2.

310 "nonpunitive letters": Fred Hiatt, "2 Rebukes Ordered in '83 Attack," *Washington Post*," Feb. 9, 1983, p. A1; John F. Lehman Jr., *Command of the Seas* (New York: Charles Scribner's Sons, 1988), p. 325.

310 Two days after": Geraghty, *Peacekeepers at War*, pp. 121, 137.

310 "Although this letter": John Lehman to Timothy J. Geraghty, Administrative Letter, Feb. 8, 1984, in ibid., pp. 163–64.

310 He had spent: Louise Carroll, "Howard 'Larry' Gerlach Survived the Beirut Bombing," *Ellwood City Ledger*, July 13, 2015, https://www.ellwoodcityledger

.com/story/lifestyle/around-town/2015/07/13/howard-larry-gerlach-survived
-beirut/18646615007/#.

311 Gerlach was: Geraghty, *Peacekeepers at War*, p. 164.

CHAPTER 63

312 "Perhaps the greatest": Thomas L. Friedman, "A Government and a Policy Fall
Victim to Inconsistency," *New York Times*, Feb. 19, 1984, p. E1.

312 On December 3: Wilson, *Supercarrier*, p. 126.

312 This prompted: Ronald Reagan diary, Dec. 3–4, 1983, in Reagan, *The Reagan
Diaries*, p. 202.

312 "If you are shot": Wilson, *Supercarrier*, p. 127.

312 The strike: Ibid., pp. 127–39; David B. Ottaway, "Syrians Down Two Planes in
Lebanon," *Washington Post*, Dec. 5, 1983, p. A1.

312 "SAMS! SAMS!": Wilson, *Supercarrier*, p. 139.

313 Commander Edward: Ibid., pp. 140–42.

313 "I found rage": Ibid., p. 144.

313 On December 14: Joseph B. Treaster, "Battleship's Guns Shell Syrian Sites in
Lebanese War," *New York Times*, Dec. 15, 1983, p. A1.

313 "Everything was shaking": "Battleship Shells Syrian Strongholds," *Buffalo
News*, Dec. 14, 1983, p. 1.

313 "We are trying": "Democrats Back Pullout," *Press Democrat*, Feb. 1, 1984, p. 1.

313 "He may be": Lou Cannon and David Hoffman, "Troop Move Was Decided a
Week Ago," *Washington Post*, Feb. 9, 1984, p. A1.

313 "Lebanon is not": "Reagan Suggests O'Neill Seeks Lebanon Surrender," *Los
Angeles Times*, Feb. 4, 1984, p. 3.

313 Other ideas: "Non Paper: Next Steps in Lebanon," undated, Box 125,
Executive Secretariat, NSC: Country File, RRPL.

314 "We must avoid": "Lebanon: Hedging Our Bets and Constructing an Outcome
We Can Live With," undated, Box 4, Donald R. Fortier Files, RRPL.

314 "This is consistent": Caspar Weinberger to Ronald Reagan, "Next Steps in
Lebanon," Dec. 30, 1983, Box 125, Executive Secretariat, NSC:
Country File, RRPL.

314 "Virtually all": "Non Paper: Next Steps in Lebanon," undated, Box 125,
Executive Secretariat, NSC: Country File, RRPL.

314 Polls showed: Barry Sussman, "Criticism of Foreign Policy Growing,"
Washington Post, Jan. 20, 1984, p. 1.

314 "How long": Richard Reeves, *Ronald Reagan: The Triumph of Imagination* (New
York: Simon & Schuster, 2005), p. 198.

314 "The solution": "Bad Scene in Beirut," editorial, *Los Angeles Times*, Jan. 5, 1984, p. 6.

314 "It is time": "Facing Lebanon," editorial, *Miami Herald*, Jan. 26, 1984, p. 28A.

314 Three former: Gene Grabowski, "CIA Alumni: Withdraw Marines,"
Philadelphia Inquirer, Jan. 2, 1984, p. 8A.

314 "The worst": Ibid.

314 The eight Democratic: Oswald Johnson, "Mondale Wants Marines Out of
Lebanon," *Los Angeles Times*, Jan. 1, 1984, p. 5.

314 This came: Nora Boustany, "U.S. Marine Is Killed in Beirut Attack," *Washington Post*, Jan. 9, 1984, p. A1; Bradley Graham, "1 Marine Killed, 3 Wounded," *Washington Post*, Jan. 31, 1984, p. A1.

314 In what no doubt: Rick Atkinson, "Jackson Scores Coup in Damascus Mission," *Washington Post*, Jan. 4, 1984, p. A1.

314 Faced with this: Ronald Reagan diary, Jan. 26, 1984, in Reagan, *The Reagan Diaries*, p. 215.

314 "We were": Martin and Walcott, *Best Laid Plans*, p. 147.

315 "Bud, what is": Cannon, *President Reagan*, p. 453.

315 For days: Cannon and Hoffman, "Troop Move Was Decided a Week Ago."

315 "The situation": "Radio Address to the Nation on the Budget Deficit, Central America, and Lebanon," Feb. 4, 1983, https://www.reaganlibrary.gov/archives/speech/radio-address-nation-budget-deficit-central-america-and-lebanon.

315 "Panic gripped": Bradley Graham, "Militiamen Seize Much of City," *Washington Post*, Feb. 7, 1984, p. A1.

315 "It's a living hell": "Capital Is in Chaos," *New York Times*, Feb. 7, 1984, p. A1.

315 In a blow: David Ignatius, "Lebanon Cabinet Quits, Spurring Concern in U.S.," *Wall Street Journal*, Feb. 6, 1984, p. 3.

315 Lebanon's army: Bradley Graham, "Beirut Split as Militias Press Gains," *Washington Post*, Feb. 8, 1984, p. A1.

315 "In the streets": David Zucchino, "Amid Terror and Chaos, West Beirut Changes Hands," *Philadelphia Inquirer*, Feb. 8, 1984, p. 1.

315 "It was just a helpless": Ernest Van Huss oral history with Benis Frank, May 21, 1984, Box 4, Operations Other Than War: Beirut Oral History Transcripts, MCHD.

315 "It was an intolerable": Martin and Walcott, *Best Laid Plans*, p. 149.

315 On February 7: Don Oberdorfer and Fred Hiatt, "Reagan Says Troops to Relocate Offshore," *Washington Post*, Feb. 8, 1984, p. A1.

316 "We don't consider": Cannon and Hoffman, "Troop Move Was Decided a Week Ago."

316 "Napoleon's Redeployment": Robert Fisk, "'If We Take Fire . . . We're Gonna Return It': How a Peacekeeping Force Took Sides," in Anthony McDermott and Kjell Skjelsbaek, eds., *The Multinational Force in Beirut, 1982–1984* (Miami: Florida International University Press, 1991), p. 181.

316 "Those who conduct": "Text of President's Statement on Redeployment of Marines," *New York Times*, Feb. 8, 1984, p. A9.

316 "The president has recognized": Steven V. Roberts, "Redeployment of Marines Is Praised," *New York Times*, Feb. 8, 1984, p. A11.

316 "Moving them out": Ibid.

316 "The work": Ernest Van Huss oral history with Benis Frank, May 21, 1984.

316 Aided by seventy-four: Frank, *U.S. Marines in Lebanon*, pp. 129–31.

316 "I'm ready to go": Herbert H. Denton, "Marines Frustrated at Not Fulfilling Their Mission in Lebanon," *Washington Post*, Feb. 22, 1984, p. A16.

316 "There's no hope": Ibid.

317 The British left: Michael Dobbs, "British Leave Beirut; French, Italians Stay," *Washington Post*, Feb. 9, 1984, p. A1; Thomas L. Friedman, "Italians Complete Lebanon Pullout," *New York Times*, Feb. 21, 1984, p. A1.

317 "No more wounded": William Claiborne, "Marines Complete Withdrawal," *Washington Post*, Feb. 27, 1984, p. A1.

317 "This place is crazy": Ibid.

317 "They were the only": Ibid.

317 "Get in there!": Thomas L. Friedman, "Marines Complete Beirut Pullback; Moslems Move In," *New York Times*, Feb. 27, 1984, p. A1.

317 "Goodbye, folks": Ibid.

318 "They sent us to Beirut": Thomas L. Friedman, "America's Failure in Lebanon," *New York Times*, April 8, 1984, SM32.

318 Within the hour: Gerald F. Seib, "Marines Complete Lebanon Withdrawal as Battleship's Guns Pound Artillery Sites," *Wall Street Journal*, Feb. 27, 1984, p. 2.

318 In January: Thomas L. Friedman, "University Head Killed in Beirut; Gunmen Escape," *New York Times*, Jan. 19, 1984, p. A1.

318 Kerr's assassination: George Boehmer, "Joyful TV Reporter Levin Reunited with Family," *Washington Post*, Feb. 16, 1985, p. A1.

318 Levin proved: Fred Burton and Samuel M. Katz, *Beirut Rules: The Murder of a CIA Station Chief and Hezbollah's War Against America and the West* (New York: Berkley, 2018), pp. 1–4; 201–4.

318 "The mission": Michael Dobbs, "Sets Out Differences with U.S. Latin Policy," *Washington Post*, March 24, 1984, p. A1.

318 "As the U.S. tide": Don Oberdorfer, "Making of a Diplomatic Debacle," *Washington Post*, Feb. 12, 1984, p. A1.

318 "These were heavy burdens": Ronald Reagan to Thomas O'Neill Jr., March 30, 1984, Box 16, Office of the Counsel to the President, RRPL.

319 "cockfight": Philip Geyelin, "The Weinberger-Shultz Debate Is a Dangerous One," *Washington Post*, Dec. 18, 1984, p. A19.

319 "The hard reality": Richard Halloran, "Shultz and Weinberger: Disputing Use of Force," *New York Times*, Nov. 30, 1984, p. B6.

319 "Employing our forces": Caspar Weinberger, "Uses of Military Power," Nov. 28, 1984, in U.S. Department of State, *American Foreign Policy, Current Documents: 1984* (Washington, DC: U.S. Government Printing Office, 1986), p. 67.

319 "Every day since the death": Reagan, *An American Life*, p. 466.

320 "The goal we sought": Jim Baker to Dick Darman, April 9, 1984, with Ronald Reagan's notes, #19799255, Box 120, WHORM Subject File: CO 086, RRPL.

CHAPTER 64

321 "The road": "Facing Lebanon," editorial, *Miami Herald*, Jan. 26, 1984, p. 12A.

321 By the mid 1990s: Yonah Alexander and Milton Hoenig, *The New Iranian*

Leadership: Ahmadinejad, Terrorism, Nuclear Ambition, and the Middle East (Westport, CT: Praeger Security International, 2008), p. 70.

321 Mugniyah, in contrast: Adam Goldman and Ellen Nakashima, "CIA and Mossad Killed Senior Hezbollah Figure in Car Bombing," *Washington Post*, Jan. 30, 2015, https://www.washingtonpost.com/world/national-security /cia-and-mossad-killed-senior-hezbollah-figure-in-car-bombing/2015/01/30 /ebb88682-968a-11e4-8005-1924ede3e54a_story.html.

321 The $5 million: Robert F. Worth and Nada Bakri, "Bomb in Syria Kills Militant Sought as Terrorist," *New York Times*, Feb. 14, 2008, p. A1; Kevin Peraino et al., "The Fox Is Hunted Down," *Newsweek*, Feb. 25, 2008, p. 40.

321 "There was an open": Goldman and Nakashima, "CIA and Mossad Killed Senior Hezbollah Figure in Car Bombing."

322 The elusive terrorist: Peraino, "The Fox Is Hunted Down."

322 But in 2007: Goldman and Nakashima, "CIA and Mossad Killed Senior Hezbollah Figure in Car Bombing."

322 "It was designed": Jeff Stein, "How the CIA Took Down Hezbollah's Top Terrorist, Imad Mugniyah," *Newsweek*, Feb. 13, 2015 http://www.newsweek .com/2015/02/13/imad-mugniyahcia-mossad-303483.html.

322 "It separated": Ibid.

322 "The world is": Joel Greenberg, "Hezbollah Fugitive Killed," *Chicago Tribune*, Feb. 14, 2008, p. 1.

322 In 1984: "Ali Akbar Mohtashamipour, Shite Clerk and a Founder of Hezbollah, Dies at 74," *Washington Post*, June 7, 2021, https://www.washingtonpost.com /local/obituaries/ali-akbar-mohtashamipour-dead/2021/06/07/2ce247c0-c793 -11eb-a11b-6c6191ccd599_story.html.

323 "We will track": Stein, "How the CIA Took Down Hezbollah's Top Terrorist, Imad Mugniyah."

EPILOGUE

325 "Lebanon has long": Fouad Ajami, "Withdraw Decently from Lebanon," *New York Times*, Feb. 12, 1984, p. E19.

326 "Success would have": Shultz, *Turmoil and Triumph*, p. 232.

326 "Contrary to some": Morris Draper statement, in *Marines in Lebanon, A Ten-Year Retrospective: Lessons Learned*, May 3, 1993, p. 42.

326 "senseless tragedy": John Vessey oral history with Thomas Saylor, Feb. 16, 2013, Concordia University, St. Paul, Minn.

326 "What were we": Ibid.

326 "For me personally": Strober and Strober, *The Reagan Presidency*, p. 213.

326 "the worst emotional": John H. Cushman Jr., "General's Kelley's Farewell," *New York Times*, June 25, 1987, p. B14; John H. Cushman Jr., "Gen. Paul X. Kelley, Top Marine Tested by a Bombing, Dies at 91," *New York Times*, Jan. 2, 2020, p. A20.

326 "What a hellish": Deaver, *Behind the Scenes*, p. 167.

326 "Lebanon was a place": Speakes, *Speaking Out*, p. 166.

326 "The loss of Marines": John Vessey oral history with Thomas Saylor, Feb. 16, 2013.

326 "My father": Michael Reagan text message, March 16, 2023.

326 "The question": Martin and Walcott, *Best Laid Plans*, pp. 152-153.

327 "It was a disaster": Caspar Weinberger interview, "Target America," *Frontline*, PBS, Oct. 4, 2001, in https://www.pbs.org/wgbh/pages/frontline/shows/target/interviews/weinberger.html.

327 On February 8, 1987: McFarlane, *Special Trust*, pp. 13–16, 337–38; Jane Leavy, "McFarlane and the Taunting Glare of Truth," *Washington Post*, May 7, 1987, p. C1.

327 "My life": McFarlane, *Special Trust*, p. 338.

327 "I so let the country": Neil A. Lewis, "Robert C. McFarlane, Top Reagan Aide in Iran-Contra Affair, Dies at 84," *New York Times*, May 14, 2022, p. B12.

327 "The story": Cannon, *President Reagan*, p. 390.

327 "The best laid": William B. Quandt, "Reagan's Lebanon Policy: Trial and Error," *Middle East Journal* 38, no. 2 (Spring 1984): 237–54.

328 "This was a tragedy": Rabbi Arnold Resnicoff, undated report, Box 14, Peter M. Robinson Files, RRPL.

328 "Even to this day": Micheline Thompson interview, Nov. 6, 2023.

328 "If Micheline Earle's husband": "Panel Backs U.S. Residency for Sailor's Lebanese Widow," *Plain Dealer*, Dec. 14, 1985, p. 4A.

329 "I miss my mom": Karen E. Henderson, "Soldier's Widow Faces Life Bravely," *Plain Dealer*, Oct. 18, 1987, p. 1B.

329 "I have a lot": Micheline Thompson interview, Nov. 6, 2023.

329 "No": James Ware interview, Jan. 6, 2023.

329 She never met: Lisa Hudson interview, Feb. 9, 2023.

330 "I have lived": Will Hudson, "Survivor to Fighter," transcript, Oct. 23, 2013.

330 "I was Sergeant": Stephen Russell email, Jan. 26, 2023.

330 "I was the guy": Henry Linkkila interview, May 30, 2023.

330 "Every day": Brad Ulick interview, Oct. 26, 2023.

330 "The failure": Geraghty, *Peacekeepers at War*, p. xv.

331 "The lawsuit": Press Release, "U.S. District Court Rules Iran Must Pay Crowell & Moring Clients $126 Million for 1983 Terrorist Bombing," Dec. 15, 2005, https://www.crowell.com/en/insights/firm-news/u-s-district-court-rules-iran-must-pay-crowell-moring-clients-126-million-for-1983-terrorist-bombing.

331 "This court": David Stout, "Court Orders Iran to Pay for Lebanon Bombing," *New York Times*, Sept. 7, 2007, https://www.nytimes.com/2007/09/07/world/middleeast/07cnd-judgment.html.

331 "I don't think": Robert Barnes, "Supreme Court Allows Families of Terrorism Victims to Collect Iranian Assets," *Washington Post*, April 20, 2016, https://www.washingtonpost.com/politics/courts_law/supreme-court-allows-families-of-terrorism-victims-to-college-iranian-assets/2016/04/20/6793f0cc-0703-11e6-a12f-ea5aed7958dc_story.html.

331 "God made it": Benjamin Weinthal, "Iran Official Admits Country's Role in Terror Bombing That Killed 241 US Military Members: Report," Fox News, Oct. 1, 2023, https://www.foxnews.com/world/iran-official-admits-countrys-role-terror-bombing-killed-241-us-military-members-report.

332 "I will follow": Author observation, Oct. 23, 2023.

332 "Civilized rules": Geraghty, *Peacekeepers at War*, p. XVI.

332 "They are not just": Randy Gaddo, 40th Remembrance, Candlelight Service, 6 a.m., Oct. 23, 2023, Action Plan and Narration.

Bibliography

ARCHIVES, LIBRARIES, AND MUSEUMS
Alfred M. Gray Marine Corps Research Center, Quantico, Va.
Charleston County Public Library, Charleston, SC
Concordia University, St. Paul, Minn.
Daniel Library, The Citadel, Charleston, SC
Dartmouth College, Rauner Special Collections Library, Hanover, NH
Library of Congress, Washington, DC
Marine Corps History Division, Archives Branch, Quantico, Va.
Marlene and Nathan Addlestone Library, College of Charleston, Charleston, SC
Miller Center of Public Affairs, University of Virginia, Charlottesville, Va.
National Archives and Records Administration, College Park, Md.
National Naval Aviation Museum, Pensacola, Fla.
Navy Bureau of Medicine and Surgery, Falls Church, Va.
Ronald Reagan Presidential Library, Simi Valley, Calif.
U.S. Naval Institute, Annapolis, Md.
University of Kentucky, Special Collections Research Center, Lexington, Ky.

SPECIFIC COLLECTIONS
Marine Corps History Division, Archives Branch, Quantico, Va.
22nd MAU Command Chronology
24th MAU Command Chronology
24th MAU SITREPS
Operations Other than War: Beirut, Lessons Learned and After-Action Reports
Report to Admiral Long
Andrew K. Mull Collection
Bill Stelpflug Collection
Fred Lash Collection
George Converse Collection
Grant McIntosh Collection
Jeremiah Walsh Collection
John Dyer Collection
Richard Blankenship Collection

Richard Dudley Collection
Steven Pitingolo Collection

Ronald Reagan Presidential Library, Simi Valley, Calif.
White House Office of Records Management (WHORM) Subject Files
Ann Higgins Files
Charles P. Tyson Files
Crisis Management Center (CMC), NSC Files
Department of State Publications
Donald R. Fortier Files
European & Soviet Affairs Directorate, NSC–Records
Executive Secretariat, NSC–Cable File
Executive Secretariat, NSC–Country File
Executive Secretariat, NSC–Head of State File
Executive Secretariat, NSC–NSDDs
Executive Secretariat, NSC–NSPGs
Executive Secretariat, NSC–Subject File
H.P. Goldfield Files
John Poindexter Files
Linus J. Kojelis Files
Michael E. Baroody Files
Michael K. Deaver Files
Morton Blackwell Files
National Security Affairs, Office of the Assistant to the President for–Chron File
Near East & South Asia Affairs Directorate, NSC–Records
Office of Correspondence Files
Office of Counsel to the President Files
Office of Media Relations Files
Office of Presidential Advance Files
Office of Speech Writing Files
Office of the First Lady Files
Office of the President, Presidential Briefing Papers
Office of the Presidential Diary Files
Peter M. Robinson Files
Philip A. Dur Files
Presidential Handwriting Files
Richard S. Beal Files
Robert B. Sims Files
Robert C. McFarlane Files
Robert H. Lilac Files
Situation Support Staff Files
William P. Clark Files

National Naval Aviation Museum, Pensacola, Fla.
Captain Michael Ohler Collection

ORAL HISTORIES

Concordia University, St. Paul, Minn.
John Vessey Jr.

Dartmouth College, Hanover, NH
Arnold Resnicoff

**Marine Corps History Division,
 Archives Branch, Quantico, Va.**
Granville Amos
Donald Anderson
Steve Anderson
Christopher Ayrey
William Barnetson
Dennis Blankenship
David Buckner
Al Butler
George Converse
Michael Ettore
Jack Farmer
Timothy Geraghty
Christopher Guenther
George Gunst
Thomas Harkins
Forrest Hunt
Charles Johnson
Robert Johnson
Jim Joy
Al Karle
Fred Lash
Michael Leonard
Frank Libutti
Charles Light
John Matthews
James Mead (speech)
James Mead (Lebanon briefing session)
James Mead
Larry Medlin
Robert Melton
Stephen Mikolaski
Reuben Payne
George Pucciarelli
Gary Rainey
Ronald Rice
George Schmidt

James Schulster
Albert Shively
Harry Slacum
Thomas Stokes
Jack Tempone
Ernest Van Huss
Arthur Weber

U.S. Naval Institute, Annapolis, Md.
Robert L. J. Long

**U.S. Navy Bureau of Medicine and
 Surgery, Falls Church, Va.**
James Ware

AUTHOR INTERVIEWS
Philip Amrhein
Mauricio Aparicio
Pablo Arroyo
Gilbert Bigelow
Rodney Burnette
Steve Combes
Blaine Cosgrove
Jack Cress
John Dalziel
Kathryn Dempsey
Paul Dziadon
Darius Eichler
Kenneth Farnan
Peter Ferraro
Randy Gaddo
Timothy Geraghty
Mark Hacala
Myron Harrington
Fraser Henderson
Don Howell
Lisa Hudson
Patrick Hutton
John L'Heureux
Robert Jordan
Henry Linkkila
Geoffrey Losey
David Madaras
Burnham Matthews
Tim McCoskey

Neal Morris
Gail Ohler Osborne
Anthony Pais
Arnold Resnicoff
Stephen Russell
Emanuel Simmons
Mark Singleton
John Snyder
Elizabeth Stephens
Robert Sundquist
George Taylor
Micheline Thompson
Michael Toma
Brad Ulick
James Ware
Richard Wells
Daniel Wheeler

**Newspapers, Magazines,
  and Journals**
American Diplomacy
Arizona Republic
Asbury Park Press
Baltimore Sun
Boston Globe
Buffalo News
Charlotte Observer
Chicago Tribune
Christian Science Monitor
Cleveland Plain Dealer
Democrat and Chronicle
Durham Sun

Fresno Bee
Guardian
Indiana Gazette
Indianapolis Star
Leatherneck
Los Angeles Times
Macon News
Middle East Journal
Military Medicine
Minneapolis Tribune
Naval History
Neurosurgery
Neurosurgical Focus
New York Times
New Yorker
Newsday
Newsweek
Observer
Orlando Sentinel
Philadelphia Inquirer
Pittsburgh Post-Gazette
Poughkeepsie Journal
Proceedings
San Francisco Examiner
State
Time
U.S. News & World Report
USA Today
Ventura County Star
Wall Street Journal
Washington Post
Winston-Salem Journal

GOVERNMENT REPORTS

Long, Robert, et al. "Report of the DOD Commission on Beirut International Airport Terrorist Act, October 23, 1983." Dec. 20, 1983.

U.S. Congress. House. *Adequacy of U.S. Marine Corps Security in Beirut: Summary of Findings and Conclusions, Report of the Investigations Subcommittee of the Committee on Armed Services.* 98th Cong., 1st sess., Dec. 19, 1983. Washington, DC: U.S. Government Printing Office, 1983.

U.S. Congress. House. *Adequacy of U.S. Marine Corps Security in Beirut," Report Together with Additional and Dissenting Views of the Investigations Subcommittee of the Committee on Armed Services,* 98th Cong., 1st sess., Dec. 19, 1983. Washington, DC: U.S. Government Printing Office, 1983.

U.S. Congress, House. *Beirut Tragedy: 'A New Crowd in Town' and Beirut Casualties: Care and Identification, Report Together with Supplemental Views of the Delegation to Beirut of the Committee on Armed Services and Committee on Veterans' Affairs.* 98th Cong., 1st sess. Washington, DC: U.S. Government Printing Office, 1983.

U.S. Congress. House. *Full Committee Consideration of Investigations Subcommittee Report on Terrorist Bombing at Beirut International Airport: Hearing Before the Committee on Armed Services.* 98th Cong., 2nd sess. Jan. 31, 1984. Washington, DC: U.S. Government Printing Office, 1984.

U.S. Congress. House. *Full Committee Hearings on the Use of U.S. Military Personnel in Lebanon and Consideration of Report from September 24–25 Committee Delegation to Lebanon.* 98th Cong., 1st sess., Sept. 27–28, 1983, Washington, DC: U.S. Government Printing Office, 1984.

U.S. Congress. House. *Hearing Before a Subcommittee of the Committee on Appropriations, Situation in Lebanon and Grenada.* 98th Cong., 1st sess. Washington, DC: U.S. Government Printing Office, 1983.

U.S. Congress. House. *"Lebanon: Limited Interest, Limited Involvement, Frequent Accounting." Report of the Delegation to Lebanon, 1983, of the Committee on Armed Services, House of Representatives* 98th Cong., 1st Sess., Oct. 18, 1983. Washington, DC: U.S. Government Printing Office, 1983.

U.S. Congress. House. *Review of Adequacy of Security Arrangements for Marines in Lebanon and Plans for Improving that Security, Hearings before the Committee on Armed Service and the Investigations Subcommittee of the Committee on Armed Services.* 98th Cong., 1st sess., Nov. 1, 2, 12, 13 and Dec. 8, 9, 14, 15, 1983. Washington, DC: U.S. Government Printing Office, 1985.

U.S. Congress. House. *Statutory Authorization Under the War Powers Resolution – Lebanon, Hearing and Markup Before the Committee on Foreign Affairs.* 98th Cong., 1st Sess., Sept. 21–22, 1983. Washington, DC: U.S. Government Printing Office, 1983.

U.S. Congress. Senate. *The Situation in Lebanon, Hearings Before the Committee on Armed Services.* 98th Cong., 1st Sess., Oct. 25 and 31, 1983. Washington, DC: U.S. Government Printing Office, 1983.

U.S. Congress. House. *The U.S. Embassy Bombing in Beirut, Hearing Before the Committee on Foreign Relations and its Subcommittee on International Operations*

and on Europe and the Middle East. 98th Cong., 1st Sess., June 28, 1983.
Washington, DC: U.S. Government Printing Office, 1983.

U.S. Congress. Senate. *War Powers Resolution, Hearing Before the Committee on Foreign Relations.* 98th Cong., 1st Sess., Sept. 21, 1983.Washington, DC: U.S. Government Printing Office, 1983.

BOOKS AND DISSERTATIONS

Baer, Robert. *See No Evil: The True Story of a Ground Soldier in the CIA's War on Terrorism.* New York: Crown, 2002.

Berman, Larry, ed. *Looking Back on the Reagan Presidency.* Baltimore: John Hopkins University Press, 1990.

Bird, Kai. *The Good Spy: The Life and Death of Robert Ames.* New York: Crown, 2014.

Brands, H. W. *Reagan: The Life.* New York: Anchor Books, 2015.

Burton, Fred, and Samuel M. Katz. *Beirut Rules: The Murder of a CIA Station Chief and Hezbollah's War Against America and the West.* New York: Berkley, 2018.

Bush, George H. W. *All the Best, George Bush: My Life in Letters and Other Writings.* New York: Scribner, 2013.

Cannon, Lou. *President Reagan: The Role of a Lifetime.* New York: Simon & Schuster, 1991.

Cannon, Lou, and Carl. M. Cannon. *Reagan's Disciple: George W. Bush's Troubled Quest for a Presidential Legacy.* New York: PublicAffairs, 2008.

Clausewitz, Carl von. *On War.* Ed. and trans. by Michael Howard and Peter Paret. Princeton, NJ: Princeton University Press, 1984.

Coleman, Bradly Lynn, and Kyle Longley, eds. *Reagan and the World: Leadership and National Security, 1981–1989.* Lexington: University Press of Kentucky, 2018.

Crist, David. *The Twilight War: The Secret History of America's Thirty-Year Conflict with Iran.* New York: Penguin Books, 2012.

Davis, Mike. *Buda's Wagon: A Brief History of the Car Bomb.* New York: Verso, 2007.

Deaver, Michael K., with Mickey Herskowitz. *Behind the Scenes: In Which the Author Talks About Ronald and Nancy Reagan . . . and Himself.* New York: William Morrow, 1987.

Diaz, Tom, and Barbara Newman. *Lightening Out of Lebanon: Hezbollah Terrorists on American Soil.* New York: Presidio Press, 2005.

Dolphin, Glenn E. *24 Mau: 1983: A Marine Looks Back at the Peacekeeping Mission to Beirut, Lebanon.* Baltimore: Publish America, 2005.

Dougherty, Kevin. *Military Decision-Making Processes: Case Studies Involving the Preparation, Commitment, Application and Withdrawal of Force.* Jefferson, NC: McFarland, 2014.

Dur, Philip A. *Between Land and Sea: A Cold Warrior's Log.* Austin, TX: Lioncrest, 2022.

Emerson, Steven. *Secret Warriors: Inside the Covert Military Operations of the Reagan Era.* New York: G. P. Putnam's Sons, 1988.

Farrell, John Aloysius. *Tip O'Neill and the Democratic Century.* Boston: Little, Brown, 2001.

Fisk, Robert. *Pity the Nation: The Abduction of Lebanon*. New York: Atheneum, 1990.

Foyle, Douglas C. *Counting the Public In: Presidents, Public Opinion, and Foreign Policy*. New York: Columbia University Press, 1999.

Frank, Benis M. *U.S. Marines in Lebanon, 1982–1984*. Washington, DC: History and Museums Division, Headquarters, U.S. Marine Corps, U.S. Government Printing Office, 1987.

Friedman, Thomas L. *From Beirut to Jerusalem*. New York: Farrar, Straus & Giroux, 1989.

Gabriel, Richard A. *Military Incompetence: Why the American Military Doesn't Win*. New York: Hill & Wang, 1985.

Gans, John. *White House Warriors: How the National Security Council Transformed the American War of War*. New York: Liveright, 2019.

Geraghty, Timothy J. *Peacekeepers at War: Beirut 1983—The Marine Commander Tells His Story*. Washington, DC: Potomac Books, 2009.

Gilmour, David. *Lebanon: The Fractured Country*. New York: St. Martin's Press, 1983.

Goldman, Peter, and Tony Fuller. *The Quest for the Presidency*. New York: Bantam Books, 1985.

Hallenbeck, Ralph A. *Military Force as an Instrument of U.S. Foreign Policy: Intervention in Lebanon, August 1982–February 1984*. New York: Praeger, 1991.

Hammel, Eric. *The Root: The Marines in Beirut, August 1982–February 1984*. St. Paul, MN: Zenith Press, 1999.

Haney, Eric L. *Inside Delta Force: The Story of America's Elite Counterterrorist Unit*. New York: Delacorte Press, 2002.

Herspring, Dale R. *The Pentagon and the Presidency: Civil-Military Relations from FDR to George W. Bush*. Lawrence: University Press of Kansas, 2005.

Hertsgaard, Mark. *On Bended Knee: The Press and the Reagan Presidency*. New York: Farrar, Straus & Giroux, 1988.

Hinckley, Ronald H. *People, Polls, and Policymakers: American Public Opinion and National Security*. New York: Lexington Books, 1992.

Jaber, Hala. *Hezbollah: Born with a Vengeance*. New York: Columbia University Press, 1997.

Jackowski, Mary Ellen, and Peggy A. Stelpflug, eds., *Voices from Beirut: The Peacekeepers Speak*. Albany, NY: Fuller's, 2013.

Kalb, Marvin, and Deborah Kalb. *Haunting Legacy: Vietnam and the American Presidency from Ford to Obama*. Washington, DC: Brookings Institution Press, 2011.

Keefer, Edward C. *Secretaries of Defense Historical Series*, vol. X, *Caspar Weinberger and the U.S. Military Buildup, 1981-1985*. Washington, DC: U.S. Government Printing Office, 2023.

Korbani, Agnes G. *U.S Intervention in Lebanon, 1958 and 1982: Presidential Decisionmaking*. New York: Praeger, 1991.

Leden, Michael A. *Grave New World*. New York: Oxford University Press, 1985.

Lehman, John F., Jr. *Command of the Seas*. New York: Charles Scribner's Sons, 1988.

Levitt, Matthew. *Hezbollah: The Global Footprint of Lebanon's Party of God.*
Washington, DC: Georgetown University Press, 2013.

Martin, David C., and John Walcott. *Best Laid Plans: The Inside Story of America's
War Against Terrorism.* New York: Harper & Row, 1988.

Matthews, John Benson. "United States Peacekeeping in Lebanon, 1982-1984:
Why It Failed." PhD diss., Washington State University, 1994.

McDermott, Anthony, and Kjell Skjelsbaek, eds. *The Multinational Force in Beirut,
1982–1984.* Miami: Florida International University Press, 1991.

McFarlane, Robert C., with Zofia Smardz. *Special Trust.* New York:
Cadell & Davies, 1994.

Meese, Edwin. *With Reagan: The Inside Story.* Washington, DC: Regnery
Gateway, 1992.

Mitchell, Neil James. *Democracy's Blameless Leaders: From Dresden to Abu Ghraib,
How Leaders Evade Accountability for Abuse, Atrocity, and Killing.* New York: New
York University Press, 2012.

Morley, Morris H., ed. *Crisis and Confrontation: Ronald Reagan's Foreign Policy.*
Totowa, NJ: Rowman & Littlefield, 1988.

Morris, Edmund. *Dutch: A Memoir of Ronald Reagan.* New York:
Random House, 1999.

North, Oliver L., with William Novak. *Under Fire: An American Story.* New York:
HarperCollins, 1991.

Norton, Augustus. *Hezbollah: A Short History.* Princeton, NJ: Princeton
University Press, 2007.

O'Hern, Steven. *Iran's Revolutionary Guard: The Threat That Grows While American
Sleeps.* Washington, DC: Potomac Books, 2012.

Persico, Joseph E. *Casey: From the OSS to the CIA.* New York: Viking, 1990.

Petit, Michael. *Peacekeepers at War: A Marine's Account of the Beirut Catastrophe.*
Boston: Faber & Faber, 1986.

Pfaltzgraff, Robert L., Jr., and Jacquelyn K. Davis, eds. *National Security Decisions:
The Participants Speak.* Lexington, MA: Lexington Books, 1990.

Pintak, Larry. *Beirut Outtakes: A TV Correspondent's Portrait of America's Encounter
with Terror.* Lexington, MA: Lexington Books, 1988.

Powell, Colin L., with Joseph E. Persico. *My American Journey.* New York:
Ballantine Books, 1995.

Prados, John. *Keepers of the Keys: A History of the National Security Council from
Truman to Bush.* New York: William Morrow, 1991.

Rabinovich, Itamar. *The War for Lebanon, 1970–1985.* Ithaca, NY: Cornell
University Press, 1985.

Reagan, Nancy, with William Novak. *My Turn: The Memoirs of Nancy Reagan.*
New York: Random House, 1989.

Reagan, Ronald. *An American Life.* New York: Simon & Schuster, 1990.

Reagan, Ronald. *The Reagan Diaries.* Edited by Douglas Brinkley. New York:
HarperCollins, 2007.

Reeves, Richard. *Ronald Reagan: The Triumph of Imagination.* New York:
Simon & Schuster, 2005.

Schiff, Ze'ev, and Ehud Ya'ari. *Israel's Lebanon War.* Edited and trans. by Ina Friedman. New York: Simon & Schuster, 1984.

Shultz, George. *Turmoil and Triumph: My Years as Secretary of State.* New York: Charles Scribner's Sons, 1993.

Simonsen, Robert A., ed. *Marines Dodging Death: Sixty-Two Accounts of Close Calls in World War II, Korea, Vietnam, Lebanon, Iraq and Afghanistan.* Jefferson, NC: McFarland, 2009.

Sloyan, Patrick J. *When Reagan Sent in the Marines: The Invasion of Lebanon.* New York: Thomas Dunne Books, 2019.

Smith, Hedrick. *The Power Game: How Washington Works.* New York: Random House, 1988.

Speakes, Larry, with Robert Pack. *Speaking Out: The Reagan Presidency from Inside the White House.* New York: Charles Scribner's Sons, 1988.

Stahl, Lesley. *Reporting Live.* New York: Touchstone Books, 1999.

Strober, Deborah Hart, and Gerald S. Strober. *The Reagan Presidency: An Oral History of the Era.* Washington, DC: Brassey's, 2003.

Sullivan, Joseph G., ed. *Embassies Under Siege: Personal Accounts by Diplomats on the Front Line.* Washington, DC: Brassey's, 1995.

Teicher, Howard, and Gayle Radley Teicher. *Twin Pillars to Desert Storm: America's Flawed Vision in the Middle East from Nixon to Bush.* New York: William Morrow, 1993.

Timberg, Robert. *The Nightingale's Song.* New York: Simon & Schuster, 1995.

Weinberger, Caspar W. *Fighting for Peace: Seven Critical Years in the Pentagon.* New York: Warner Books, 1990.

Weinberger, Caspar, with Gretchen Roberts. *In the Arena: A Memoir of the 20th Century.* Washington, DC: Regnery, 2001.

Wills, David C. *The First War on Terrorism: Counter-Terrorism Policy During the Reagan Administration.* New York: Rowman & Littlefield, 2003.

Wilson, George C. *Supercarrier: An Inside Account of Life Aboard the World's Most Powerful Ship, the USS John F. Kenney.* New York: Macmillan, 1986.

Wright, Robin. *Sacred Rage: The Wrath of Militant Islam.* New York: Touchstone Books, 1986.

Index

About the Authors

Jack Carr is a #1 *New York Times* bestselling author and former Navy SEAL sniper. He lives with his wife and three children in Park City, Utah. He is the author of *The Terminal List, True Believer, Savage Son, The Devil's Hand, In the Blood, Only the Dead*, and *Red Sky Mourning*. His debut novel, *The Terminal List*, was adapted into the #1 Amazon Prime Video series starring Chris Pratt. He is also the host of the top-rated podcast *Danger Close*. Visit him at OfficialJackCarr.com and follow along on Instagram, X, Twitter, and Facebook @JackCarrUSA.

A Pulitzer Prize finalist and former Nieman Fellow at Harvard, James M. Scott is the author of *Target Tokyo, Black Snow, Rampage, The War Below*, and *The Attack on the Liberty*. In addition, Scott is a sought-after public speaker, who leads battlefield tours and lectures at institutions around the world. He lives with his wife and two children in Charleston, South Carolina, where he is the Scholar in Residence at The Citadel. Visit him at JamesMScott.com.